Blueprint for Action

Achieving Center-Based Change Through Staff Development

Second Edition

Paula Jorde Bloom

NEW HORIZONS

EDUCATIONAL CONSULTANTS AND LEARNING RESOURCES

LAKE FOREST, ILLINOIS 60045-0863

New Horizons
Educational Consultants and Learning Resources
P.O. Box 863
Lake Forest, Illinois 60045-0863
847-295-8131
847-295-2968 (FAX)
newhorizons4@comcast.net
www.newhorizonsbooks.net

Design – Stan Burkat

Publisher's Cataloging-in-Publication Data

Bloom, Paula Jorde
   Blueprint for action : achieving center-based change through staff development / Paula Jorde Bloom
   —
   p. cm.
   Includes bibliographical references and index
   ISBN 0-9621894-8-0
   1. Day care centers — United States — Administration
2. Education, Preschool. 3. Organizational change
4. Employees — Training of. I. Title.

HV854   372.21
                    QBI91-1106
                    MARC

Library of Congress Control Number: 2005920004
ISBN 0-9621894-8-0

Printed in the United States of America

Acknowledgements

Like many writers, my personal life intersects my professional life in interesting and memorable ways. This is especially true when I think about *Blueprint for Action*. The shrink-wrapped copy of the first edition of the book arrived from the printer the same day I brought my youngest daughter, Kristine, home from the hospital. Next fall she will be heading off to high school. A lot has happened during those intervening 14 years. Needless to say, an updated and revised edition of this book is long overdue.

This second edition reflects the research, trends, and new developments in leading and managing organizational change that have emerged over the past decade. My goal was to highlight the universal truths that apply to all organizations while providing specific examples that relate to the unique context of early care and education.

My collaborators for the first edition, Joan Britz, Marilyn Sheerer, and Norma Richard, have moved on to other personal and professional pursuits, but I remain indebted to them for the insights that emerged from that initial collaborative process. The theoretical framework and organizational change concepts embedded in this edition clearly show the influence of their sharp, insightful thinking.

I owe much to my colleagues at the McCormick Tribune Center for Early Childhood Leadership at National-Louis University for their continued support. The leadership and management training we conduct at the center has served as a living laboratory for refining the concepts and case studies that uniquely capture the distinctive elements of change in early childhood settings.

I am grateful to Jill Bella, Eileen Eisenberg, and Janis Jones for their assistance in revising the assessment tools and to Teri Talan and Jennifer Bergmann for their help in updating the information on performance appraisal and career ladders.

This edition has also benefited from the wisdom and expertise of literally hundreds of early childhood administrators who have used *Blueprint for Action* as a practical guide for describing, monitoring, and improving their programs. I am particularly appreciative for the feedback I received from Marilyn Brink, Lisa Downey, Eleanor Gardner, Leonette Hall, Marsha Hawley, Deborah Jaye, Gail Kulick, and Marcia Orr.

Finally, I extend special thanks to Catherine Cauman for her wonderful editing and to Stan Burkat for his patience and skill in the design and production of the book.

► Table of Contents ◄

Introduction

Anyone who has chased the shadow of a center director for even a brief time knows that being an effective administrator means wearing many hats—budget analyst, fund-raiser, receptionist, supervisor, community liaison, maintenance engineer, record-keeper, curriculum developer, public relations coordinator, event planner, counselor, nutritionist, nurse, and child advocate. The list is long and varied. While administrating an early childhood program has never been easy, the director's job has become even more complex in recent years.

When veteran directors get together, one of the most common topics of discussion is how their administrative role has changed. Increased regulatory requirements, multiple funding sources, more complicated fiscal reporting procedures, a greater number of families with special needs, more complex networks of social services to coordinate, and a host of societal changes have dramatically altered the scope of responsibility and the demands placed upon early childhood center directors.

The director stands center stage. Like the architect, engineer, and construction foreman all in one, the director is the individual responsible for designing and constructing a model program. The construction metaphor is apropos. Administering a high-quality early care and education program is an awesome responsibility, one which few directors feel their training and education have adequately prepared them.

From my discussions with center directors, I am convinced that a critical element is missing in the training and education of most early childhood program administrators—a theoretical framework for understanding child care centers as organizations. A theoretical framework is important because it serves as a blueprint guiding actions and behavior. Without a perspective for interpreting the dynamics of center life, directors tend to tackle problems in piecemeal fashion, scrambling to put out one fire at a time and not making the critical changes needed to improve the quality of their programs.

I have found that even in those centers that regularly engage in staff development activities, there seldom exists a coherent model or philosophy of professional development. In other words, when asked to explain why they implement the practices they do, few directors can articulate a rationale for their approach. A philosophy of professional development is important because it gives substance to action.

Blueprint for Action is designed as a practice resource for directors who are serious about improving the quality of their programs. It will help you move beyond a quick-fix notion of staff development and center improvement by serving as a guide for program analysis and action. It details a comprehensive method for analyzing the different components of your program. It will help you diagnose common organizational problems and select appropriate strategies for implementing change and evaluating progress. It will also help you reduce, even eliminate, the *us* versus *them* adversarial climate that exists in many programs. In its place you'll develop a sense of shared responsibility for center change.

The premise for this book rests on two assumptions: first, every center has areas of strength and areas in need of improvement. High-quality programs are distinguished by their willingness to deal with their imperfections. Lightfoot (1983) used the term *consciousness of imperfection* to describe this organizational characteristic of the exemplary high schools she observed. This term is equally fitting for early childhood settings. The role of the director then is that of catalyst, setting the climate that allows staff to reflect on how program practices might be improved.

The second assumption of this book is that organizational change can come about only through change in individuals. That is why the emphasis in *Blueprint for Action* is on linking individual needs to organizational needs. The blueprint presented here will serve as a guide for enhancing the professional development of all who work together in a center to achieve a shared vision.

In this book, the terms *professional development* and *staff development* are used interchangeably. This usage reflects common parlance in the literature. Technically, however, professional development refers to the growth and change of an individual while staff development refers to the collective professional development of teachers on a staff. It is appropriate in the context of this discussion to use the terms interchangeably because the model of staff development presented in these pages is one that is truly individualized.

A word about how this book is organized

The first three chapters of *Blueprint for Action* provide a global perspective on the issues. Chapter 1 presents a social systems model to help you better understand the significance of events in the day-to-day life of your center. At first glance, this chapter may appear weighty, perhaps "too

theoretical." I encourage you to read it carefully, though, because it will give you a better understanding of how early childhood centers function. Chapter 1 also introduces you to a case study featuring Martha, the director of the Children's Corner. Martha's experiences applying the ideas presented in this book will breathe life into the theoretical concepts that serve as the foundation for this approach to center improvement.

Chapter 2 addresses the nature of change, providing an overview of how change occurs in early care and education programs. Change, as discussed in this chapter, implies altering the people, structure, and processes of a center to achieve more desirable outcomes. This chapter sets the stage for Chapter 3 which describes more specifically the director's role in the change process. In addition to the case study of the Children's Corner, real-life vignettes connect the concepts presented to practical situations similar to those you may have encountered. As you read these vignettes, think of your own center. Jot notes in the margins. This will help you make that important link between theory and practice.

In the second half of the book you will see how the theoretical concepts introduced in the first three chapters become a blueprint for action for helping you implement change in your own program. Chapter 4 provides the essential tools that will help you assess the needs of your center as a whole. This chapter explores issues regarding communication, supervisory processes, goal consensus, leadership style, center climate, and a host of other organizational characteristics. It presents a step-by-step process for collecting data about your center along with practical assessment tools that you can readily adapt to your unique situation.

Chapter 5 looks more specifically at how you can assess the needs of the individuals who work at your center. It presents a framework for developing individual profiles for each member of your staff. This information serves as the springboard from which to implement the staff development model you will learn about in Chapter 6.

Chapter 6 takes you through a step-by-step process for designing an individualized model of staff development. This model serves as a template for putting your philosophy of center improvement into action. The model of staff development presented is in sharp contrast to what is customarily called in-service education. In-service is typically viewed by teachers as something done to them to remedy a defect or deficiency. Sadly, most in-service training is nothing more than an indoor spectator sport—an inspirational speaker is invited, a smorgasbord of workshops offered, gallons of coffee and dozens of donuts consumed—but little in the way of sub-stantive behavioral and attitudinal change result.

Chapter 7 links the notion of individualized staff development to the supportive organizational structures that ensure its success. This chapter presents information that will help you design a comprehensive performance appraisal system and a career ladder for professional advancement. Chapter 8, the final chapter, will help you learn how to connect organizational needs and individual needs in a unified approach for achieving change. It underscores the importance of thinking of your center as a professional learning community, a place where collaboration, shared decision making, and team building are the driving forces that make your vision of center-based change possible.

To help get you started in implementing the ideas presented in *Blueprint for Action*, I have included an extensive appendix of assessment tools and worksheets that you can adopt or adapt to meet the specific needs of your program. The accompanying CD-ROM can be used to print out reproducible versions of the assessment tools and worksheets.

I am a strong believer that the blueprint for action detailed in this book really works. Since its first publication nearly 15 years ago, I have received hundreds of letters from directors who provide examples of how they wove the principles described in this book into the fabric of the daily life of their centers. The changes in staff morale and job performance they describe provide compelling evidence that incremental changes in program quality are possible when directors and teachers work together toward shared goals. I am confident you can experience the same success at your center. Best of luck!

Paula Jorde Bloom,
December 2004

Chapter 1

Child Care Centers as Organizations: A Social Systems Perspective

There are many different ways of thinking about early childhood centers as organizations. Typically when directors are asked to draw a picture of their organization, they respond by illustrating some version of an organizational chart. This kind of model reflects the formal reporting relationships among jobs and the formal work units that make up a center. While this is one way to think about early care and education programs, it is a very limited view. It only addresses one aspect of the structure of the center and captures only a small part of what goes on.

With a limited view of how centers function as organizations, directors are apt to think of individual incidents that occur in the everyday life of their programs as isolated events. Such a narrow perspective can hamper their ability to respond appropriately to situations. The result is that they are more likely to deal with problems that arise in a piecemeal fashion, failing to see the interconnection between isolated problems.

This book proposes another view of early childhood centers that takes a broader perspective of organizational life. This approach views centers as dynamic and open social systems. A social systems perspective draws on the literature of organizational theorists such as Beer (1980), Bronfenbrenner (1979), Hoy and Miskel (2005), Nadler and Tushman (1983), Oshry (1996), Owens (2000), Senge (1994), and Zmuda, Kuklis, and Kline (2004).

In this chapter I connect the observations of these well-known theorists with my own and others' experiences in the field of early childhood to construct a model of how child care centers function as organizations. This perspective is important because as directors consider the serious business of improving their programs, it is critical that they look at the whole as well as the parts, viewing their center as a true ecosystem. This chapter provides the framework for that analysis.

What Is a System?

The concept of social systems is a general one that applies to groups regardless of size or purpose. You can think of a family, club, or a corporation as a social system. In simplest terms, a system is a set of interrelated parts. A system is characterized by the interdependence of its parts, its differentiation from its environment, a complex network of social relationships, and its own unique culture. When the organization interacts with the external environment, it is an open system. Now let's take this abstract concept and see if we can come up with some concrete examples of how systems theory can be applied to early childhood programs.

Central to a systems theory approach is the notion that the system is comprised of subsystems or components. On a very rudimentary level, for example, we could say that a child care center is comprised of different classrooms, or even different groups within the classroom. This is just one way of thinking about programs as an integrated whole made up of interacting parts. It's analogous to an automobile. A car is made up of many different parts, all interacting to perform a specific function. This conceptualization, however, is still too basic; it doesn't capture the complexity of the interacting components of centers. The sections that follow describe a more detailed model of child care centers when viewed from a social systems perspective. This model includes several components.

Components of the System

Each component or subsystem of the model described here is definable and separate but also interrelated and interdependent. These components consist of the external environment, people, structure, processes, culture, and outcomes. Table 1.1 will serve as a useful reference. It summarizes the key elements of each component. Figure 1.1 graphically represents the relationship between these components. As you read the description of each component, think of your own program and make margin notes about the elements of your setting that seem to fit the description provided.

External Environment (the Outside World)

Early childhood centers do not exist in a vacuum. Every organization exists within the context of a larger environment that includes individuals, groups, other organizations, and even social forces, all of which have a potentially powerful impact on how the organization performs.

Early childhood centers, for example, exist in an environment from which they receive input such as money, personnel, and clients (parents and children) and for which they produce outcomes. The environment also includes governmental and regulatory bodies, competitors, and special interest groups. The external environment makes demands on the center. For example, it may require a certain kind of service or a certain level of quality. It is critical to organizational functioning.

The environment may also place constraints on organizational action. It may limit the types of activities in which the center can engage. For example, in many states, licensing requirements put constraints on the child care center to conform to certain standards. In another example, a few years ago the insurance industry raised rates for programs. Many centers had to shut down; others found they needed to raise tuition fees and adjust expenses in order to cover the cost of their increased premiums.

Finally, the environment provides opportunities the organization can explore. For example, a program sponsored by a large social service agency may be able to tap other resources of the agency, such as volunteers or expertise in program management. The local resource and referral agency may offer quality enhancement grants to support center accreditation.

Centers as social systems can be viewed as *open systems* because they interact with their external environment. The environment in which centers exist has certain values, desired goals, information, human resources, and financial resources. In many respects the external environment creates the context for the organization. It is the source of the input and in return receives the output.

The values of the broader society and the immediate community in which the program exists also influence the center. These are two other facets of the external environment that must be considered. Problems often occur when directors perceive their centers as closed systems, downplaying their dependency on the broader environment. But centers are indisputably affected by the values of the community, by politics, and by history. Here are some examples of influences from the external environment.

▶ Sponsoring agency—for example, Head Start grantee agency, church or synagogue, public school, YMCA, United Way, or military command

▶ Local community—the immediate neighborhood surrounding the center; mental health and family support services in the community

Table 1.1

Components of the System

ENVIRONMENT	PEOPLE	STRUCTURE	PROCESSES	CULTURE	OUTCOMES
Sponsoring agency	Individuals	Legal governing structure	Leadership style	Shared values	Organization
Local community and immediate neighborhood	personal history (age, gender, ethnicity, family background)	Size (student enrollment, total number of staff)	Decision-making and problem-solving processes	Norms	reputation of the center
Professional community (professional organizations, colleges, unions, other centers)	educational level, specialized training, and experience	Program type, hours, services provided	Communication processes	History of the center	fiscal viability
		Funding structure	Planning and goal setting	Traditions (rituals, celebrations, and customs)	internal efficiency
					professional orientation
Legislative bodies and regulatory agencies	knowledge and skill	Division of labor	Group meeting processes	Organizational climate	
	interests and special talents	Accountability and decision making	Interpersonal relations	Ethics	Staff
Economic, social, and political climate	beliefs and values	Reporting relationships	Conflict management		absenteeism
Business community	dispositions	Policies regarding children (enrollment, group size, group composition, ratios)	Supervisory and training processes		turnover
Technological environment	flexibility and openness to change		Center evaluation processes		level of competence
	energy level	Policies regarding parents' roles and responsibilities	Performance appraisal processes		job satisfaction
	cognitive capacity	Policies regarding staff recruitment and training	Socialization practices		commitment to center
	learning style	Performance appraisal policies	Teaching practices		professional fulfillment
	psychological type	Pay and promotion system	Child assessment practices		
	communication style	Accounting, budgeting, and fiscal management system			Children
	self-efficacy				social competence
	needs and expectations	Written philosophy			cognitive competence
	adult development stage	Program mission, strategic plan			overall health
	career stage	Written curriculum			
	level of commitment	Size (square footage)			Parents
	level of motivation	Arrangement of space			satisfaction with center
	professional orientation	Materials and equipment			perceived support
	concomitant roles				
					Community/society
	Groups				service provided
	dominant coalitions				

Figure 1.1

Child Care Centers as Organizations: A Social Systems Perspective

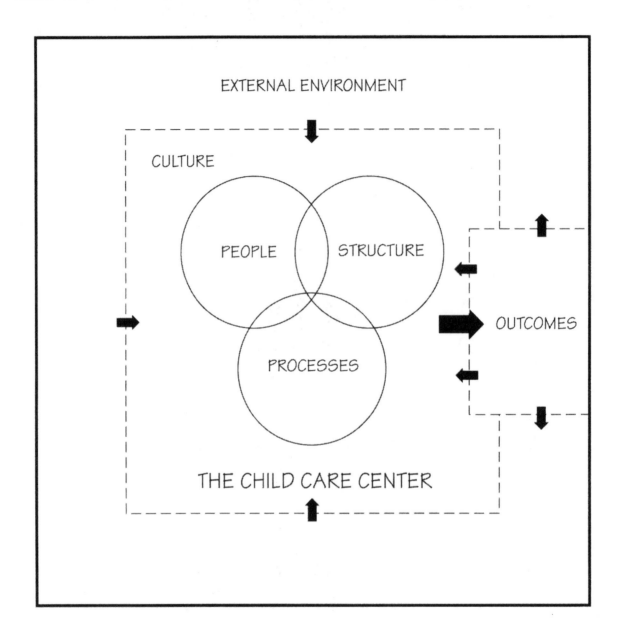

EXTERNAL ENVIRONMENT

CULTURE

PEOPLE

STRUCTURE

PROCESSES

OUTCOMES

THE CHILD CARE CENTER

- Professional community—professional organizations, colleges, teachers' unions, other child care centers

- Legislative bodies and regulatory agencies whose policies impact the program—for example, the state's Department of Education or the Department of Children and Family Services

- Current economic, social, and political climate

- Business community and civic organizations—support, expertise, resources

- Technological environment—e-mail and Internet connectivity, access to computer software and hardware, resources for duplicating or faxing

Case Study: The Children's Corner

Martha is the director of a Head Start program in a large metropolitan area. Her program, The Children's Corner, is one of five Head Start programs operated by a large nonprofit social service agency. The agency also operates a nursing home and recreation center for senior citizens. Martha's program is housed in a small church.

Martha is keenly aware of the constraints as well as the benefits of the external environment in which her program operates. On the downside, she feels she is inundated with paperwork in both meeting Head Start's Performance Standards and the administrative demands of the social service agency that sponsors her. She also has to accommodate the demands of the church that houses her program. That means putting away all her equipment and supplies on Friday afternoon so the church can use her classrooms for Sunday School.

On the positive side, Martha recognizes that she receives many benefits from her external environment. Her agency, for example, is able to get a discount on food, equipment, and supplies because it purchases products in bulk quantities for all its centers. Martha also doesn't have to worry about trying to recruit new teachers. Finding qualified candidates for teaching positions is taken care of by the central administrative office of her agency. Since the agency also operates a nursing home and recreation center for the elderly, Martha was able to tap into this resource for a pool of volunteers to start an intergenerational program at her center.

Because the context of each early childhood center is unique, so too are the constraints posed by its external environment. Programs that are funded by the military, for example, have a very different set of issues to deal with than those confronting Martha in her Head Start program. Likewise, the effects of the external environment are quite different for programs in the for-profit proprietary or corporate sector.

Mark and Jennifer are co-owners of a large, for-profit proprietary child care center. Their goal is to provide high-quality care at affordable rates. They believe that with cost-effective measures, they can make a profit while providing a needed service for their community.

Mark and Jennifer are fairly autonomous in their decision making, not hampered by having to get things approved by a board of directors. They also feel lucky they are not burdened by having to complete tons of paperwork for a sponsoring agency. This part of their arrangement they like. They find, however, there are other aspects of the external environment that impact them adversely. These have to do with stereotypic perceptions held by people in the local community about private, for-profit child care.

Mark and Jennifer sometimes feel they are swimming upstream against the tide of public opinion and negative press regarding poor quality care offered by some in the for-profit sector. They believe that parents enrolling children in their program are far more critical of center practices and tuition rates even though their rates are competitive with nonprofit programs in the area. They even sense that their licensing rep is more demanding of their program just because it is a private, for-profit program. Changing these impressions is emotionally draining. Mark and Jennifer are dedicated to doing a good job, but they often feel unappreciated.

People (the Cast of Characters)

 Organizational theorists refer to the people component of the system as the psychosocial subsystem. The psychosocial subsystem is made up of individuals (psycho) and groups of individuals (social) within the center. People are the raw material of any social system. This component includes the values, attitudes, motivation, morale, and personal behavior of each individual who works for the center. Also included are relationships with others and interpersonal issues such as trust, openness, and the group dynamics that ultimately help or hinder the center in its effort to achieve a common goal (Kast & Rosenzweig, 1985).

The people subsystem is based on the idea that a set of individuals is more than an aggregate of persons. As people interact in a social setting, networks of social relations have important effects on behavior (Hoy & Miskel, 2005). Social systems are composed of personalities. Although people occupy roles and positions in the center, they are not simply actors devoid of unique needs. No two teachers or directors in the same situation behave exactly the same way. They have different personalities, needs, and expectations that are reflected in their behavior. Thus individuals shape their roles with their own styles of behavior.

Beer (1980) reminds us that it is important to distinguish between the *can do* or abilities of an individual and the *will do* or motivational aspects of performance. Motivation ultimately is the energizing force needed to coalesce people into action to meet organizational goals. Indeed, when individuals accept jobs to work in early care and education programs, they enter into what Schein (2004) calls a *psychological contract:* the expectation of certain rewards in return for meeting organizational expectations. For each individual this reciprocal relationship will be slightly different because of the unique motivational characteristics of each person.

Just how do people differ? The following describes some of the things that go into making each individual so unique. (A more complete description of characteristics will be offered in Chapter 5.

- ▶ Personal history—age, gender, ethnicity, socio-economic group, family background

- ▶ Level of formal education, specialized training, and previous work experience

- ▶ Knowledge (e.g., child development, effective instructional practices, classroom management practices, different curricula, principles of leadership) and skill—the ability to effectively use knowledge (e.g., maintain classroom order, assess children's growth and development, lead circle time, conduct a staff meeting)

- ▶ Interests and special talents in areas such as music, art, drama, literature, athletics

- ▶ Beliefs and values about different educational practices such as appropriate goals for children, the role of the teacher, the importance of diversity, the role of parents, and the importance of inclusion

- ▶ Dispositions (e.g., tendency to be nurturing, playful, curious, optimistic, reflective, resilient, risk-taking, or self-starting)

- ▶ Flexibility and openness to change

- ▶ Energy level and physical limitations

- ▶ Cognitive capacity—level of abstract thinking

- ▶ Learning style and sensory modality preference (visual, auditory, or kinesthetic)

- ▶ Psychological type and temperament

- ▶ Communication style—direct, spirited, considerate, or systematic

- ▶ Self-efficacy—sense of confidence and conviction that one can successfully achieve desired outcomes

- ▶ Needs and expectations for autonomy, structure, security, variety, neatness, control, acceptance, intellectual challenge, achievement

- ▶ Adult development stage

- ▶ Career stage—survival, consolidation, renewal, maturity

- Level of organizational commitment

- Level of motivation

- Professional orientation—perceptions about work as "just a job" or as a career; degree of involvement in career advancement opportunities

- Concomitant roles—outside commitments and obligations (e.g., works at a soup kitchen on weekends, cares for an elderly parent, or sings in the church choir)

When individuals come together in a group, the group takes on a kind of collective personality that is the composite of the background characteristics, needs, values, interests, skills, talents, expectations, and dispositions of the individuals comprising the group. Typically people seek interaction with those they like and avoid interaction with those to whom they are not attracted. Some groups are actively sought out and admired; others are not. And groups have their own personality as evidenced by their degree of cohesiveness (Barker, Wahlers, & Watson, 2001).

Groups can also be viewed as dominant coalitions. These may be formal coalitions (e.g., by role—administrators, teachers, support staff, parents) or informal coalitions (cliques). Some coalitions have more status, power, and influence than others. The different patterns of interaction among individuals and groups, and the status structure defined by them, shape the social structure of the group (Hoy & Miskel, 2005).

Case study: The Children's Corner
Prior to accepting the directorship at The Children's Corner, Martha was the director of a parent cooperative preschool. In that position she was confronted daily with the realities of a very influential dominant coalition—the parents who comprised her board of directors. After three years as director, Martha decided to leave her position because on too many occasions she felt she had to compromise her professional judgment in order to appease this outspoken group of parents.

When she accepted the position at The Children's Corner, Martha had no idea how strongly the people dynamic in her new job would similarly influence her sense of professional fulfillment. At her first scheduled staff meeting she was struck by the level of resistance and defensiveness of three members of the staff. These three teachers were clearly a dominant coalition. They considered themselves the old guard, having taught in this Head Start program for several years. Martha was determined not to be intimidated by them, but she also recognized that they were a force to be reckoned with. Whenever one of the other teachers would suggest a new idea, Mary, Bea, or Georgia would snap back with, "We tried that years ago. It didn't work then, and there's no reason to think it should now."

Martha felt stymied. She knew she had to contend with this powerful threesome or she would be frustrated in her efforts to make her staff work as a unified team.

Structure (Formal and Informal Arrangements)

 The structure of an organization is similar to the frame of a house. Like the supporting beams of a building, the structure is the skeleton or supporting framework that holds the center together. We can think of the structure of a child care center as including several elements: the legal structure and program composition; the decision-making structure (lines of authority and division of labor); the formalized policies and procedures guiding behavior (usually detailed in a center's bylaws or parent and employee handbooks); the philosophical structure (mission and curriculum); and the actual physical arrangement of space.

"We shape our buildings, and afterwards our buildings shape us," Winston Churchill once quipped. We could easily say the same for all the structural components of our early childhood centers. The structures of an organization are like invisible forces that impact program outcomes in subtle yet profound ways. The key feature of the formal structure is that the roles, goals, and division of labor are consciously designed to guide the activities of members (Hoy & Miskel, 2005). Implicit in this formal structure is the power and status relationships of individuals working at the center.

Not every center formalizes all the following elements of structure, nor can we assume that what is written is actually how practices are carried out. We will get to this later when we talk about organizational processes. The following are common structures of early childhood programs:

Legal structure, size, program composition

- ▶ legal governing structure—for-profit or nonprofit; public or private

- ▶ size—total student enrollment and total administrative, teaching, and support staff

- ▶ program type (e.g., part-day or full-day), hours, services provided (e.g., infant care, preschool, school-age child care)

- ▶ funding structure—percentage of operating income generated from parent tuition and fees, government subsidies, grants, and in-kind services and donations

Division of labor and decision-making structure

- ▶ division of labor—job titles, roles, and assignments

- ▶ accountability and decision making—who is responsible for making what types of decisions

- ▶ reporting relationships—lines of authority, status

Policies and procedures

- ▶ policies regarding children—enrollment, teacher-child ratios, group size, group composition

- ▶ policies regarding parents' roles and responsibilities

- ▶ policies regarding staff recruitment and training—requisite qualifications, hiring guidelines (e.g., affirmative action, ADA compliance)

- ▶ performance appraisal policies

- ▶ pay and promotion system—salary scale, career ladder

- ▶ accounting, budgeting, and financial management system

Philosophical and business structure

- ▶ written educational philosophy

- ▶ program mission, strategic business plan

- ▶ written curriculum

Physical structure

- ▶ size—square footage of indoor and outdoor space

- ▶ arrangement of space for children and adults

- ▶ materials and equipment

No doubt in your own work you can think of numerous examples of the impact of different structural aspects of your program. The following vignette captures the relationship between the structural components of a center and program outcomes.

Connie had taught kindergarten in the public school system for 20 years. With a small inheritance from her uncle, she decided to leave the security of her job and open a preschool of her own. In starting her new school, Connie thought a lot about the structural elements of her program. Things like establishing the legal governing structure, deciding on program composition, developing a marketing plan, and formalizing her financial management system all seemed fairly straightforward. When it came to making decisions about the supervisory and performance appraisal structure, however, or how she would go about delineating roles and responsibilities, Connie was less sure how to proceed.

She had previously worked for a district that she perceived was a bureaucratic straightjacket. It had so many rules and regulations that she felt constricted and stifled. Connie was intent on not creating the same kind of bureaucratic climate in her new school. She also felt strongly that job descriptions, reporting relationships, supervisory and training policies, program philosophy, and educational objectives should be developed once she had her teaching staff in place.

When Connie hired her first teachers, she was disappointed to find that they floundered with the informal structure of her program. While they were excellent teachers in the classroom, they wanted and needed more definitive guidelines about center policies and practices. They complained that the lack of formal job descriptions clearly delineating roles and responsibilities created confusion in knowing who was expected to do what, how, and when. Further, they complained that the lack of a formalized pay and promotion system bred competition between staff and intensified feelings of job insecurity.

During the first year of operating her new school, Connie experienced a 50% turnover in staff. It really hurt her to see such capable teachers leave her center. The experience convinced her she needed to take action to clarify the personnel policies and procedures of her program.

Processes (How Things Get Done)

 This component of the system includes all the behaviors and interactions that occur at the individual or group level. While the structure provides the framework, processes occur when individuals interact within a given structure. The processes of a center are the cement that holds it together. The processes tell us how things actually get done. Centers often have written policies, but the way those policies are carried out is quite different than what appears in print.

The following are some of the more common processes that characterize early childhood programs:

▶ Leadership—how authority and influence are exercised by those in leadership roles

▶ Decision-making and problem-solving processes—how decisions are actually made and problems are solved (or not solved)

▶ Communication processes—the ways in which oral and written information is communicated both formally and informally; the vertical and horizontal communication networks of the center

▶ Planning and goal-setting processes—the ways in which a program's philosophy and objectives are translated into action

▶ Group meeting processes—how often meetings take place, who is expected to attend, and the patterns of behavior that characterize interactions during meetings

▶ Interpersonal relations—the type and quality of daily interactions between individuals; the degree of cohesiveness and esprit de corps that characterize human relations in the workplace

▶ Conflict management—how differences in style, beliefs, and opinions are resolved

▶ Supervisory and training processes—how the day-to-day supervision of novice and experienced employees is carried out; the type and frequency of in-service staff development

▶ Center evaluation processes—how the program as a whole is evaluated

▶ Performance appraisal processes—the formal and informal ways that administrative, teaching, and support staff are evaluated

▶ Socialization practices—how new staff are socialized into the life of the center; how the center shapes the behavior of personnel to make individual beliefs and values correspond with those of the center

▶ Teaching practices—the behaviors that characterize teacher-child interactions in the classroom

▶ Child assessment practices—how children's progress is evaluated

One of the things that impressed Martha when she interviewed for the position of director of The Children's Corner was the written philosophy of the program. The statement that appeared in the parents' handbook stressed the importance of developmentally appropriate experiences, a child-centered curriculum, and a learning environment that encouraged exploration and experimentation. What Martha saw in action when she visited the program, however, was quite different.

She was distressed to see teachers distributing dittoed worksheets to 3- and 4-year-old children. She saw children waiting in line to go to the bathroom, waiting at the table to get their snack, and waiting to be called on in large-group activities that stretched their patience and attention span. When she questioned the teachers about what she saw, to her surprise they stated that they felt they were providing children with a developmentally appropriate educational experience.

Martha realized that the incongruence in what she had read as the center's educational philosophy and what she actually saw as everyday teaching practices would provide a real challenge for her in the months ahead. She wasn't sure how she would accomplish it, but she knew she had to begin to reduce the discrepancy between the stated philosophy of the program (structure) and the everyday teaching practices (processes) that were in place. Martha knew she had her work cut out for her.

Culture (What Makes the Center Unique)

 The culture of an organization describes the basic assumptions, shared beliefs, and orientations that emerge to unite members of a group (Schein, 2004). The culture often exists outside our conscious awareness, but it shapes everything in the center. Firestone and Corbett (1988) define the culture of a school as the socially shared and transmitted knowledge of what is and what ought to be, symbolized in act and artifact. The culture, they state, "provides points of order and stability in the blooming, buzzing confusion of everyday life. It helps to clarify what is important and what is not" (p. 335). In early care and education programs, the culture of the center includes the following elements:

▶ Shared values—the collective beliefs about what is important in life (e.g., openness, trust, honesty, cooperation, teamwork)

▶ Norms—expectations for what is appropriate and acceptable in everyday interactions

▶ History of the center—key events and milestones that have shaped the center's reputation

▶ Traditions—rituals, celebrations, and customs that distinguish the center from other centers

▶ Climate—the collective perceptions of staff about different organizational practices

▶ Ethics—a shared code of moral conduct guiding professional obligations and practice

The distinction between *values* and *norms* is sometimes a fuzzy one. Generally values define the ends of human behavior and social norms describe the explicit means for pursuing those ends (Hoy & Miskel, 2005). When we make a value judgment, we make a subjective estimate of quality. That estimate is based on the principles and beliefs we feel are important in life. Norms, on the other hand, are the standards or codes of expected behavior.

As people work together, implicit agreement develops about the ways in which they are expected to behave in a variety of situations. These patterns become stable over time and define what is appropriate and acceptable behavior. We use the term *norms* to describe these rules about behavior. Most child care centers have norms about everyday demeanor, the use of space and materials, the appropriate allocation of time and expectations for workload, professional conduct with children and parents, collegiality, communication, decision making, and change (Bloom, 1986).

Jeff had never thought much before about the norms of his early childhood program until he happened to walk into the 3-year-old classroom one morning to help orient a new teacher who had just been hired. Jeff observed a series of incidents that made him reflect on how subtle

the norms of appropriate conduct are in each work setting.

The new teacher, Valerie, had worn an old pair of tattered jeans and a sweatshirt to work that morning. She had just come out of the kitchen with a coffee cup in her hand and was wandering around the classroom introducing herself to the children. "Hi Jason," she said from across the room in a loud voice to a child who had just entered the classroom and was getting his name tag from his cubbie. At that moment Jeff was called back to the office to attend to an administrative issue.

It wasn't until the end of the week that he had a chance to revisit Valerie's classroom. When he walked into the classroom, he couldn't believe he was observing the same teacher. Valerie was wearing a nice pair of pants and sweater. She was quietly making her way around the classroom assisting children with their projects. She did not have her coffee cup in hand. When a child entered the classroom, she quietly made her way over to the cubbies, knelt down, and in a soft voice greeted the child with a friendly hello and pat on the head.

Jeff was impressed. He talked to the lead teacher to find out if she had taken Valerie aside and instructed her about the do's and don'ts of appropriate behavior at the center. "I didn't need to," she said. "Valerie just figured it out herself by watching the teachers and checking their reactions to her behavior. I guess we send a pretty clear message about what is expected at this place."

The history of a center is also part of its culture. Centers are strongly influenced by events in the past. A center that has had allegations of child abuse levied against it or negative press for unethical or professional conduct will surely feel the effect of the adverse publicity for many years. Some early childhood centers have even had to close their doors and start fresh, reorganizing with a new name in a new location.

Related to the history of a program are the traditions, ceremonies, and rituals that help define its uniqueness. Your center may host an annual May Day picnic for families, decorate a float for your town's Fourth of July parade, or sponsor a holiday food drive for needy families. These traditions are often infused with deeper meaning. They provide a way for people to bond with each other and give voice to your center's mission. As Deal and Peterson (1999) state, "Without ceremony to honor traditions, mark the passage of time, graft reality and dreams onto old roots, or reinforce our cherished values and beliefs, our very existence would become empty, sterile, and devoid of meaning. Without ritual and ceremony, any culture will wither and die" (p. 31).

Culture is often used as a synonym for climate. The two concepts, *organizational culture* and *organizational climate*, though related, are conceptually distinct. Culture is the more inclusive concept, taking in values, norms, ethics, traditions, and the history of a center in addition to its climate. In the context of early care and education, we can think of organizational climate as a kind of global perception of the quality of a center. These perceptions are subjective interpretations that vary between people. This is because people perceive reality differently depending on their role in the center, their value orientation, and the context of the situation. Organizational climate is thus the collective perceptions (shared beliefs) about the people, processes, and structure. It is akin to the *personality* of a center.

Systems are not simply collections of individuals, they are constantly shifting patterns of human relationships.

Barry Oshry

These perceptions about organizational practices can be viewed from several dimensions: degree of collegiality; opportunities for professional growth; degree of supervisor support; clarity of communication, policies, and procedures; the center's reward system; decision-making structure; degree of goal consensus; task orientation; the center's physical setting; and the degree of innovativeness or creativity. While perceptions in each of these areas certainly are related, research has shown that they are distinct enough to warrant separate dimensions (Bloom, 1997).

One of the hallmarks of a true profession is that it has a code of ethics guiding the decision making of practitioners. Individuals working in the early childhood education field have a working set of assumptions that guide their behavior when confronted with moral dilemmas. The ethics that undergird their behavior may or may not conform to the stated ethics of the early childhood profession (NAEYC, 1998). An example of this discrepancy would be the director who knowingly enrolls more children in the program than are allowed by the state's licensing code. The collective sense of ethics of the teachers and administrators working for a particular program can be said to be part of its culture. To be sure, the center's code of ethics is a powerful force shaping individual and collective behavior.

Outcomes (the Effects of the Program)

Think of outcomes as the result of three intersecting components: people, structure, and processes. Figure 1.1 (p. 8) visually captures this relationship. Outcomes can be conceptualized on several different levels: the organizational level, the group functioning or staff level, the client level (both parents and children), and the community or broader societal level.

- ▶ Organization—professional reputation of the center; fiscal viability; internal efficiency; the center's professional orientation

- ▶ Staff—level of absenteeism and turnover; overall level of competence; job satisfaction; degree of commitment to the center; sense of personal and professional fulfillment

- ▶ Children—social and cognitive competence; overall health

- ▶ Parents—satisfaction with the program; degree of perceived support from the center

- ▶ Community and society—quality of the service provided

The outcomes of a center are a kind of barometer of organizational effectiveness. Keep in mind, however, that organizational effectiveness is a multidimensional concept. No single criterion can capture the complex nature of organizational functioning. Some center outcomes are readily apparent and easy to measure; others, however, are more subtle and difficult to assess. Problems can arise when directors and boards lack adequate data and base decisions about outcomes (center effectiveness) on inference. The following three examples underscore the importance of using multiple sources of evidence to assess an organization's effectiveness.

- ▶ *When a center has full enrollment and long waiting lists, it might seem logical to infer that the program has a strong reputation in the community. But that inference might be incorrect. Full enrollment could also be due to the lack of other viable options for parents in the community.*

- ▶ *In looking at a high teacher turnover rate at a center, its board of directors might conclude that the director was not doing a good job in supervising staff or providing an enriching work environment. This may or may not be the case. A high turnover rate among teachers could be due to faulty hiring practices on the part of the board. The board could be hiring individuals who are overqualified for their positions and quickly become dissatisfied with the pay and lack of challenge in their jobs.*

- ▶ *Parents are often quite vocal when they are dissatisfied with some aspect of an early childhood program. And parents who are pleased with the program often do not take the time to compliment the staff or provide positive written feedback. Directors who base their assessment of their program's effectiveness only on unsolicited feedback may be getting an unrepresentative sample of parents' true perceptions about their program's quality.*

Look again at Figure 1.1, and note that the arrows extend outward from the outcomes component back to the external environment. This completes the loop of influences. Sometimes the effects of outcomes on the external environment are strong as in the case of a higher demand for services when a program has achieved a strong reputation. Other times the effect can have far-reaching consequences. We have read, for example, how a few well-publicized cases of child abuse in child care centers resulted in legislation in several states for mandated fingerprinting of all child care workers and systematic child abuse reporting procedures. On a more positive note, we have also seen how the highly publicized program outcomes of the High/Scope Perry Preschool Project (Schweinhart, et. al., 2005) have been used by child advocates to achieve increased funding for disadvantaged children.

Characteristics of Centers When Viewed as Social Systems

Now that we have looked at all of the components of the center as a social system, let us turn our attention to some of the common characteristics of centers when viewed as systems.

Change in One Component Has an Effect on Other Components

Central to a social systems perspective is the notion that change in one component of a center will have a ripple effect throughout the social system of the center. For example, the hiring of a new director or lead teacher will most certainly alter certain processes at the center. Likewise, a change in the structure of a center (e.g., a new salary scale or change in reporting relationships) will have a strong influence in shaping the attitudes, behavior, and expectations of individuals who work in the program.

Changes in the external environment as well impact a center in different ways. State and federally funded programs, for example, are keenly aware of how the external environment affects organizational practices, particularly when there are changes in funding levels or regulatory requirements. The recent push for accountability and testing of Head Start children is an example of the impact the external environment can have on center practices. Likewise state mandates for

establishing interagency working agreements that foster cross-agency staff training, common planning for new programs, and information and resource sharing are impacting program practices at the center level.

Shortcomings of our current early care and education system are that it is fragmented, often fosters competition and inequities, and doesn't direct sufficient investments to achieving and sustaining quality. Policymakers and child advocates (Helburn & Bergmann, 2002; Kagan & Neuman, 2003; Lombardi, 2002) are calling for dramatic changes in the infrastructure of the external environment that would, if implemented, have profound consequences on an individual program's capacity to achieve positive outcomes for children and families.

Something as small as the flutter of a butterfly's wing can ultimately cause a typhoon halfway around the world.

Edward Lorenz

Organizational Equilibrium Is a Desirable Goal

Most organizational theorists believe that maintaining a sense of equilibrium is essential for the continued adequacy and viability of an organization's ability to carry out its functions. An example will help illustrate this point. People work in early childhood education in order to satisfy certain needs—for example, the need for achievement, the need for security, the need for affiliation. The center where they work also has needs that are fulfilled by the employees who function in various roles. Getzels and Guba (1957) describe this reciprocal relationship as the interplay between the *nomothetic* (the organization's needs) and the *idiographic* (the personal needs of the individuals who fill various roles). From this perspective, organizational equilibrium means maintaining that delicate balance between meeting the needs of the organization and those of the individual. As long as this state of equilibrium exists, the relationship presumably will be satisfactory, enduring, and relatively productive (Owens, 2000).

Organizations Must Change and Adapt

Social systems theory is not a static model of how organizations function. To the contrary, early childhood centers as organizations are dynamic in nature—always in flux, adapting and changing. It goes without saying that to remain vital and thriving to maintain a sense of equilibrium, centers must be flexible and able adapt to changing trends and shifting needs in the external environment. The ability to reexamine the current structure and processes of a program in light of changing trends is the key to this adaptation.

> *An organization capable of continuous renewal must have built-in provisions for self-criticism.*
>
> *John Gardner*

Sometimes these changes are abrupt and organizations must respond quickly. A tragic incident in a suburb of Chicago illustrates the point. A young woman went on a shooting rampage in an elementary school. Within hours of the incident, virtually every educational institution in surrounding communities had instituted stringent security procedures. This single incident in the external environment had a strong and immediate impact on early childhood centers in the area. Directors of these programs knew they had to implement swift changes in order to ensure children's safety and allay the fears of parents and teachers.

At other times the changes are more gradual. The increased numbers of mothers in the workforce during the last several decades has created an increased demand for infant and toddler care, prompting directors of early care and education programs to expand their menu of program options. Concurrently the demand for parent cooperative preschools has diminished. While this program model was a robust and thriving in the 1960s and 70s, today the number of parent cooperative preschools has decreased significantly.

Organizational Health Is Related to the Congruence Between Components

Matthew Miles (1965) defines a healthy organization as one that "not only survives in its environment, but continues to cope adequately over the long haul, and continuously develops and extends its surviving and coping skills" (p. 390). Organizational health can be viewed as the relative degree of congruence or *fit* between different components of the system.

A healthy early childhood center is one that has norms of continuous improvement, engaging in an ongoing self-examination aimed at identifying incongruities between components. For example, one aspect of the center's structure is the division of labor and the tasks associated with each job. The individuals assigned to do these tasks have certain characteristics (e.g., skill, knowledge, motivation, interest). When the individual's knowledge and skill match the knowledge and skill demanded by the task, performance (an outcome) will be more effective. Likewise, when the physical environment (structure) and philosophy (structure) of a program support the teaching practices (processes), better outcomes in the way of staff satisfaction and fulfillment will be ensured.

From these two examples, it is possible to see how a web of connections between the people, structure, and process components directly affects outcomes. Nadler and Tushman (1983) state that just as each pair of elements within and between components has a low or high degree of congruence, so too does the aggregate model display a low or high level of system congruence. They believe that the greater the total degree of congruence or fit between the various components, the more effective an organization will be. The director's role in assessing congruence is central. In Chapter 4 you'll be introduced to some practical tools to assist in assessing the degree of fit between various components of your program.

A Final Word

A systems approach for describing early childhood centers can lead to a better understanding of the impact of change and a more accurate estimate of anticipated outcomes. A systems view of organizations in itself is not a planning strategy nor does it predict outcomes or results. It is merely a way of looking at centers as an integrated whole that is made up of interrelated, interacting parts. By asking what impact a particular change may have on all components of the system (external environment, people, structure, processes, culture, and outcomes), it is possible to be more aware of, and thus better prepared to manage, the potential negative aspects of change.

A social systems perspective also helps early childhood administrators understand the potential sources of conflict that are part of organizational life. Many of the problems centers experience arise from the fundamental conflict between the needs and motives of an individual and the requirements of the organization. Individuals attempt to personalize their roles so their idiosyncratic needs can be met, whereas centers attempts to mold and fit individuals into prescribed roles in order to best achieve center goals. It is natural that there is inherent tension between these two elements in the system, and how this tension is handled impacts center outcomes. High morale, for example, results when organizational goals and expectations are compatible with the collective needs and expectations of individuals.

One important implication of a systems perspective is that effective organizational improvement (change) efforts necessitate first understanding the unique system of the organization, then identifying and diagnosing potential problems in the system (the degree of fit between components), and finally determining strategies that promote better equilibrium in the system. This model of change implies that different configurations of key components result in different outcomes. Thus it is not a question of finding the *one best way* of managing change, but rather determining effective combinations of components that will lead to desired outcomes.

Chapter 2

The Dynamics of Organizational Change

In today's world the question of whether change will occur is no longer relevant. Instead, the issue is how directors can cope with the inevitable barrage of changes that confront them daily in an attempt to keep their centers viable and vibrant. As Hersey, Blanchard, and Johnson (2001) state, "Although change is a fact of life, if managers are to be effective, they can no longer be content to let change occur as it will. They must be able to develop strategies to plan, direct, and control change" (p. 376).

This chapter looks at the nature of change in early care and education programs. This overview sets the stage for Chapter 3, which looks more specifically at the director's role in the change process. Two important points are central to this discussion. First, change is an integral part of thriving early childhood centers. It is not something to be avoided. To the contrary, change should be welcomed and to the extent possible, even anticipated. Second, directors who understand the nature of change will not be seduced by quick-fix solutions to the complex problems that beset their programs. As Kilman (1984) stresses, it is time we stop perpetuating the myth of simplicity. Organizations generate complex problems that cannot be solved by simple solutions. The only viable alternative is to develop a truly integrated approach to organizational improvement.

Before proceeding, take a moment to complete Exercise 2.1. Reflect back on a change or innovation you have been involved in and recall why or why not that change or innovation was or was not successful in achieving the desired outcomes.

What Is Change?

In many respects change is really an abstraction; it takes on personal meaning only when we can link it to specific examples that have some relevance. By definition, change is any significant alteration in the status quo that affects an individual or organization. Educational change, for example, is usually intended to improve school outcomes. Change usually entails some alteration in the roles and responsibilities of the people involved. For instance, in order to improve parent relations at a center, a director may decide to institute new policies in the way staff report children's progress or keep anecdotal records.

Change—only babies like it.

Roberta Newman

Although closely related to change, innovation has a slightly different meaning. Innovation refers to any proposed change or set of changes intentionally implemented that represent something new or novel to the people experiencing the change. Innovations vary in type, in complexity, and in the values associated with them. It is important to stress, though, that it does not matter if the particular innovation under consideration is new by some objective standard; it is the perceived newness of the innovation by the potential adopter that counts. For example, even though computers have been around for some time now, implementing

Attitudes and Experiences Regarding Educational Change

Over the past decades, many educational innovations have been introduced and implemented in early childhood programs. Some of these innovations, such as bilingual education, inclusion of special needs children, or the provision of infant care, have entailed major alterations in the way programs are run. Others, like incorporating mixed-aged groupings of children, adopting different curricula, implementing new assessment procedures, or introducing new technology, may have required only minor adjustments.

Think back during the past three years and name one innovation or educational change you implemented in your classroom or your center. That innovation could have been a procedural change in the way your classroom or program was run or a structural innovation that changed the operation of your program.

Describe the innovation/change: _____

_____

What was the impetus for the change? Was it self-initiated or mandated?

_____

At the time you implemented this change, what was your degree of confidence that it would work?

I was _____% sure it would succeed

If you are still using this innovation, how successful would you rate your efforts at implementing the change?

_____ not successful   _____ somewhat successful   _____ successful   _____ very successful

How has your innovation been modified since you first initiated it? Describe.

_____

_____

If you have abandoned the innovation/change, describe your reasons. If it was a change that you initiated, what would you do differently if you were to make the implementation decision again? If this was a change that was mandated for you, what could have been done differently to ensure greater success?

_____

_____

a computer billing system at a center that has always invoiced parents by handwritten notes would be considered an innovation for this center. Likewise, implementing a new curricular approach, adopting computer-based child assessment practices, or instituting new admission procedures to allow for the inclusion of special needs children could also be considered innovations.

The Impetus for Change

The impetus for change can come from many sources. Often change is mandated from our external environment. For example, the American's with Disabilities Act (ADA) sets forth mandated requirements for accommodating children and adults with special needs. The power behind mandated change is derived from the sanctions imposed if the center does not comply— for instance, funding may be taken away or a license may be revoked.

At other times, the impetus for change comes as the result of a crisis at the center. An uncontrollable case of head lice, for example, may prompt a director to institute procedures for sanitizing the children's toys and equipment daily. Parental complaints, as well, can also be the stimulus for change. Parents may be unhappy about the way behavioral problems are handled in the classroom or the lack of communication between home and school.

Programs sensitive to parental needs and expectations will feel an obligation to make program-matic changes to accommodate parental wishes. Programs sensitive to children's needs will also institute changes when necessary. For example, an influx of immigrant families enrolling in a program may prompt the director to institute a variety of programmatic changes to meet the needs of dual-language families.

Program outcomes, as well, are a powerful impetus for change. A director faced with high turnover and teacher dissatisfaction may feel the necessity to review the center's pay and promotion system and make some changes to improve staff stability. Other outcomes such as declining enrollment may prompt a director to expand enrollment options for the community. For instance, the decision might be made to expand services from part-day to full-day care or from serving preschool-age children to also serving infants and toddlers.

The Magnitude of Change

Not all change is of the same magnitude. Some organizational changes are an extension of the past. They are incremental, consistent with prevailing values and norms, more focused in nature, and can usually be implemented with existing knowledge and skills. Some organizational theorists refer to this kind of change as *first-order* or *technical change* (Fullan 2001; Heifetz, 1998; Waters, Marzano, & McNulty, 2003). Implementing new emergency and risk management procedures might be an example of this kind of change. First-order change is usually designed to solve a specific problem (what to do if the sewer system backs up or a tornado sweeps through town).

Other organizational changes are more complex, greater in magnitude, and break with past traditions and practices. These *second-order* or *adaptive changes* are more challenging because they usually require changes in people's attitudes or mental models about the ways things should be done. They also usually require new knowledge and skills to implement and may involve redefining roles and expectations. They definitely take more time. Moving a program from a highly structured, didactic, and teacher-directed curriculum to a more child-centered, individual-ized, and developmentally appropriate curriculum would be an example of second-order change. This kind of change can transform a program from the inside out.

The Nature of Change

How can we take an abstract concept like change and translate it into some fundamental principles that will serve to guide our center improvement efforts? The results of research in this area provide us with a convenient starting point. From the multitude of change efforts that have been studied in educational settings, researchers have extracted some basic principles that can help us be more successful in our change endeavors. The work of Fullan (2001), and Hord (2001), Havelock and Havelock (1973), and Berman and McLaughlin (1976) is particularly helpful in this regard.

Change Is a Process, Not an Event

Perhaps the most serious mistake directors make is to view change as a single event. To the contrary, change takes time and effort to enact. Change should really be thought of as evolutionary. It is an incremental process that is achieved in stages. Most organizational problems do not fit into the category of being solved in a short period of time. Indeed, most major educational changes take several years, not months, to implement. Many innovative educational programs fail not because they are poorly conceived but because they are rushed.

One of the characteristics of directors who experience job burnout is their inability to accept change as an integral element of organizational life (Bloom, 1982). They have a linear view of their jobs and treat change as a singular event. They view change as having a precise beginning and a definitive end. Thus, they tend to have unrealistic expectations for program stability following their change efforts and view themselves as failures if they can not control change.

Not everything that is faced can be changed; but nothing can be changed until it is faced.

James Baldwin

Directors who are successful in their administrative role view change as an integral and necessary component of a thriving center. They see it as a continuous and never-ending cycle of identifying problems, exploring change options, implementing new strategies, evaluating those changes to redefine the problem, and then developing new strategies to improve their centers. Later in this chapter you'll be presented with a diagram of the change process. This diagram captures the cyclical, ongoing nature of change. Regardless of how successful a center is in one year, there is always a new year around the corner, one that will hold a new set of issues to be addressed.

What Works Well in One Setting May Not in Another

We have all heard stories of directors who implemented procedures that were highly successful in one center, only to find that they flopped in another center. This should not come as a surprise. The teachers at different centers vary considerably in years of experience, level of education, teaching style, instructional skills, and willingness to change. There are many variations among centers, both in people's willingness to adopt new procedures and in their capacity to implement new approaches. The conditions that support the adoption of an innovation in one setting may not be present in another. This does not mean that the innovation is not worthwhile; it only means that it may not be appropriate for all settings.

On a broader scale, we can relate this principle to the early childhood program models that were promoted in the 1970s. These program models were part of the Planned Variations study and were designed to serve as exemplar prototypes. The inherent assumption, as Kagan (1990) explains, was that "what worked well in one locale would work equally well in another." Kagan goes on to say that "not only were there problems encountered because different settings had their own unique cultures, but numerous challenges emerged as programs attempted to move from small to large scale" (p. 18). The problem, of course, is that new models are often not incorporated into the life of the organization; they never become institutionalized. The most successful educational experiments in the adoption of educational innovations have been those where models have not been adopted wholesale, but rather adapted to meet the unique needs of the school (Berman & McLaughlin, 1976; Fullan, 2001; Rust & Freidus, 2001).

Success Depends on the Felt Need for Change

Change is more likely to occur and be successful when it relates to a felt need or resolves a problem that is important to those implementing the change. Teachers, for example, are more likely to try out a new approach to classroom management when they feel their current methods are not working well. The research on successful educational change consistently underscores the principle that individuals are more likely to change when they focus on problems significant to them and have input into how to best resolve those problems.

While this principle makes good common sense, it also presents a dilemma for directors. Often a director has a clear idea of how a center should be changed, but his or her perceptions may not be broadly shared by others. In fact, considerable evidence exists that directors' views of organizational practices are significantly different from their staffs' view (Bloom, 1988a).

Beer (1980) states that change will occur only when sufficient dissatisfaction exists with the status quo among those who must change. Sufficient dissatisfaction creates momentum for change. But even then, Beer adds, individuals may be reluctant to change unless they are convinced the proposed new approach will really solve their problem. Unilateral pressure to change can create resistance and hostility directed at the source of pressure. Sometimes all it takes is direct discussion between a director and teacher to provide an awareness of problems that will stimulate change. But other times the recognition of the need for change is more difficult to communicate.

All Change Isn't Necessarily Good
This principle can be summed up by the old adage, "If it ain't broke, don't fix it!" Some administrators think that there is no progress unless things are in a constant state of flux. But change for the sake of change can be detrimental. When people are made to change for no apparent reason, they will develop resistance to the concept of change. Wu (1988) believes effective leadership is not characterized by either constant or radical change. If no valid reason for change exists, then chaos may result.

Change Has a Ripple Effect
Some of the most successful organizational changes have happened in small increments. A director may not be able to convince her whole staff to adopt a new curriculum or instructional technique, but she may be able to convince one teacher to try it out. Success experienced by that one teacher can have an impact on others. Thus change in one person or one classroom may provide the impetus for change in another person or in another classroom.

Change Is Highly Personal
How individuals react to change depends in large part on their personal values and dispositions. If a proposed change is consistent with what they believe, they are more likely to embrace it and implement it enthusiastically. If it contradicts what they believe to be important, resistance is more likely to occur. Likewise some individuals are flexible and more willing to take risks; others are more rigid in their thinking and risk averse. Some people eagerly embrace innovations and want to be on the cutting edge of change; others are more cautious in their approach, adopting new ideas only after they have stood the test of time. There is no formula to predict how people will react to any specific proposed change.

Models of Change
With this overview of the change as a backdrop, let's look now at the advantages and disadvantages of different approaches to change. The framework for this comes from Beer (1980), who defines three models of change that are characteristic in organizations: top-down, bottom-up, and collaborative change.

Top-Down Change
Many decisions regarding center change are mandated by decree; they are essentially top-down directives of new procedures to be implemented, oftentimes rapidly. They may be decisions about new policies, new organizational structures, or new ways of doing things. Some top-down changes are mandated by legislation and public policy and impact virtually all programs. The Americans with Disabilities Act is

an example of a top-down change that required compliance across the field of early care and education. Other times changes may be mandated by the central administrative office of a child care organization and impact policies and practices in only a few centers. Many of the decisions that directors make are also implemented using a top-down model of change. A top-down approach is essentially a directive model.

Top-down changes are usually unilateral. Only a few people make the decisions. For this reason, the changes can be introduced very rapidly. If the solution is appropriate for the problem that triggered the need for the change in the first place, the changes will probably obtain immediate results. A directive top-down model of change can work if people anticipate some positive outcomes of the change, support it, and are committed to it. It is the speed of the top-down approach that makes it attractive to directors under pressure to obtain immediate results.

One of the shortcomings of this approach is that the proposed solutions are not always the most appropriate because the people who know the most about the problems are not consulted. Top-down changes often do not reflect the needs of the individuals impacted unless those mandating the changes are attuned to their needs. As a result, staff may not be committed to implementing change because they do not understand the rationale behind it or do not have sufficient information to successfully put it into practice.

The likelihood that a top-down approach will result in psychological stress is strong. Staff may perceive the change as a directive. Even when teachers agree that change may be necessary, top-down models risk making them feel manipulated and powerless. The result may be animosity, hostility, and overt behavior to undermine or sabotage the proposed change.

Juanita is the director of a small, private, for-profit child care center. She is also a technological whiz and has always used a personal computer to do her work. Juanita was dismayed that Nancy, the office secretary, still did all the billing of parents by hand. She perceived this to be both too time consuming and tedious, so she purchased and installed a financial management software package on the office computer. Juanita assumed Nancy would enthusiastically embrace this new software as being a labor-saving device for monitoring accounts receivable.

The following day when Nancy turned on her computer and noticed the new icon for the financial management software on her screen, she was visibly upset. Next to her computer was a detailed set of instructions on how to use the program that Juanita had prepared. Now Nancy was angry. While she understood that the software would make her job more efficient, she was hurt that she was not consulted about whether or not she even wanted to use this software package to do the accounts receivable. She felt the least that Juanita could have done was consult her if she wanted to convert to this automated way of doing billing.

Fortunately Juanita was a seasoned director, sensitive to differing points of view. She apologized to Nancy for not consulting her and acknowledged that it was insensitive of her to think that Nancy would embrace new software as much as she did. With this acknowledgement, Nancy began to open up. She confessed it wasn't so much the technology itself that she was opposed to, but the change in the relationship with the parents that she feared would take place. Nancy believed that her handwritten notes to parents each month with their tuition invoice provided a personal touch that conveyed that the center really cared about them as individuals and wasn't only concerned about their financial support. She feared that a computerized system might make the whole financial billing process too institutional and cold.

This incident was a clear case of making a hasty decision based on only partial information. Juanita perceived that others viewed technological conveniences as she did. She did not seem to consider Nancy's feelings or value her expertise.

Fortunately, however, she was a sensitive administrator who took the time to better understand the point of view of her subordinate.

Kevin was recently hired as the director of a state-funded prekindergarten program. He had always felt that accurate record keeping was the hallmark of a professional. One of his first directives in taking over the program was to send a memo to the teachers telling them about the importance of keeping anecdotal notes on each child. He indicated that all teachers would now be required to make one anecdotal note on every child each day. He stressed how this new procedure would improve the quality of parent conferencing at the center.

The teachers at the center were a very experienced group of educators. They did not feel there was a need for this additional paperwork. They felt they had been conducting parent conferences just fine without reams of anecdotal notes. They followed the directive for about three weeks and then gradually stopped taking notes altogether.

Kevin's directive was destined to fail. First, he did not anticipate that a group of seasoned teachers might interpret such a directive as a challenge to their professional autonomy. Second, his decree was communicated in a written memo. From the teachers' perspective, this made the directive very impersonal and easier to dismiss. Third, the teachers were simply not convinced of the need for more anecdotal notes. Finally, Kevin did not make any structural changes in the program, such as allotting additional planning time for the teachers to write up their notes. This kind of structural change may have helped sustain the new procedure he proposed.

Despite the drawbacks of the top-down model, it appears it is the prevailing model for making organizational changes in early childhood programs. Top-down unilateral decisions can be an effective approach where circumstances dictate that quick action be taken (Bloom, 2000). For example, an increase in neighborhood vandalism may prompt a director to institute new security precautions for the center. Staff in this kind of situation are more apt to comply with a directive. They understand the urgent nature of the directive and the rationale for the decision.

A top-down model of change can also be effective when the focus of the change only tangentially concerns staff. For example, teachers may not be very interested in change decisions regarding routine managerial aspects of running the program. The decision to change janitorial services or landscape maintenance services may have little consequence for teachers. A top-down model of change may be quite appropriate for these kinds of decisions.

Bottom-Up Change

In bottom-up change, the responsibility for defining and developing a solution is left to the teaching or support staff of the center. This responsibility may be delegated or assumed. This kind of change model is often present in programs where directors take a hands-off approach to management. Their nondirective leadership style assumes that people can implement changes that are necessary for them to do their jobs efficiently. The problem with this approach, though, is that it often results in a clash over the goals or the direction of change. Also, because the director or the center's governing board are not involved (or perhaps not even aware of the change), they are not in a position to implement the administrative structures that can sustain the change, assuming it is a positive one. The following example illustrates this point.

Gayle is a preschool teacher. At her local AEYC conference she attended an interesting workshop on the Reggio Emilia approach to documenting children's learning. During her spring break, Gayle decided to enroll in a three-day intensive institute on documentation that was being offered at a local college. She was really excited about what she learned and

*came back from vacation enthusiastic to imple-
ment the new documentation strategies in her
classroom. Given the frenetic activity of the
program and all the other demands tugging at
her sleeve, though, Gayle just couldn't seem to
find the time to get herself organized to
implement all the great ideas she had learned.
After a month, she packed away her notes from
the institute and abandoned all hopes of
making her classroom a Reggio-inspired show-
case for the center.*

Gayle's innovation did not fail because it was
not well suited for her classroom. It failed because
she lacked the appropriate incentives and
administrative support to sustain her enthusiasm in
it. Had Gayle been more actively encouraged to
try out some new documentation strategies by her
director or her peers, her level of interest in Reggio
Emilia instructional methodologies would have
been sustained. If she had worked at a center
where supervision and performance appraisal
processes were in place to ensure that she had the
resources and technical support to adopt new
ideas for her classroom, her attempt at implementing documentation strategies probably would have
met with greater success.

*The teachers and support staff at a large
urban child care center felt discontent because
of their salaries, benefits, and lack of job
security. They met with the staff from another
center that had recently unionized to learn
more about their labor rights. They decided
they had nothing to lose by confronting their
director with the possibility that they, too,
wanted to unionize if their current conditions
were not improved. Under pressure, the
director convinced her board to implement a
small salary increase and some paid planning
time.*

*The teachers were jubilant. They felt empow-
ered by their success at changing the center's
policies. What they hadn't anticipated, though,
was the increased strain and tension with the
director that resulted from their actions. The*

*director felt she had been coerced to take
action. She viewed the whole incident as a
direct challenge to her authority. What had
been an amiable working relationship between
the director and staff turned sour.*

We see, then, that there are several shortcomings to the bottom-up model of change. If the
administration of a center delegates completely to
staff the right to define the change, it gives up its
influence in the definition of problems and their
solutions. Even if one classroom adopts a change,
the likelihood that the whole center will adopt the
change will be less. Second, there is a high
potential for clash if the outcomes of the change
are not valued or if they conflict with the center's
values. Finally, the likelihood that the change will
not become institutionalized is high. Virtually all
changes in a program in order to be sustained
have to be supported from the top.

Collaborative Change

Top-down and bottom-up change strategies
represent extremes in the distribution of decision-
making authority in a center. For most organizational changes, the most successful model is
simultaneously top-down and bottom-up—
collaborative change. Here both the administration and the staff are involved in identifying
problems and developing viable solutions.

The concept of collaboration as having power
with, not *over,* colleagues is central to success in
this approach. Parity in status and equal
responsibility for work characterize the relationship
between teachers and directors in centers where
this model of change prevails. In such
environments, teachers are active partners in
some or all of the stages, including clarifying the
problem, collecting and analyzing the data,
generating solutions, and evaluating results.

Behaving collaboratively does not mean that
the director relinquishes the responsibility to
provide expertise and leadership in the change
process. Necessary technical assistance and
support are clearly vital contributions of the
director. What collaboration does imply is that the

expertise of others is recognized and incorporated into the center's improvement efforts. As Saxl (1989) states, a collaborative approach is focused and directed, but not directive in a controlling sense. It is a helping and facilitative orientation that supports cooperative learning, mutual growth, reciprocal openness, and shared problem solving. Collaboration rests on trusting relationships.

The drawback of collaborative change is that it takes longer to implement. Collecting data to clarify the nature of problems, holding meetings to clarify the direction of change, and providing feedback to clarify what's working and what isn't can't be done on the fly. No way around it, collaborative change takes time and lots of it. Immediate turn-around of a problem is not likely to occur.

For this reason, it is understandable why a collaborative approach to change is not widely embraced in organizations, big and small, educational or otherwise. But the positive benefits that result from adopting a collaborative approach clearly outweigh the disadvantages in terms of the time commitment. In a collaborative model, staff have a clearer idea of expectations and what their roles and responsibilities will be in the change process. Most important, however, is that a collaborative model results in a higher level of trust, a deeper level of commitment, and greater overall satisfaction with the process by all involved.

A collaborative model tends to be appropriate for working with individuals and groups who are achievement motivated, seek responsibility, and have a degree of knowledge and experience that may be useful in solving problems. As we saw in the example with Kevin, an experienced group of teachers may become oppositional if change is implemented in a directive manner. A directive approach is inconsistent with their perceptions of themselves as mature, responsible, self-motivated people who should be consulted on issues that directly affect them. At the same time, a collaborative approach may be less successful when working with a group of inexperienced teachers who need more guidance and structure. In Chapter 6, you'll learn how these models of change (top-down, bottom-up, and collaborative) relate to different supervisory styles.

In sum, there is no fail-proof recipe for implementing change in early childhood programs. Participation is important at all levels of the organization, but its form will vary from center to center. One cannot assert that any particular change model is most effective; it depends on the situation and the nature of the problem being resolved.

The basic assumption of this book is that bringing about change is an important task of early childhood administrators. But forcing changes—even good ones—endangers the goal of fostering human relations in a center. Moreover, forced change rarely results in lasting changes in teachers' behavior. The role of the director, then, is to create the interpersonal context that frees, encourages, and helps people to embrace new ideas and adapt new strategies that improve the quality of program services.

Change is inevitable, but growth is optional.

Michael Fullan

Factors Influencing the Adoption of Innovations

There are many interrelating factors that can potentially influence one's behavior with respect to decisions about the adoption or rejection of educational innovations. These factors relate to the attributes of the innovation itself.

Attributes of the Innovation

Embodied in the decision-making process to adopt a specific innovation is the assumption that the individual or group responsible for the decision weighs alternatives in an effort to discern the relative advantages of a particular innovation over existing practices or other potential innovations. These alternatives generally center on various attributes of the innovation and thus serve as incentives for adopting or rejecting a new approach. The individual's perceptions of these attributes are of considerable importance because they help explain why some innovations enjoy rapid and widespread dissemination while others fade to obscurity. It also helps explain the rate and ease with which different innovations are implemented.

Drawing predominantly on the work of Rogers (2003), Gladwell (2000), and Fliegel and Kivlin (1966), it is possible to develop a taxonomy of some of the characteristics used to classify a wide range of innovations. These eight criteria are not intended to be exhaustive, nor are they intended to be mutually exclusive. Considerable overlap exists among them. Nevertheless, taken together they represent a fairly comprehensive set of criteria for making decisions to adopt or reject an innovation.

Cost effectiveness. Cost is clearly a critical factor for many innovations. But economic considerations also involve more than initial capital investment, particularly when supplies and ongoing maintenance may be an issue. In considering cost, a distinction must be made between initial costs and continuing costs (or operating costs). It must also be remembered that cost effectiveness is a relative attribute and must be assessed in relation to other variables such as increased output, reduced production costs, and other economic or social factors deemed important. It is for this reason that computers as an administrative tool are such a popular innovation. While their initial cost is high, the perceived benefits in terms of increased output and time savings generally make them an attractive innovation for early childhood directors to consider.

Nothing endures but change.

Heraclitus

Social approval. This is a noneconomic attribute associated with the status and prestige that different innovations confer. Social approval is clearly an important motivator with respect to adoption and rejection decisions. The social cost of an innovation may come in the form of ridicule, ostracism, or even exclusion from a group. Some educational innovations are clearly seen as conferring more status than others. The widespread appeal of NAEYC's center accreditation initiative, for example, is due in large part to the perceived professional status it confers on those centers that achieve accreditation.

Complexity. The degree of complexity associated with an innovation may also have an important bearing on acceptance or rejection. Complexity is the degree to which an innovation is perceived as difficult to understand and use. Some innovations are readily understood; others are more complicated. Innovations that are challenging yet have a high likelihood of success are more apt to find wider acceptance than those that are too simple or those that are highly complex. The wide-spread adoption of the Creative Curriculum (Dodge, Colker, & Heroman, 2002) and the High/Scope Curriculum (Holmann & Weikart, 2002), for example, can be attributed to the fact that while these curricula require some specialized training to successfully implement, the training and the curricula are not perceived as too complex.

Efficiency. Efficiency is a broad attribute and can be measured both in terms of time saved and the avoidance of discomfort. The saving of time clearly has direct economic implications. The efficiency attribute is one of the strongest motivators for directors using e-mail. As with most technological advances, what is often not anticipated is the considerable time and patience required during the initial learning phase of a new technological application. This is discouraging for many new users expecting quick results and immediate gratification.

Trialability. The degree to which an innovation may be experimented with on a limited basis before one decides on full scale adoption also influences whether or not it is adopted. Trialability reduces the uncertainty associated with complex or costly innovations. The possibility of trying out the innovation on a limited scale allows one to minimize possible unanticipated negative consequences and to postpone decisions regarding large investments of educational resources. Many programs that provide inclusion for children with special needs, for example, start out with a limited number of children in a classroom.

Observability. The degree to which the results of an innovation are visible to others also has an impact on adoption decisions. In other words, the easier it is for individuals to see the results of an innovation, the more likely it is that it will stimulate peer discussion. This may increase the likelihood of adoption. The enthusiasm generated for the project approach is a good example of this principle. Having the opportunity to observe a classroom where one can see firsthand the results of the project approach to curriculum planning and instructional convinces many teachers it is a worthwhile innovation for their own classrooms.

Compatibility. The individuals' or group's present values and past experiences have a considerable influence on adoption decisions. If an innovation is too incongruent with current practices, it may be perceived as too threatening and thus unacceptable.

Terminality. Terminality describes the ease with which a particular innovation or change can be ended if it isn't working out. Terminality can serve as a strong motivation to adopt or resist an innovation. Innovations that can be more easily reversed are more apt to be adopted. It is for this reason that many school districts have been slow in adopting a career ladder approach to professional advancement. Once implemented, a career ladder is difficult to terminate given the contractual agreements that it may have imposed.

It is important to underscore the salience of individual differences in people's perceptions with respect to these various attributes. What may appear to be a simple and easily understood innovation to one person may seem highly complex and intimidating to another.

The Center Improvement Process

Implementing centerwide change is essentially a problem-solving process involving a series of steps to remedy an unsatisfactory situation. These steps move from initial problem identification to action based on an agreed-upon solution. The following diagram graphically highlights the different steps in this process.

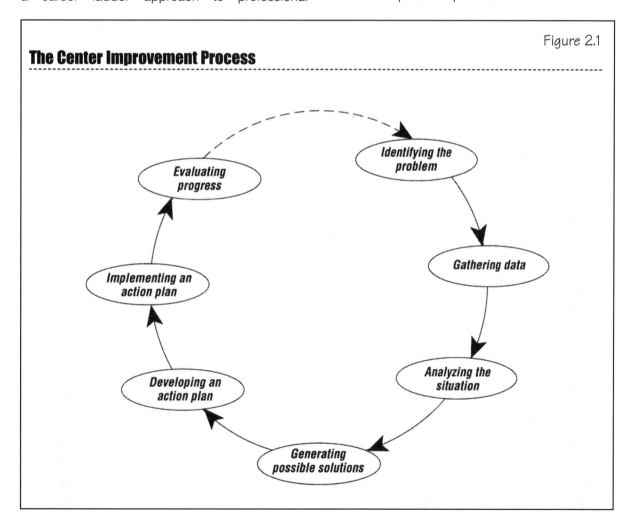

Figure 2.1

The Center Improvement Process

The first step in the center-improvement process involves defining the most pressing organizational problems that need to be addressed. This step sounds fairly straightforward, but in reality involves careful analysis of present conditions and how these differ from ideal conditions. Change efforts, in other words, should focus on attempting to reduce the discrepancy between real (actual) and ideal (desired) conditions.

In order to form a clear picture of problem areas in a program, it is necessary to gather data. Clear, accurate data on the situation helps the director and staff avoid the mistake of focusing on mere symptoms of the problem (e.g., high turnover, parental dissatisfaction, or low commitment to center goals) rather than on the deeper core problems that may need to be addressed. Chapter 4 provides guidelines that will help you assess the needs of your program.

The third step in the change process involves analyzing the situation. This step results in generating possible solutions and weighing alternative courses of action. From this analysis an action plan is developed to address areas in need of improvement.

Change is not just about having new ideas; it's about seeing old things with new eyes.

Dee Hock

The final step in the process is evaluating the effectiveness of the change effort. The information gleaned from evaluating program improvement efforts results in reformulating and redefining new areas that need to be addressed. While the cycle depicted in Figure 2.1 appears two dimensional, you can also think of the program improvement process as being a three-dimensional spiral where each successive loop of the cycle helps a center achieve higher levels of program excellence. Implementing this model is essentially the essence of instilling norms of continuous improvement.

A Final Word

After reading the overview of the change process presented in this chapter, it is probably clear to you why many organizational change efforts fail to result in lasting improvements. Good intentions simply don't guarantee good results. In reviewing the research on the topic, Parkay and Damico (1989) conclude that failure to achieve positive lasting benefits from organizational changes are usually due to two reasons. First, there is usually a lack of staff input. The result is improvement goals and proposed change that are not compatible with the needs, values, beliefs, and expectations of the staff. Second, many (if not most) change efforts are viewed too narrowly; they do not take an ecological systems view that considers the political, social, demographic, economic, and technological forces in the organization's environment. The result is that changes can't be sustained or they end up creating new problems that negate the positive outcomes of the initial change effort.

So far we've looked at the broad issues surrounding center-based improvement. Now let's turn our attention to the role of the director in the change process and how a systems perspective of early childhood programs can help to achieve lasting change.

Chapter 3

The Director's Role in the Change Process

R are is the director who does not feel caught in a whirlwind of activity. With new staff to orient, new procedures to implement, new curricula to evaluate—where is the calm, the expected, the anticipated? Change and child care administration go hand in hand.

How is it, though, that some directors are so successful in implementing substantial, significant changes in their programs? Who is it that initially senses the need for change and nurtures the change process? Where do the innovative ideas come from? And how can staff be motivated to support needed change? This chapter explores these and other questions in an attempt to set the stage for how directors can take charge in implementing change that improves center life and achieves program goals.

The perspective of change proposed in this chapter takes a systems view of centers as dynamic entities constantly interacting with their external environment, changing and adapting to ensure greater congruence between people, structure, and processes. The underlying assumption of this model is that when these components are not congruent, the program cannot achieve desired outcomes. When this condition does not exist, people in the center perceive barriers to accomplishing their work and meeting their personal needs. The director's job, in a nutshell, is to maintain a sense of congruence within and between these components of the program.

The Director as Change Agent

The director's role is central in the change process. In a number of powerful ways, the director shapes the center as a workplace. The director as leader plays a pivotal role in both assessing the current situation and structuring change to improve conditions. More than anyone else, directors are the agents of change. This does not mean that they impose change, but rather they encourage and support it by developing the interpersonal context that frees, encourages, and helps people to assess their program and become actively involved in the change process.

> *What you leave behind is not what is engraved in stone monuments, but what is woven into the lives of others.*
>
> *Pericles*

The important thing to remember is that directors are facilitators of change, not dictators of change. Mobilizing and empowering people means helping others create new behavioral expectations. But keeping change efforts on target is not easy. Managing change is not a haphazard process. It is a delicate balance of providing direction yet suppressing the urge to overmanage. Leading change efforts means providing sufficient leadership and support but resisting the temptation to micromanage. Facilitating the process means helping to maintain the momentum, the pace, and the spirit.

Facilitating organizational changes requires directors to use both the leadership and management functions of administration. As Figure 3.1

captures, leadership functions relate to vision building, securing buy-in from stakeholders, promoting commitment and creativity, and overcoming resistance. Management functions relate to the actual orchestration of tasks—gathering data, making timelines, creating procedures, and securing the resources to ensure the work gets done.

Building a Vision for Change

Fundamental to successful change is directors' ability to have a clear, informed vision of what they want their centers to become. This sounds basic, yet often directors can articulate what is wrong with their programs but have difficulty articulating just how their ideal program would look and function. Further, directors need to know how to translate that vision into realistic goals and expectations for teachers and children. This means creating the climate that supports progress toward goals and expectations.

A vision statement provides the direction and driving power for change. It is not some elusive abstraction, but rather the heart and soul of what guides a strategic plan of what one's program will look like in three to five years. A vision statement helps directors develop a set of realistic goals that are both purposeful and achievable.

Before reading on, take a few moments to complete Exercise 3.1. What would you like to hear when people describe your program? Write a dozen or so words or phrases that would describe your ideal program. What would you like to see more or less of in your program? Now take those impressions and weave them into a short statement of your vision of what you would like your program to become in three to five years. While your vision statement will embody elements of your ideal, it should also be reality based. These thoughts will be incorporated into an organizational profile you will develop at the end of Chapter 4.

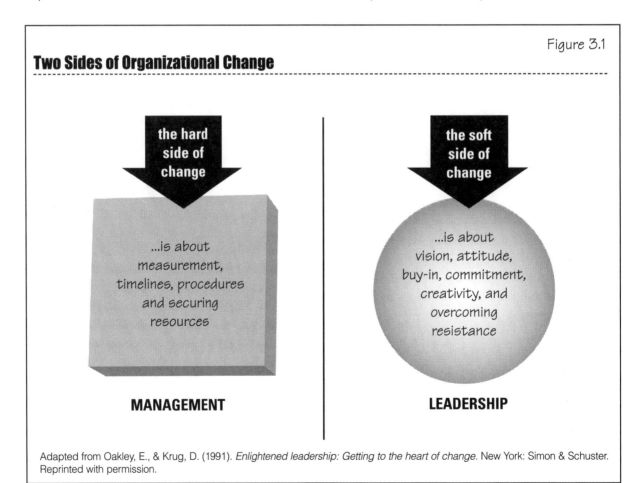

Two Sides of Organizational Change

Figure 3.1

the hard side of change

...is about measurement, timelines, procedures and securing resources

MANAGEMENT

the soft side of change

...is about vision, attitude, buy-in, commitment, creativity, and overcoming resistance

LEADERSHIP

Adapted from Oakley, E., & Krug, D. (1991). *Enlightened leadership: Getting to the heart of change.* New York: Simon & Schuster. Reprinted with permission.

Vision Building: Clarifying Your Ideal

What would you like to hear when people describe your program? Write a dozen or so words or phrases that describe your ideal program.

_____   _____

_____   _____

_____   _____

_____   _____

_____   _____

_____   _____

What are some of the things you'd like more of in your program?

_____   _____

_____   _____

What are some of the things you'd like less of in your program?

_____   _____

_____   _____

Now take the words and phrases that describe your ideal program and your impressions of things you'd like more or less of in your program and weave them into a short statement of your vision of what you'd like to see your program become in three to five years. While your vision statement will embody elements of your ideal, it should also be reality based.

My vision of what my program could look like . . .

_____

_____

_____

_____

_____

Serving as a Catalyst for Change

The director is the one who must sense the need for change and communicate that need to others. This means being informed about new trends in the field, interpreting changes in the external environment that may influence organizational effectiveness, and actively eliciting feedback from others about the quality of program services. In other words, regularly assessing the pulse of the center. Chapter 4 presents a variety of assessment tools that will help you gather the data you need to become and stay informed.

Huszczo (1996) believes that unless 80 percent of the members of an organization see a need for change, it will be difficult for any proposed change to take hold. This does not mean that 80 percent of the people must rally enthusiastically behind the plan, it just means that to begin the change process, at least 80 percent of the people need to be unhappy enough with the current situation to want some kind of change. Serving as the catalyst for change means stepping to the plate and taking the initiative to propose needed changes. It means being proactive, rather than reactive, and willing to take risks. This is an uncomfortable stance for many early childhood administrators.

Finally, if directors are to be effective change agents, they need to keep abreast of new methods, approaches, and current research in the field. Studies have shown a strong relationship between directors' professional orientation and their degree of innovativeness (Bloom & Ford, 1988). It stands to reason that directors who regularly participate in professional organizations, subscribe to journals, visit other centers, and attend conferences to enhance their expertise are likely to be exposed to a wider variety of innovative practices. They are also more likely to develop a network of resources to help implement and support desired changes.

Acknowledging that the director is the one who serves as the primary catalyst for change does not diminish the importance of others as a source for innovative ideas. Many good suggestions for improving programs come from teachers, parents, and the children we serve. The key is to manage in such a way that divergent thinking and creative problem solving are promoted at all levels.

In assessing a center's readiness for change, timing is everything. Many good change efforts fail not because the ideas are poor, but because the timing for implementing the change is not good. As the catalyst for change, directors need to assess a program's readiness for change. This entails determining the accessibility of resources and support, the internal press for change, the stability of the staff undergoing change, and the overall spirit of risk taking. Table 3.1 details these elements.

Creating the Climate for Change

The director is the key person for establishing the organizational norms that support or inhibit change. By a combination of position and sheer persuasiveness, directors can initiate or inhibit, build or erode, expand or contract the norms that bear critically on center quality. Developing a sense of trust, openness to experiment, and the willingness to risk failure are all norms that will impact a center's ability to incorporate needed change. Further, the director must know how to deal with institutional cynicism (the "we've tried that before" syndrome) and be able to assess the underlying causes that breed cynicism and defensiveness. As director, the comments you make in formal staff meetings or informal hallway conversations can reinforce or inhibit norms of experimentation and risk-taking.

Case Study: The Children's Corner

Christine was the newest teacher to be hired by Martha at The Children's Corner. She was young, enthusiastic, and a recent graduate of the early childhood program at the local college. At one of the first staff meetings in the fall, teachers discussed the problems they were experiencing with tote bags getting mixed up and papers being sent home with the wrong children. "I have an idea," Christine chimed in. "At the lab school we color coded the tote bags. It really helped organize everything. We bought plain canvas tote bags, and dyed each group's bags a different color. Then we put the children's names on the bags in big bold letters. The parents paid for the cost of the bags." Bea immediately countered, "Well, that may have worked at the lab school, but it sure won't here. You forget what kind of background these Head Start kids come from. Their parents surely don't have money to throw away on a new tote bag every year!"

Table 3.1

Assessing a Center's Readiness for Change

Accessibility of Resources and Support

- ► Availability of technical knowledge within the center
- ► Accessibility of technical knowledge and expertise outside the center
- ► Availability of financial resources
- ► Support from board or key administrators

Internal Press for Change

- ► Proportion of individuals who are dissatisfied with the present situation
- ► Proportion of individuals who value the proposed change
- ► Proportion of individuals who have confidence that the proposed change will bring positive benefits to the center

Stability of the Staff Undergoing Change

- ► Proportion of turnover of staff
- ► Commitment of key administrators to remain in current positions during the early stages of change
- ► Proportion of individuals involved in other change endeavors

Spirit of Risk-Taking

- ► Proportion of individuals who are willing to risk new action on behalf of the center
- ► Presence of leadership
- ► Proportion of individuals willing to undergo training to achieve desired changes
- ► Proportion of staff who experience stress due to center-related or personal factors

Adapted from Arbuckle, M., & Murray, L. (1989). *Building systems for professional growth: An action guide.* Andover, MA: The Regional Laboratory for Educational Improvement of the Northeast and Islands, pp. 1–3.

Inside Martha was furious at the way Bea just dismissed Christine's suggestion. But she also realized there was much more going on in this brief exchange than met the eye. Martha knew that Bea actually felt a bit intimidated and perhaps even threatened by the youthful exuberance Christine exhibited. Her comments were really a defensive posture intended to put Christine in her place. Martha calmly intervened: "You're right on target, Bea. Our parents don't have the money to buy new tote bags. But I think Christine has an innovative idea here that is worth exploring. How could we take this idea and turn it into a workable solution to our tote bag problem? Think we might have a small fund-raiser to cover the cost of the tote bags? Bea, you've had a lot of experience with fund-raising. Do you have any suggestions on how we might proceed?"

The director also has a strong impact on institutionalizing norms of self-reflection—individually and collectively looking for ways to do things better. Norms of self-reflection can't be imposed, they need to be nurtured over time. Many programs have a culture characterized by inertia. Coaxing the system to be less complacent is not easy, but it is essential if a program is to work on resolving problems. Thus, the director's role in creating a climate for change is essentially one of energizing the self-reflection process.

Providing Resources, Support, and Recognition

Another vital function the director plays in the change process is that of resource provider. The director brings together a variety of needed resources. These can be financial resources such as money for substitutes, materials, trainers, travel, equipment, or evaluation. Resources may come from professional associations, publishers, vendors, or outside consultants.

Another leadership task is providing encouragement and recognition to staff for their efforts. The importance of this task can't be overstated. Reinforcing positive behaviors, listening, providing emotional support, and allowing people room to make mistakes are all part of the director's role in providing support for change. In a defensive climate, people do not have the time or emotional

energy to be creative because their energies are dissipated in trying to protect themselves from critical feedback.

Beer (1980) states that in order for change to spread through an organization and become a permanent fixture, early successes are needed. It is desirable but not necessary for the results of a change to be able to be measured. But feelings of success are more important than quantitative measures. When individuals or groups feel more competent than they did before a specific change was implemented, this increased sense of competence reinforces the new behavior and solidifies learning associated with the change.

But intrinsic feelings of success are not sufficient for patterns of organizational behavior to be changed permanently. Self-confidence will quickly erode if extrinsic rewards in the organization do not immediately follow the early indicators of improved performance. Rewards can include recognition by the director, the board, or peers. The structure and processes of the center, such as personnel policies and practices, performance appraisal procedures, promotion guidelines, and budget allocations, must also support the new behaviors being sought.

Managing (and Protecting) Time

Time is clearly a huge barrier to implementing thoughtful and constructive change. The press of everyday events typically requires teachers and directors to be more concerned with just maintaining the status quo than envisioning change. In fact, time is a central ingredient in the change process itself. Time is needed to share knowledge and information about the content of a planned change or innovation. Time is needed to develop the skills necessary to ensure a smooth change process. And time is needed to make the coffee, order the donuts, and set up the chairs for meetings to plan and carry out a proposed change.

As an administrator, you know that time is a scare commodity. As such it must be judiciously used and jealously protected if change endeavors are to be successful. Unfortunately, it is the kind of resource that is typically neglected in the planning process. It is easy to underestimate the amount of time needed for information sharing, training, group meetings, and administrative coordination. Change initiatives will make little progress without adequate time being allocated.

We know that carving out sufficient time to address organizational issues is a persistent problem for directors. As you undertake change endeavors in your program, no doubt you will ask yourself, "Where will I possibly find the time to do a proper diagnosis of center needs?" "How can I ensure that staff will actually devote the time needed for this change?" "Do I have the time to manage all the activities, locate appropriate resources, and follow through in a way that will ensure success?" "And how can I help my staff so they do not become impatient with the amount of time it takes to achieve workable long-range solutions?" An important part of your role in ensuring success in any change endeavor, then, is to assess how time is currently being used, set priorities for the judicious use of time, and eliminate time wasters whenever possible. In fact, the use of time in a center may even become a focus of your change efforts.

The Challenge of Balancing Individual and Organizational Needs

Schein (2004) calls the interaction between the individual and organization a dynamic, two-way process. This interaction, he believes, consists of a mutual sense of obligation between the interacting parties. He refers to this as *reciprocation*. Centers employ individuals because their services are essential for the center to successfully achieve its goals. Individuals, in turn, relinquish some of their personal autonomy and independence to the center in order to fulfill their personal needs. This relationship is cooperative only when it offers both entities—the individual and the center—the opportunity to fulfill their respective needs.

If we could distill the essence of what leadership means in the context of early childhood program administration, perhaps it could best be summed up by the challenge that directors face in balancing individual and organizational needs. The

center must achieve a balance between helping individuals meet their personal needs and meeting its organizational goals. Successful directors acknowledge the importance of being goal-oriented, but they are also mindful that "people are not willing to sacrifice themselves at the altar of the organization" (Dyer, 1984, p. 123).

The issue of how to best balance individual and organizational needs has caused many a restless night for Carlos. As the program administrator of a multisite early childhood organization, he is keenly aware of the staff's dissatisfaction with their level of pay. He's heard their grievances and listened patiently and attentively to their complaints. Yet he struggles to come up with a satisfactory resolution to the issue. From the teachers' perspective, the solution to the problem seems clear—raise tuition rates and let the parents assume a greater share of the cost of providing a quality program. The teachers feel that for too long their low wages have subsidized the center's low tuition rates. Carlos is sympathetic to their situation. He feels, however, that the teachers don't understand how difficult it is to balance the center's budget. He has worked hard to structure tuition rates to ensure full enrollment. He feels certain if he raises tuition, he will lose some families and cause dissatisfaction among others.

Leadership Behavior

As the director, you see the big picture. Metaphorically speaking it is like being privy to the image on the front of the jigsaw puzzle box. Your teachers are the individual pieces of the puzzle. And linking their individual needs to achieve a unified whole is the challenge of effective leadership. Often it comes down to achieving a balance between order and coordination (getting the job done) and respecting the individual's professional right to autonomy and individual expression.

The organizational management literature is replete with references about the effects of different leadership styles as they relate to organizational effectiveness. The work of Blake and Mouton (1994), Blanchard, & Johnson (2002), and Yukl

(2002) are particularly useful in understanding how different leadership behaviors can help directors to balance organizational and individual needs, while making needed changes to keep their organizations thriving. The following conceptualization is a synthesis of their work.

Task-oriented style. Directors with a *task-oriented style* stress institutional or organizational needs. These directors tend to emphasize the requirements of the center and the achievement of centerwide goals. They "go by the book" and stress following appropriate procedures. Staff are expected to conform to organizational expectations. Directors employing this style try to be conscientious in applying the same rules and procedures to all staff. Conformity and control are emphasized. The director assumes that if roles are well developed, clearly articulated, and closely monitored, then center goals will be achieved. The message is clear: the center's needs come first. Job descriptions are precisely defined and staff are expected to conform to the role. While this style tends to promote efficiency, staff working in centers with this type of leadership may complain that it is too bureaucratic and neglects individual needs.

People-oriented style. Directors with a *people-oriented style* focus on people and their individual needs more than organizational requirements. This type of director puts a premium on human relations and believes happy employees are productive employees. The director thus devotes considerable attention to maintaining comfortable, friendly, and satisfying relationships among staff. This leadership style stresses the importance of allowing staff to exercise control, allowing them to actualize their individual needs and become more self-directed. Although acknowledging the necessity of some policies and procedures, the people-oriented director believes that rules and regulations should be tailored to fit the needs of individual staff. Job descriptions are designed with specific individuals in mind. While positive human relations are a desirable outcome of this style, staff working in centers with this style of leadership may complain about the lack of order and coordination.

Integrated style. Directors who have achieved an *integrated style* stress a high concern for both the center's needs and the needs of individual workers. Directors who adopt this style want to promote conditions that integrate high productivity and high morale through focused teamwork. They understand the necessity of having explicit roles and expectations for staff, but also understand that people have individual needs that must be met.

An integrated style is situational in that it rests on the premise that the director should not simply steer a middle course between organizational and individual needs, but rather assess the correct balance for different situations. In other words, different situations require different leadership behaviors, and the effectiveness of an approach will depend on the situation in which it is used. The integrated style stresses that the demands of the center need not clash with the needs people have for satisfaction and recognition from their work. This leadership style is most likely to yield optimum results in a center. Results, in this case, means achieving center goals and maintaining a high level of morale among staff.

Managing the Change Process

Being successful in managing the change process in any organization means being tuned in to the phases through which individuals progress as any major change strategy is being implemented. It also means developing a keen understanding of the critical elements that need to be in place to ensure success.

Transition Phases

Drawing on the work of several change theorists (Bridges, 1991; Conner, 1993; Scott & Jaffe, 1989), Figure 3.2 captures five phases in the change transition process as they relate to building acceptance, competence, and capacity to implement organizational change. The key factors impacting successful transition from one phase to the next, from old to new, are time and support.

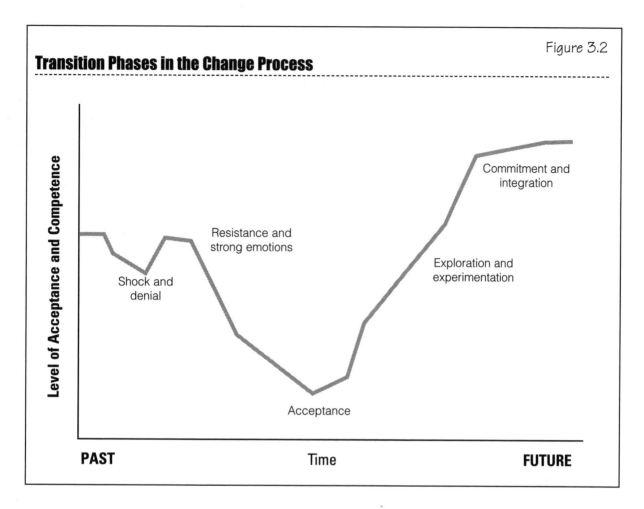

Transition Phases in the Change Process

Figure 3.2

Level of Acceptance and Competence

Shock and denial

Resistance and strong emotions

Commitment and integration

Exploration and experimentation

Acceptance

PAST   Time   FUTURE

Shock and denial. The first phase people experience when any new change strategy is announced is often shock and denial. It is not uncommon during this phase to see business as usual and people focusing on the past—those good ol' days when life was more predictable. This is because most people prefer working in a stable work environment and any change (even a good one) threatens their comfort level. During this phase it is important to expect and accept signs of grieving. Provide people with information and explain (as often as necessary) what to expect, suggesting actions they can take to adjust to the change. It is critical to allow time for things to sink in, honoring the past but shining a positive light on the future.

Resistance and strong emotions. When the reality of the change endeavor hits, strong emotions and outright resistance often occur. During this second phase, it is not uncommon to see anger,

blame, and high anxiety. Some people may "retire on the job," exhibit passive-aggressive behavior or outright noncompliance. This phase is often accompanied with intense frustration as individuals cope with the loss of what was and the unknown of what is to come. Your role during this phase is to listen, acknowledge feelings, respond empathetically, and continue to encourage buy-in. It is important during this phase not to try to talk people out of their feelings, but rather respect the internal turmoil they may be experiencing.

Acceptance. Gradual acceptance of the proposed change is often accompanied by what many organizational theorists refer to as an *implementation dip*, an actual decrease in performance and level of competence. Patience is critical at this stage as you continue to provide information, support, and resources that help people meet the changing demands of the job.

Exploration and experimentation. As time progresses, as support and resources are put in place and a fuller understanding of the expectations for new behaviors are understood, people move to an exploration and experimentation phase. While this phase has lots of energy, it often lacks focus and may be accompanied by confusion and chaos. During this phase it is important to help people focus on priorities and to continue to provide needed training, goal setting, and feedback on performance.

Commitment and integration. The final phase of the transition process is when the change has been fully integrated into the daily life of the center. It is the time when *hopeful realism* turns to *informed optimism* (Conner, 1993). This phase is marked by cooperation, commitment, and pride at achieving and mastering new behaviors, knowledge, and attitudes. This is the time to set long-term goals, concentrate on team building, and validate the hard efforts of all involved.

Clearly the time needed to successfully move from one phase to the next depends on the type of change being implemented, the competence level and dispositions of the people involved, and the support you are able to provide as the change agent. Small changes introduced in supportive ways may even help people skip the shock and denial phase and move through the resistance and strong emotion phase rapidly, while larger more complex changes may immobilize people, creating a climate of uncertainty and high stress for an extended period of time.

Critical Elements to Ensure Success

Managing successful change in early care and education programs really boils down to ensuring that five essential elements are in place—vision, education, incentives, resources, and an action plan (APQC, 1993; Hendry & Johnson, 1994; Kotter, 1996; Ritvo, Litwin, & Butler, 1995). When all these elements are present, the likelihood is greater that the change will result in positive outcomes and sustainable improvements.

If one or more of these elements is missing, than your change efforts are bound to produce disappointments. If a vision is not present, then confusion will follow. When education and skill development is not offered, then anxiety will follow. When incentives are not present, then resistance will follow. When resources are not present, then frustration will follow. And when an action plan is not in place, then a treadmill of false starts will follow. Figure 3.3 visually captures this critical combination of elements.

Kathleen is the kindergarten teacher at a private school serving children 3 to 6 years of age. She received a flyer from her principal suggesting that she attend a Math Their Way workshop at the local university. Kathleen resented the implication that her math program was inadequate, but since the school offered to pay her workshop registration fee and provide a substitute teacher to cover her classroom during the two days she would be away, she agreed to go. Much to her surprise, she was amazed at how the workshop expanded her awareness of important math concepts. She realized how much more she could be doing in her classroom.

Kathleen came back to the school energized and very much a convert to the Math Their Way approach. She offered to share what she had learned at a staff meeting but she was told the meetings for the next several months were already scheduled with other more important business. Still, Kathleen was eager to try out the Math Their Way approach in her classroom. She submitted a purchase requisition to her principal for $80 to purchase some new manipulatives for the Math Their Way activities. She also asked if she might have $25 to pay the school's high school student aide to help her make the games on a Saturday. The principal wrote back a note explaining that the budget was very tight and all the school could afford was $30 toward supplies. Further, the principal felt it would be too much of an imposition to ask the aide to work on a Saturday. She reminded Kathleen that the school had already paid her registration fee for the workshop and for a substitute teacher in her absence. If she wanted to make some new games, she would have to do it in her free time.

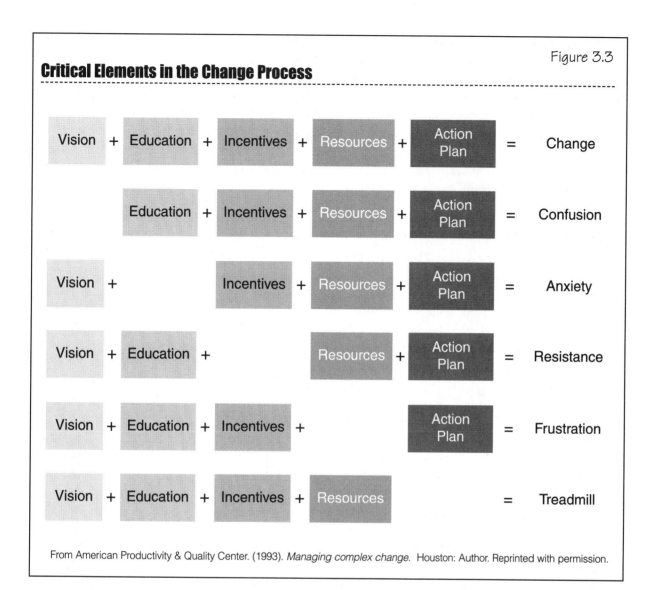

Critical Elements in the Change Process

Figure 3.3

Vision	+	Education	+	Incentives	+	Resources	+	Action Plan	=	Change
		Education	+	Incentives	+	Resources	+	Action Plan	=	Confusion
Vision	+			Incentives	+	Resources	+	Action Plan	=	Anxiety
Vision	+	Education	+			Resources	+	Action Plan	=	Resistance
Vision	+	Education	+	Incentives	+			Action Plan	=	Frustration
Vision	+	Education	+	Incentives	+	Resources			=	Treadmill

From American Productivity & Quality Center. (1993). *Managing complex change.* Houston: Author. Reprinted with permission.

Kathleen was hurt and disappointed. She never found the time to make all the new math games she wanted to. Gradually her enthusiasm for Math Their Way disappeared.

The above scenario is not uncommon. There are no villains in this story, only miscommunication about expectations. The training did achieve its objective in increasing Kathleen's awareness, but the lack of school resources to support her after the training meant that real change in behavior never really occurred. Kathleen was left frustrated and the school missed out on an opportunity to capitalize on Kathleen's enthusiasm and expertise about Math Their Way (Barratta-Lorton, 1994).

Change Viewed from a Systems Perspective: Linking People, Structure, and Processes

There are different schools of thought about the best way to implement changes to improve early childhood programs. Some approaches focus on changing individuals through staff training and educational programs; others focus on changing the structures of the organization (e.g., pay and promotion policies); still others emphasize direct intervention in the processes of the center (e.g., changing decision-making processes or group-meeting processes). The central point of this book, though, is that lasting change must consider all three components of the program—people, structure, and processes. Directors need a variety of interventions to effect change, and these changes may need to happen simultaneously.

And what about the other two components of the system, the external environment and the culture? While it is true that impacting the external environment through different advocacy efforts can produce change, your control over many elements in the external environment is limited. Because of this, the external environment is much slower to respond to change efforts. Those efforts are important, but they are not the focus of this book.

Changes in the culture of a center are a by-product of changing people, structure, and processes. For example, there may be a strong prevailing norm at a center that divergent points of view are not welcome and that the center's governing board makes all key decisions. By changing decision-making processes at the center to those that are more participative in nature, this norm would change. Likewise, if a norm exists that staff do not talk about their salaries or benefits, this could be changed quickly if a center adopted a career ladder and salary schedule detailing rates of pay and benefits for positions with differing qualifications and experience. We see, then, that the culture changes as a result of our efforts to change people, structure, and processes.

The bottom line is that change will be more successful in your center if it takes a total systems approach. Changes in one component of the system will be more enduring if they are supported by changes in other components of the system. For example, if teachers are trained to use new procedures for assessing children's progress, their use of these new procedures will be short-lived unless accompanied by structural and process changes in the program, such as changes in teachers' work schedules, the center's reward system, or the center's performance appraisal processes.

People Strategies

Educational change is fundamentally dependent upon change in people's knowledge, attitudes, and behavior. The changes that occur in a program's structure (use of space, delineation of roles, curriculum content) or that occur in the processes of the center (teaching practices, decision-making processes) cannot happen without changes in the people responsible for those elements of the program. The importance of changing people to achieve organizational change is essential. People's needs, expectations, beliefs, and abilities strongly influence all other components of the social system.

Changes in knowledge tend to be the easiest to make—they can occur as a result of reading an article or hearing something new from another person. Attitude changes are more difficult to make. This is because attitudes relate to one's values and may be emotionally charged in a positive or negative way. Changes in people's behavior are even more difficult and time-consuming. Most people who smoke, for example, are well aware of the health risks associated with smoking (knowledge). They may even want to stop smoking (attitude). But to actually stop smoking (behavior) is just too difficult a change to make. Likewise, merely telling a teacher that a new approach will make classroom routines smoother does not ensure the teacher will actually follow through and use the approach. Directors often assume that just because they provide information about something, teachers will automatically be persuaded to change their behavior; clearly an erroneous assumption.

LaToya is the director of a small preschool. She recently attended a workshop at a local conference on the topic of emergent literacy. She was really inspired by the presentation and arranged to visit the presenter's preschool. LaToya was quite impressed with what she saw—teachers actively engaged in taking student dictations, words and phrases displayed around the classroom, and handmade books of children's stories displayed in the library corner. The emergent literacy approach these teachers used obviously worked.

LaToya asked the presenter if she would do a workshop at her center. She paid her teachers to attend the workshop on a Saturday morning. The teachers reluctantly attended, but afterward complimented LaToya on her choice of presenters. In their evaluations of the workshop, they indicated they were impressed with both the presenter and the content of the presentation.

Given this level of enthusiasm about emergent literacy, LaToya was disappointed to see over the next several months that virtually nothing changed in the way the teachers taught in the classroom. She was perplexed. They had obviously learned a lot from the workshop and thought the emergent literacy curricular focus was worthy. Why hadn't they changed their instructional methods to incorporate this new approach?

LaToya was actually quite successful in changing the teachers' knowledge and even their attitudes about emergent literacy. But thinking that she could change their behavior by exposing them to one workshop was not a realistic goal. Behavior change is difficult because it usually entails unlearning old behaviors in order to substitute new ones; this is not something that can be accomplished quickly or easily.

There is an undeniable comfort in the status quo, even if that status quo is not perfect. The teachers at LaToya's center were clearly impressed with the possibilities of the emergent literacy instructional approach they learned but obviously not dissatisfied enough with their present instructional strategies to want to change. Success in implementing change is related to the felt need for change. The teachers in LaToya's center didn't feel there was a compelling enough need to change. They may have also even resisted the change because of the perceived additional work they thought implementing the different approach would entail.

Hall and Hord (2001) remind us that change is a highly personal experience. Too often directors and administrators involved in staff development ignore the perceptions and feelings of people experiencing the change process. The personal dimension may be more critical to the success or failure of the change effort than the actual merits of the innovation or change being considered. Since change is incumbent on individuals, their personal satisfaction, frustrations, concerns, motivations, and perceptions must be taken into consideration.

Particularly when teachers have limited ability, flexibility, and confidence, it is crucial that staff development be an integral part of the change process. The purpose of staff development is to create the right set of conditions that will enable lasting change to occur. The process begins with self-diagnosis—the individual's perceived problems and needs. Chapter 6 provides a framework for helping individuals take charge of their own professional change. The director's job, then, is to ensure that individual change supports the goals of the center.

Wu (1988) cites research showing that the most crucial learning for teachers occurs in their first two years on the job. After that, in-service education becomes a matter of unlearning as well as learning. That is why change is so difficult with staff who have been teaching for many years. The process of unlearning old behaviors may be more difficult than learning new skills. Recall, for example, the last time you drove a rental car, how awkward it felt trying to adjust to the positioning of the controls. You may have even reached for the knob to turn on the lights and mistakenly turned on the windshield wiper.

What happens if individual change is not forthcoming and an individual is not willing to adapt behavior to be consistent with center goals? Often in joint planning, it will become clear that the needs and expectations of the individual do not match those of the organization. If this is the case, you may be faced with decisions about replacement or termination. There may be problems with personal style or philosophy, or a lack of flexibility, skill, and innate ability.

While making decisions about termination are painful for any director, successful leaders

> *Leadership begins where management ends, where rewards and punishments used to control behavior give way to a common purpose, innovation, teamwork, and the courage of convictions.*
>
> *David and Roger Johnson*

understand that the replacement of key individuals can speed up changes in a group's performance and in achieving desired outcomes. The goal in the termination process is not to assign blame, but rather to help the individual understand that there is a mismatch between the individual's needs and the center's needs. Such an awareness conveys respect and allows the individual to be terminated with his or her integrity intact. With an open, direct, and supportive approach, it is possible to turn the termination process into an opportunity for personal growth.

Structural Strategies

While people strategies are fundamental to achieving center-based change, a systems view of early childhood programs supports the proposition that change at the individual or group level is not likely to be sustained unless it is supported by structural changes in the way a center operates. Increased competence in the classroom as the result of staff development, for example, is not likely to be sustained unless there are changes in the reward and promotion system or the performance appraisal system of a program.

Structural changes tend to be highly visible and can often be implemented relatively quickly. But structural changes alone cannot create permanent change. The open classroom educational experiments of the early 1970s provide a case in point. Many districts knocked out walls, regrouped teachers, and changed teaching assignments. To the casual observer, it appeared that these programs had implemented open classrooms. But while the physical structure of the schools changed, teachers in many cases had not. They still treated children in the same way and taught under the same assumptions as before. The teachers, it seems, had either not really bought into or fully understood the philosophy of open education. It is not surprising, then, that many open classroom experiments were considered a failure. Within a year or two, the walls went back up and the schools took on a more traditional look.

The lesson learned from these failures is that changes cannot be adopted wholesale; they must be modified and tailored to the unique conditions of each context and each group of teachers. Making a few structural changes in the program will not achieve lasting impact unless the people implementing the changes also adopt new attitudes and behaviors that support the structural changes.

Process Strategies

We have seen that a director who wants to improve center outcomes can do so by redesigning organizational structures or by changing the behavior of key individuals. But often, direct intervention is required in modifying center processes that may be blocking center effectiveness. Effective working relationships between people and groups depend on their capacity to communicate feelings and perceptions. This can only be achieved by getting people together to listen to one another, negotiate differences, problem solve, and work through the thorny issues that block mutual understanding. Most process interventions center on helping people learn new behaviors and develop new relationships.

Janet and Maria both work part-time for a faith-based preschool program. They share a classroom, with Janet teaching in the morning and Maria teaching in the afternoon. For the past year they have felt they have not been able to carry out their tasks effectively because they have conflicting ideas about how the learning environment should be arranged. They also have quite different work styles, particularly in their tolerance for clutter. Their interpersonal relationship is clearly tense.

Their director has essentially ignored the situation, hoping the two would resolve their personal differences. But Janet and Maria are both strong willed; neither is willing to confront the situation directly. Instead, they make highly critical remarks to the other teachers and to parents about each other's style.

The interpersonal relationship that characterizes the interactions between these two teachers is clearly blocking their ability to carry out their roles effectively. Their friction is also having a negative impact on other teachers.

Janet and Maria need help. The hands-off leadership style of their director is not improving the situation. Clearly a process intervention is needed to support a change in the behavior of these two teachers. Their inability to appreciate their differing styles is having a negative impact on the program.

Sometimes process interventions are best facilitated by an objective outside party. Depending on the severity of the problem, outside support may be needed to improve interpersonal relations, problem-solving processes, or communication processes at a program. Other times all that may be needed is for the director to intervene and support needed changes. Process interventions are critical because they impact the culture of a center.

In most centers, an assessment of group meeting processes and decision-making processes is a good place to start. Virtually all organizations experience some problems in communication, trust, and interpersonal relationships that block organizational efficiency and effectiveness. Process interventions can help deal with these problems directly. This book provides some assessment tools that will help you evaluate the effectiveness of these and other center processes. You'll learn more about these in Chapter 4.

Tuning In to Staff's Levels of Concern

Hall and Hord (2001) underscore the point that change is a personal experience for each individual involved. This means that each person will have somewhat different concerns about any particular change or innovation being considered. If the implementation of an innovation is to be successful, it is critical that directors tap into staff's level of concern.

Many teachers, for example, are well aware of the importance of individualizing instruction for children, but they may resist approaches to individualize because they fear they will lose control of the group. Other teachers may have a fear of failure that may prevent them from embracing new educational ideas. These concerns need to be addressed up front. Before initiating any major change, it is helpful to tap into staff's feelings, assumptions, fears, values, defenses, and worries about the specific change being considered.

Directors can do this in a couple of ways, depending on the type of change or innovation being considered. Simply asking each person, "When you think about this change, what concerns do you have?" This informal, open-ended approach can be used anytime a change is being proposed.

Another approach would be to solicit feedback using an informal questionnaire or survey. Assessment Tool #1, found in Appendix A, is an example of a survey. Using a survey to gather data about people's perceptions of an anticipated change has the ancillary effect of moving individuals from vague global feelings of concern to being able to pinpoint those specific areas that are most important to them. With this feedback, you'll be in a better position to counter potential resistance. An analysis of the feedback generated from such a survey can help directors address those initial informational needs and personal concerns. These may be issues having to do with planning, time, or organization.

There is a correlation between the size of an organization and its capacity to change. It's the difference between turning around the Queen Mary and a speedboat.

Bryan Kinnamon

Hall and Hord (2001) have developed another approach for understanding staff's concerns that is appropriate for curricular innovations or new instructional techniques. They believe that an individual's concerns move through several stages—from self, to task, to the innovation's impact. Nonusers, for example, are typically less concerned about the implications of an educational innovation for students than they are about what the innovation means to them personally (e.g., added time for planning). Table 3.2 summarizes these stages of concern.

Assessment Tool #2 in Appendix A is an abbreviated version of Hall and Hord's instrument using the Work Sampling System curriculum (Meisels, et al., 1994) as an example of an innovation. The data generated from the administration of this questionnaire can be used in

Table 3.2

Typical Expressions of Concern About an Innovation

	Stage of Concern	Expression of Concern
I M P A C T	REFOCUSING	I have some ideas about something that would work even better.
	COLLABORATION	How can I relate what I am doing to what others are doing?
T A S K	CONSEQUENCE	How is my use of this innovation affecting the children? How can I refine it to have a greater impact?
	MANAGEMENT	I seem to be spending all my time getting materials ready.
	PERSONAL	How will using this innovation affect me?
S E L F	INFORMATIONAL	I would like to know more about this innovation.
	AWARENESS	I am not concerned about this innovation.

Adapted from Hall, G., & Hord, S. (2001). *Implementing change: Patterns, principles, and potholes.* Boston: Allyn and Bacon. Reprinted with permission.

a variety of ways. It is possible to simply note the stage that received the highest score for the individual (or for the entire staff if scores are combined). This indicates the kinds of concerns that are most intense for the individual or group at that particular point in time. The implications of generating a group profile for planning staff development are seen in the following example.

Kelly attended a conference where the Work Sampling System was being showcased. She did some additional reading about the performance assessment approach and talked to several directors in her community who had gone through Work Sampling System training.

Kelly was convinced she needed to implement the assessment system at her center. She took a proposal to her board asking that the center allocate money to pay for three Saturday staff development days to train staff in the Work Sampling approach. Kelly met with the trainer to ensure that the in-service sessions would be well designed to include intensive training in both materials and techniques.

Before embarking on the training, however, Kelly followed the suggestion of one of the board members who thought it would be a good idea for her to administer Assessment Tool #2, "Concerns Questionnaire," to the staff prior to the training. Kelly was sure glad she did. She discovered that the staff was primarily concerned about how much time this new approach was going to take (management concerns). Further, several noted comments at the end of the questionnaire that they weren't sure if this innovation was even needed. It seems they were really quite content using the teacher checklist and portfolio approach they had been using for years. Kelly also noted their concern about having to give up a weekend day to attend training.

Realizing her enthusiasm for this innovation might be met with a wall of resistance, Kelly quickly changed her plans. Based on the results she got from administering the "Concerns Questionnaire" about the Work Sampling System, a decision was made to address information and personal concerns first. She decided to spend only a portion of the money she had allocated for training and have the trainer provide a half-day overview of the assessment system. Staff could elect to attend or not. Those who did would be paid at their regular hourly rate. After the overview, staff would be given the option to decide if the Work Sampling System was an innovation that would be worthwhile implementing in their classroom. If so, additional staff development days would be scheduled for those who wished to participate.

Had Kelly not assessed the staff's level of concerns about the Work Sampling System, there was a high probability that her attempts to implement change would have failed. By tapping into staff's concerns, she was able to redesign her in-service training to address the issues that were most pressing to the teachers. Hall and Hord (2001) believe that by using such an assessment tool, a director's gut feelings about what teachers need are replaced with reliable data about their genuine concerns. The stages of concern profile that is generated by using this instrument can be helpful in planning interventions, evaluating progress, and identifying potential problems that might surface during the change process.

A Final Word

Wu (1988) underscores the importance of linking what we know about change to what we know about staff development. "If staff developers apply the research with common sense, we will have a notably better chance to effect change in people and in programs" (p. 13). This chapter has stressed that one of the factors involved in improving early childhood programs is empowering the people engaged in the day-to-day life of the center and supporting their change efforts. The remaining chapters in this book provide the tools necessary to help you make collaborative change possible.

Chapter 4

Assessing Organizational Needs

irectors often have a global impression that things are either going well or not so well at their centers, but they lack specific information on just what areas of program operations contribute to these impressions. Without a clear sense of how the people, structure, and processes of a center interact to produce desired outcomes, directors can't ensure their program will be as effective as possible.

The information gleaned from assessing organizational needs can help you turn those vague, amorphous feelings into more precise data about what aspects of your program can be improved. Assessing organizational needs helps you identify the issues that are most pressing so you can prioritize your time and resources to address these concerns. When used properly, organizational assessment provides a sound basis for determining the objectives, content, and emphasis of staff development programs. It is the first step in linking organizational goals to individual goals.

This chapter presents a systematic approach to assessing the external environment, people, structure, processes, culture, and outcomes of a program in order to improve a center's effectiveness in solving its problems and achieving desired outcomes. The chapter's focus is on assessment tools you can use to gather data at the organizational level. Chapter 5 addresses issues pertaining to the assessment of individual needs. Later chapters discuss how to mesh organizational and individual needs. The approach is issue-oriented, focusing on

existing and anticipated problems and generating possible strategies to neutralize the forces that create the problems.

Why Is Organizational Assessment Important?

Ongoing assessment is important at the organizational level not only because it gives structure to your center improvement efforts, but because it also conveys respect to staff, encouraging a team approach to problem solving. Staff can be incredibly resourceful at generating solutions to center-wide problems if provided the opportunity to participate in a meaningful way. The implicit message conveyed through assessment is a powerful one—improving the center is a shared responsibility. Indeed, the most effective early care and education programs are those where administrators, teachers, parents, and students together engage in problem solving, decision making, and implementation of program improvement plans. Obtaining perspectives on any particular issue helps ensure that fewer obstacles are encountered in the change process.

The two-way communication that emerges from assessing organizational issues can lead to a collaborative approach to problem solving and establish a precedent for future change. Since change is more likely to occur in work settings where individuals feel that new ideas are welcome, such data can be used to unfreeze existing norms and attitudes. When the information is perceived as valid, accurate, and unbiased, the description of organizational conditions arrived at through the assessment process can be a potent force in helping bring about needed change (Bowditch & Buono, 1982).

Even if you are not aware of any immediate problems, it can be helpful to conduct periodic assessments of different aspects of your center's functioning. Monitoring center outcomes in particular is one way to ensure the center stays healthy. When used in this way, assessment is preventative in nature. It helps direct people's energies from potential griping to coming up with solutions before issues develop into difficult problems.

Diagnosing a Center's Need for Change

When we feel sick and go to our doctor seeking relief, we expect that our doctor will do some kind of diagnostic assessment of our condition before prescribing a remedy for our illness. Doctors generally ask us to describe the symptoms we are experiencing. They may listen to our heart with a stethoscope, take x-rays, and even run a series of blood tests. All these diagnostic assessments provide the data needed to make an accurate diagnosis of our condition.

Directors of early childhood programs, as well, need diagnostic data to help them improve their centers. Unfortunately, most directors lack a systematic way to diagnose and monitor their center's effectiveness. They may sense that their program has a low-grade fever or a few minor aches and pains, but lack the specific diagnostic skills to identify the problem or problems that may be causing these symptoms. Without concrete tools to focus their assessment, directors may end up misdiagnosing the situation or merely treating the symptoms of problems. Worse yet, a haphazard approach to organizational assessment may even end up aggravating the ailment.

Looking back, I think it was more difficult to see what the problems were than to solve them.

Charles Darwin

Pinpointing Problems

 The diagram in Figure 2.1 presented on page 31 stresses the point that the first step in the change process begins with the identification of a condition that someone feels needs to be improved. The success of the change plan will be affected by the degree to which everyone involved realizes that a problem exists, defines the problem in the same way, and agrees that improving the condition is desirable (Dyer, 1984). Change is bound to get off track if some people see the problem one way but others see it differently or do not see it. Identifying the problem means achieving consensus as to why there is a problem as well as what the problem is. This sounds rather straightforward; in reality, problem identification is quite difficult to achieve.

A problem is the discrepancy between current and ideal conditions. Hersey, Blanchard, and Johnson (2001) state that a problem exists when there is a discrepancy between what is actually happening (*the real*) and what you or someone else would like to be happening (*the ideal*). They stress that unless you can explain precisely what you would like to be occurring and unless that set of conditions is different from the present situation, no problem exists. "Change efforts involve attempting to reduce the discrepancy between the real (actual) and the ideal" (p. 378).

Hersey, Blanchard, and Johnson caution, however, that change efforts should not always involve attempting to move the real closer to the ideal. Sometimes after diagnosis, you might realize that your ideal is unrealistic and should be brought more in line with what is actually happening. In other words, you and your staff need to ask yourselves, Where are we now and where would we like to be? The problem is essentially the gap between where you are now and where you would like to be.

Problems should not be confused with symptoms. Most problems manifest themselves in a variety of symptoms. For example, students may be disruptive, teachers may be apathetic, or parents may not follow through on their obligations. These situations imply the possibility of a problem, but such behavior is usually only symptomatic of the problem rather than the problem itself. Even so, symptoms should be noted because they signal where to search for the cause. Remember, a problem is defined as a difference between the present situation and the ideal situation.

Recall the vignette in Chapter 1 where Connie was experiencing high turnover among her employees. The turnover, while troublesome, was really only a symptom of a far deeper problem—the lack of role clarity in personnel policies. Recall, also, the case study of Martha, who encountered cynicism and overt hostility from several teachers at the first staff meeting she conducted in her role as director of The Children's Corner. This unproductive staff meeting was symptomatic of a far deeper problem at Martha's center—the lack of collegiality, trust, and cooperation among the teachers.

A problem is more than a frustration. Schmuck and Runkel (1994) caution that we should not mistake frustrations for real organizational problems. Some frustrations, they state, go away by themselves; others may remain as minor irritations. When we listen to teachers discuss their frustrations, we hear them say or imply that they would prefer something to be different. Often, however, they are not able to specify the features of that improved state of affairs. Schmuck and Runkel state that teachers who complain about the present without conceiving a better alternative have not yet conceived a problem and are therefore not ready to solve a problem. "A problem is a discrepancy between a present state of affairs and a more preferred state of affairs—sufficiently more preferred that one is ready to spend some energy to get there. Without the two parts—the current situation and the more desirable one—no problem has been specified. Frustration, irritation, anger, or confusion is often a feature of a problem—part of the present state of affairs—but it is not in itself a problem" (pp. 234–35). Frustrations are usually only symptoms of underlying problems.

A problem depends on one's point of view. We know that directors and teachers often have differing perceptions of organizational practices. Research has provided convincing evidence that

directors uniformly rate organizational conditions far rosier than their staff (Bloom, 1996). Moreover, teachers typically look at problems from a fairly narrow perspective; directors hold a broader perspective of organizational issues. Whether the perspective is narrow or broad is of secondary importance in problem identification, however, because individual behavior is guided by one's own perceptions, regardless of how accurate those perceptions are in some objective sense.

Armando is the owner/director of a small proprietary child care center located in the Southwest. The seven teachers on his staff are a close-knit group of young women with limited training in early childhood education. Armando has been frustrated by his inability to instill child-centered practices in the teachers. While they clearly find fulfillment in their work, are generally responsible in meeting the basic obligations of their jobs, and are nurturing and protective of the children, Armando is frustrated by what he perceives as many missed opportunities for engaging the children in developmentally appropriate learning experiences.

Armando's biggest concern is outdoor time. The teachers see scheduled outdoor play periods as time to sit back and socialize with one another. Armando thinks the teachers' "lifeguard behavior" is unacceptable. He wants the teachers to be more active with the children, using the outdoors as an extension of the indoor learning environment.

At a staff meeting Armando presented to the teachers his perception of the problem and shared his expectations for outdoor supervision. He gave the teachers some handouts on gardening with children, making obstacle courses, and outdoor art activities. Unfortunately, the teachers didn't see the situation the same way he did. Outdoor play periods were simply not a problem in their minds. They felt the children got plenty of teacher time in the classroom. They felt they deserved some downtime, a chance to observe children to ensure they were safe but not be actively engaged in their play.

Not surprising, Armando's plan for getting the teachers to change their behavior was only half successful. When he was present, the teachers complied; they did what he expected. When he wasn't around, though, they reverted to their established patterns of noninvolvement and socializing with one another.

Armando's situation points out that there is a big difference between compliance and commitment, and that the difference is often due to differing perceptions of the problem. An understanding of point of view is critical to accurate diagnosis in center assessment. Because point of view is one's frame of reference for assessing a given situation, it is important to determine through whose eyes the situation is being described or observed—your own, those of the board, the parents', or the staff's. Ideally, to get a full picture of the situation, you should get as many points of view as possible—particularly from those people who will be affected by any proposed changes.

> The measure of success is not whether you have a tough problem to deal with, but whether it's the same problem you had last year.
>
> John Foster Dulles

Schmuck and Runkel (1994) point out that problems lie in people's heads, not in the real world. In other words, when a person says a center has problems, what that means is that the individual believes things should be different. But people may have very different images in their heads of the present situation. The implication is obvious; one of the first steps in problem solving is to ascertain with some precision the different images the people concerned have of the present situation. Achieving clarity about differences in perceptions of any situation is critical for effective group action. The goal of problem identification is thus to build a shared vision of what the center should be like and be able to articulate in meaningful images how the center will get there.

A problem usually involves more than one component in the system. One way to approach problem identification is to ask yourself a series of questions about each component of the system (external environment, people, structure, processes, culture, and outcomes). This preliminary diagnosis can help you identify problems in congruence within and between components. Looking at program outcomes is particularly useful. For example, you can ask yourself if there is a discrepancy between what you want or expect you should be achieving and what you actually have achieved. In this type of analysis you can view a problem as the difference between actual and ideal outcomes. A problem exists when a meaningful difference is observed between outcomes at the organizational, staff, child, parent, or community level and what is desired. Remember, however, this information tells you only that a problem exists; it does not specify what the causes are or how to remedy it.

We have seen in this section that agreeing on the problem isn't quite as easy as it may appear, but that should not dampen your desire to move forward. Finding the problems and choosing the right solutions to those problems is at the heart of center-based improvement. Exercise 4.1 provides a number of questions to get you started on the road to identifying the most important problem areas for your center. As you read through the series of questions, jot some notes to yourself in the margins. When you have finished, write about two or three problems as you presently view them.

Pinpointing Organizational Problems

External Environment

► How have changes in federal or state regulations affected the center in recent years?

► How have mandated requirements from the center's sponsoring agency helped or hindered it from achieving its mission?

► How does the physical location of the center affect its performance?

► Does the community support the center? How does the immediate neighborhood react to the presence of the center?

► How does the presence of other early childhood programs in the community impact the center? How would you characterize your professional relationship with other centers in the community?

► What experiences has the center had with respect to the vendors it uses for materials and equipment, food service, landscape maintenance, and other goods and services?

► How does the current political, social, and economic climate affect the program?

► Have there been any significant technological changes impacting the center over the past few years?

► Has the center been able to use the resources of local universities, colleges, and professional organizations effectively?

People

► Do employees possess the knowledge, skills, and attitude needed to carry out their jobs effectively? Are any employees overqualified for their assignments?

► What do employees say they like or dislike about their work? To what extent do their positions allow them to improve and grow personally and professionally?

► Do staff in supervisory positions provide good role models for new or less-qualified staff?

► Are there any dominant coalitions in the center? How have they changed over time? Do they help or hinder the program in achieving its goals?

► Have there been any noticeable changes in the clientele (families and children) over the past few years? How have these changes impacted the program?

► Are the current members of the board of directors supportive or critical of the program's functioning? Why?

Structure

▶ What is the philosophy of the center? How has it changed over time?

▶ Does the center have a written mission statement? Are the center's goals clearly defined? Are they understood and accepted by the board and staff?

▶ Does the written curriculum accurately reflect the philosophy and goals of the center?

▶ How are teaching roles and responsibilities defined and communicated?

▶ Are reporting, supervising, and evaluating relationships clearly defined? Are interdependence and collaboration supported by job descriptions and reporting relationships?

▶ Is there a sound rationale for each level in the decision-making hierarchy of the center? Is the decision-making structure adaptable to change?

▶ Are parents' roles clearly defined and communicated during the enrollment process?

▶ Does the physical environment support program goals and desired teaching practices? Does the physical environment facilitate team behavior?

▶ Are space and materials allocated on the basis of task and need or on the basis of status?

▶ How equitable is the pay and promotion system?

▶ Do budgeting priorities reflect the goals of the center?

Processes

▶ How would staff characterize interpersonal relations at the center—warm and supportive or tense and competitive? Do staff appear at ease? Do they laugh with one another and appear to enjoy each other's company?

▶ How are interpersonal differences handled?

▶ Are personnel recruitment practices effective in attracting staff with the right knowledge, skills, and attitudes to do an effective job?

▶ How are new teachers and substitutes treated? How are employees oriented to their new positions?

▶ Do supervisory practices match the career level and professional needs of individuals?

▶ How are staff evaluated? Do they perceive performance appraisal practices as fair? Do they perceive performance appraisal practices as being supportive in helping them grow in professional competence?

▶ Are meetings productive? How are they planned? Who speaks most and to whom?

▶ How are organizational problems solved?

▶ Are teaching practices consistent with the stated goals and educational objectives of the center?

▶ Do leadership practices provide a clear vision for the center?

Culture

- ▶ What are the center's shared values and beliefs?

- ▶ What are the critical events in the history of the center?

- ▶ What norms describe the culture of the center with respect to everyday demeanor, communication, risk taking, and how employees are valued?

- ▶ How would you characterize the general organizational climate of the program?

- ▶ Do individual and group behavior reflect a shared code of ethics?

Outcomes

- ▶ What is the general reputation of the center in the community?

- ▶ Are families satisfied? Do they communicate positive feedback when they are pleased, or do they tend to focus feedback only on negative impressions of the program?

- ▶ Does the center have full enrollment? Is the program fiscally healthy?

- ▶ Does the center seem to be running efficiently? Is it able to anticipate and prepare for change or does it operate in a crisis orientation?

- ▶ How would you rate general employee satisfaction and overall staff morale? Do teachers appear to be personally and professionally fulfilled?

- ▶ How would you evaluate overall employee competence in performing their respective roles and responsibilities?

- ▶ Do teachers seem to be committed to the center? Is there high absenteeism and turnover among teachers? Are there indications of undue stress or work overload?

- ▶ Are children achieving at expected levels? Do indicators of social and cognitive competence allow one to conclude that children are thriving in the environment?

- ▶ How would you characterize the general health of the children enrolled? Is there excessive absenteeism due to illness? Are there any indications of child abuse or neglect?

Perceived Problem

Describe what is actually happening now in a particular situation.

_____

_____

_____

_____

_____

Describe what is likely to happen in the future if no change takes place.

_____

_____

_____

_____

_____

Collecting Accurate Data

 In most cases your first attempts at stating a problem will be incomplete. Additional data are usually needed to define the problem more clearly and ascertain underlying causes for the problem. The goal of data collection is to form a valid picture of the needs and problems of a center as a basis for action. Valid information is fundamental to understanding and dealing with problems that staff face. The instruments used to collect data should allow staff the opportunity to both describe the factors which contribute to their perceived problems and their feelings associated with the problems. Collecting accurate data is integral to center-based improvement. It is part of the program improvement process described in Chapter 2. Before proceeding

with the actual data collection, however, several questions need to be addressed.

When should data be collected? It should be clear from the preceding section that center assessment is not a one-time phenomenon—assessing centerwide conditions needs to be ongoing. After all, situations and people change and centers must respond. You'll definitely want to collect data when a problem seems to have surfaced to which there may be multiple perspectives or when additional information is necessary to clarify the problem situation. In most cases, an annual assessment of conditions is sufficient. Many directors feel that late spring is the best time to do this. Even if a center operates year 'round, there is a typical school-year pattern of enrollment and staffing that seems to exist, with changes being made during the summer months. If data are collected in the May or June, they can be summarized during the summer months and shared with staff as they prepare for the new academic year.

Data should also be collected before undertaking any kind of major organizational improvement effort, even if it occurs mid-year. This is important because such data can serve as baseline information on progress toward achieving goals. Centers will sometimes implement exciting organizational changes but have no benchmarks to measure their progress. Initial baseline data provide a starting point for directors to chart their progress in improving organizational functioning. Virtually all of the assessment tools described in this book can be used as a pre and post measure. In this way, both directors and staff can see the incremental progress they are making in achieving desired outcomes.

How much data should be collected? Data collection begins with an assessment of the existing state of affairs. Diagnosis can be simple and straightforward or complex and involved. It can include a few people or many. But in any case it should give sufficient information about the existing situation so that plans for the future can be made with confidence. Diagnosis of any situation should provide enough data to allow the director to find out the following:

▶ What is actually happening now in a particular situation?

▶ What is likely to happen in the future if no change takes place?

▶ What would people ideally like to happen in this situation?

▶ What are the blocks or restraints from achieving the ideal?

One caution, however: in their zest to take an accurate pulse on organizational conditions, some directors end up overdiagnosing. This can unwittingly have a negative effect on staff, who may

sense a kind of paralysis of analysis setting in. Too much time spent on diagnosis can convey the impression that the center isn't really interested in moving forward with constructive change.

Who should collect the data? This is a difficult question to answer because each situation is different. In most cases, the director or administrator of a center will be in charge of overseeing the assessment process. However, in some instances it may be wise for an impartial outside party to collect the data. The key is to make people feel comfortable in stating problems without blaming anyone or arousing defensiveness. They need to be convinced that their perceptions are valued and important and that the data generated from assessment will help the center develop realistic goals that address key issues.

Regardless of who collects the data, it is critical to assure staff of the confidentiality of their responses. They need to feel confident that they can be as open as possible about sharing both positive and negative feedback and that the results of assessment will in no way be used against them. They need to be told up front who will have access to the data, how they will be summarized, and the extent to which the results will be shared with those who participated in the assessment process.

Because confidentiality is the most essential prerequisite for obtaining accurate information, any doubts respondents have about where the information will go and who will be identified can cloud the accuracy of your findings. If staff do not feel that their responses and their identity will be safeguarded during the assessment process, they may choose not to be completely truthful about answering some questions.

This presents a problem for administrators wishing to develop a questionnaire and tally the results themselves. Employees may not be totally candid if they know that someone directly associated with the center will be collecting and analyzing the results. The data generated from surveys conducted in this manner may be biased and of limited value. If the issue being assessed is a contentious one, then it may be wise to have an agreed-upon third party collect the data and summarize them. Sometimes those in supervisory positions may be perceived by staff to be the source of the problem. Under such circumstances, it is essential to have an impartial outside person conduct and analyze the data collected from surveys or interviews.

Should the results be shared? Unless the issue facing the center is very sensitive, it is important to be as open as possible about sharing all feedback—both positive and negative. This process builds trust and confidence that staff do have an important role to play in improving the center and that it is the collective responsibility of all concerned to both identify strengths of the program and come up with possible solutions to problem areas.

As an expression of administrative concern for their welfare, this step is what conveys your intent to be open and supportive of needed organizational changes. This demonstration of concern in itself can contribute to healthy staff relations. It can also open channels of communication and stimulate group problem solving. As feedback is translated into follow-up activities, staff will feel a greater sense of shared responsibility for implementing change and incorporating new practices.

Different Approaches for Data Collection

There are many different ways to gather data. The assessment tools in this book provide several examples of different data collection techniques. It will be up to you to decide which assessments should be used to collect data about the problems you have described as a result of doing Exercise 4.1. The five most popular approaches to data collection include questionnaires, interviews, observations, records and documents, and standardized tests.

Surveys and questionnaires. Surveys and questionnaires are probably the most widely used data-gathering technique in educational settings. They are particularly useful when you are interested is assessing the attitudes, beliefs, and values of a particular group of people. Moreover, they can provide useful information on changes in attitudes over a period of time.

The main strength of using questionnaires for data collection is that the approach is quick and, if the instrument is constructed well, the results can be easy to summarize. There are, however, some inherent limitations to using surveys. Questionnaires tend to be impersonal. Moreover, the questions may not adequately tap the desired information. Staff can also misinterpret a question or skip over a question (or even a whole block of questions). Since most surveys are conducted anonymously, there is usually no way that missing information can be updated or probed more fully. This could be a problem because nonresponses may pose a threat to the validity of the data collected.

The primary issue with respect to questionnaires has to do with their validity and reliability—whether the questionnaire measures what it purports to measure, and whether it does so reliably and consistently. For this reason, it is probably wisest to use established validated instruments when they meet your purposes. The success of questionnaires depends in large part on the trust of the respondents. If individuals suspect the data will not be kept confidential or be used in the ways intended, they may give socially desirable answers instead of truthful responses.

The questionnaires in this book include several different types of response formats. There are both open-ended response formats (where the respondent is required to construct the response) and forced-response items (where the respondent is required to select their preferred choice from two or more alternatives). Forced-choice formats include multiple choice, yes/no, or rating scale questions. Table 4.1 provides a list of ten questions to guide you in selecting a questionnaire for your center-based assessment or in constructing your own questionnaire.

Interviews. Personal interviews are another approach to collecting data about your center. This approach is more direct and can lend deeper insight into the meaning of the issues addressed. Face-to-face interviews provide greater flexibility to probe more fully certain issues that would be too difficult to elicit in a questionnaire. Like questionnaires, interviews can be open-ended or

Table 4.1

Some Things to Think About in Selecting or Designing a Questionnaire

1. Are the directions on how to complete the questionnaire written in a manner that is easy for staff to understand? Are the directions concise, clear, and complete?

2. Is the purpose of the questionnaire clearly explained in the cover letter or the directions?

3. Does the title of the questionnaire clearly communicate what the questionnaire is about?

4. Is each question worded clearly and concisely, and does it address only one issue?

5. Are any questions too personal?

6. Is the response format appropriate for the questions being asked?

7. Is the questionnaire too long?

8. Are respondents provided with clear directions as to what to do with the questionnaire when they are finished?

9. Is the instrument clearly reproduced?

10. Overall, is the layout and design attractive?

highly structured. Successful interviews, however, require considerably more time to administer. Scheduling staff for interviews, transcribing interview notes, and summarizing the results of interviews, for even a small sample, is enormously time consuming.

Observations. Perhaps the most effective way to obtain information about what is actually happening in a given situation is to watch people's behavior as they work or interact with others. Such observations can be casual, with anecdotal notes taken, or highly structured, using checklists to code precise behaviors. Most directors are familiar the use of observational techniques to code children's and teachers' behavior in the classroom. But observational techniques can also be used to provide greater insight into organizational

processes other than teaching practices. For example, observing organizational processes such as group meeting behavior and providing feedback to participants can help group members increase their understanding of how to improve group meetings.

There are, of course, shortcomings in using observational techniques for collecting data. The most obvious is that observational methods are open to perceptual biases. Since what we view is influenced by our own subjective feelings and experiences, it is possible to distort reality. We have all been in situations where we have witnessed an event with others only to hear later multiple versions of the event being told. Objective reality varies with the lens one is using to view any situation. This underscores the importance of using observers who are highly trained and skilled in observational techniques. Saying that observers should be highly skilled does not necessarily mean that the observational tools need to be elaborate. Sometimes it is helpful to have a frequency tabulation on how many people said what or how many times a behavior or an event occurred in a given situation.

Records and documents. Records and artifacts are another rich source of data for directors that can be collected to document certain patterns in organizational performance. Attendance records, staff memos, and parent notes are all examples of documents that may provide clues to problem areas that need attention. Analyzing staff absenteeism records or assessing annual turnover for the center may provide clues as to staff's level of commitment to the center.

Standardized tests. While the use of standardized tests with preschool children is generally discouraged, they can serve a useful role in helping staff assess areas of the curriculum or instructional methodologies that may need to be improved. Children's scores on the Peabody Picture Vocabulary Test, for example, may provide useful clues for teachers on ways to improve instructional strategies to enhance language development. With staff who have limited training, the director may also want to use some type of standardized knowledge base test to assess level of knowledge in child development or specific areas of the curriculum. Such a test may be useful as a pre and post measure of changes in knowledge if a staff development program is implemented that addresses teachers' training needs in specific child development or curriculum content areas.

Tools for Assessing Organizational Needs

Collecting adequate data to assess the many elements of center effectiveness will undoubtedly necessitate using several different types of instruments, each with a different focus. Using multiple sources of evidence is important because no single instrument can capture the complex nature of organizational functioning with respect to people, structure, processes, culture, and outcomes.

A comprehensive, valid, and reliable tool available to assess overall leadership and management practices of center-based early care and education programs is the *Program Administration Scale* (PAS) (Talan & Bloom, 2004). This instrument measures organizational quality using 25 different items clustered in 10 subscales. These include human resources development, personnel cost and allocation, center operations, child assessment, fiscal management, program planning and evaluation, family partnerships, marketing and public relations, technology, and staff qualifications. The resulting profile can serve as a useful tool for developing a program improvement plan and for measuring change in program quality over time. The PAS is inexpensive and easy to use. (It is available from Teachers College Press and New Horizons.)

While the PAS is excellent for generating an overall picture of organizational functioning, there are times when you will want more detailed information about a specific aspect of your program. In Appendix A of this book are a number of assessment tools you can use to gather detailed information about different organizational practices. For example, whereas the PAS measures group meeting processes, it does so with just a couple of indicators. The group meeting assessment tool in this book assesses this important aspect of program functioning in far greater detail.

There are times when you will want to use the assessment tools from this book in the format in which they are presented. At other times, only a part of an instrument may suit your needs. It is hoped that the many examples presented in this book will assist you in gathering data about your center, diagnosing existing problems, and measuring your progress in achieving your objectives. The following provides a brief description of the range of organizational issues addressed in the instruments. More detailed information about administering and scoring these assessments is included with each instrument in Appendix A.

A word of caution. It should be underscored that many of these assessments measure staff's perceptions about different organizational practices. These perceptions may or may not mirror objective reality. Objective reality is not as important, however, as what people perceive to be the case. For it is the internalized filtered perceptions that guide and shape staff behavior.

Organizational Climate

Organizational climate describes the collective perceptions of staff regarding the overall quality of work life at the center. Assessment Tool #3, the short form of the *Early Childhood Work Environment Survey* (Bloom, 1996), can be used to assess the organizational climate of a program. This instrument measures staff's perceptions about a wide range of organizational practices. It is short and can be administered to the staff annually to take a quick pulse of the staff's perceptions of the quality of their work life.

Leadership Style

The first part of Assessment Tool #4 assesses three different leadership styles: the task-oriented style, emphasizing organizational needs; the people-oriented style, focusing on people and their individual needs; and the integrated style, stressing an appropriate emphasis on both the center's needs and the individual worker's needs, depending on the situation. The second part of this assessment is an overall evaluation of the director's management and administrative behavior.

This instrument is designed to be completed by all staff who work at the center. The composite results summarize the staff's perceptions of the director's leadership style.

Goal Consensus and Communication Processes

Whether in business and industry or educational settings, the hallmark of any successful organization is a shared sense among its members about what they are trying to accomplish. Agreed-upon goals and ways to attain them provide the foundation for rational planning and action. When the goals of a program are broken down into attainable, short-term targets, they are called objectives. These constitute the tasks individuals must accomplish in order to meet the organizational

goals. They are important because they help prioritize activities.

One cannot assume, however, that because a center's goals and objectives are committed to paper, there is uniform agreement about those goals and objectives. Indeed, consensus on program goals and objectives is often lacking. This is because the goals of the center may not be fully embraced by individual staff members or people may interpret them differently. Assessment Tool #5 assesses staff's rankings of various educational goals and objectives. From this information you will be able to determine the degree of agreement that exists among staff regarding various educational objectives.

Goal consensus depends largely on the effectiveness of communication in the center. Communication is the degree to which information is transmitted clearly among employees at all levels of the organization. Communication assumes many forms—oral or written, formal or informal, personal or impersonal. Communication networks also vary in centers. They may be vertical (from supervisor to teacher) or horizontal (between teachers). Assessment Tool #5 assesses staff's perceptions of the effectiveness of communication processes at the center.

Collegiality and Collaboration

Assessment Tool #6 assesses staff's perceptions regarding their overall co-worker relations, particularly the extent to which they feel teaching is a team effort. Whether or not teachers work collaboratively depends in large part on the harmony of their interests within the center—the degree to which they share similar goals and objectives. As Rosenholtz (1989) states, "Communal goals, problems, and values offer common substance from which to share" (p. 44). It should not be surprising, then, if the results of this assessment are similar to those of the goal consensus assessment tool described earlier.

Decision-Making Processes

The opportunity to participate in centerwide decision making is an important factor impacting the morale of teachers. We know from previous research, however, that the degree of desired decision-making influence by teachers varies from center to center and from situation to situation. We can't assume that all teachers want the same degree of decision-making influence in all areas of program functioning. Thus the roles that teachers and director play in decision making needs to vary according to the nature of the issue being considered and the background and interests of the parties involved.

Assessment Tool #7 was designed to assess staff's perceptions of their current and desired levels of decision-making influence in 10 areas: staff supervision and professional development; instructional practices and scheduling; enrollment and grouping; fiscal policies and practices; human resources allocation; centerwide goals and educational objectives; parent relations; community relations; facilities management; and evaluation practices (child, staff, center).

The purpose of this assessment is to measure the discrepancy between current and desired levels of decision-making influence. Assessment Tool #7 also includes questions about how the staff perceive the decision-making processes of the center. The information yielded by this instrument gives you a clearer picture of the areas in which staff desire a greater role in decision making. A more comprehensive treatment of this topic can be found in *Circle of Influence: Implementing Shared Decision Making and Participative Management* (Bloom, 2000).

Supervision and Evaluation Processes

The cornerstone of a center's capacity for self-renewal rests on the ability of staff to grow and adapt to change. It is the supervisory and performance appraisal practices in place at the center that allow this to happen. Assessment Tool #8 measures staff's perceptions of the extent to which the supervisory and performance appraisal processes of the center pose restraints or opportunities for professional growth. Using this assessment to tap staff's perceptions can provide important clues as to how to better motivate them to

higher levels of performance. This assessment tool can also serve as a useful pre and post measure of the center's attempt to improve supervisory and performance appraisal processes.

Organizational Norms

When individuals work together in a work setting, implicit agreement develops about the way things are supposed to be done. Over a period of time, these shared patterns of behavior become standard and define the appropriate range of acceptable behavior in a variety of situations. The term *norm* is used to describe these shared assumptions and expectations. Every center varies in the types of norms it has and the intensity with which they are felt.

Although the existence of a norm is neither good nor bad per se, certain norms can facilitate or inhibit behavior. This in turn may have a positive or negative impact on the effectiveness of how group members carry out their respective roles. Norms can be both prescriptive (do's) and proscriptive (don'ts). Assessing staff's perceptions about the prevailing norms can serve as a starting point for understanding those norms and how we can best implement needed changes to impact the norms.

Assessment Tool #9 assesses the prevailing norms at the center in seven areas: everyday demeanor; use of space and materials; time and task orientation; professional conduct regarding children and parents; collegiality; communication and decision making; and change and experimentation.

Group Meeting Processes

In most organizations people spend considerable time in meetings of one sort or another. Despite their importance to organizational functioning, few workers speak favorably about meetings. Many view them as a burden and waste of time. In early childhood programs, directors rely on meetings as the primary vehicle for communicating information, identifying and solving problems, and making new decisions and modifying old ones. Whether it's a weekly staff meeting, a monthly parent meeting, or an annual board meeting, well-run meetings are essential for achieving center goals. Assessment Tool #10 assesses staff's perceptions of the effectiveness of the staff meetings conducted at the center. The information gleaned from this assessment should prove useful in making center meetings both more efficient and effective.

Parent Satisfaction

Meeting the needs of parents is central to our mission of educating young children. It is incumbent upon us, therefore, to regularly assess parental satisfaction regarding the range and quality of services provided. Assessing parental perceptions about program functioning communicates the message to families that they are important and that their opinions are taken seriously. The information generated from Assessment Tool #11 will provide you with rich data about parents' perceptions of the overall effectiveness of the center and ways you can improve the quality of the program to be more family responsive. It is probably best administered in late spring each year.

Moving Forward: Considering Different Strategies for Change

We've stressed in the previous section that diagnosis of organizational practices is the cornerstone of problem solving in early childhood programs. Without complete and accurate data, problems tend to multiply. Problem identification and data collection naturally flow into data analysis. Once a discrepancy (problem) has been identified, the goal of analysis is to determine why the problem exists. Analysis consists of identifying aspects of people, structure, and processes that can be altered or changed to reduce the problem.

Now that you have collected additional data regarding the initial problem you identified as a result of completing Exercise 4.1, you are ready to restate the problem, identify the symptoms, and summarize the results of the data you collected. This can be done on Worksheet #1 "Identifying the Problem," in Appendix B. Completing this worksheet will yield a clear, succinct goal statement. This is nothing more than a precise description of

the ideal situation you want to achieve. Bean and Clemes (1978) state, "When a group defines goals, it gives substance to what people feel is important. People's feelings, attitudes, and expectations are critical to the success of achieving goals. They provide the energy and commitment that are necessary to do the work required to fulfill goals; motivation to action arises from feelings" (p. 72).

Some examples of goal statements might be:

▶ The program will achieve NAEYC Accreditation.

▶ Teachers will engage in collaborative planning and positive interactions with one another.

▶ The spatial arrangement of the physical environment will encourage children to engage in cooperative play.

▶ Parents will play an active role in center governance and daily activities.

Having goals that are explicitly stated and focus on the future helps you and your staff direct your energies and encourages cohesiveness. In sum, the purpose of this step is to generate a shared image of what the center will become. The importance of having a clear and shared vision for the change process cannot be overemphasized. All staff should be able to visualize a picture of what the center will be when the effort has been achieved.

Analyzing the Situation:
Assessing Helping and Hindering Forces

 In the early 1950s, Kurt Lewin (1951) introduced a useful model for analyzing problem situations. His Force-Field Analysis Model is helpful in understanding the pressures and counter-pressures of various forces that act to block or bring about change. He called these *driving forces* and *restraining forces*. Lewin believed that organizational life can be characterized by a dynamic balance of forces working in opposite directions.

The approach is useful because it helps us to think about problem situations in terms of factors that encourage and facilitate change (helping forces) and factors that work against change (hindering forces). These forces may originate inside the organization (people, structure, processes, or culture) or outside the organization in the external environment.

Using this model as a framework for problem analysis helps us think of the present state of the problem as a balance between opposing forces. The task, then, becomes one of enumerating all the forces that are on either side. The helping forces are those that support change efforts in moving toward an ideal; hindering forces are those that block movement toward the ideal. Lewin's force-field analysis is a useful technique because it identifies the positive and negative factors affecting change, targeting the cause rather than the effects of a problem. Worksheet #2, "Analyzing the Situation," in Appendix B, can help you identify the helping and hindering forces as they relate to the present situation and your conception of the ideal you would like to achieve.

Generating Possible Solutions:
Weighing Alternatives

 The next step in the problem-solving process is to determine how the helping or positive forces can be strengthened or increased and how the hindering or negative forces can be reduced or decreased. It is usually recommended that a program's first priority be given to reducing negative forces, since this usually has a stronger effect in achieving a desired ideal state than trying to increase the helping forces.

The solutions that are generated will probably involve all components of the system: changing people (through staff development or supervisory practices); changing structures (by implementing new policies or redefining roles); and changing organizational processes (by altering the way business is done). The internal components of the system are typically easier to change than the external environment. That is not to say that some of the strategies might not entail changing aspects of the external environment that the center may have control over. Changing the culture of the program will probably not appear as an immediate solution. That is because a center's culture changes as a by-product of changes in people,

structure, and processes. In other words, it will automatically change as a result of your efforts to modify other components of the program.

The next step is to determine the viability of each proposed solution. Some solutions will simply be impractical. Others will be too costly or take too long to put in place. In determining the viability of each solution, think of the possible effects that each solution will have on other aspects of people, structure, and processes. This involves anticipating the probable consequences of using each alternative strategy. The process implies trade-offs. Worksheet #3 in Appendix B, "Generating Possible Solutions," can be used to guide your analysis.

At the top of this worksheet state your goal. This will describe the ideal state you hope to achieve. Then proceed to list all possible solutions. Do not begin to assess the merits of each until you have noted all the possible solutions to your problem. Next jot down the possible consequences of each. After doing so, you will be able to assess which solutions are the most viable.

Developing an Action Plan

 Once viable solutions have been generated and alternative strategies for change have been carefully considered in terms of their intended and unintended consequences, it is then possible to develop a concrete plan of action. Putting your plan in writing not only helps avoid the ambiguity about who is to do what by when, but it also serves as a terrific way to benchmark your progress in achieving your goals. Worksheet #4, "Action Plan," in Appendix B, is designed to guide the planning process. The process is essentially one of translating the solutions generated from the previous exercise into concrete objectives and action steps that will achieve your goal. This is the step that will help you transform intentions into reality.

The first step in completing your plan of action is to state as clearly as possible your objectives. Objectives are statements that define measurable, observable behaviors that lead toward a goal. Objectives are typically stated in phrases that begin with the word to. They should also define time

Table 4.2

Writing Clear Objectives

WHAT will be accomplished

- ▶ the presence of new behavior
- ▶ the absence of a previously observed behavior
- ▶ the performance of a particular task
- ▶ the completion of a concrete product

WHO the persons are whose behavior will be measured

- ▶ everyone
- ▶ a part of a group
- ▶ a person

WHEN the specific behavior will be measured

- ▶ a specific date
- ▶ a contingent date (e.g., three months after training was conducted)
- ▶ a general period of time (e.g., within one year)

HOW MUCH of the behavior will show that some standard has been reached

- ▶ a score on a test
- ▶ a relative reduction in something (e.g., half as many absences...)
- ▶ a relative increase in something (twice as many enrollment applications...)
- ▶ an absolute number of something (10 curriculum modules completed)

Adapted from Bean, R., & Clemes, H. (1978). *Elementary principal's handbook: New approaches to administrative action.* Upper Saddle River, NJ: Prentice Hall.

limits. When writing objectives, think of what observable outcomes will provide evidence that you are making progress toward achieving a goal. While goals are often quite broad statements of what we hope to accomplish, objectives are more precise statements of what needs to be done to achieve a specific goal. As Table 4.2 notes, well-written objectives should contain four elements: what will be accomplished, who the persons are whose behavior will be measured, when the specific behavior will be measured, and how much of the behavior will show that some standard has been reached.

The next thing to do is to detail all the activities (action steps) that are necessary to accomplish each of the objectives. Next to each action step should be noted the individual or individuals responsible for carrying out the specific activities delineated, the total amount of time necessary to accomplish the task, a proposed timeline, and any additional resources needed (e.g., people, dollars). Try to estimate as closely as possible any direct expenses that may be incurred by carrying out the action step.

Finally, the action plan should include checkpoints for evaluation. In other words, how will you know you have accomplished your objectives? These may be actual products if your objective is to produce something tangible, or they may be points in time when you will assess your progress. This last category is important because it will help you know how to measure progress in achieving your goal.

While the planning process is presented in a worksheet format in this book, it may be easier for you to make a separate task card for each activity. Each card could detail the task, the person responsible for carrying out the task, and how long the task should take to accomplish. These cards can then be arranged on a wall in the appropriate sequence to make a visual timeline of the tasks to be done.

This process is recommended for undertaking goal setting when it involves several objectives entailing multiple activities over an extended period of time. The process is useful because it provides all parties involved with a very visual blueprint of the scope of the change process to be undertaken.

In the following section we see how Martha, the director of The Children's Corner, defined her problem and detailed a plan of action. At the end of the chapter are the worksheets that Martha completed for her program. These examples of completed worksheets will help you identify problem areas you may want to improve in your own program.

Case Study: The Children's Corner

Given the newness of her position and the gravity of the situation, Martha decided that time was scarce. The first couple of weeks on the job had convinced her that she would have to take the initiative to implement some changes. She would start with a top-down model of change and gradually increase staff's involvement as they were ready and willing. Martha knew that certain unproductive norms had found acceptance over the years and that patterns of behavior would be difficult to change. But she had one thing going for her: she sensed that the teachers were also dissatisfied with the present situation. If she could implement a few structural changes and work on modifying some of the processes of the center, she might be able to establish the norms of collegiality and collaboration that would lead staff to begin to examine their own teaching practices.

Martha's first step was to clarify her problem. At first blush, she thought her problem was the hostility directed at her at staff meetings. But after she pondered the issue a while, she realized this might be a symptom of a far deeper problem. She decided to collect some data regarding the staff's perceptions of center policies and practices.

Martha was encouraged by how open and candid staff were in completing the assessment tools. She saw how the process of asking teachers their opinions signaled her interest and respect for them.

When Martha analyzed the data from the assessments, she realized that the teachers on her staff were generally distrustful of one another. Because of their lack of influence in decision-making processes and staff meeting processes in recent years, they had reacted by becoming overly protective of their own turf. Martha knew that if she was to make any impact on this program, she first needed to improve the cooperative nature of relationships and establish an environment that encouraged collaboration. This became her goal.

Martha's objectives for accomplishing her goal were ambitious. First, she would try to increase staff's knowledge of different learning and teaching styles. Her hope was that this would lead to a greater appreciation of individual differences. At the same time, she would develop an individual profile for each teacher highlighting his or her teaching strengths. This information would be used to encourage collaboration between teachers.

Second, she would work to modify some of the structures of the center that seemed to discourage collaboration. Staff work and planning schedules in particular seemed to be a real problem. Martha knew that meaningful interactions between teachers were often difficult, given teachers' overlapping and conflicting schedules. Even getting everyone together for staff meetings was almost impossible. She wanted to free up time to allow teachers to plan activities together, observe other centers together, and go to conferences and workshops together.

Finally, she would make some bold changes in the way staff meetings were conducted. She realized that valuable time was being wasted talking about trivial details that could be covered in a memo. Meetings did not start on time and people did not have a stake in the agenda or in supporting productive interaction processes. Martha decided she would involve teachers in setting the agenda and facilitating discussions. She would also work to help them examine the roles that each of them played in meetings. She believed that increasing their knowledge of group dynamics would have the added benefit of actually improving group functioning.

Implementing the Action Plan

 Picking the right problems and finding the right solutions only points you in the right direction. Implementing the plan is what actually leads to center improvement. If goals and objectives are important to the individuals involved, and if they are doable, then implementing the action plan should be a fairly straightforward process. In a top-down model of change, the director has control over this process. In a collaborative model of change, however, the director's role is a delicate balance of providing sufficient supervision and oversight, ensuring tasks actually get done, and at the same time providing leeway so that individuals internalize a sense of ownership in the change process.

In Chapter 3 you learned about the vital role that you play in providing resources, protecting time, and giving staff the support and recognition they need during the change process to ensure feelings of success. It is critical that the change process not be viewed as a linear event. All kinds of circumstances can arise that necessitate modifying action plans and timelines for carrying out activities. Being flexible and viewing your action plan as a blueprint that may have to be revised from time to time will help you keep staff motivated to achieve desired goals.

Evaluating Progress

 The final step in the change cycle is to evaluate progress in achieving desired goals (outcomes). Without evaluation, the actions implemented toward change would not be understood. Thus, evaluation should not be seen as the end of the process, but rather as a stepping-stone toward further identifying new areas in need of change. This is a cyclical process, one that addresses the needs of a complex social system in action. What is the purpose of evaluating change? And what is the best way to pursue practical and useful evaluation procedures? Perhaps a good way to begin is to define what evaluation means in this context.

During the implementation process, directors play a monitoring role. The easiest way to get a sense of how things are going is what Peters and Waterman (1982) call *management by wandering around,* talking informally with staff involved in the change process. "How's the new literacy program working?" "What insights did you get from the emergent literacy workshop you attended last week?" "Have you noticed a change in the children's behavior since you rearranged the writing and listening center?" Informal pulse taking is critical in keeping change on target. This type of formative evaluation also serves to provide information on how the action plan might be improved.

At a designated point in the change process you'll also want to gather data in a more formal, systematic way. A summative evaluation assesses the degree of success of the change endeavor in achieving desired outcomes. Formal evaluation occurs when the outcomes of these investigations are described in terms that can be measured. If the goals and objectives on the evaluation plan are described precisely, then this process is a fairly straightforward one. It may be done using some of the assessment tools discussed earlier as a posttest measure of the degree of improvement made in a specific area. This type of evaluation provides useful data about the success of the change endeavor and any alteration to resources that may need to be made to make it more successful in the future.

Loucks-Horsley (1987) believes that the most important evaluation question to ask is whether the new changes are thought of as an improvement by those most affected by them. To assure objectivity in the formal evaluation process (particularly when the results of the evaluation will be used to document the need for additional funds from a sponsoring agency or external funding source), it is best to use an impartial third party to collect evaluation data and summarize the results of the change efforts. In sum, evaluation is both a basis for assessing whether intended outcomes have been achieved and pinpointing alterations in the action plan that should be made in subsequent change endeavors.

Identifying the Problem

Problem: _Lack of cooperation among teachers. Inability (lack of willingness) to collaborate._

Symptoms: _Low involvement in staff meetings. Mistrust, competition, and very little sharing of ideas and teacher resources. Teacher isolation._

Results of data collection: _Assessment Tool #10: Staff perceptions of meetings show they believe meetings are boring and a waste of time._

Assessment Tool #6: Staff perceptions of collegiality and collaboration show that they feel alienated from one another but want to find ways to reduce the tension in their interpersonal relations.

Assessment Tool #3: Organizational climate score = 65.

Assessment Tool #7: Staff desire greater decision-making influence in all areas of center functioning, particularly in determining the content of staff meetings and in determining work schedules.

Goal (ideal situation): _Staff will engage in collaborative planning and in more cooperative, supportive interactions with one another._

Analyzing the Situation

Goal (ideal situation): <u>Staff will engage in collaborative planning and in more</u>
<u>cooperative, supportive interactions with one another.</u>

Helping Forces	Hindering Forces
isolated instances of some teachers helping each other →	← protecting classroom "turf"
director willing to support collaboration →	← time
teachers' interest in greater involvement in staff meetings →	← some staff are afraid or unwilling to share ideas
staff willing to give honest feedback when asked →	← distrust of others
staff aware of tension →	← physical arrangement of space promotes isolation in classrooms
low staff turnover →	← conflicting work schedules
some new teachers have lots of enthusiasm and interest in sharing resources →	← history (norm) of lack of sharing and collaboration

Present Situation

Generating Possible Solutions

Goal (ideal situation): <u>Staff will engage in collaborative planning and in more cooperative, supportive interactions with one another.</u>

Proposed Solution	**Possible Consequences**
create resource bulletin board ▶	some staff may not use it
change work schedules to encourage joint planning and time to visit other centers together ▶	more opportunities to work together but may result in cliques forming
involve staff in planning meetings ▶	greater sense of involvement in decisions
conduct training on learning styles and psychological types ▶	may increase appreciation of individual differences
director to model cooperative behavior ▶	some staff may perceive this as disingenuous
hire substitutes so teachers can observe each other's classrooms ▶	will be expensive and some staff may resist

Action Plan

Goal: Staff will engage in collaborative planning and more cooperative, supportive interactions.

Objectives	Action Steps	Person Responsible	Time	Resources Needed (people, materials, $$$)	Evaluation Checkpoints
To increase staff's knowledge of different teaching and learning styles	• invite speaker for fall workshop • have staff complete Assessment Tools #14, 15 • photocopy handouts • purchase books on learning styles	director	• 2 hrs to plan workshop and write letter to speaker • 2 hrs to score assessments	• guest speaker $125 • teachers $35 each for attending workshop • $110 photocopying handouts and books for staff library • $30 food	• feedback from workshop • see if reference is made to different styles during the year
To change center structures to encourage more teachers to share ideas and resources	• set up bulletin board and resource center • rearrange schedules to encourage joint planning time and opportunities to visit other centers together	director and teachers	• 3 hrs to set up resource center • 16 hrs for individual conference time with teachers	• $200 supplies for resource center • substitutes for staff who want to observe—approximately 40 hrs	• see how staff utilize the resource center • administer Assessment Tool #6 as posttest in May
To increase staff involvement in planning and conducting meetings	• ask for volunteers to help plan and lead meetings • provide staff with handouts on group dynamics and how to conduct effective meetings	director and teachers	• approximately 35 hrs released time for staff to plan meetings between Sept. and May	• substitutes to cover planning time—approx. 35 hrs • misc. photocopying, $8 per meeting • $10 food per meeting • $75 for books on group dynamics	• administer Assessment Tools #3 and #7 as posttest in May to see if change in perceptions • administer Assessment Tool #10 after six meetings; share results

A Final Word

We have seen in this chapter that picking the right problems and finding the right solutions to them is the heart of center-based improvement. We have also seen that a systems model can serve as a viable framework for organizational analysis and problem solving. Effective directors collect information on the quality of their center, compare the information with desired outcomes, identify discrepancies, and search for underlying causes to problems. From this information it is then possible to develop a plan to alleviate the problems.

Your role is to act as a catalyst, moving the center toward its goals. Data analysis is the step that links the present to the future. If teachers can have an active role in collecting data, analyzing data, and generating alternatives, they'll feel a greater sense of shared responsibility for implementing change and incorporating new practices. Examining the changes the staff would like to see leads naturally to developing objectives and designing appropriate strategies for change. The goal in the change process is to turn problem solutions into goal statements that clearly state what will be done in a specific, realistic, observable, and measurable way.

The assessment process is essentially a self-renewing process—it is dynamic rather than static. It is concerned with both outcomes and processes. It is a means for developing organizational teamwork and building collaborative action to bring about an understanding and acceptance of changes necessary to achieve center objectives, and the responsibility for implementing those changes. Ongoing assessment should be an integral tool for creating, designing, improving, and maintaining effective early childhood programs.

Chapter 5

Assessing Individual Needs

Most early childhood administrators are well steeped in the principles of child development and developmentally appropriate practices. They understand the importance of providing educational experiences that address the developmental stages, experiences, abilities, and unique cultural and linguistic backgrounds of individual children. But when they turn their attention to the professional development needs of the teachers on their staff, they often forget that adults too need developmentally appropriate, individualized experiences (Vartuli & Fyfe, 1993). Without this perspective, they are likely to implement cookie-cutter, one-size-fits-all supervision and staff development practices as if all their teachers had the same background, interests, and needs.

This chapter stresses the importance of assessing the needs of individual teachers in light of a host of factors including their learning style, previous educational experiences, career stage, special talents and abilities, and unique life circumstances and backgrounds. It underscores the point that your knowledge and understanding of the teachers in your program rest on collecting accurate data. And it provides a template to help you think about the most important assessment areas in identifying the strengths and professional needs of your teachers.

Adults as Individuals

In the world of personal psychology it is easy to think of ourselves as the norm and anyone not quite like us as an aberration. When put to the test, we acknowledge, of course, the importance of diversity, but the pull to want to associate with people who think and act like us is strong. The pull to want to change other people so they also think and act like we do is even stronger. But effective directors know that such thinking is flawed. They understand that the heart of effective interpersonal relations is recognizing and appreciating differences. And the heart of motivating people to achieve peak performance rests on integrating this belief into a philosophy of supervision and staff development. Put simply, effective leaders know what makes people tick and what ticks them off.

There are many ways to conceptualize human differences. The following categories are in no way intended to be exhaustive, but they do capture the key areas that highlight the amazing diversity in the people who work at your center. While there is some overlap among areas, for the most part they represent separate aspects of the developing adult.

Personal History

The gathering of basic background information on individuals begins during the interviewing and hiring process. To address family history and other background variables in more depth, however, it is necessary to devote some focused time getting to know teachers during their first few months on the job. In addition to strengthening personal connections that build rapport, the resulting information can provide greater insight to help structure supervision from a developmental perspective.

Knowing, for example, that a teacher has a twin, or grew up on a farm milking cows, or moved from one military base to another as a child, or was a star athlete on a high school sports team can help illuminate why the person has certain preferences or deeply held beliefs. Even recognizing a teacher's lack of exposure to different ethnic groups can help you better understand why the teacher may be having difficulty relating with parents and children of different cultures. In the same way, knowing that a teacher has recently experienced a painful loss or is going through a separation or divorce helps you extend the emotional support needed during difficult days.

Establishing open and trusting interpersonal relationships that take into consideration the whole person, both personal and professional, is essential if you are going to be successful in implementing an individualized model of supervision and staff development. Obviously such information cannot be obtained through questionnaires or quick assessments. Rather it is gradually acquired through many informal conversations with staff. It is the stuff of hallway conversations, lunchroom chatter, and parking lot exchanges. But it can also surface through sensitive and tactful intervention as in the following two examples, in which Martha talks about the connection between personal history and job performance:

Case Study: The Children's Corner

"My relationship with Margaret was quite formal when she was first hired. Although I encouraged her to call me by my first name, she continued to use 'Mrs.' when she addressed me. She was also extremely nervous every time I observed in her classroom. After about four months I decided to take the risk and confront her about the tension in our relationship. I told her that I sensed she was upset by my presence when I observed in her room. That broke the ice. Margaret opened up and talked to me about her relationship with her mother, who is my age. She described her mother as very demanding and critical, a real perfectionist. Margaret explained that as a child she disliked having her mother attend any event where she performed for fear of a harsh assessment. Once Margaret could express her feelings and her fear of being critiqued, we were able to establish a healthier relationship as supervisor and teacher."

Case Study: The Children's Corner

"Scott had been late for work several mornings over a two-week period. He apologized to me and to his classroom aide, who had handled the children on her own in his absence, but he offered no explanation for his tardiness. In the late afternoon when his session was over, he appeared rushed and anxious to depart. He would leave the center just as soon as the last child was gone.

"I invited Scott to have lunch with me and talked with him about his tardiness. Reluctantly, he opened up and shared his personal situation. He wouldn't give me the specific details, but he said his wife was having some medical problems, and the care of his two school-age children fell on his shoulders. Since he worked in child care, he was guarded about letting others know about his situation. After all, he reasoned, all the other parents are able to manage busy schedules; certainly he should be able to deal with his children and still get to work on time! He felt his self-esteem was on the line.

"Scott and I talked about his situation, and I offered some helpful suggestions. Even though his tardiness was the reason for our meeting, I felt he really benefited from having someone tell him it was okay to reach out and ask for help; that he didn't need to shoulder the burden of an immediate family crisis alone."

Educational Level, Specialized Training, and Work Experience

In most states licensing regulations require that centers document each teacher's level of formal education. Well-maintained personnel records reflect specific educational degrees, the completion of specialized training programs, and the years and type of teaching or volunteer experience. Unfortunately, in most centers, once this information is collected it is filed away, never to see the light of day unless the licensing rep stops by or the center is preparing for an accreditation validation visit.

Directors don't often think of themselves as career counselors, but that is precisely the role they play when they tune in to the individualized professional development needs of each of their teachers. Knowing that one teacher is just two courses shy of completing an associate's degree, that another would benefit from some specialized training being offered by the local child care resource and referral agency, or that still another would be well suited for an online degree-completion program is what guiding the professional development of staff is all about. This means that those transcripts and other records documenting knowledge and skill don't stay buried away, but are referred to and used regularly to guide decision making about appropriate professional development opportunities.

Likewise, with respect to work experience it is important for directors to be aware of the many and varied roles teachers have performed over the years. Some may have worked in family child care or parent cooperatives while their children were young. Others may have volunteered in different capacities in public schools or community social service agencies. Still others may have been camp counselors or Girl Scout and Boy Scout troop leaders. Taking time during the initial hiring process to learn as much as you can about the various experiences of individual staff members will help you tap their expertise and involve them in your program in more meaningful ways.

Knowledge and Skill

Perhaps the most vital information to assess about the teachers on your staff is their level of knowledge and skill. Knowledge—the facts and information teachers have attained through formal study, independent reading, life events, and on-the-job experience—provides the foundation for effective teaching practices. In early care and education settings we want teachers to be well versed in theories of child development, effective instructional practices, classroom management techniques, family support strategies, and different curricula.

Skill, on the other hand, is the actual ability to carry out or apply the knowledge one has gained. As director, you certainly care about your teachers' knowledge base, but you are probably more concerned about their skill levels—their ability to connect the theoretical principles they've learned to actual classroom practice. No doubt you know a teacher or two that has a wealth of book knowledge about children's growth and development, classroom management, or effective teaching strategies, but is

inept at effectively applying that knowledge in different classroom situations. The only way to ascertain teachers' skill levels is to observe them in action.

Interests and Special Talents

Also important to note is information related to particular interests and talents of staff. Sadly, in many centers teachers who have special gifts or talents go unrecognized; their potential to enhance the curriculum is missed. Whether it is in the area of music, art, drama, puppetry, sports, photography, foreign language, or cooking, integrating teachers' special interests and talents into the curriculum not only enriches the program for the children, but also bolsters teachers' sense of self-worth.

Sometimes teachers have unusual talents that are not readily apparent. One director told of a teacher who could imitate more than a dozen bird calls. She used different bird chirps to communicate different commands to the children (time to clean up, time for snack, time to go home). The kids loved it. In another center, a teacher who was an avid gardener worked with the children to design and plant a vegetable garden. This project ultimately became a small fund-raiser for the center as neighbors happily relieved the center of its extra zucchinis and tomatoes each harvest. At Martha's program, The Children's Corner, young Shelley, who loved aerobics and jewelry making, turned these two passions into special after-school activities for the older children attending the center. Martha also tapped Christine's special interest in graphic design to take over production of the center's monthly newsletter.

Beliefs and Values

In Bill Ayers's book *The Good Preschool Teacher* (1989), much of the focus is on the beliefs of the six teachers who are profiled. Anna thinks of herself as a substitute mother and "struggles to achieve an intensity and investment in each child that will truly support and nurture and challenge" (p. 127). Chana has come to some solid conclusions about the issue of separation in children's lives. She thinks of herself as a person "who understands what makes separations successful experiences from which to grow and build" (p. 127). Joanne's strongest belief is that children need to be empowered—that they need to be able to make decisions for themselves. For Darlene, patience is the key attribute of a good teacher. Michele emphasizes the importance of order and organization and productive work for children. And finally, Maya infuses her teaching with a strong belief in warmth and respect. "She tells stories of her grandmother, who told her to respect herself and never to put herself in situations where she wasn't respected, and who insisted that she associate only with other children who were doing interesting things" (p. 129).

The rich, descriptive profiles drawn by Ayers underscore the importance of looking at the values and beliefs of teachers in order to understand the meaning teachers give to their work. A value is a deeply held view of what we believe to be important and worthwhile. Our personal values shape our beliefs about what is important to pursue, how we treat others, and how we choose to spend our time. A belief is different from a value. It is our personal conviction that certain things are true and that certain statements are facts.

Our core values cut across all aspects of our lives. They serve as a point of reference, a kind of moral compass for making daily decisions. They give rise to our fundamental commitments, the things in life that we consider worthy for their own sake. While values certainly reflect our family upbringing and cultural backgrounds, they are also shaped by personal experiences, education, and societal influences.

It is a central task of directors to listen closely to teachers to hear what values and beliefs support their teaching practices. Through attentive listening, directors can assist teachers in identifying, clarifying, and articulating the values and beliefs that they bring to their present role, which have been developed during their childhood, their educational training, or years of teaching experience.

The following comments illustrate some of the beliefs that undergird the classroom practices of teachers:

> *If we were all alike, we'd only need one of us.*
>
> Lilian Katz

"This article on the Corporate Community School of America says that they have been able to teach children regardless of background to read and enjoy it. I'll bet they selected only the smartest kids!" (Belief: Home background and inherited ability are more important than teaching as factors in learning.)

"I don't think teachers should dictate to children how they should spend their time, so I have long periods of free play for children; group time is just 10 minutes a day." (Belief: Autonomy is important; teachers should not intrude on children's learning.)

"Children, first of all, need structure. They feel safer with firm limits and rules. I can't buy into all of this talk about letting children make their own decisions." (Belief: Adults are the experts; they know what is best for children.)

"Families need to be more connected to the classroom operation in child care. I'd like to see us encourage more visitation at lunch time and more discussion sessions with parents." (Belief: My role is only secondary to that of parents; I cannot affect change without parents' support.)

Often we can trace our beliefs back to the way we have been raised or educated. The values our families and teachers inculcated during childhood make a deep and lasting impression on our developing belief system. Regardless of their origin, it is important that values and beliefs be identified and articulated. Otherwise teachers may try to implement new curriculum approaches and not understand that their beliefs may not be aligned with the underlying assumptions of the curriculum model they are using.

Kim, a young first-grade teacher, accepted a job in a primary wing where the teachers were experimenting with an open-classroom approach. In the job interview, she was able to articulate quite well the theory and philosophy underlying open-classroom practices; it had been part of her undergraduate pre-service training program. She had also done quite well in her student teaching placement in a traditional kindergarten program. However, once she got assigned to a classroom with real children and real situations within an informal structure that promoted autonomy and flexibility, she became very frustrated with allowing children a lot of freedom and choice. Kim began using a loud, harsh voice to try to maintain a better sense of order.

In a discussion with the principal following his observation of her teaching, Kim began recalling her own school experience. She was the product of a rigid parochial school. While she disliked aspects of her own educational experience, she also began to see that she had embraced and internalized certain core values of the approach—namely that children should always be attentive and defer to authority figures. She came to realize that her value and belief system conflicted with the educational philosophy of the program in which she now taught.

Those teachers who move to a higher level of abstract thinking and altruistic motivation have reflected on their own values and beliefs in an attempt to clearly identify the linkages between their beliefs and their behavior. As director, you can be instrumental in assisting teachers to move in this direction.

Dispositions

Teacher dispositions are critical elements impacting performance; something early childhood administrators can't ignore. A disposition is one's natural tendency or inclination—a habitual way of acting toward others or thinking about things (House, 2004). A disposition is different than knowledge or skill. The construct is descriptive, designating actions or thought processes that are characterized by their frequency.

For example, a teacher who is thoughtful, asks deep questions, and ponders important issues before making decisions could be described as having a *reflective disposition*. A teacher who encourages children, helps them set new and challenging goals, and gives abundant praise for effort could be described as having a *supportive*

disposition. And a teacher who has an insatiable curiosity for new information and is always reading books or researching topics on the Internet might be described as having a *disposition for lifelong learning*.

Dispositions set the tone for interpersonal interactions in a program and they have a profound impact on program outcomes. In early care and education settings, most directors would agree that being nurturing, compassionate, enthusiastic, reflective, flexible, patient, respectful, collaborative, tolerant, conscientious, and creative are desirable dispositions that promote positive program outcomes. These are dispositions we want teachers to show as well as those we want teachers to foster in children.

Lilian Katz (1993) reminds us that because not all dispositions are desirable, we need to find ways to strengthen positive dispositions and weaken or diminish those less undesirable. While directors readily connect professional development with opportunities to expand teachers' knowledge base or build new skills, they usually don't think of professional development as a means of nurturing desirable dispositions and providing critical feedback on less desirable dispositions.

Katz argues that the dispositions that support effective teaching should constitute goals for teacher development. But changing, even modifying, a person's disposition does not happen overnight. This is because dispositions are often grounded in a person's values—values such as caring, fairness, honesty, responsibility, and social justice. As such they are part of a person's more enduring traits and acquired patterns of behavior. Change can only come about by helping individuals build self-awareness and consider alternative ways of thinking and behaving.

Flexibility and Openness to Change

The disposition to be flexible and open to change is clearly important in early childhood settings and warrants separate discussion. Individual variance is great with respect to flexibility. Some teachers are firm believers in routine, finding comfort in established order and tried-and-true solutions. When any change is proposed, their knee-jerk reaction is to resist. These people are predictable. They drive the same route to work every day, wear the same hairstyle year after year, and haven't changed the arrangement of their classroom since they joined the staff. Others teachers seem to thrive on change, risk taking, and exploration of alternatives. They eagerly embrace each new fad, change their hairstyle on a whim, and love to surprise their students by rearranging their classrooms. Having both extremes on a staff can be a definite challenge for a director. Fortunately, most people fall somewhere between these two extremes on the continuum.

Understanding each teacher's orientation as it relates to flexibility and openness to change is essential when implementing an individualized model of supervision and staff development. If you know in advance that several teachers tend to be inflexible and skeptical of any change, you will be in a better position to handle their initial resistance. For example, if you are proposing the adoption of a new curricular approach, you may need to allow these teachers a longer trial period before fully committing to the proposed change. They may need change introduced in baby steps. Presenting change as an option rather a mandate is also preferable, allowing discussion and evaluation along the way.

The degree of flexibility reflected by a particular staff member can also be described by the terms *adaptor* and innovator coined by Kirton (1976). Kirton conceptualizes the trait of innovativeness as a behavior preference related to two contrasting cognitive styles. He sees people as adaptors or innovators based on their preference *to do things better* or *to do things differently*. Adaptors are characterized by precision and conformity; innovators prefer to approach tasks in unusual and different ways. Knowing where teachers fall on this continuum will help you gain insight into the diverse thinking and functioning preferences of the individuals on your staff.

When one moves from theoretical constructs to practical application, Kirton's conceptualization of innovativeness is particularly appealing because it may assist in promoting collaboration in an organizational setting, especially in times of change. The approach emphasizes that a staff comprised of both adaptors and innovators is important in order to be prepared for all contingencies. Thus we should not discuss the noninnovative person in pejorative terms.

Under pressure, adaptive personalities and innovative personalities usually disagree on what steps are appropriate to take, and they often hold negative viewpoints of each other when collaboration would be a more fruitful strategy. Innovators perceive adaptive individuals as dogmatic, stodgy, timid, inflexible, and compliant to authority. Adaptive people tend to see innovators as being unsound and unreasonable. Kirton states that an organization needs to allow for mutual appreciation of those with different modes of problem solving.

Energy Level

From a physiological standpoint, adults have very different energy levels. Two teachers who seemingly have the same family demands, responsibilities, and outside interests may come to work in very different states. One complains constantly of being tired and worn out; the other seems to possess unlimited bounce and stamina. In conversations with these teachers, one says she can get by on a midnight-to-six sleep routine, while the other says she needs her full nine hours of beauty rest.

The physical differences in people are particularly important to consider in early care and education settings as you structure work assignments and staff development opportunities that maximize the fit between an individual's physical limitations and the demands of the job. To be sure, working in early childhood education is physically demanding—kneeling, bending, and lifting are core physical requirements of most teaching jobs. But that does not mean that considerations can't be made to accommodate legitimate differences among people's energy levels and physical limitations.

Cognitive Capacity

Certainly individuals differ in their cognitive capacity and fundamental thought processes. As the product of both nature and nurture, some people have the capacity to process complex abstract concepts while others struggle to make sense of simple concrete ideas and concepts. David Hunt and his associates define level of abstract thinking as one's ability to determine relationships and to make comparisons and contrasts between information and experience that can be used to generate multiple possibilities in formulating decisions (Hunt, et al., 1978). Glickman (2004) classifies the abstract thinking of teachers as low, moderate, or high. Understanding a teacher's level of abstract thinking is essential for designing professional development opportunities that will challenge but not cognitively overwhelm the individual.

Teachers who have a low level of abstract thinking describe experiences in simple, concrete language. They evaluate problems in clear-cut, black-and-white terms and have trouble determining the subtle gray areas of complex issues. They may have difficulty making changes in their classroom or adjusting their behavior to the shifting demands of their students. They often respond to the same problem in a habitual manner despite the fact that the response does not resolve the problem. Often they do not see the relationship between their own behavior and a problem they may have identified. They may want quick answers, structured work assignments, and clear direction from a supervisor. Such a perspective is apparent in one teacher's plea to her director:

These kids won't sit in a group for more than five minutes! All the boys want to do is play in the block area; and they all come to me constantly for help or to tell about somebody. What should I do, throw this developmentally appropriate stuff out the window? This approach just doesn't work with this group!

Teachers with moderate levels of abstract thinking, according to Glickman, can define a problem and generate a limited number of possible solutions but may still have difficulty formulating a comprehensive plan or thinking of the consequences of alternative approaches. Individuals with a moderate level of abstract thinking may realize that the problems they are experiencing relate in some way to what they are doing. However, they may still

be unable to find an appropriate remedy, as the following example illustrates:

Some children want to spend all their time in art or blocks. So I've decided to move small groups through each interest area for 20 minutes at a time. That way everyone will experience each area, and I won't have to nag the children to get them to try new things!

Finally, teachers who have achieved a high level of abstract thinking use a rational process of problem solving by incorporating several sources of information and applying their own knowledge and experience. They can generate many alternative responses to a situation and before making a final decision about changing something, they will consider all available data. They regularly reflect on the lessons learned form past experiences in order to arrive at the best solution. In the following scenario, a teacher discusses with her director her problems concerning Omar, one of her students:

I've been trying to find some new strategies to use with Omar when he becomes so frustrated and angry. I talked yesterday with his mother to see if we could come up with a consistent approach. It may be that excluding him from certain activities is warranted. I've resisted removing him from the block area, but I'm beginning to think this is necessary. His behavior is threatening the safety of others. I think it's important, however, for Omar to be involved in constructive things after he has been removed. In other words, I don't think he should just remain alone, unattended. He seems so vulnerable emotionally, and he needs my support.

Learning Style

The term *learning style* describes the multiple ways that people make sense of their world. It includes the diverse ways we decode, encode, process, store, and retrieve information as well as the emotional and environmental elements that affect motivation and desire to learn. A person's learning style clearly influences his or her receptivity to different instructional strategies and the degree to which concepts are internalized.

Although each person's learning style is shaped by biology, it is also modified by experience (McCarthy, 1996). Teachers' learning styles influence their selection of learning activities and situations. Some teachers learn best by reflecting, others learn by observing, and still others acquire new skills best by doing. While some teachers relish the idea of using the group setting to discuss problems and situations at length, others see this approach as time consuming and cumbersome.

The work of Anthony Gregorc (1982) provides a useful framework for thinking about different learning styles. He proposes that there are two ways that individuals perceive information—concretely and abstractly—and two ways they process and organize information—sequentially and randomly. Although everyone uses all these perceptual and processing modes to some degree, the unique combinations of where people fall on these two intersecting continua create unique learning styles. The following typologies will be useful as you consider how you can meet the diverse styles of teachers on your staff.

Practical learners (concrete-sequential). More than anything else, practical learners want to see the real-life application of the ideas they are learning. Their favorite question is "How can I use this?" They learn through direct experience and want tangible evidence of learning in the form of handouts, products, notes, and recipes. In meetings, it is important for practical learners to have a sense of where the discussion is heading and what is going to be accomplished, so a detailed agenda is essential. In workshops, they get impatient when other participants ramble or stray from the point. Practical learners strive for perfection, so they may press for the one right answer. They are interested in facts and details, so step-by-step directions are essential. Sometimes practical learners are so busy studying the details of an issue that they miss the big picture.

Analytic learners (abstract-sequential). Analytic learners weigh the pros and cons, advantages and disadvantages, and good and bad of each issue presented in different learning experiences. They

are interested in the credentials of trainers and want to make sure the person is an expert on the subject. They tend to be verbal—the ones tossing out the hard questions and challenging you for your rationale, the logic, or the research backing your statements. Their favorite question is "How do you know this is true?" They live in the world of abstract ideas, see the big picture, and enjoy analyzing every angle of a situation. They use facts to prove or disprove their theories. Analyzers are quite content to sit through lectures as long as they have an opportunity for vigorous debate and discussion following the presentation. They are usually impatient with cooperative learning strategies or activities where participants process information in small groups.

Imaginative learners (abstract-random). Imaginative learners are people-people. They wear their hearts on their sleeves and focus on the processes of learning more than the content. For them, learning must be personalized; their emotions influence their ability to concentrate. It is essential with imaginative learners to tend to their emotional, social, and physical needs. They thrive on personal meaning and personal involvement in any learning situation. They also recognize the emotional needs of others. Their favorite question is "Why is this important?" They want to know how they can make a difference. Time is irrelevant to imaginative learners, so they may not return from breaks on time. Small group discussions and in-depth sharing with a learning partner are favorite instructional strategies with these individuals. Imaginative learners need a lot of time to reflect and process ideas. They often engage in flights of fantasy, sprinkle their conversation with superlatives, and focus on the big picture at the risk of missing the details.

Inventive learners (concrete-random). Inventive learners need a lot of mental elbowroom. They use experimentation as well as insight and instinct to solve problems. Inventive learners make intuitive leaps and take risks to come up with novel ways to solve problems. They might test poorly because they think too much about the nuances of questions. Inventive learners need flexibility in instructional strategies so they can create innovative spin-offs. Their favorite question is "What if...?" While inventive learners are inquisitive and independent learners, they can also be impulsive. They think fast on their feet. Don't be discouraged if they don't follow directions exactly; they need room to come up with alternative paradigms.

In Table 5.1, "Four Types of Learners," you can see why a wide repertoire of strategies is essential if you are going to meet the needs of these four learning styles. An appreciation of different learning styles helps you discern linkages between the teachers' learning preferences and their expectations of you as their supervisor.

Some teachers prefer a supervisory style that promotes self-directed learning, independent decision making, and indirect guidance. Others, however, look for clearly delineated curriculum guides, specific directions, and director-initiated decisions and answers. The following examples illustrate two different learning styles:

After the first in a series of in-service workshops on conflict resolution, Belinda complained to her director Sandra that the role-playing sessions conducted by the consultant were too time consuming. She asked Sandra if she could just read the handouts and try implementing the approach on her own. The group sessions, as Belinda described them, were too touchy-feely; she did not like being observed while trying new ideas and strategies.

Another teacher at the same center, Constance, mentioned to the director that she didn't feel that the conflict resolution training was being tied closely enough to the actual classroom situations. She asked if the consultant could come back to observe her as she taught and give her specific feedback and suggestions. She felt she needed more concrete support and direction in trying to implement something new.

These two teachers probably represent the two learning styles analytic and practical. Belinda would prefer to get the ideas from written material and try them out on her own. Analytic learners usually learn best in impersonal learning situations,

guided by theory and their own analyses. On the other hand, Constance would like to carry out the suggested theories and have someone observe her doing so. Practical learners are task oriented and want direct practical payoffs.

Adults also differ in terms of their preferred perceptual modality, another way to conceptualize learning style. Some people are visual learners and enjoy detailed flipcharts, overhead transparencies, and handouts. Others are mainly auditory, preferring lecture, debate, and group discussions. And still others have a kinesthetic modality preference, preferring to learn new things by moving, touching, and engaging in action-oriented activities.

Visual learners. Visual learners learn best when information is written out. They prefer diagrams, charts, and tables as learning aids and enjoy media such as films, videos, and pictures. They are the teachers who always comment on the outfit you are wearing or the earrings you have chosen as an accessory. When given a choice of where to sit at a meeting or workshop, they'll choose to sit near the front of the room so they can easily see the presenter and the visuals being used. Visual learners like working in a classroom that is aesthetically pleasing, not too distracting or cluttered. They appreciate handouts and will often notice small details like a misspelled word on a transparency. Visual learners often have trouble remembering verbal instructions and would rather read than be read to. They like to take notes or doodle during meetings or workshops, although there is no guarantee they will refer to these notes once they leave the session.

Auditory learners. Auditory learners learn best by hearing things spoken. They prefer small- and large-group discussions, lectures, storytelling, and audiotapes as instructional aids. Auditory learners appreciate good speakers. They are able to recall the specifics of what was said as well as how it was said. Auditory learners often have an inner dialogue going on during a meeting or presentation and play with the pros and cons of an issue to clarify concepts internally. They are generally talkative and love discussions, but they can get carried away with lengthy descriptions.

Table 5.1

Four Types of Learners

Practical Learners (concrete-sequential)

Their Comfort Zone	Their Frustration Zone	Instructional Strategies for Leaders
Learn through senses, direct experience, models, manipulatives, practice, ordering, patterning, logic, and facts. Want direct practical payoff. Are task oriented and give attention to detail. Like time limits and deadlines; need closure.	May get frustrated with tasks requiring divergent thinking, unexpected changes, too many choices, loose structure, conflicting data, or open-ended requirements.	Use samples, visuals, charts, note-taking guides, advance organizers, outlining, time lines, self-correcting activities, and situational how-to's. Incorporate hands-on activities such as puzzles, manipulatives, task cards, and constructions.

Analytic Learners (abstract-sequential)

Their Comfort Zone	Their Frustration Zone	Instructional Strategies for Leaders
Learn through the exploration of ideas using comparison-contrast and weighing pros and cons. Rely on facts and logic. Analyze various angles and seeks evaluative feedback. Give attention to larger picture.	May get frustrated with divergent strategies with no obvious relevance to task at hand. Don't like picky and apparently unrelated details or expectations. Dislike activities that deal with emotions.	Teach through lectures, brainteasers, readings, surfing the net, debates, and independent work. Provide privacy to think through "why" questions. Provide opportunities to analyze and discuss merits of different issues.

Imaginative Learners (abstract-random)

Their Comfort Zone	Their Frustration Zone	Instructional Strategies for Leaders
Learn through sixth sense, from people and surroundings. Are reflective and flexible in thinking. Highly imaginative, sensitive, and attuned to emotions. See global picture.	May get frustrated by rote memory and tasks, outlining, organizing, deadlines and pressures about time. Don't like detail-oriented tasks requiring precision and concentration.	Provide group discussions and one-on-one peer sharing. Give time to explore and generate possibilities. Use color, images, visuals, fantasy, and role play. Stress personalized applications.

Inventive Learners (concrete-random)

Their Comfort Zone	Their Frustration Zone	Instructional Strategies for Leaders
Learn through intuitive leaps, experimentation, and creative endeavors. Seek alternatives and takes risks. Visualize the future and creates change. Are curious and invent unusual solutions.	May have difficulty meeting deadlines and following specific procedures. Frustrated with tasks requiring detailed notetaking, choosing one answer, ordering and prioritizing, or requiring linear input.	Use open-ended questions and tasks, trial and error, and choices with room for independence and creativity. Stress application to real world, metaphors, inventions, explorations, and problem solving,

Adapted from Herman, B. (1999). *Teach me—Reach me!* Deerfield, IL: Pathways to Learning; and Tobias, C. (1994). *The way they learn.* Colorado Springs, CO: Focus on the Family Publishing.

Kinesthetic learners. This perceptual modality style learns best by touching, moving, and feeling. Kinesthetic learners like to be actively involved in learning new things. They learn best by manipulating objects, acting out scenarios, and playing games. When given a choice, kinesthetic learners sit at the rear of a meeting or workshop room so they can stretch out, move around, or get up and go to the restroom when needed. Kinesthetic learners use action words and gestures when speaking. They enjoy role-playing, dramatizations, games, and any type of activity where they are physically engaged in the learning process. Kinesthetic learners tend to gesture more than visual or auditory learners. They may touch another person to get their attention and use a finger to guide their reading. Variety in action is crucial for kinesthetic learners. They can't sit for long periods of time.

Table 5.2 presents the behavioral indicators relating to the visual, auditory, and kinesthetic sensory modalities.

Psychological Type

Many of the differences between people are reflected in various aspects of their personality and behavior. Some adults seem to thrive on constant interaction and communication with their colleagues, while others need and want more alone time and may recoil from constant chatter and exchange. Some people respond in very flexible ways to unexpected demands and changing situations, while others may react quite negatively when routine and order are disrupted. The latter personality types want everything planned carefully and exactly; the former are more situational decision makers and can thrive with a flexible, less-structured approach.

Carl Jung (1923) believed these similarities and differences in personality are not random, but rather predictable. In studying patterns of human behavior, particularly the way people perceive information and interpret reality, Jung concluded that people are born with a predisposition for certain personality preferences. In Jungian theory, behavior relates to basic functions involved in gathering information about one's world and making decisions based on that information. Jung's

theory of psychological types was expanded by Katharine Briggs and her daughter, Isabel Briggs Myers. They developed the Myers-Briggs Type Indicator (MBTI) (Myers, 1998).

The MBTI assesses preferences for how we function along four continua: extraversion/ introversion, sensing/intuition, thinking/feeling, and judging/perceiving. Table 5.3 summarizes the key characteristics of each dimension as they relate to preferences in different work situations. The extravert sees people as a source of energy, while the introvert prefers solitude to recover energy. The sensing type is more practical and concerned with the here and now, while the intuitive type tends to be more visionary and innovative. Thinking types base decisions on logic, data, and facts; feeling types base their decisions on their personal gut feelings of what is right. People who have a strong need for closure are likely to be judging types, while people who prefer to keep things open and fluid are perceiving types. Use of the MBTI yields one of 16 psychological typologies.

David Keirsey (1998) has taken the work of Jung and Myers and adapted it to educational settings. He refers to differing personality preferences as one's temperament. Temperament is a somewhat broader concept than "function type." As such, he believes it is a better explainer of behavior. Keirsey defines temperament as that which places a signature or thumbprint on each of one's actions, making it recognizably one's own. Keirsey states that because people have a preferred style or temperament, they are often baffled by others who do not see the world as they do. An awareness of similarities and differences in personalities can help foster interpersonal understanding.

Communication Style

Clear, understandable, and unambiguous communication with teachers, families, and community representatives is at the heart of effective leadership in early care and education. But communication is more than carefully crafting a message. It also means being acutely aware of the nuances in people's communication styles that shape the way a message is sent, received, and interpreted.

Table 5.2

Perceptual Modality Indicators

Visual	Auditory	Kinesthetic
Organized Neat and orderly Observant Quieter Appearance oriented More deliberate A good speller Memorizes using mind pictures Less distracted by noise Trouble remembering verbal instructions Would rather read than be read to	Talks to self Is easily distracted Moves lips, says words when reading Can repeat back Finds spoken language easy Finds math and writing difficult Speaks in rhythmic pattern Likes music Can mimic tone, pitch, and timbre Learns by listening Memorizes by steps, sequence	Responds to physical rewards Touches people and stands close Is physically oriented Moves a lot Has larger physical reactions Early large muscle development Learns by doing Memorizes by walking, seeing Points when reading Gestures a lot Responds physically
Voice Chin is up, voice high	"Marks off" with tone and tempo	Chin is down, voice louder
Learning Needs overall view and purpose and a vision for details	Dialogues both internally and externally; tries alternatives verbally first	Learns through manipulating and actually doing
Recall Remembers what was seen	Remembers what was discussed	Remembers an overall impression of what was experienced
Conversation Has to have the whole picture; very detailed	Talkative, loves discussions, may monopolize; has tendency for tangents and telling whole sequential event	Laconic, tactile, uses gestures and movements, uses action words
Spelling Most accurate of three modes; sees words and can spell them. Confused when spelling words never seen before	Uses phonetic approach, spells with a rhythmic movement	Counts out letters with body movements and checks with internal feelings
Reading Strong, successful reader; has speed	Attacks unknown words well, enjoys reading aloud and listening; often slow because of subvocalizing	Likes plot-oriented books, reflects action of story with body movement
Writing Having it look OK is important, learning neatness is easy	Tends to talk better than write, and likes to talk when writing	Thick, pressured handwriting that's not as good as others'
Imagination Vivid imagery; can see possibilities	Sounds and voices heard	Intuitive; weak on details

Adapted from Barbe, W., & Swassing, R. (1988). *Teaching through modality strengths: Concepts and practices*. Columbus, OH: Zaner-Bloser.

Table 5.3

Effects of Preference in Work Situations

EXTRAVERSION	**INTROVERSION**
Like variety and action	Like quiet for concentration
Are often impatient with long, slow jobs	Tend not to mind working on one project for a long time uninterruptedly
Are interested in the activities of their work and in how other people do it	Are interested in the facts/ideas behind their job
Often act quickly, sometimes without thinking	Have trouble remembering names and faces
Develop ideas by discussion	Like to think a lot before they act, sometimes without acting
Like to have people around	Develop ideas by reflection
Learn new tasks by talking and doing	Like working alone with no interruptions
	Learn new tasks by reading and reflecting
SENSING	**INTUITION**
Like using experience and standard ways to solve problems	Like solving new complex problems
Enjoy applying what they have already learned	Enjoy learning a new skill more than using it
May distrust and ignore their inspirations	Will follow their inspirations
Seldom make errors of fact	May ignore or overlook facts
Like to do things with a practical bent	Like to do things with an innovative bent
Like to present the details of their work first	Like to present an overview of their work first
Prefer continuation of what is, with fine tuning	Prefer change, sometimes radical, to continuation of what is
Usually proceed step-by-step	Usually proceed in bursts of energy
THINKING	**FEELING**
Do not show emotion readily and are often uncomfortable dealing with people's feelings	Uses values to reach conclusions
Want mutual respect among colleagues	Want harmony and support among colleagues
May hurt people's feelings without knowing it	Enjoy pleasing people, even in unimportant things
Tend to decide impersonally, sometimes paying insufficient attention to people's wishes	Often let decisions be influenced by their own and other people's likes and dislikes
Tend to be firm-minded and can give criticism when appropriate	Tend to be sympathetic and dislike, even avoid, telling people unpleasant things
Look at the principles involved in the situation	Look at the underlying values in the situation
Feel rewarded when job is done well	Feel rewarded when people's needs are met
JUDGING	**PERCEIVING**
Work best when they can plan their work and follow the plan	Enjoy flexibility in their work
Like to get things settled and finished	Like to leave things open for last-minute changes
May not notice new things that need to be done	May postpone unpleasant tasks that need to be done
Tend to be satisfied once they reach a decision on a thing, situation, or person	Tend to be curious and welcome a new light on a thing, situation, or person
Reach closure by deciding quickly	Postpone decisions while searching for options
May decide things too quickly	Adapt well to changing situations and feel restricted without variety
Feel supported by structure and schedules	Focus on the process of a project
Focus on completion of a project	

Adapted from Barbe, W., & Swassing, R. (1988). *Teaching through modality strengths: Concepts and practices.* Columbus, OH: Zaner-Bloser.

Misunderstandings between people often occur simply because the sender and receiver have different communication styles and expectations. If one person is slow, deliberate, and thorough and the other is fast-paced and decisive, their interpersonal relationship may be tense unless they are aware of each other's communication preferences. Knowledge of communication styles helps reduce the likelihood of such frustrations occurring.

While there has been an abundance of research on different communication and behavioral styles (Alessandra & O'Connor, 1994; Bolton & Bolton, 1996; Hunsaker & Alessandra, 1980; Norton 1983), most conceptualizations build on the work of David Merrill, who conceptualized behavior along two dimensions (Merrill & Reid, 1981). In relating his theoretical framework specifically to communication styles, Russo (1995) labels these two dimensions assertiveness and expressiveness. The dimension of assertiveness is the effort that a person makes to control the thought or actions of others. Assertive communicators tend to be direct, task-oriented, and confident. Nonassertive communicators defer; they are more reserved, deliberate, and easygoing.

The dimension of expressiveness describes the degree to which people exhibit or control their emotions and feelings while communicating. People who are expressive tend to show more vocal variation in their speech patterns and are more outgoing and demonstrative when talking. Russo (1995) describes four styles resulting from the intersection of these two dimensions: direct, spirited, considerate, and systematic.

Direct. Direct communicators tell it like it is. They are decisive, take-charge people who like to be in control. They possess strong leadership skills, have the ability to get things done, and work single-mindedly toward their goals. Sometimes direct communicators can be perceived as being too strong-willed and overbearing. In their quest to get things done quickly, they may overlook important details. Focusing on feelings is not generally a strength of direct communicators, so they may be viewed in some interactions as lacking empathy.

Spirited. Spirited communicators are enthusiastic, friendly, and optimistic. They love to be around other people and enjoy the spotlight. They are good at building alliances and are able to motivate others and generate excitement about issues and projects. They enjoy a fast pace and are decisive decision makers. Spirited communicators are not always the best listeners. They can also exaggerate to make their point, behave impulsively, and gloss over important issues in an effort to rally support for their cause.

Considerate. People with a considerate communication style value warm, personal relationships with others. They are good listeners, reliable and steady, and supportive of others in a group. Because considerate communicators are easygoing, they may be reluctant to change, preferring to stick with what is comfortable. And because they want to avoid conflict, they may keep their opinions to themselves, give in too easily, and not achieve what they want.

Systematic. People with a systematic communication style value accuracy and objectivity. They are analytical in their approach to problem solving and base their decision making on facts and data. They are persistent, orderly, and organized in their approach to their work and their relations with others. Systematic communicators can also be viewed as impersonal and detached, putting accuracy and details ahead of other's feelings.

Self-Efficacy

The issue of self-confidence or self-efficacy is a central factor in assessing why some teachers approach their own development in positive, constructive ways while others seem hesitant about doing so. According to Bandura (1997), self-efficacy is the conviction that one can successfully execute the behaviors required to achieve a desired outcome. Such judgments are important since they affect the decisions individuals make, how much effort they expend on a particular task, and how persistent they will be in the face of obstacles. In other words, those teachers who have a strong sense of efficacy usually exert greater effort to master new challenges. According to Bandura, there are four principal sources from which people form estimates of themselves: past accomplishments, vicarious experiences, verbal persuasion, and emotional arousal.

Past accomplishments. A teacher who has been able to implement an educationally engaging classroom learning environment where children thrive is likely to have a strong sense of personal self-efficacy. Past performance provides the basis for future growth. Likewise, a teacher who has had previous negative experiences may feel inadequate and ineffective and have difficulty approaching new experiences with any sense of confidence.

Vicarious experiences. Teachers who have the opportunity to observe other teachers in different settings often come away with a renewed sense of self-confidence. They may say to themselves, "I do a lot of the same things that the teacher who everyone else says is fantastic does. I must be good too!" Vicarious experiences rely on judgments of how similar one is to the person modeling a particular behavior. Observing others who are seen as being similar in ability carry out teaching practices that are successful can raise self-efficacy expectations.

Verbal persuasion. You know from previous experience that when you tell a teacher that he or she is doing something well, it does not mean that the teacher will necessarily believe it. Verbal persuasion is not as strong a source of efficacy information. Yet if the teacher perceives the verbal reinforcement you provide as sincere, specific, and supportive, it may contribute to that person's sense of self-confidence.

Emotional arousal. The teacher's state of emotional arousal is another source by which self-efficacy expectations are acquired and/or altered. High arousal generally inhibits performance because teachers are less likely to expect success when they are tense or anxious. Thus, feelings of self-efficacy can be context-specific in that a teacher may feel very confident in one area of his or her teaching and less so in another.

The following examples illustrate different perceptions held by teachers of their of self-efficacy expectations:

Sharon was pleased when her director asked her to co-present at a state conference on the topic of infant-toddler caregiving. She had been refining her infant-toddler curriculum over the past five years and knew she had done a good job. Her ideas for the physical environment, napping arrangements, supervision, and parent involvement had met with praise from different sources. At the last state conference she had attended, she felt that she had better ideas than some of the people who were presenting. She left her director a note the next day: "Thanks so much for inviting me to join you at OAEYC. I think I can do a good job with this, and I appreciate your including me. One thing I know is good programming for infants and toddlers!"

The staff met to discuss the parent open house scheduled for the fall. It was decided that teachers would conduct an information and discussion session in their classrooms on the topic of developmentally appropriate curriculum relative to the particular age group they taught. After the meeting, Jarrod came to the director's office to express his anxiety: "I don't think I can do this talk to the parents. I know what developmentally appropriate is, I think, but I'm not ready to try to explain it to the parents. It gets too confusing with all of this Piaget stuff and questions about academic and reading readiness. And anyway, I hate talking to big groups. Maybe I could combine my group with LaToya's group and she could do the talking."

Clearly, these two teachers reflect very different perceptions of their own self-efficacy. Sharon had had experiences and observations that had confirmed her feeling that she knew a lot about infant-toddler programming and could present that knowledge in a formal workshop. Jarrod, on the other hand, confessed that he was unsure of his ability to articulate the essence of developmentally appropriate practices to a group of parents. Most likely, he had had little experience in public speaking to give himself the confidence he would need to speak comfortably about the center's educational philosophy.

Directors who are sensitive to the differing levels of self-confidence in their teachers will be better able to adjust their supervision and professional development strategies to provide the right amount of challenge to help teachers. Sometimes it takes verbal persuasion to help teachers take the risk to try new tasks that will increase their self-efficacy expectations. Other times it is just reminding teachers about previous challenges they have successfully accomplished. The key, though, is modulating support and intervention so it addresses the needs of each teacher.

Needs and Expectations

Any group of teachers working together will have differing needs and expectations relative to themselves and the center. An individualized model of supervision and staff development rests on the premise that you as director make a conscious and concerted effort to become aware of those needs and expectations. At the same time, you must also be aware of your own expectations relative to your supervisory role and be able to honestly communicate those to each teacher you work with.

Expectations are the assumptions—whether conscious or unconscious—that we have for our own or another person's behavior. In other words, we anticipate that the other person will act in a manner consistent with our expectations. At the same time, the other person also has expectations for his or her own behavior. If there is a misalignment of expectations, then frustration, resentment, and interpersonal tension may occur. Consider the following interaction between a director, Marcy and one of her teachers, John.

Marcy: "You don't seem to be taking as much initiative as I thought you would in keeping anecdotal records on the children. In your initial interview, I can remember you saying that this was a priority of yours."

John: "Yes, but I thought someone would provide me with some guidance on doing it. It seems like part of your job as my supervisor should be to assist teachers in setting up record keeping."

Marcy: "I guess my assumption is that you've had practice doing this type of thing in the courses you took at the community college. Wasn't observation and documentation a key focus of one of your curriculum classes?"

John: "Not where I went to school. Anecdotal records were discussed, but we never had real experience writing them. The rational behind them makes sense to me, but the problem is finding the time to do them.

In this example, both players had different expectations relative to their roles. John expects Marcy, as his supervisor, to provide a lot of direction in an area that she sets as a priority. Marcy, on the other hand, assumes that John has the training and is proficient in carrying out such a process on his own. Without open communication on this issue, both John and Marcy would continue a cycle of blame, resentment, and disappointment.

Teachers at any center represent a variety of needs, some of which are unconscious. The need for equity is an issue for Pat at The Children's Corner, whereas recognition seems to be a strong need for Shelly.

Case Study: The Children's Corner

Pat is a seasoned, talented teacher at The Children's Corner. The competitive climate of the center in recent years, however, has heightened Pat's basic need for equity and fairness. During the first month of school Martha became conscious of how important equity and fairness were to Pat. This need first came to Martha's attention in late August when classroom art supplies were being distributed. Pat made a big fuss about how important it was that every teacher receive a fair and equitable portion. Equity issues for Pat also carried over into space, lunch hours, and expense reimbursement. Martha surmised that in a more collaborative, cooperative environment, these equity issues might not be quite so important to Pat. Unfortunately, the negative climate of the program tended to bring out the worst, even in this excellent teacher.

Shelly, a young, new teacher at The Children's Corner, has a strong need for recognition. Shortly after she was hired, Martha became aware of Shelly's need to be recognized for her hard work and contributions to the center. If praise wasn't forthcoming, Shelly tended to pout or make a sarcastic comment about how unappreciated she was. As a rule, Martha was not the kind of director who doled out lavish amounts of praise to teachers. She wanted to establish a work environment where teachers gained their fulfillment more from intrinsic sources rather than relying on external praise from her. In the case of Shelly, however, she felt she needed to modify her supervisory style and recognize Shelly's hard efforts on a more frequently.

Surfacing each teacher's individual needs and expectations can only happen in a climate of trust. Establishing that climate and keeping the lines of communication open so individual needs and expectations can be addressed is a fundamental part of effective supervision.

Adult Development Stage

The literature in the area of adult development has expanded greatly over the past 30 years. Research has found that cognitive, social, and language development do not solidify at adolescence or early adulthood but continue to develop throughout life (Erikson, 1968; Glickman, 2004, Levine, 1989; Loevinger, 1976). Unlike children, however, in whom changes are rapid and readily noticeable, the changes in adult development are more gradual and subtle.

The literature in this area focuses on two aspects of development—the study of adults' capacity to improve over time and research on life span stages and transitions. Many different theories have been proposed to account for changes in people over their life span. In this section, we look at three key theorists whose work provides insights into effective supervision and professional development.

Levine. Levine (1989) describes the three stages of adulthood (early, middle, and late) as characterized by different orientations and outlooks. Young adults are still experimenting with a variety of roles and relationships. They are dominated by life dreams, idealism, and feelings of omnipotence. In middle adulthood, people become more aware of their limitations. Becoming established in the workplace is the main objective along with the realization of possibilities in regard to marriage and home. In late adulthood, the focus becomes the reassessment of priorities and a consequent reallocation of their energies.

As adults move through these phases, they go through periods of transition. These transitional times are often characterized by questioning, confusion, discouragement, and personal crises. Levine suggests that our transitional periods take up almost half of our adult lives. Working with individuals at such points in their lives can be particularly challenging for supervisors and peers.

Adult development theorists consistently emphasize that adults need to take an active role in helping to define their own developmental stage and needs. The challenge for you as director is to listen closely to individuals on your staff so you can assist in this process of self-definition.

Loevinger. Loevinger's (1976) research on ego and personality development identifies 10 developmental stages from self-protective to integrated. At the lower levels, people are more impulsive and symbiotic in their thinking. They are more dependent on others for decisions. At the middle of the continuum, individuals tend to conform in terms of socially approved codes but begin to develop self-evaluation standards. At higher levels, people show more autonomous, integrated thinking and respect for individuality.

Just what does this mean in terms of behavior? A person in the self-protective stage is rule bound and tends to assign blame to others or to circumstances when things do not go well. At Loevinger's conscientious-conformist level, rules remain important, but there is a growing awareness of self as an agent of responsibility. In place of one right way, multiple right ways can be assessed and understood. At the highest level, the integrated stage, conflicts and polarities are transcended. Individuals have high respect for themselves and others. Loevinger's theory underscores the fact that interpersonal relations are altered as people move through the ego stages.

Erikson. In Erikson's (1968) theory of psychosocial development, each stage evolves into a new stratum of social interactions establishing new possibilities for building relationships between oneself and others. Erikson believed that the decisions people make during a lifetime continuously mold and shape the tenor of their relationships with other people. Each dimension of interaction can be viewed from the perspective of two extremes on a continuum—trust and mistrust; intimacy and isolation. Growth and development occur when a balance is achieved. For example, too much trust can be as problematic as no trust at all.

According to Erikson, there is a continuous search for identity because adulthood is not a static phase. Interactive experiences designed to meet the psychological needs of adults in different phases will promote growth throughout the life cycle. Such experiences allow adults to continue to interact with others and to feel productive, to guide the less experienced, and to consolidate their life experiences.

How can an awareness of Erikson's life stages help directors and teachers better understand themselves? Directors and teachers can gain insight into interpersonal experiences by stepping back and assessing their reactions to different situations. For example, does working at the center promote feelings of safety and security? Do daily interactions give workers a sense of control over their environment and promote feelings of support and belonging?

As director of a small nursery school, Sonja worked hard to develop a strong esprit de corps among her staff. She frequently planned social activities in addition to professional development sessions and tried to promote open communication and a sense of community. One teacher, Anna, however, did not seem to appreciate Sonja's efforts. Although she attended staff meetings and training sessions when required, Anna never came early to chat or stayed afterward to enjoy a snack and coffee with her fellow teachers. She always seemed in a deliberate hurry to get away. Moreover, she was conspicuously absent at social gatherings organized by the staff.

Sonja was concerned about Anna's pronounced isolation and decided to have a talk with her. The initial interaction felt awkward and strained; Anna indicated in many ways that she did not wish to share information about herself. Finally, Sonja asserted that she felt Anna's colleagues would be enriched by Anna's presence. This appeal seemed to open a floodgate of emotions for Anna, and she shared with Sonja her reasons for being so reclusive. It seemed that over the past six years she had suffered many losses—the death of her husband and her sister; a relationship with a man who later left her for someone else; and the breaking of a confidence by a close friend whose support she had counted on. Consequently, Anna was fearful of forming close ties with anyone. She openly admitted she did not want to be vulnerable again. She stated that she would rather not be dependent on anyone anymore. She would carry out all her responsibilities, but she didn't wish to be part of the family Sonja seemed to want to create.

Committing to a model of staff development that addresses individual differences requires an understanding of the many ways in which adults change over the life cycle. Overall, adult learning theorists believe that adults become increasingly self-directed if they are stimulated by real life tasks and problems that fit their developmental levels.

Career Stage

The idea of stages in people's careers is intricately related to adult development. Lilian Katz (1972) identifies four stages in teachers' professional growth patterns. Table 5.5 summarizes these stages and their corresponding concerns. In Stage I, *survival*, the teacher's main concern is coping with the day-to-day demands of the job. A new teacher is frequently overwhelmed by all the tasks and responsibilities required. This stage may last a full year; it is dominated by feelings of self-doubt and a strong need for acceptance.

In Stage II, *consolidation*, teachers move beyond an egocentric focus and begin to focus on individual children and problem situations. They expand their knowledge base about children's behavior and learn how to apply educational concepts to new situations. In Stage III, *renewal*, which often occurs during the third or fourth year of teaching, teachers seem to tire of doing the same things. Recent research has shown that the third year of teaching is a critical time; many teachers leave the profession at that point. Gehreke (1988) notes that teachers in the third year begin to perceive the job as basically unchanging. They grow bored and unchallenged.

Teachers who decide to remain in the field may permanently remain in Stage III and continue to battle professional fatigue, or they may internalize a renewed spirit for their work and move on to Stage IV, *maturity*. These teachers now ask deeper, more abstract questions. They begin to integrate their knowledge and experiences and take on more

responsibility in the center and in the early childhood field.

It is important to note that not all teachers move on to Stage IV. As many directors are aware, some teachers remain stagnant and unmotivated, no matter what kind of energy and time are invested in them. These teachers are essentially rustouts (Bloom, 1982), going through the motions of teaching but devoid of any real joy or zest. They present a real dilemma for directors, who must consider whether to overlook their diminished enthusiasm and less-than-adequate performance or terminate them.

VanderVen (1988) describes a five-stage sequence in her model of professional development that extends the work of Katz. Her formulation examines each stage in terms of level of professionalism, roles and functions, variables in adult and career development, adult cognition and affect, the concept of lifelong careers, male and female differences, guidance of practice, and educational preparation.

Burden (1987) also identifies career stages for teachers that support Katz's model. He describes the beginning stage as one in which the new teacher is struggling for survival; the middle stage as a time in which the teacher is adjusting, growing,

Table 5.5

Developmental Stages of Teachers' Concerns

Stage	Concern
Stage IV Maturity	Finding new perspectives and insight Sharing knowledge and experience
Stage III Renewal	Sustaining enthusiasm Maintaining interest in new developments
Stage II Consolidation	Handling individual problem children Solving problem situations
Stage I Survival	Surviving on the job Being accepted by colleagues

and exploring; and the final stage in which the teacher functions as a mature professional.

In her research, Fuller (1969) found that teachers with different stages of professional experience show different concerns. Like Katz, she found that beginning teachers were concerned mainly about their own survival. Adequacy, classroom control, and others' perceptions of their capabilities are the main issues. Experienced teachers are more concerned with the impact that they have on students. And master teachers always focus on pupil progress. Fuller states that when concerns are mature, they focus on pupil gain and self-evaluation as opposed to personal gain and evaluation by others.

Fessler and Christensen (1992) identify eight stages of the career cycle—preservice, induction, competency building, enthusiasm and growth, career frustration, stability, career wind-down, and career exit. The research conducted by these authors indicates that appropriate incentives need to be linked to the respective career stages of teachers. The differences in teachers' career stages point to the need for models that advocate personalized, individualized support systems.

The complexities of human behavior do not allow for an oversimplified use of the career stage model. Often, for example, teachers who change jobs or who are assigned to work with a different age group can temporarily regress to an earlier stage. Fessler and Christensen (1992) suggest that teachers may experience many reoccurring cycles or loops within their career. They might work in the profession for several years, drop out to raise their children, and then reenter at a later point. Others may decide to enter a teacher training program for the first time in their late thirties or early forties. Thus, the interface between adult stages of development and career stages is not necessarily parallel. The director must draw on information about the individual teacher from both perspectives when looking at personal and professional development.

The case examples that follow present portraits of two teachers employed at The Children's Corner whose career and adult development stages appear to overlap.

Case Study: The Children's Corner

Shelly is 22 years old and in her first year of teaching. She has come from a teacher training program that emphasizes developmentally appropriate curriculum and practices. In her conversations with Martha, she expresses her frustrations with her job. "This group of children just doesn't respond to all the things I learned. They don't listen! They're always fighting and calling for my help. Maybe it's because there are so many hyperactive boys in my class! I'm not sure. But it would probably be better if we had more help. It's really a zoo! I thought 4-year-olds would be fun to work with, and I thought I would be a great teacher with them. But I'm beginning to think I'm not cut out to be a teacher. I worry all the time that parents will complain to you. But honestly, I think it's partly their fault. They've allowed their kids to be so disrespectful to people. And then I'm supposed to straighten them out!"

Shelly's remarks reflect several points identified in adult and career stage theory. First, she seems to be in a self-protective stage as evidenced by her tendency to blame others and blame the circumstances for her problems. Secondly, she alludes to her dream of what teaching 4-year-olds would be like. She is not comfortable with her identity as a teacher but feels the need to commit to a profession.

Shelly clearly represents the new teacher in the survival stage. Her responsibilities seem somewhat overwhelming to her. She has feelings of self-doubt and is striving for acceptance by the children, her colleagues, and her supervisor. She is struggling to achieve a level of confidence in dealing with everyday problems and issues.

Case Study: The Children's Corner

Georgia has taught different age groups at The Children's Corner and at another preschool for over 12 years. She always appears prepared and has a good attendance record, but her comments to Martha show an underlying lack of enthusiasm. "I'm not sure where I go from here. I like the kids, but I'm so tired of hearing the same old complaints from the parents. And I know you try to get us more money, but still the pay is low and the hours are so long. Quite frankly, I hate all these in-service workshops we've been having. If I hear one more person tell me

> how to manage a classroom or interact with parents, I'll scream! I know how to teach; I just need better conditions to do it in! I guess I really don't know where I go from here. I'm drained! My husband says I shouldn't take it so seriously. In fact, he probably wouldn't mind if I quit so I could give him more time. Maybe that's not such a bad idea."

Georgia seems to be trying to reconcile some inner conflicts in relation to teaching in the field. She has a good sense of her worth and effectiveness, but she appears to need a lift. She seems to be in the process of reassessing herself and reallocating her energies. As Levine (1989) suggests, she seems to be trying to reassess her priorities.

Georgia appears to be in Katz's Stage III, where teachers tire of doing the same things. They perceive their jobs as basically static and grow bored and unchallenged. Georgia, now in her late thirties, is reflecting upon why she is doing this work. She recognizes that she may need to be re-energized, but her job description doesn't seem to give her avenues to do so.

Level of Commitment

Organizational commitment is the relative strength of a teacher's identification with and involvement in a particular center (Bloom, 1988b; Mowday, Steers, & Porter, 1979). It is characterized by at least three related factors: a strong belief in and acceptance of the organization's goals and values; a willingness to exert oneself on behalf of the program; and a strong desire to remain working at the center.

To a large extent, organizational change depends on the degree to which individuals can integrate the goals of the center into their own structure of needs and values. This sense of belongingness represents the anticipation that one will be able to achieve personal satisfaction within an organizational framework. It is the essence of organizational commitment. Interdependence through achieving a common goal leads to relationships of trust and respect.

Hall (1988) defines commitment as "the soul of work." He states, "It is the sense of purpose that guides one's activities; it is the meaning that justifies one's investment of self; it is the feeling of responsibility that defines one's role and reason for being; and when shared, it is a common bond which holds people together in ways that transcend differences and personal gratification" (p. 100). Commitment is a personal desire to contribute to the success of the center.

The challenge for directors, then, is to help teachers develop a strong sense of personal ownership and responsibility within the context of an organization. According to Hall, three conditions are essential in order to achieve this: impact, relevance, and community.

Impact. People need to know that what they are doing makes a difference. Teachers, in particular, may feel they make a difference in the lives of young children and may derive a great deal of personal satisfaction from their work each day, but they also need feedback that the work they do has a positive impact on what happens in the center. Impact relates to our personal feelings of importance. For feelings of importance to be enhanced and sustained, people must receive affirmation of the important role they play in achieving centerwide goals. This affirmation supports a sense of purpose and commitment to something larger than one's own personal satisfaction.

Relevance. Particularly in early childhood work settings, people need to expect that their talents are being used appropriately and the time they spend on important tasks helps move the center forward in achieving its mission. Many times staff perceive they are stuck with meaningless tasks that take time and seem pointless. Hall states that irrelevant tasks undermine the sense of purpose so critical to commitment; they spawn frustration, resistance, and stifle motivation. Listen to the words of Twanya, a head teacher at a state-funded prekindergarten program.

> "I've been teaching for 15 years in this district and have consistently been evaluated as an exemplary teacher. Last year the program administrator decided it would be a good idea if

we turned in our lesson plan books showing our detailed educational objectives for each activity. I wouldn't mind doing this task if I felt somebody cared. My sense is that these lesson plans just get filed anyway. Nobody even looks at them. If the purpose of this exercise is accountability, then somebody ought to use the information. All this added paperwork takes so much time away from other activities that I feel are so much more important."

How widespread irrelevant work has become! It not only diverts energy, it undercuts commitment. When people are asked to spend their time doing mindless paperwork or attending meetings that have little relevance to what they are doing, a sense of frustration and indifference can't help but surface. The director's task, then, is to ensure that people spend time on core activities. People need to perceive they are doing activities that are germane to their work.

Community. Hall states that for relevance to become a shared experience, and for the sense of personal challenge and contribution to become a collective feature of the organization, there must be a norm of interdependence and mutual reliance. Judith Warren Little (1982) calls these *norms of collegiality.* Collegiality and interdependence foster mutual respect and a sense of shared responsibility for each other's well being. Community refers to the sense of oneness or a spirit of belonging. It is the belief that people can depend on one another.

Striking the balance is difficult. In supporting individuality, some directors end up encouraging too much independence and unwittingly foster competition. Other directors are so focused on achieving organizational goals, they end up eroding norms of collegiality. The goal is to try to focus both on people and their individual needs and on the conditions in which they can work together to achieve common goals.

As a director of an early care and education program, you are keenly aware of differences in your teachers' levels of commitment. The teacher with a strong sense of commitment demonstrates active involvement in the center and in the field of early childhood. That teacher arrives early to prepare the classroom, turns in requested paperwork on time, and takes an active role in outside professional activities.

Conversely, the teacher who does not demonstrate a strong commitment may not be eager to initiate or participate in opportunities for personal development. It becomes your task, then, to address this lack of commitment if you feel it is interfering with job performance. Perhaps there are basic unmet needs; or perhaps the teacher is not clear about your expectations or the organization's vision. Helping such teachers build greater self-awareness of the factors that contribute to their personal and professional satisfaction is a start. Determining the degree of fit between a teacher's needs and expectations and those of the center will help you determine if the person should continue employment at your center.

Level of Motivation

Commitment to a center is directly related to the level of motivation an individual exhibits. Directors frequently find themselves asking why some teachers show a lot of initiative and desire to contribute to the organization while others do not. Directors also wonder why certain incentives motivate some teachers to peak performance and not others. Put simply, there is a difference between the *can do* and *wanna do* factors that regulate behavior in all employees. The first has to do with level of competence, the latter relates to attitude. The attitude part of the equation rests squarely on one's level of motivation.

Bernard Weiner (1980) defines motivation as the complex forces, drives, needs, tension states, or other mechanisms that start and maintain voluntary activity directed toward the achievement of personal goals. Motivation results from the expectation that one's efforts will lead to anticipated outcomes.

Numerous theories of motivation have been proposed over the years, but perhaps the most well known in the field of education is Maslow's hierarchy of needs (1954). The fundamental premise of Maslow's theory is that higher-level needs become activated as lower-level needs are satisfied. For example, if children come to a preschool program not having had breakfast in the morning, hunger presents itself as the prime motivator. It will be difficult for them to attend to other higher-level needs like achievement. Likewise, if teachers feel there is little job security where they work, they may be unable to focus on other goals.

A director reported that one of her most enthusiastic and dedicated teachers resisted attending staff meetings scheduled for late afternoons. Upon a closer look, the director discovered that this teacher, a single parent, did not have the financial means to cover the child care costs that would result from her attendance. She also found that the teacher was too embarrassed to admit to her colleagues how financially strapped she was. Lower-level needs must be largely satisfied before higher-level needs can be felt and pursued. An understanding of Maslow's theory can assist directors in considering whether an individual's basic needs are met and whether that person is able to focus on higher-level goals relating to self and the organization.

Herzberg's (1966) landmark research on motivation supports Maslow's hierarchy of needs. Herzberg distinguishes between the positive aspects of an individual's job that are *satisfiers* and the negative aspects of the job that are *dissatisfiers*. The two categories, Herzberg asserts, are quite distinct as they relate to motivation issues.

Dissatisfiers include such things as salary, working conditions, status, job security, technical supervision, and organizational policies. Satisfiers, on the other hand, include the nature of the work itself, the individual's degree of responsibility, opportunities for growth and advancement, and a sense of achievement. Herzberg believes that eliminating dissatisfiers seldom improves an individual's performance; it merely reduces the irritations and frustrations in doing one's job. To motivate individuals to higher levels of performance, changes in the structure and nature of the work itself (the satisfiers) need to be addressed.

While the available theories may not explain exactly why individuals demonstrate so much

variance in motivation, they may be helpful in assessing adults and designing appropriate staff development strategies. The following example shows the relationship between one teacher's personal situation and her lack of motivation as it relates to her work commitments.

Maureen, and infant-toddler teacher, came in to discuss her annual evaluation with her supervisor. Maureen didn't disagree when they reviewed the low ratings in a number of areas— disorderly storage area, late lesson plans, cluttered classroom shelves, and inconsistency in keeping high chairs and equipment clean. But the reason for the disorganized aspects of the classroom operation related to something very personal. Maureen stated that she was having marital problems. Her perceived lack of stability in her personal life was keeping her from approaching her job responsibilities with the enthusiasm she knew she should have. She seemed unable to keep her professional life in good order when her personal life was in shambles.

This information allowed the director to gain new insight into the reasons for some of Maureen's difficulties. She now realized that Maureen was quite capable of being an excellent teacher, but the personal issues that were consuming Maureen were sapping her energy. The result was a lack of motivation.

Professional Orientation

Commitment to a center and overall motivation to perform certainly relate to commitment to the field of early childhood education. It stands to reason that those who are more committed to the field will have a stronger professional orientation. Professional orientation is characterized by an individual's emphasis on growth and change, skill based primarily on knowledge, and autonomy in decision making, as well as a reference-group orientation, the achievement of goals, and loyalty to clients and professional associations (Bloom, 1989; Corwin, 1965).

Most directors have an idea of where individual teachers fit on a continuum relative to this concept. Some teachers are very active in NAEYC and ACEI Affiliate Groups, read professional books and journals on a regular basis, and see themselves as members of the early childhood profession. Many others, however, see their work with young children as a tolerable job and have little incentive to connect to a professional organization. They perceive their work as a job as opposed to a career.

> *"I am a person. Do not bend, fold, spindle, or mutilate."*
>
> picket sign at Berkeley, 1964

As director, you may not be able to inspire all your teachers to embrace a career orientation. Like other professions, some people see teaching young children only as a means of earning an income. They may plan to exit the field just as soon as something better comes along. This reality is no doubt frustrating for you. What it means is that for the purposes of implementing an individualized model of supervision and staff development, it is crucial to know where individual teachers stand with respect to their level of professional orientation.

As the profession of early childhood education gains greater credibility and career ladders become more established, the factors impacting teachers' levels of professional orientation—compensation, benefits, status—will also receive more attention.

Concomitant Roles

Also important for any director to consider is the number of roles teachers assume in their personal lives outside the center. This is a particularly important focus given that the early childhood profession is dominated by women, most of whom wear many hats. One director expressed her feelings about this issue well:

I'm amazed at how many different things my staff, all of whom are women, are involved in. Most of them are mothers; some of them single parents. Two women in particular are very active in their husbands' work. Others are quite active in community, religious, and civic activities. Three of my teachers are pursuing graduate degrees; two of them are finishing their bachelor's degrees. In general, I believe that all of this involvement makes them better teachers; but it does mean adjustment on my part at times. For example, when a teacher's child becomes sick, I try to make it possible for her to leave early. I also provide a child care benefit for teachers who have preschoolers. I think this practice promotes staff retention. And I've been trying to provide release time for staff development activities like attending courses at the college. Like I said, it's rough to respond to all of these things sometimes, but I think overall the program reaps the benefits.

Being aware of the concomitant roles of individual teachers means that you can be more sensitive about when you plan staff development activities. The trick is to allow for optimum flexibility while still maintaining high standards for the program.

Tools for Assessing Individual Needs

In order to collect adequate data on individual staff members at your center, many different types of instruments can be used—both formal and informal. Because of the inherent complexity of measuring human behavior, using multiple data collection methods is important. In Appendix A of this book are a number of assessment tools to get you started. Some are questionnaires you can distribute to staff or use in an interview of a prospective employee. Others are observation tools you can use to measure different aspects of your center's quality. You may not find all of them relevant to your specific needs, but they should prove helpful as you seek more information about the unique strengths of each of your teachers and how you can best design individualized plans to support their professional growth.

The following provides a brief description of the areas assessed by these instruments. More detailed information about administering and scoring is included with each assessment tool in Appendix A.

Preschool Teaching Practices

There are different types of teaching practices that you'll want to evaluate in your center and direct observation is the best way to collect this kind of data. Assessment Tool #12 looks at preschool teaching practices in four areas: interactions among teachers and children; curriculum; the physical environment; and health, safety, and nutrition.

Infant-Toddler Teaching Practices

Over the past decade infant-toddler programs have burgeoned. The issues of infant-toddler programming are distinctly different than those for preschool programming, particularly as they relate to the stability of teachers and classroom health and safety issues. Thus, measuring effective teaching practices for the youngest children in your center's care warrants criteria that relate specifically to this age group. Assessment Tool #13 was designed for this purpose.

Learning Style

The essence of successful staff development is making connections—connections between the individual and the content to be learned. An understanding of different learning styles can help ensure better learning outcomes. Assessment Tool #14 can be used to ascertain the learning style preferences of the individuals on your staff. Part 1 looks at preferences for processing and organizing information. Part 2 looks at environmental, emotional, sociological, and physical elements related to learning style. And Part 3 zeros in on perceptual modality preferences—visual, auditory, or kinesthetic. The results of this assessment can be used to plan staff development opportunities that match individuals' preferred learning styles.

Psychological Type

An understanding of different psychological types can help teachers develop a deeper appreciation for those who function differently than they do. Assessment Tool #15 is based on the work of Jung (1923) and Myers (1980, 1998) and provides a brief assessment of psychological type along four dimensions: extraversion/introversion, sensing/intuition, thinking/feeling, and judging/perceiving.

The information gleaned from this assessment will help you consider the implications of different typologies for your work situation.

Beliefs and Values

Assessment Tool #16 is designed to assist you in determining the particular beliefs and values that shape teachers' attitudes and guide their behavior. A teacher's answers to the eight questions in Part 1 can serve as a springboard for a discussion about classroom environment, parent interactions, discipline, preferred instructional strategies, and other important issues related to teaching. Answers to Part 2 can serve to help teachers understand what traits they value in children and how they encourage the development of those traits in the classroom.

Communication Style

Assessment Tool #17 is a quick and easy-to-use instrument to assess teachers' communication styles. As a topic for discussion at a staff meeting, the results of this instrument can serve as a catalyst for helping teachers understand the strengths of different styles and the importance of appreciating styles different from their own.

Job Satisfaction

Achieving a work climate that promotes a high level of employee job satisfaction is on every director's wish list. Job satisfaction can be defined as teachers' personal assessments of the degree to which their jobs meet their personal needs, values, and expectations. From a practical standpoint, it can be conceptualized as the discrepancy between real conditions and ideal conditions. When job satisfaction is high, the discrepancy between existing and ideal conditions is small.

Assessment Tool #18 is a modified version of the *Early Childhood Job Satisfaction Survey* (Bloom, 1988b). It assesses five facets of job satisfaction: co-worker relations, supervisor relations, the nature of the work itself, working conditions, and pay and promotion opportunities. Being aware of the factors that promote high levels of job satisfaction in each of your teachers is essential information as you work with them to design and implement individualized professional development plans.

Professional Orientation

Assessment Tool #19 is a useful tool for assessing a teacher's level of professionalism. It measures such things as their perceptions of their work as *a job* or *a career*, their level of involvement in professional associations, their interest in pursuing higher levels of education, and their commitment to the field of early childhood. You may want to use this assessment in the initial hiring process to gather information about an individual's level of involvement in different types of professional activities. It is also a good tool to benchmark staff's level of involvement in professional activities over time.

Role Clarity

Clarification of roles and expectations is essential for effective organizational functioning. Program effectiveness is increased when role conflict and role ambiguity are low. *Role conflict* occurs when one's formal position has conflicting organizational expectations. For example, teachers are sometimes asked by parents to have their children skip naptime in the afternoon so they will be tired for bedtime at an early hour. For teachers, this presents a conflict in expectations between what the center requires (mandated naptime) and what the parent wants. There is an inherent tension in making decisions in the best interest of the child because different parties will interpret the child's best interest differently.

The role of a teacher may be subject to a variety of different and incompatible expectations from divergent groups such as the center's board, the funding agency, families, and his or her supervisor. *Role ambiguity* occurs when individuals do not have a clear understanding of the scope and nature of their jobs. Role ambiguity is often the result of vague job descriptions, center policies, and operating procedures.

Assessment Tool #20 assesses staff's perceptions about their roles. The resulting information can assist you in seeing where teachers' perceptions differ from your own. Assessment Tool #21 is specifically designed for new staff. It should be given to staff approximately four weeks after they have begun their position. The results of this assessment should help alert you to potential misunderstandings on the part of the new employee.

Organizational Commitment

Earlier in this chapter organizational commitment was defined as the relative strength of a teacher's identification with and involvement in a particular center. Assessment Tool #22 yields important information about a teacher's level of commitment. Because the items in this tool are sensitive in nature, it is important that you make it available as a voluntary self-assessment rather than a mandated one. The goal of the assessment is to stimulate a teacher's reflection on his or her own level of commitment to the center. This information may be useful in stimulating discussion between you and the teacher about ways to increase commitment and motivation. Identifying a lack of commitment could lead to the identification of underlying problems and concerns.

Perceived Problems

Teachers often feel overwhelmed by the many problems they confront working with young children and families. Helping them to zero in on the precise nature of their problems can serve as a first step in solving them. Johnston (1984) developed a Preschool Teacher Problems Checklist, which is provided in Appendix A as Assessment Tool #23. This tool can be used as a vehicle for building staff development programs around teachers' perceived problems. The 60 items that comprise this instrument were generated by teachers and represent the problems they identified as most frequent and/or most bothersome.

Flexibility and Openness to Change

Teachers vary greatly with respect to their willingness to accept new approaches and alternative ways of doing things. If you are going to implement meaningful change in your center, it is essential that you be aware of potential resistance on the part of your staff. Assessment Tool #24 was designed as a self-assessment to provide insight into a person's approach to risk and change. The resulting flexibility profile can serve as the focus for a discussion about people's different responses to change. It is important, however, that you emphasize that there are no right or wrong answers on this assessment and no one best profile. Understanding teachers' different profiles will help you introduce change in thoughtful, nonthreatening ways.

A Final Word

The process of assessing teachers from an individualized, developmental perspective does not lend itself to quick-and-easy methods of analysis. Instead, you must view this type of supervision as an ongoing, continuous process of collecting relevant information that contributes in a meaningful way to individual growth. This may necessitate a paradigm shift, a new mindset for thinking about your role. The process conveys respect for individuals by communicating that they have an important role in defining their own professional development. Any and all information concerning an individual teacher becomes data from which to build a comprehensive and personalized staff development action plan.

To be sure, the process is both time consuming and complex. It is built on the premise that the most important part of your job is supervision and staff development. Directors and other administrators give many excuses for not devoting time to such an in-depth process. Some of the excuses are valid; directors wear many hats and are indeed very busy. But the energy and time devoted to individualized staff assessment pays off in rich dividends. When teachers are challenged in meaningful ways, when their personal goals are tied in with the organization's goals, and when they feel valued and respected, organizational commitment will increase and staff turnover will assuredly decrease.

Procedurally, recording developmental information on individual teachers is an ongoing process that is similar to anecdotal record keeping of children's behaviors and interests. Having a small notebook readily available is one way you can jot down notes on individual staff members. These notes can include specific comments and examples of verbal interactions. From this notebook more permanent entries can be made for each teacher's file.

A word of caution. In your quest to develop a comprehensive profile of each teacher, try not to overdiagnose people. If you spend too much time collecting personal information, assessing needs, and diagnosing trouble spots, a paralysis of analysis can settle in and the important issues that need to be addressed in your program may be neglected. Strive for a good balance between assessment and action. The next chapter will help you make that possible.

Chapter 6

Implementing an Individualized Model of Staff Development

The overall purpose of implementing a model of staff development is to improve the quality of the experiences of the children in your care. Beyond this overarching goal, it is useful to keep in mind the many other purposes that provide a rationale for engaging in staff development. Stonehouse (1986) provides a useful summary of these reasons in Table 6.1.

As is apparent from the variety of reasons detailed in this table, staff development goes far beyond the traditional notion of training. Training programs are usually short-term and skill oriented, and they typically address only one aspect of teaching. For the most part, training deals with specific behavioral changes in people. The individualized model described in this chapter, on the other hand, addresses the overall education and professional development of a person. This model focuses on long-term growth and addresses change in individuals' thinking processes. It rests on the assumption that as individuals become more self aware and their thinking progresses to higher levels of complexity, they become more flexible and open to a wider range of ideas (Dillon-Peterson, 1981; Seligson & Stahl, 2003). When viewed from this individualized perspective, the goal of staff development, then, is to move the individual to the next stage of professional competence.

Robert Kegan (2000) describes this subtle distinction using two contrasting terms—*informational learning* versus *transformational learning*. Informational learning focuses on what a person knows; it is technical in nature. Transformational learning focuses on how a person knows what he or she knows; it is adaptive in nature. Good professional development programs incorporate both aspects—moving individuals to higher levels of skills and knowledge (what they know) while altering the very thought processes by which they deepen their understanding of their professional practice (how they know).

Elizabeth Jones (1993) uses the phrase *growing teachers* to capture the notion that teacher development is an emergent, open-ended process, where philosophy and practice are defined, but outcomes less clear. Similarly the individualized model of staff development described in this chapter rests on the premise that teachers are active agents in constructing knowledge about their work and need to be involved in making choices about options for their personal and professional growth.

Everyone has peak performance potential—you just need to know where they are coming from and meet them there.

Ken Blanchard

Facilitating Change in Individuals

As stressed in previous chapters, adults, like the children they teach, are at different levels of development and therefore have different needs and abilities. Thus their professional development plans should be differentiated based on a holistic view of the life span. What this means in practical

Table 6.1

Why Have Staff Development?

- ► To provide basic skills and an orientation to the profession for teachers who are untrained

- ► To extend teachers' expertise in specific areas

- ► To provide opportunities for teachers to learn about new developments in a rapidly changing field

- ► To remind staff about center expectations

- ► To identify resources (people and materials) that staff can access

- ► To decrease professional isolation

- ► To broaden teachers' perspectives and world view of early care and education

- ► To promote the establishment of informal support networks among teachers

- ► To empower teachers to take a more active role in their work, their education, and their professional development

- ► To increase the enjoyment of work

- ► To boost morale and self confidence

Adapted from Stonehouse, A. (1986). *For us, for children: An analysis of the provision of in-service education for child care centre personnel in Australia.* Canberra: Australian Early Childhood Association, pp. 13–16. Reprinted with permission.

terms is that staff development activities must be planned so as to accommodate individuals at different stages in their careers. Table 6.2 describes a model of staff development that embraces this principle. For each career development stage, a supervisory style, corresponding staff development goals, strategies, and content areas are suggested. Before launching into a description of the specifics of the model, though, it is perhaps useful to review the assumptions upon which such an approach is premised.

Underlying Assumptions

The primary assumption upon which an individualized model of staff development rests is that teachers are unique learners in various stages of adult growth and development. Research suggests

that there are differences in adult learners on developmental variables such as cognition, ways of thinking, and interpersonal orientation. These differences account for variation in teachers' levels of interest and in their levels of performance. Teachers at higher levels function in more complex ways in the classroom. Thus, if we wish to improve the quality of education in the classroom, we need to consider the relationship between adult development and effective teaching.

A second assumption of the model is that teachers need to engage in identifying and helping solve their own concerns and problems related to their development as professionals. Such involvement empowers people by focusing on strengths and insights into their own developmental processes. Cookie cutter approaches, where

A Model of Staff Development

Table 6.2

Career Stage	Supervisory Style	Goals	Strategies	Content Areas
Survival	Directive	Help teachers develop specific competencies in the classroom and realistic expectations for measuring success. Increase perceived level of competence and effectiveness.	▲ Modeling ▲ Direct coaching ▲ On-site workshops ▲ College classes ▲ Support and encouragement ▲ Articles and books selected by the supervisor or mentor ▲ Hands-on activities	▲ Instructional methods in art, music, science, math, early literacy, drama ▲ Child development ▲ Nutritional practices ▲ Health and safety ▲ Arrangement of physical environment
Consolidation	Directive, collaborative	Help teachers apply what they have learned about children to new situations. Help them begin to analyze their belief system and the effectiveness of different instructional strategies.	▲ Release time to visit other centers ▲ Conferences and workshops ▲ College classes ▲ Feedback from videotaped segments of instruction ▲ Self-selected books and articles ▲ Peer observation and coaching	▲ Anti-bias curriculum ▲ Multiculturalism ▲ Parent relations ▲ Child observation, documentation, and assessment techniques ▲ Children with special needs ▲ Children's learning styles ▲ Childhood stress
Renewal	Directive, collaborative	Help teachers sustain their enthusiasm about work. Help them explore their many interests and find ways to generate more challenging responsibilities.	▲ In-depth institutes ▲ Collegial support groups ▲ Sharing ideas with new staff ▲ Involvement in development of new curricular materials ▲ Visiting other centers ▲ Expanded role in local professional organizations	▲ Time management ▲ Stress management ▲ Child advocacy ▲ Cross-cultural childrearing ▲ Adult learning styles ▲ Conflict management ▲ Curriculum models and innovations (e.g., Reggio Emilia, technology)
Maturity	Nondirective	Provide opportunities for teachers to expand their expertise in related areas. Help them broaden their sphere of responsibility for the training and supervision of others.	▲ Classroom research ▲ Presentations at conferences ▲ Leadership role in professional organizations ▲ In-depth institutes and seminars ▲ Involvement in development of new curricula and policies ▲ Mentoring others	▲ Budget/finance ▲ Grant writing ▲ Program evaluation ▲ Group dynamics ▲ Supervision techniques ▲ Public speaking and presentation skills ▲ Legal issues and social policy

in-service training is planned by the director for whole-group participation, are bound to fail because there is no way they can meet the different professional needs and interests of individual staff members.

Third, individualized staff development relies on a strengths-based model, not a deficit model. A deficit model implies that the teacher is unprepared or incompetent and that by using prescriptive techniques, a supervisor can fix the teacher as we might fix a broken pencil sharpener. A strengths-based model focuses on the individual's strengths. A strength is an area of performance in which an individual excels and does so consistently. It is also an area in which a person experiences intrinsic satisfaction. A strength can be defined as a combination of talents (those naturally recurring patterns of thought, feelings, or behaviors), knowledge (facts and lessons learned), and skills (the how-to or steps of an activity) (Buckingham & Clifton, 2001).

Each time we ask someone to change, we ask him or her to take a journey into incompetence.

Tynette Hills

A strengths-based organization is built on the premise that individuals will excel by cultivating and maximizing their strengths rather than fixing their weaknesses. The underlying message is that teaching and learning are complex activities in which no one ever masters the totality of the profession. By focusing on strengths, a supervisor builds on natural talents and interests.

The philosophical premise of this model is rooted in a Theory Y tradition of leadership rather than Theory X (McGregor, 1960). Theory X directors assume that their employees dislike work, and that they need coercion and tight supervision to get the job done. Theory Y directors, on the other hand, assume that people have integrity, will work hard toward objectives to which they are committed, and will respond to self-control and self-direction as they pursue their objectives. The Theory Y director's role thus becomes one of facilitating growth.

Supervisory Style

An individualized model of staff development necessitates a developmental approach to supervision. This approach focuses on the fact that individuals who function at different conceptual or developmental levels and who are at different stages of their careers should be supervised in qualitatively different ways. Individuals require differentiated learning environments for optimal development. For example, teachers who are more concrete in their conceptualization or are in their first year of teaching will probably benefit more from a structured supervisory approach. At the other end of the spectrum, mature teachers who function at a high level of conceptualization or abstraction appreciate more loosely structured approaches to supervision and staff development.

Glickman (2004), in delineating a model of developmental supervision, proposes that it is the job of supervisors to promote higher-level thinking in teachers. He believes that teachers in general are in a relatively low stage of ego and conceptual development, one characterized by dependence, simplicity, and concreteness. In order to move teachers forward in their thinking, the director needs to begin where each teacher functions by presenting ideas and opportunities that meet the identified developmental level. Sound familiar? This process parallels the developmental approach we advocate for young children.

At this point you may want to assess your own supervisory beliefs and preferred style. Glickman (2004) has developed an instrument to determine one's tendency toward directive, collaborative, or nondirective supervision (Assessment Tool #25 in Appendix A). Assessing yourself from this perspective will allow you to see how much control you believe is necessary when supervising staff.

In ascertaining approaches to use with teachers who may function at very different levels, it is important to remember that developmental levels of teachers are not static. Therefore a director should take into account the current status of the individual and work to structure professional development opportunities that stimulate growth to higher levels. Again, this emphasis directly parallels the cognitive-developmental philosophy being implemented in our early childhood programs. Lev Vygotsky's concept of the *zone of proximal development* is just as applicable to adults as it is to children. Vygotsky (1978) believed that development should not be viewed as a fixed entity, but rather as a dynamic and constantly changing continuum of behavior. Your role as supervisor, then, is one of assisting or *scaffolding* the teacher to higher levels of conceptual thinking and behavior.

While there are certainly exceptions to the rule, less developmentally mature individuals usually profit most from highly structured staff development environments. Conversely, individuals who are professionally mature are likely to profit more from less-structured staff development environments. Translating this principle into practice means that directors should supervise staff differently according to their assessed developmental levels.

Glickman (2004) puts a slightly different spin on this concept. He provides definitions of different supervisory styles that directly relate to the issue of control. *Directive supervision* is characterized by high supervisor control and low teacher control. When control is conceptualized more equally, the strategy is labeled *collaborative supervision*. Finally, low supervisor control and high teacher control is referred to as *nondirective supervision*.

According to Glickman, all three approaches are valid as long as they are linked to the developmental needs of teachers and aim to increase teacher self-control. When teachers are unskilled and unmotivated or are very new to the profession, a directive orientation may be the best approach. On the other hand, when teachers have had some experience, have shown some success and competency, and appear motivated, collaborative strategies will probably be a more successful approach. And for teachers who have had extensive background and experience, have demonstrated independence and autonomy, and have high problem-solving abilities, a nondirective orientation is most appropriate.

Glickman's Supervisory Behavior Continuum (Figure 6.1) provides a sequencing of supervisory behaviors matched to the three general approaches identified above. When the supervisor determines the actions for the teacher to follow by directing what will be done, standardizing the criteria of expected results, and reinforcing the consequences, the approach falls into the directive category (far left on the continuum). A collaborative approach is evident when the supervisor participates in the discussion by presenting his or her ideas, problem solves with the teacher by proposing alternatives, and then negotiates to find a common course of action. In this case control over decisions is shared by teacher and supervisor. On the far right of the continuum, the behaviors fall into the nondirective category of supervisory behavior. With this approach, the supervisor listens to the teacher, clarifies what the teacher says, encourages, and reflects. In this nondirective approach, the supervisor serves as a sounding board for the teacher.

Interactions between directors and teachers in early childhood programs are presented below to further clarify different supervisory styles and behaviors.

Directive Approach

Director: Have you looked through the new science materials that came in a few weeks ago? I haven't seen anything on your lesson plans that looks like you're using them.

Teacher: I just haven't had time to review them. We need a lot more planning time to do things like that!

Director: I know you're busy, but science is an important part of our curriculum. I'd really like to see more science activities in your lesson plans. Perhaps you could take some of the things home this weekend and consider using them the following week.

Teacher: Well, actually, I'm not sure what I'd want to do with them. The sand and water tables seem to be enough for my kids.

Director: Why don't we get together next week to talk about this some more? I'll get your room covered and put a note in your box. Make sure you bring your lesson plans along, okay?

Teacher: All right. Any help would be appreciated.

Supervisory Behavior Continuum

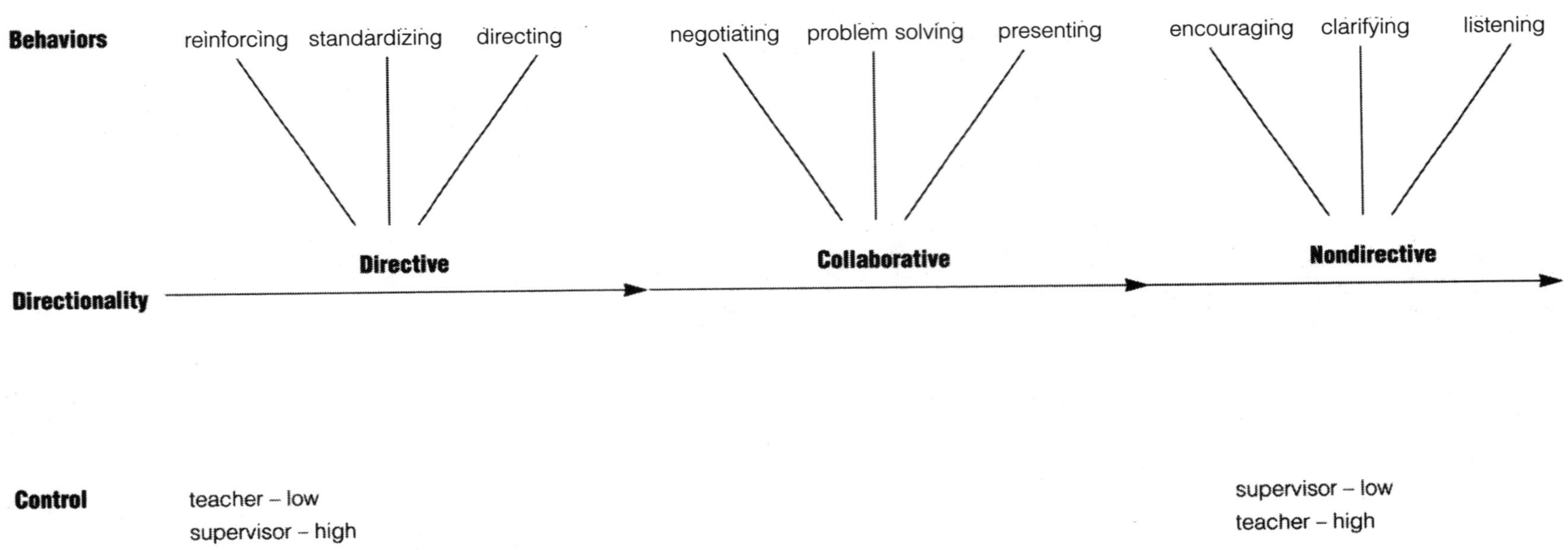

Figure 6.1

Behaviors

reinforcing standardizing directing negotiating problem solving presenting encouraging clarifying listening

Directive   **Collaborative**   **Nondirective**

Directionality

Control

teacher – low
supervisor – high

supervisor – low
teacher – high

Adapted from Glickman, C. D. (2004). *Supervision and instructional leadership: A developmental approach.* Boston: Pearson Allyn & Bacon, pp. 132–33. Reprinted with permission

A directive supervisory style can be useful when, as in this case, the teacher possesses little expertise in an area and doesn't seem motivated to find out about the subject on his or her own. Directive behaviors are also useful when the director cares about an issue, but the teacher doesn't see it as a priority.

Collaborative Approach

Teacher: I really think 4-year-olds still need naps!

Director: In general, I agree. But in the case of Josh, I'm not sure it's true. Having to lie on the cot for an hour and a half seems difficult for him.

Teacher: But even resting is good for the kids. Otherwise they get real cranky later in the afternoon.

Director: That might be true for a lot of children, but is it for Josh? Josh's mom is asking that we let him read books quietly during naptime. She says he's very upset over having to lie there so long. Perhaps we should think about an adjustment of some kind for him.

Teacher: But you know the problems that causes. Once one child is allowed the privilege, they'll all want it!

Director: On the surface, that's true. But maybe there's some other way to do it.

Teacher: Maybe you're right. I was just thinking that maybe if we had him lie on his cot until everyone else was settled or asleep and then let him go to the book area it would work. I don't know. But it's probably worth a try.

Director: Sounds so simple, but I think you might have something!

The collaborative approach encourages a frank exchange of ideas. Differences of opinion are encouraged, not suppressed; equality in problem solving characterizes the nature of the exchange. Collaboration should be used when the teacher and supervisor have approximately the same degree of expertise on an issue (Glickman, 2004). In addition, for collaboration to work, both teacher and director must intensely care about the problem and be committed in carrying out the decision. In the case

above, both teacher and director would deal with the parent to communicate the decision about naptime and explain the adjustment.

Nondirective Approach

Teacher: Boy, we sure had a mess in that room today!

Director: What happened? Sit down and relax a minute. You look exhausted!

Teacher: Well, two of the volunteers did the footprint activity today and didn't prepare for it well enough. You wouldn't believe all the paint drips that got on the floor. They didn't bring enough newspaper and paper towels. I thought I told the volunteers at their orientation session what they needed, but they came unprepared. I didn't notice until too late!

Director: I know how frustrating that is. You must have been upset!

Teacher: Upset is right! I'm going to have to think of how to inform these volunteers so they hear. I know they mean well, but they have to be better prepared.

Director: Do you still give out the guideline sheets you developed last year? They seemed so clear.

Teacher: Yes, I still do. But apparently I'm not placing enough emphasis on them.

Director: You think they don't read them carefully.

Teacher: That's the issue. They probably stick the papers in with everything else I give them about the center. I shouldn't be trusting that they read them without being prompted.

Director: Well, you've always been good at setting expectations for our volunteers.

Teacher: Yeah, I've thought so, too. I'll just have to get back to being more thorough again. Thanks for your ear!

Nondirective supervision is based on the assumption that a teacher knows best what changes need to be made and has the ability to think and act on his or her own. The role of the supervisor is one of assisting the teacher in the process of thinking through different courses of action. However, if the teacher lacks the expertise or capability, the nondirective approach is definitely an unwise choice. Only when teachers have expertise, take responsibility, and care about the issue will the nondirective supervisory approach prove viable.

A final consideration with respect to supervisory style is the recognition of the director's developmental level and continual growth. Caruso and Fawcett (1999) postulate that supervisors go through a series of phases as they move toward maturity—beginning, extending, and maturing. Like teachers, directors may move back and forth from one phase to another during their careers. Caruso and Fawcett note that even mature, educated, and talented directors may demonstrate some characteristics of beginners when they work in new roles, in unfamiliar settings, or with people they don't know.

> *Treat people as though they were what they ought to be and you will help them become what they are capable of being.*
>
> Goethe

An awareness of their own growth and development can assist directors in realizing that they cannot be all things to all people or know all the answers at all times. As directors gain experience, they are more comfortable in making decisions and soliciting group input in those decisions. There are times, though, when directors have to acknowledge that they may not have control over all the variables affecting their programs. Supervisors, just as teachers, are individuals with their own strengths and limitations.

Staff Development Strategies

Teachers who are in the survival or early consolidation stages, and who may function at a low level of abstraction, tend to focus on the practical. They are concerned with determining what to do in specific situations rather than reflecting on philosophical principles and abstract ideas that can be generalized to multiple situations. Consequently, these teachers need more concrete, precise information on what to do, how to do it, and the circumstances under which it should be done. They benefit from lectures on specific topics related to classroom situations and visits to other centers. Sample materials for their use should be clearly organized and sequenced.

Glickman (2004) identifies this group of teachers as low in abstract thinking and emphasizes the importance of demonstrating and/or modeling new practices, skills, or techniques. Since these teachers are hesitant and inexperienced, workshops should focus on teachers' understanding of the personal advantages to be gained from any proposed change. In early childhood centers, such inexperienced teachers benefit initially from a fairly structured program of in-service activities and clearly organized goal plans. They'll need your support in managing their classrooms and dealing with problem children.

Teachers who function at the career stage of consolidation or renewal and who exhibit a moderate or high level of abstract thinking may resist mandatory staff development programs that appeal to teachers in the survival group. Although they may not have clarified their own point of view, these teachers express their criticisms of the way things are conducted and want to apply principles they have learned on their own. With this group, it is important that staff development activities allow opportunities for alternatives both with respect to content and presentation. Teachers at this level benefit from group discussions in which participants are given the chance to express and elaborate their own points of view.

Glickman sees this group of teachers as benefiting from applying newly learned principles to classroom activities. However, they are still in need of help from a supervisor in defining what they want to do and how to do it. Direct assistance from the director or supervisor still needs to be provided.

At the mature level of the career-stage continuum, teachers frequently function at a high level of abstraction. They require very different approaches with respect to staff development activities. Dillon-Peterson (1981) suggests that democratic decision-making procedures are particularly applicable at this level. By involving these teachers in the planning process, directors are allowing them to express their own uniqueness, knowledge, and experience. This group is expected to focus on the link between theory and practice, philosophical underpinnings, and more complex concerns. Glickman (2004) sees these teachers as contributing actively to brainstorming and group problem-solving processes in a center.

Mature teachers function well in mentoring roles with new or inexperienced teachers, in conducting parent education programs, and in articulating the goals, curriculum, and philosophy of a center to the public. Presentations by these individuals at conferences provide opportunities for sharing their knowledge and experience and keeping them actively involved in the profession.

As Table 6.2 (p. 105) shows, there are many and varied staff development strategies that can be used with teachers at different developmental levels. While it is not the intent of this book to offer an in-depth discussion of each of these strategies, an overview of some of them is appropriate.

Mentoring. The idea of using a knowledgeable and experienced person to guide another has gained credibility in education over the two decades. Formal mentoring, if implemented carefully, can meet the specific needs of beginning teachers and provide increased professional satisfaction to mature teachers acting as mentors.

Mentors, according to Zachary (2000), are more than master teachers; they also serve as coach, positive role model, developer of talent, opener of doors, protector, sponsor, and successful leader. Driscoll, Peterson, and Kauchak (1985) studied teachers' perspectives of the actual functions performed by mentors that were considered most important. These are the top four items:

► observes and comments on classroom performance;

► gets involved in solving specific problems with curriculum, instruction, and people;

► provides clear feedback about how well you are doing as a teacher; and

► helps you to cope with the practical details of being a teacher.

These researchers also present criteria for screening prospective mentors. The criteria include the amount of time the individual has available to devote to mentoring, his or her concern for the needs of beginning teachers, the presence of a communicative supportive personality, and the person's overall level of professional competence. Carter (1998) emphasizes that it is crucial that mentors understand their role is not to evaluate or seek compliance but rather to nurture the learning process by helping individuals construct their own understandings and become reflective teachers.

Change is not something you do to people. It is something you do with people.

Also important is the need for some types of structured support systems for mentors. Driscoll and her colleagues emphasize that if mentors are to work closely with teachers in the classroom, they need expertise in observation, conferencing, and reflective supervision. This assistance must be an integral part of a mentor system. If such a support system is in place, mentoring benefits the new teacher, the teacher mentor, and the children in the program.

Workshops. Workshops have long served as a vehicle for staff development in early childhood settings. The drawback of workshops, Caruso and Fawcett (1999) point out, is that we tend to expect too much from them. "In one or a few sessions, participants are supposed to develop new skills or understandings, or to change attitudes toward children and parents. They are then presumed to be ready to demonstrate what they have learned on their return to the classroom. It is no wonder the results are often disappointing" (p. 219).

Workshops will be more successful as a staff development strategy if the following considerations are kept in mind. First, workshops need to be geared to the interests and developmental needs of participants. That means ensuring that there are multiple options for staff to select from. By having multiple options, teachers can self-select those workshops that will be of most interest to them. A single topic workshop designed for all staff is bound to disappoint half or more of your teachers.

Second, the presenter should have an awareness of the specific context of the program and the real-life concerns of the teachers attending the session. There is nothing more disconcerting than a presenter who laces his or her presentation with examples that have no resemblance to the concerns or issues experienced by participants.

Third, as Carter and Curtis so passionately advocate in their book *Training Teachers* (1994), workshop trainers need to be grounded in constructivist theory so they design professional development experiences where participants are active and given opportunities to reflect on what they know. Good trainers "watch and listen and build on participants' ideas and stories; help interpret and connect people, their experiences, and ideas to each other; pose questions that may uncover contradictions; and expose further complexity to be explored" (p. 157).

Finally, sufficient follow-up needs to be planned to ensure that teachers have integrated the ideas and concepts into their day-to-day practice. Workshops can be a viable means for increasing the knowledge and skills of teachers and even changing attitudes and behaviors if follow-up by supervisors reinforces what has been learned. Stonehouse (1986) emphasizes that the most successful, well-planned workshops embody both educative and supportive functions. In other words, they not only increase participants' knowledge and skills, they also enhance their self-esteem.

Professional reading. An important staff development strategy is to stimulate regular professional reading by teachers. Finding time for professional reading is a worthwhile goal for staff at all levels of professional responsibility, but it is essential for teachers in the early stages of their careers. Many directors have found that one way to instill expectations for professional reading is to assign an article to read for each staff meeting. Short, high-interest articles can be the substance of a brief discussion at the meeting where teachers exchange points of view and reflect out loud on the relevance of the topic for professional practice.

Clearly there are less structured ways to encourage professional reading as well. Having a staff library that is well stocked with journals, books, and other resources will help promote professional reading. Developing a resource file for parents will also prompt staff to search for new articles and useful ideas to pass on.

Classroom research. The idea of teachers functioning as action researchers in their classrooms has been given renewed emphasis in the last decade (Stremmel, 2002). This strategy is best used with mature teachers who are ready to systematically study and reflect upon some aspect of their classroom operation.

For teachers to undertake an action research project, they'll need your support and guidance. Released time will most likely be necessary if their research question necessitates the need for structured observations either in their own classroom or in the classroom of one of their co-workers. Assistance will also be necessary for designing the study as well as time to address data collection issues, procedural problems, data analysis, and implications.

Directors who have provided time for teachers to engage in action research have found the investment worthwhile. This staff development strategy allows seasoned teachers to go beyond informal assessment of their classroom to learn new skills in a systematic way. Such involvement usually serves to energize and challenge a teacher at this level.

In addition to the more formal strategies detailed above, there are numerous informal strategies that you can use: visits to other centers to observe programs; opportunities to meet with teachers from other centers for informal discussions; opportunities to meet with staff from community agencies that serve for children and families to discuss issues of mutual interest; individual on-site consultations with resource people possessing specialized expertise; participation in short courses, conferences, and seminars; and involvement in professional organizations.

Staff Development Content Areas

In the staff development model presented in Table 6.2 (p. 105), a number of different content areas are identified that match teachers' career stages and goals. In general, these content areas move from concrete topics to those that are more abstract and complex. Thus, beginning teachers in the survival stage are usually not interested in or ready for staff development on grant writing or child advocacy. Beginning teachers are focused on their classrooms and on issues related to curriculum, health and safety, and the physical environment. Likewise, mature teachers will probably be bored with topics that center on these issues; they are ready for discussions that are more philosophical and esoteric in nature or that help them refine their expertise in new curricular areas or mentoring approaches.

Another way to think about content areas is to group topics into categories. Abbott-Shim (1990) provides a fairly comprehensive list of topic areas for staff development. Table 6.3 summarizes these areas. She suggests that such a list could be used as a needs assessment survey. It could be distributed to staff to assess their level of interest in different topics.

Table 6.3

Content Areas for Staff Development

Child Care
Before- and after-school programs
Infant programming
Legal issues
Licensing
Program evaluation
Public policy
Resource and referral
School-age programs
Summer camps

Child Development
Child assessment
Cognitive development
Documenting learning
Gender identity
Language acquisition
Moral development
Physical development
Social and emotional development

Exceptional Children
Developmentally delayed
Gifted
Physically disabled
Referrals

Curriculum
Anti-bias
Art
Block play
Children's literature
Computers
Curriculum models
Dramatic play
Emergent literacy
Environments, design
Equipment and materials
Health
Language arts
Math readiness
Movement and dance
Multicultural/multilingual
Music and movement
Nutrition
Play
Reading readiness
Safety
Sand and water play
Science
Social studies
Teacher-child interactions

Families
Blended families
Death and divorce
Family-friendly environments
Intergenerational programming
Parent education
Parent involvement
Single-parent households
Teen parents

Staff Needs
Building team relationships
CDA credential
Career ladders
Child abuse awareness
Child advocacy
Communication skills
Community resources and services
Learning styles
Stress management
Time management

Adapted from Abbott-Shim, M. S. (1990, January). In-service training: A means to quality care. *Young Children, 45*(2), 14–18. Reprinted with permission.

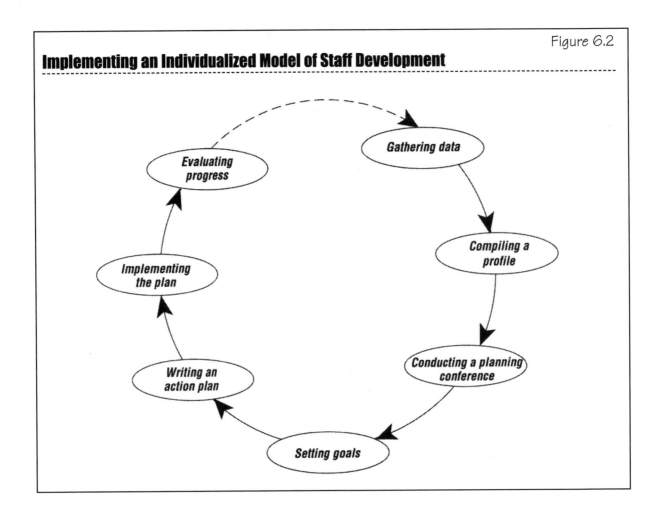

Figure 6.2

Implementing an Individualized Model of Staff Development

Gathering data

Compiling a profile

Conducting a planning conference

Setting goals

Writing an action plan

Implementing the plan

Evaluating progress

Implementing Individualized Staff Development

The goal of implementing an individualized model of staff development is to have teachers develop a clear understanding of their own strengths and dispositions as well as their professional development needs. The hope is that as you allow teachers more choice and control in structuring their own professional development, they will become more committed to self-improvement and to the mission of your center.

Individualized professional development plans cannot be done haphazardly; a systematic approach is needed. Figure 6.2 details a seven-step process that can be used as a framework for conceptualizing the process. While the seven steps here are visually displayed in a cycle, it is probably more useful to think of them as a professional spiral,

where new data are added, goals are refined, and new targets for professional growth are set each year. The seven steps in this process parallel the organizational problem-solving process of change detailed in Chapter 2. Where Figure 2.1 on page 31 focuses on the center as the target of change, Figure 6.2 focuses on the individual as the target of change.

Gathering Data

 The initial interview with a new employee is a good time to begin collecting data. The open and trusting relationship you establish at this time lays the groundwork for future interactions. As director, it is important to acknowledge that you want to get to know this person better, that you want the person to come to you with concerns and problems, and that you wish to establish a good working relationship. Ask questions, look interested, and be concerned!

With veteran staff, as well, it is important to regularly check in. How are things going? What's happening on the home front? Have any problems surfaced since we last talked? As director, you set the tone for open communication. Your knowledge of individual staff increases daily through many and varied informal and formal contacts. All of these contacts generate data for planning individualized professional development opportunities.

Relative to the job itself, there are many sources of data that you can use. Teachers can be observed in action to assess the quality of their teaching practices using Assessment Tools #12 and #13 (Appendix A). This data can be supplemented with informal anecdotal notes that you keep. Teachers frequently complain that their supervisors do not spend enough time observing in their class-rooms. Brief, frequent visits are less threatening to teachers than formal observations. Frequent visits convey a sense that you are in touch with what is going on in the classrooms. This supervisory style pays off. In a planning conference or performance appraisal conference with a teacher, if you are able to relate specific instances of particular classroom practices, your credibility is greatly enhanced.

In using observational data for professional development purposes, try to suspend judgment on what is observed. As Katz (1993) cautions, there is a strong tendency when observing teachers to immediately evaluate (judge) whether the person is doing it your way (the preferred way). But if your intention is to gather data to support someone's professional development, the filter through which you observe should be different. Instead of compar-ing and evaluating behavior against your personal yardstick of what is good or best, ask yourself, How can I account for what I am observing? Why is the teacher responding to the situation this way?

The anecdotal notes you keep are a valuable source of data for compiling a profile on each teacher. Although time consuming to write, anec-dotal notes provide rich, descriptive examples of the way a teacher functions. These examples can be used in discussing a more abstract concept. For example, one director recorded the following exchange between a new teacher and a parent:

Parent: I thought you would be working on the alphabet with Jenny by now. She is certainly ready for it.

Teacher: Our program is more play oriented. We don't believe in prereading activities.

The director was able to refer to this exchange when discussing parent communication with the teacher. Although this particular early childhood program was indeed play oriented, the answer the teacher gave to this parent's question did not assist the parent in understanding why play and social interaction had been established as emphases of the program. Moreover, stating that there were no prereading activities was erroneous. Children were read to frequently, print was readily available in the classroom, and artwork was often enhanced with children's dictations. This simple interaction identified several areas in which the director could work with the teacher. Having a specific example facilitated a meaningful discussion on important issues.

To simplify the recording of anecdotal entries, many directors carry a small notebook or three-by-five-inch index cards around with them. The task is quite similar to teachers' efforts to record anecdotal data on the children in their classrooms. The goal of data gathering is to pinpoint teachers' needs so you can help them address rather than avoid problems. Without adequate information on an individual, it is impossible to develop a meaningful professional development plan.

The feedback you receive from parents and co-workers will also be helpful. Directors can gain valuable information about teachers through ongoing, informal exchanges with parents and through conferencing with other staff. While data from direct observations and from colleagues and parents is useful, no doubt the most valuable data you'll collect will come from the teachers them-selves. Using the assessment tools in this book, or adaptations of them, will help you generate mean-ingful data in a number of areas—learning style, level of job satisfaction, commitment, perceived problems, and so on.

Compiling an Individual Profile

 After sufficient information has been gathered on an individual, it is time to create a profile. Appendix B includes blank worksheets you can use for this purpose. At the end of this chapter are examples of completed worksheets on two teachers from The Children's Corner—Shelly, a new, inexperienced teacher, and Pat, a mature, seasoned teacher. The areas noted on Worksheet #5, "Individual Profile," reflect the use of many of the different assessment tools previously discussed. For example, there is a space for learning style, psychological type, communication style, and so on. The accompanying Worksheet #6, "Observations," show anecdotal entries on Shelly and Pat that provide evidence for statements made on the profile. Obviously, these entries will be far more extensive after the individual has worked at the center for a period of time.

This first profile you prepare should be considered tentative until you have a planning conference with the teacher where you will elicit further information and clarification. Also, as you observe the classroom and receive ongoing feedback on the teacher, other modifications may need to be made.

Conducting a Planning Conference

 It is important that a formal get-together, a planning conference, be conducted to begin the process of developing a professional development plan with each teacher. This conference is important not just for the content and information that will be communicated, but also for its symbolic value—the ritual being established of formally meeting to talk about professional development issues. Such a ritual will help you structure your work with the teacher and serve as a framework for building a supportive relationship.

For new teachers it is suggested that a planning conference be conducted six weeks into a new job and then annually thereafter. For veteran teachers it is usually sufficient to meet once a year. Many directors like to schedule their professional development planning conferences in late August or early September because it is a logical time to think about setting individual and organizational goals for the new academic year.

Prior to the scheduled conference, it may be helpful to allow the teacher to prepare answers to some of the questions that will be discussed. Worksheet #7 in Appendix B, "Preparing for the Planning Conference," is provided for this purpose. Sample completed worksheets are included with the profiles for Shelly and Pat at the end of this chapter.

The goal of the planning conference is to create the kind of supportive, trusting atmosphere where a teacher will openly share information and concerns. Luft and Ingham (1973) developed the concept of the Johari Window to describe four types of information about a teacher that might surface during such meetings. This is graphically illustrated in Figure 6.4.

The open self. Much of what we know is information that is known both to the teacher and others in the center. *Gina is a good piano player; she loves music activities.*

The secret self. Some information is known to the teacher but not to others. *Gina is terrified each time she has to conduct a parent conference.*

The blind self. There is information about the teacher's behavior that is known to others but not to the teacher. *Gina seems to reinforce sex role stereotypes in her classroom.*

The undiscovered self. There is information that is unknown both to the teacher and to others. Through professional development opportunities these qualities may emerge. *Gina has the potential to be an outstanding mentor to less experienced staff.*

The challenge to the director is to motivate the teacher to go beyond the open self and to delve into the secret and the blind self when identifying improvement areas. Figure 6.5 represents this shift graphically.

Be sure to allow sufficient time for the teacher to initiate questions or raise concerns. Remember, the focus of planning conferences is to build on teachers' strengths and expressed interests, not their perceived deficits. This meeting provides a prime

The Johari Window

Figure 6.4

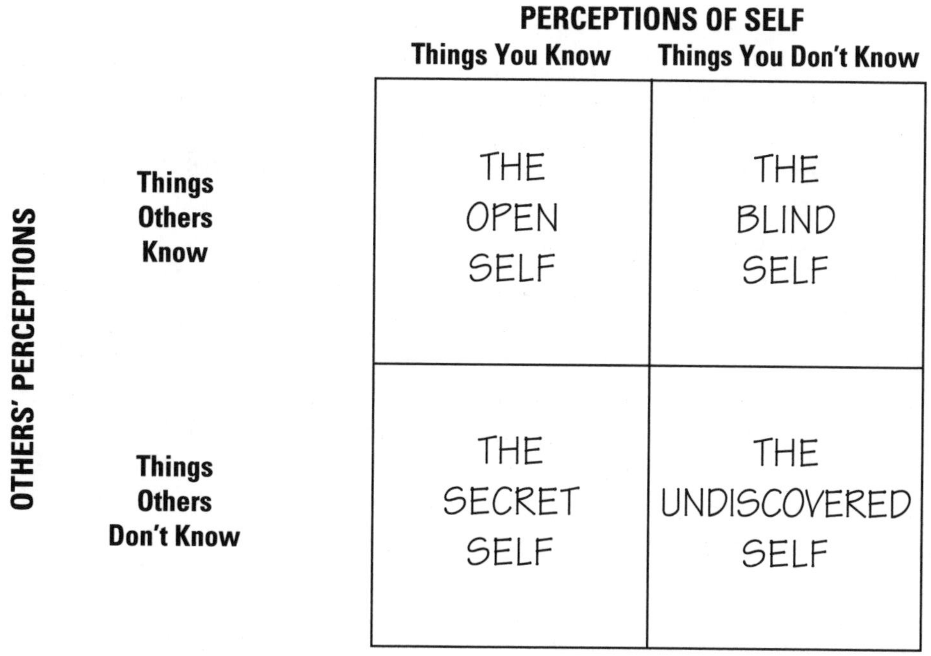

PERCEPTIONS OF SELF

	Things You Know	**Things You Don't Know**
Things Others Know	THE OPEN SELF	THE BLIND SELF
Things Others Don't Know	THE SECRET SELF	THE UNDISCOVERED SELF

OTHERS' PERCEPTIONS

Figure 6.5

When a teacher has been motivated to go beyond the *open self* and delve into the *secret self* and the *blind self* in identifying improvement areas, the proportions of known and unknown information shift.

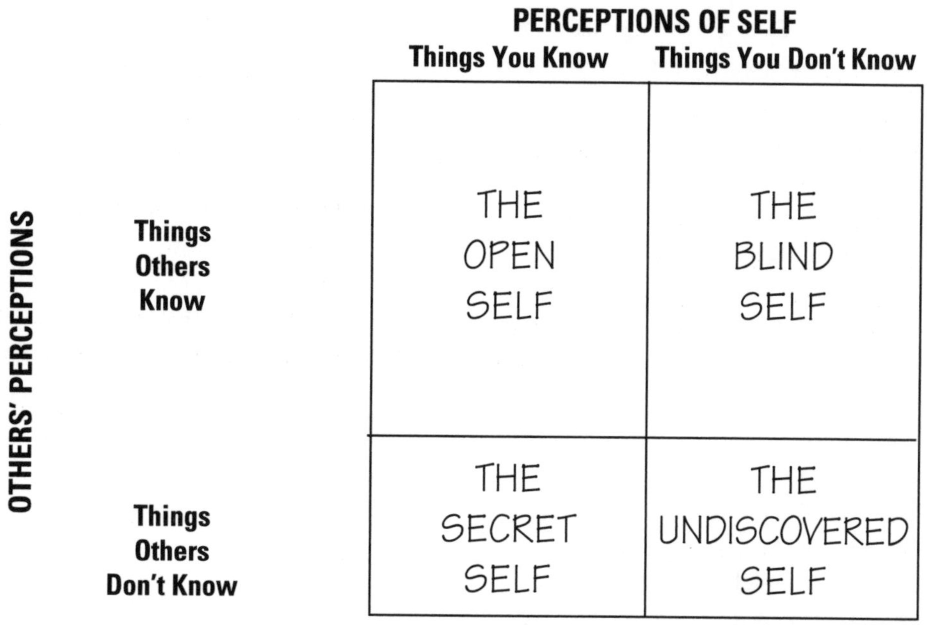

PERCEPTIONS OF SELF

	Things You Know	**Things You Don't Know**
Things Others Know	THE OPEN SELF	THE BLIND SELF
Things Others Don't Know	THE SECRET SELF	THE UNDISCOVERED SELF

OTHERS' PERCEPTIONS

Adapted from Luft, J., & Ingham, H. (1973). The Johari Window. *Annual handbook for group facilitators.* San Diego, CA: University Associates.

opportunity for teachers to identify their new interests and passions and together with you explore ways that will allow them the time and resources to pursue them.

From the responses to Worksheet #7, "Preparing for the Planning Conference," you will begin to get an idea of what kind of support the teacher needs. Looking at Pat's answers, for example, we see that she is interested in learning more about program management issues. She has also expressed a desire to improve her presentation and group facilitation skills. Perhaps a break from the long hours in the classroom might be appropriate for a teacher like Pat.

Don't shortchange this important step in the staff development model. The planning conference is a potent motivational tool because the focus is on the individual teacher—a dedicated time where teachers can articulate their perceived needs and dream out loud of new possibilities for the future. Everyone relishes the opportunity to do this in relation to his or her work!

Developing a Goals Blueprint

Toward the end of the planning conference, the focus should move to goal setting. Goal setting should be a joint process. When directors include teachers in goal setting, they express confidence in them as reliable sources of information. Your role is facilitative in the sense that you help ensure that individuals set realistic and achievable goals that are congruent with their developmental profiles.

Begin the goal-setting process by identifying and discussing the strengths of the teacher. By doing so, the process of setting goals begins on a positive note. Next, specific areas in need of improvement or growth can be noted. From this point, goals can be articulated. Worksheet #8, "Goals Blueprint," is provided for this purpose. Goals need not be grandiose, but they do need to be meaningful and moderately challenging.

The approach advocated here is a needs-analysis approach, one where teachers are helped to identify strengths they can build on as well as problem areas they want to address. They then work with you to target specific objectives and activities that will reduce or eliminate those problems. A needs-analysis approach in working with individuals is essentially the same model we used to assess centerwide needs. It is one that defines a problem as the discrepancy between what is and what is required or desired. In this case it is the discrepancy between the knowledge, attitudes, or skills possessed by the teacher and those deemed desirable for the position.

It is important for directors to be mindful that there is often a difference between inferred and expressed needs. Many staff development programs in early childhood centers operate on an inferred needs basis. In other words, directors infer the training needs of staff based on their expert judgment alone. When teachers are permitted to express their own training needs, different themes often emerge (Peters & Kostelnik, 1981).

Writing a Staff Development Action Plan

A direct outgrowth of working together on goals is writing a staff development action plan. This plan breaks the goals down into activities, time, resources needed, and the how and when of evaluation. Worksheet #9, "Staff Development Action Plan," was designed for this purpose. You'll notice at the end of this chapter that the action plans for Pat and Shelly are quite different. Pat's activities reflect her maturity both in terms of her development and her career stage; they are directed beyond her classroom and emphasize her move into assuming a leadership role in the center. Shelly's plan, on the other hand, is focused on her classroom, as this is where she needs and wishes to concentrate her energies. Developmentally, this focus is appropriate because it addresses her survival orientation. Let's take a closer look and see how these action plans evolved.

Case Study: The Children's Center

Martha and Shelly scheduled a time to meet to work on Shelly's goals blueprint action plan for the year. Martha thought a lot about how to handle this conference. Clearly there were many areas of Shelly's performance that needed attention, including her lack of control of the children in the classroom, her overly structured instructional style, and her inability to deal with parents effectively. The list seemed to go on and on. But Martha also realized that Shelly's self-esteem as a teacher was fragile. She was convinced that with the right kind of supervision and mentoring, Shelly could develop into a competent and capable teacher. That is why this first planning conference was so crucial. If Shelly left the conference overwhelmed by having to tackle too many improvements all at once, there was a good chance, Martha felt, that Shelly would simply burn out before she ever really made a commitment to the profession.

Martha decided to proceed cautiously. First Martha and Shelly talked about some of the ways Shelly's talents could be tapped. Shelly loved the idea of doing a special jewelry-making project with the after-school program. She also jumped at the idea of developing an obstacle course and outdoor aerobics activities for the preschool-age children.

Martha let Shelly take the lead in the discussion regarding her perceived problems in the classroom. She was pleased at how Shelly opened up and how receptive she was to Martha's suggestions on ways they might work together to help solve some of Shelly's classroom problems.

Martha quickly realized that what Shelly needed most was to feel some sense of control over the management of her classroom. Trying to take on other goals right now, such as improving her interactive style with parents, would just be too much. First and foremost, Shelly needed to see herself as a competent teacher in control of her classroom. Once that happened, Martha felt confident Shelly would be more ready to take on some of the other areas that needed improving such as parent relations.

In talking to Shelly, Martha began to see how instrumental her own role was in helping to create a collegial and supportive atmosphere in the center. She talked to Shelly about doing some observations in Georgia's room. While Martha knew that Georgia wasn't ready to be a mentor, she did know that Georgia had a wonderful interactive style with children and would serve as a good role model for Shelly in the area of classroom management. Martha also thought that this just might be the shot in the arm that Georgia needed to re-energize her own teaching.

All kinds of possibilities were racing through Martha's mind. She thought, Why couldn't Pat serve as Shelly's mentor, the person to meet with her each week to go over her progress in meeting her professional development goals? When she suggested this to Shelly, Shelly liked the idea. Shelly said that she always felt like she was bothering Martha when she came to her with a problem because Martha was busy with so many other administrative responsibilities. Shelly liked the idea of having a big sister to go to with problems she was experiencing. Martha wasn't sure what she was getting herself into, but she said she would talk to Pat the next day at Pat's goal-setting conference and see how Pat felt about the idea of mentoring Shelly.

When Pat and Martha met to work on Pat's action plan, the conference was, of course, far less directive. Martha listened intently as Pat talked about wanting to take on a more active role in the local AEYC group and how she wanted to "get up her nerve" to make a presentation at the state conference the following year. Martha proposed the idea of mentoring to Pat, thinking that Pat might graciously decline given how much additional work it would entail. She told Pat that she would revise Pat's schedule to give her two hours a week for mentoring—one hour to observe Shelly and one hour for feedback and consultation with Shelly. Much to Martha's pleasure, Pat was eager to take on the assignment. She told Martha how honored she was to be asked and that no supervisor had ever shown that much confidence in her before. Martha loaned Pat some books on mentoring and they scheduled a three-way meeting with Shelly to work out the details. Martha was elated.

At the conclusion of the goal-setting conference, you might want to have the teacher complete Assessment Tool #26 in Appendix A. This instrument was designed to assess the individual's level of motivation in tackling the goals and objectives that have been outlined on the action plan. If the assessment results reveal that the teacher has very little motivation for achieving the stated goals and objectives, then it will be important for the two of you to meet again to revise the action plan to more accurately reflect those goals that the teacher is sincerely interested in accomplishing. Otherwise the entire goal-setting endeavor will become merely a paper exercise.

Implementing the Action Plan

 Action plans often need revision as they are implemented. For this reason it is important that you and your teachers view them as being flexible, making changes as warranted. Depending on how large your program is, you will probably be the key person monitoring the staff development action plans that have been initiated. Without the exercise of leadership on your part, the entire process will crumble. Staff development does not happen just by talking about it. There must be active follow-through to keep the process moving and relevant.

On Shelly's plan, for example, her third goal was to keep anecdotal records on the classroom operation. Through a review of these records as well as observations of the classroom, Martha and Pat (as Shelly's mentor) will try to determine if Shelly is more aware of interactions in the classroom and what might be influencing them. Once this awareness develops, the record keeping can be dropped and a new goal established.

> *The magnitude of change you ask people to make is inversely related to their likelihood of making it.*

Much of your time will be spent scheduling activities and providing resources as needed for individuals to achieve their goals. Often staff members need assistance in managing their time so they can attend to the action plan that has been agreed upon. Keeping people on-task and maintaining the momentum is crucial.

Evaluating Progress

 It is the director's responsibility through monitoring the action plans to evaluate teachers' progress on a continuous basis. Evaluation in this sense relates specifically to whether the goals have been attained, not to how well the teacher is doing his or her job from an overall perspective. Sometimes this responsibility can be delegated to a mentor, as in Shelly's case. Martha is still responsible, however, for ensuring that the mentor-mentee relationship is progressing smoothly. If not, she must intervene and make adjustments in supervising Shelly's progress in meeting her goals. Overall it can be assumed that teachers in the survival or consolidation stages will require more time in assessing progress in meeting the goals stated on their individualized staff development plans. Teachers at more independent levels of functioning will require a less directive supervisory style.

Evaluation from this perspective is linked specifically to the accomplishment of the staff development activities that have been identified. The outcomes will be an important piece of evidence in the performance appraisal process when considering merit and pay increases or promotion to a new position of responsibility. Staff evaluation as it relates to overall performance appraisal from a more global framework will be addressed in the next chapter.

A Final Word

This chapter has focused on strategies and supervisory approaches for implementing an individualized model of staff development. The emphasis has been on the match between teachers' developmental levels and the degree and type of support provided by their supervisor. Just as teachers facilitate the growth of children, your role as director in implementing an individualized model of staff development is to stretch teachers, helping them to move with confidence into the next level of professional competence. Clearly the process is a time-consuming one. By focusing your attention on the most important asset of your program—your staff—you will save time in the end by reducing, if not eliminating, many of the staff-related problems that impact the quality of program services.

Individual Profile

Name: __Shelly__   Age: ___22___

Personal history __Only child; father encouraged her in sports; parents divorced when__ __she was 15. Recently married her high school sweetheart. Went to a parochial__ __school as a child.__

Education/training ___Associate's degree in early childhood. CPR certificate.___ __Is familiar with the principles of developmentally appropriate practice, but unsure__ __how to put them into practice.__

Work experience ___Lab experience at the community college. No formal teaching___ __experience. Worked at a summer camp for two years.__

Interests and special talents ___Runs in local marathons; has assisted as an aerobics___ __instructor; makes jewelry; terrific bulletin board displays.__

Beliefs and values ___Believes children learn best in a structured well-planned___ __environment; values well-disciplined children who show respect for authority;__ __values consistency, routines, and standardization.__

Dispositions ___Talkative, friendly, and outgoing. Gives praise and likes to receive___ __praise. Is cooperative and promotes a good team spirit.__

Flexibility and openness to change ___Has a right/wrong orientation to teaching. Seems___ __overwhelmed when presented with change. Likes established routines.__

Energy level ___Has a high energy level, is peppy and always active. Participates___ __fully with the children on the playground.__

Cognitive capacity ___Low level of abstract thinking. Identifies problems but doesn't___ __consider their relationship to her behavior. Looks for quick solutions.__

Learning style___A practical learner (concrete-sequential). Wants to know real-life application of ideas. Enjoys discussions. Very visual. Likes detailed handouts. Creates little cartoons and pictures in her lesson plans.

Psychological type___ESFJ. Outgoing, cooperative, eager to please. Likes routines clearly laid out. Likes definitive answers.

Communication style___Spirited and outgoing. Enthusiastic and loves to be around other people. Can be impulsive; sometimes speaks before thinking.

Self-efficacy___Seems uncertain of herself in the classroom. Confident in interpersonal interactions with other teachers, even those much older than she.

Needs and expectations___Appears to have a strong need for approval. Important to be validated that she is doing a good job. Wants to be recognized as a professional and not just a caregiver. Was insulted when a parent asked her to babysit.

Adult development stage___Young adult stage. Beginning to seriously consider career options. Wants to purchase a home. Reluctant to make certain decisions. Frequently consults with others for the "right way" to do things.

Career stage___Survival. Frequently frustrated. Says it's difficult to keep track of all the things she's supposed to do as a teacher. Wants the children to like her. Energy and focus is on classroom control.

Level of commitment and motivation___Brings a lot of enthusiasm to her work with young children, but seems centered on having her own needs met instead of the center's goals. Concerned with increasing financial incentives.

Professional orientation___Belongs to NAEYC and local affiliate. Reads Young Children and Pre-K Today. Not sure, however, if ECE will be her lifelong career.

Concomitant roles___Husband is in sales, away from home frequently. Belongs to women's fitness group. Works in a local soup kitchen every weekend.

Observations

Name _____Shelly_____

Date: _____August 6_____

Shelly came into the office very frustrated. "These boys are out of control! They all want to be in the block area, but all they do is fight. I'm think of closing the block area for a while."

Date: _____September 8_____

Shelly was talking to a parent outside the classroom. "Joe will have to learn to behave in here. He's been very disrespectful! I think you should talk to him about his behavior."

Date: _____September 12_____

At a staff meeting we discussed the problem of the lack of planned activities on the playground. Shelly chimed in, "I have an idea. Maybe a couple of days a week I could lead the children in doing some aerobic activities and exercises. I could even set up an obstacle course." The other teachers were very receptive to Shelly's suggestion.

Preparing for the Planning Conference

Dear Shelly:

As you prepare for our planning conference, think about the following:

▶ What aspect of your job gives you the greatest personal satisfaction?

I really like doing outdoor activities with the kids. Then I don't need to worry about the noise level.

▶ What aspect of your job is most frustrating?

Trying to get the kids to listen to me.

▶ What keeps you from being as effective as you would like to be in your position?

Some of the children are really disrespectful. I can't even get through a story time without a major disruption.

▶ If you had the power to change anything about your job, what would you change? Why would this be an improvement over existing conditions?

I wouldn't be so stressed out if I could get the kids to cooperate. Maybe if the parents were involved more they would help control them.

▶ What do you see yourself doing five years from now?

I'm not sure—maybe teaching, maybe something else.

▶ What new skills or knowledge would you like to learn this next year?

I'd like to learn more about classroom management and discipline techniques. I'd like to learn how not to get so wound up when things don't go right. I'd also like to try doing some activities in the after-school program. Maybe I'd do better with older kids.

▶ How can I or other staff help you achieve your personal and professional goals?

I'd really like to go to the AEYC conference. I've never attended before.

Goals Blueprint

Teacher's name: **Shelly**   Date: **September 15**

Strengths as a teacher

1. Enthusiastic; eager to learn

2. Conscientious in preparing classroom and completing lesson plans

3. Promotes cooperation and a team spirit among staff

Identified growth areas

1. Expand knowledge about the importance of the physical arrangement of space in the classroom

2. Learn effective classroom management strategies

3. Take time to reflect on her role and the impact of her actions on children's behavior in the classroom

Goal: More positive interactions among children and better use of space, equipment, and materials.

Objectives

1. To improve the physical arrangement of the classroom learning environment

2. To improve classroom management strategies: redirection, prevention, and intervention

3. To monitor classroom interactions by keeping anecdotal notes

Staff Development Action Plan

Name __Shelly__   Date __September 25__

Objective #1 __To improve the physical arrangement of the classroom learning environment__

Activities	Time Needed	Resources Needed
1. Read <u>Designs for Living and Learning</u> Read <u>Caring Spaces, Learning Places</u> View video "Room Arrangement as a Teaching Strategy" View High/Scope video "Setting Up the Learning Environment"	1. Approx. 10 hours reading and viewing time	1. Borrow books and videos from college library and media center
2. Experiment: restructure space and observe behavior	2. 1 hour weekly with mentor	2. 1 hour per week coverage for classroom

Evaluation (how/when) __Weekly meeting with mentor. Use Assessment Tool #12 as pre/post__

Objective #2 __To improve classroom management strategies__

Activities	Time Needed	Resources Needed
1. Observe Georgia's preschool class during free-choice period	1. 2 hours per week for 3 weeks	1. Coverage for classroom 6 hours
2. Experiment with different strategies: prevention, redirection, and intervention Keep journal to reflect on progress	2. Ongoing—one entry per week	2. Notebook

Evaluation (how/when) __Weekly meeting with mentor to discuss progress__

Objective #3 __To monitor classroom interactions by keeping anecdotal notes__

Activities	Time Needed	Resources Needed
1. Observe each child. Note examples of positive behavior	1. Ongoing in classroom	1. Note cards
2. Read <u>The Art of Awareness</u> Read <u>The Power of Observation</u> View video "Observing Young Children: Learning to Look, Looking to Learn"	2. Approx. 8 hours	2. Borrow books from college library

Evaluation (how/when) __Weekly meeting with mentor to discuss entries__

Individual Profile

Name: ___Pat_____   Age: ___38_____

Personal history___Has two children. Stayed at home when they were young and was__
active in a parent co-op preschool. Adopted one child. Experienced the death of
_her father last year._____

Education/training _B. A. in early childhood education. Interested in pursuing_
_master's degree. Attended Reading Recovery institute._____
_____

Work experience __Lead teacher—3 years. Assistant teacher—3 years._____
_Volunteer (parent co-op)—6 years_____
_____

Interests and special talents _Active in a support group for adoptive parents. Plays piano_
_and sings in her church choir. Strong supporter of the community arts program._____
_____

Beliefs and values _Believes that people are inherently good. Believes children are_
intrinsically motivated to learn and need a certain amount of freedom to express
_themselves. Values diversity._____

Dispositions __Even-tempered, very nurturing, and curious about new ideas._____
_____
_____

Flexibility and openness to change __Believes that change is healthy. Quite open to new_
_curricular approaches and teaching techniques._____
_____

Energy level _Moderate energy level. Puts a lot into her work, but has to monitor_
_hypoglycemia._____
_____

Cognitive capacity _High level of abstract thinking. Good problem solver. Considers_
many sources of information before making a decision. Able to evaluate her
_actions and the actions of others objectively._____

Learning style _Identifies herself as an auditory learner. Enjoys and learns from group discussions. Loves books on tape. Very self-directed._

Psychological type _ENFJ. Outgoing with parents and colleagues. Concerned about the feelings of others. Always dependable. Likes a sense of closure._

Communication style _Considerate communicator. Warm and friendly interactions. Very attentive listener. Will defer to people who are more direct or spirited. Will avoid conflict at all costs._

Self-efficacy _Confident in her abilities. Sometimes gets frustrated at not being able to be all things to all children._

Needs and expectations _Equity issues are important to her. Wants to know that everyone is pulling their fair share and that pay and benefits are distributed equitably. Often uses the word "fair" in her decision making._

Adult development stage _Midlife stage. Can reflect and explain why and how she has integrated particular goals and priorities. Able to respect diverse points of view and alternative lifestyles. Show autonomy in thinking and decision making._

Career stage _Maturity. Still gets excited about her teaching. Integrates her knowledge and experience well. Asks philosophical questions about the meaning of educational experiences._

Level of commitment and motivation _Self-motivated and committed to improving the center. Works to develop herself maximally. Understands the concept of quality from multiple perspectives and is committed to giving it her all._

Professional orientation _Reads widely—professional literature and current events. Subscribes to Education Week. Attends conferences and is active in local AEYC Affiliate Group. Has made a presentation to local parent group._

Concomitant roles _Wife and mother. Active in son's PTA. Serves on two local boards—women's shelter and community arts center._

Observations

Name Pat

Date: August 8

In the classroom, Pat was sitting on the floor in the block area. The children had built a stage out of hollow blocks, and Pat extended and enhanced their play by assisting them in making signs, tickets, and programs for audience members. She was flexible in dropping her scheduled plans to capitalize on their interest in dramatic play.

Date: September 6

Pat came in to discuss Michael. She observed that Michael's mother advocates a stronger discipline program with Michael than what she perceives he is getting in our program. Pat's comment: "This is a tricky situation. I think we need to respect her ideas, yet provide some guidance by offering alternative strategies for handling Michael's behavior." NOTE: Pat's interactions with this family focus on solving problems, NOT judging their actions or beliefs.

Date: September 15

I observed Pat supervising an aide in the classroom. She was pointing out some of the possible reasons for a child's negative behavior. She said to the aide, "It's frustrating, isn't it? It requires a lot of patience to be as understanding as we need to be." She seemed to convey just the right amount of empathy to her to help her through this difficult moment.

Preparing for the Planning Conference

- -

Dear Pat:

As you prepare for our planning conference, think about the following:

▶ What aspect of your job gives you the greatest personal satisfaction?

I get such satisfaction from charting the children's progress from September to June. Day by day you don't notice the change, but when you compare what they are able do after nine months, it is amazing. It is such a pleasure to share this information with the parents. They are so proud when they hear about their children's developmental strides.

▶ What aspect of your job is most frustrating?

I don't have any major frustrations, but it does annoy me that a few of the other teachers don't pull their weight. It doesn't seem fair that a few of us always get stuck cleaning the art area and kitchen. It also bugs me the way some people waste supplies (for example, by leaving caps off the markers).

▶ What keeps you from being as effective as you would like to be in your position?

I wish we could achieve a better team spirit as a staff. I don't like the gossiping that goes on. I think it petty and undermines our professionalism.

▶ If you had the power to change anything about your job, what would you change? Why would this be an improvement over existing conditions?

I wish everyone on the staff were as committed to early childhood education as I am. I think some staff treat teaching as a job and not a career.

▶ What do you see yourself doing five years from now?

I've been thinking I might want to get my master's, but I'm not sure exactly what in. I'd like to do more administrative tasks, but I don't want to leave the classroom entirely. I love my work with families.

▶ What new skills or knowledge would you like to learn this next year?

I'd like to learn more about documentation and developing electronic portfolios for children. I'd also like to plan a workshop for the state AEYC conference, but I need to learn more about presentation techniques. I have a lot of ideas, but I need time to organize them.

▶ How can I or other staff help you achieve your personal and professional goals?

I could use your feedback on the ideas I come up with for workshops. I really trust your judgment. Also, there is a 3-day institute on documentation I'd love to attend. I would be appreciative if the center could cover the registration fee.

Goals Blueprint

Teacher's name: __Pat_____   Date: __September 20__

Strengths as a teacher

1. __Excellent ability to integrate curriculum areas_____

2. __Excellent communication skills with children and adults_____

3. __Well-organized learning environment and efficient use of time_____

Identified growth areas

1. __Expand opportunities to practice and refine mentoring skills_____

2. __Learn strategies for documenting children's learning_____

3. __Expand knowledge about effective workshop presentation techniques__

Goal: __Greater sense of confidence and competence in communicating expertise to__
__others—parents and other early childhood professionals_____

Objectives

1. __To increase knowledge and skill in mentoring others_____

2. __To increase knowledge and skill in documenting children's learning__

3. __To plan and present a workshop_____

Staff Development Action Plan

Name <u>Pat</u>   Date <u>September 30</u>

Objective #1 <u>To increase knowledge and skill in mentoring others</u>

Activities	Time Needed	Resources Needed

1. Take course at the university on reflective supervision and adult learning theory
   View video "Side by Side: Mentoring Teachers for Reflective Practice."
   Read <u>Growing Teachers: Partnerships for Staff Development</u>
2. Serve as mentor to Shelly (meet with her weekly to help her implement her action plan)
	1. 4 hrs/wk class time, 4 hr/wk study time
	
	2. 1 hr/wk observation 1 hr/wk consultation
		1. Books for course, $75 Borrow video from college media center
		
		2. Classroom coverage, 2 hrs per week

Evaluation (how/when) <u>Meet with Martha in Dec., Feb., and April to review progress of #2</u>

Objective #2 <u>To increase knowledge and skill in documenting children's learning</u>

Activities	Time Needed	Resources Needed

1. Attend weekend documentation institute
   Read <u>Windows on Learning</u>
   Read <u>Focused Portfolios</u>
 	
2. Create electronic portfolios for 15 children
	1. Approx. 20 hours institute and reading time
	
	2. Approx. 4 hours per portfolio
		1. Registration fee $199 Borrow books from the community college library
		
		2. CDs and scanner Borrow camcorder and digital camera

Evaluation (how/when) <u>Share completed portfolios at May staff meeting</u>

Objective #3 <u>To increase confidence in making presentations</u>

Activities	Time Needed	Resources Needed
1. Present workshop to parents on the importance of block play 2. Present workshop on block play at Spring AEYC conference	1. Released time for preparation 6 hours in January) 2. One day released time	1. Classroom coverage for 6 hours 2. $125 to cover conference registration and travel expenses

Evaluation (how/when) <u>Copy of AEYC program documenting presentation</u>

Chapter 7

Linking Staff Development to Performance Appraisal and a Career Ladder

One of the key concepts emphasized in this book is that to achieve lasting change in one component of a system, the change must be reinforced by change in other components of the system. The staff development process provides a prime example of this principle. Changes in teachers' knowledge, skills, and attitudes that result from implementing an individualized model of staff development will have a far better chance of taking hold if they are supported by changes in other organizational structures and processes. Two organizational structures are particularly important in this regard—the center's performance appraisal system and a career ladder for professional advancement.

Most centers already have in place some form of performance appraisal system, but few tie that system to their staff development processes. This chapter provides recommendations on how that can be done. Likewise, few centers have implemented a career ladder for professional advancement. As you'll see later in this chapter, a career ladder makes good sense, both from an economic standpoint and from a staff motivation standpoint. Career ladders have helped professionalize the field of education at the elementary and secondary levels, and there is no reason why the same principles can't be applied to staff working with younger children.

Linking Staff Development to Performance Appraisal

A performance appraisal is a natural extension of the individualized staff development cycle described in Chapter 6. It lays the foundation for ongoing planning and the charting of new goals and objectives for individual performance. So often we think of evaluation only as a way to judge performance, as a way to provide evidence on whether or not to renew a teacher's contract. But the performance evaluation process should serve as an effective tool for supporting change in individuals. Reviewing progress against previously set goals gives the evaluator and the teacher a yardstick by which to measure growth. This growth (or lack of growth) is the basis for change—change in knowledge, skills, and attitudes.

People don't care what you know until they know that you care.

The performance appraisal is a pivotal activity around which good directors manage their programs for staff development. When done right, it makes teachers aware of those areas of teaching performance in which they excel and those areas in need of improvement. In good programs, evaluation of staff is a continuous and ongoing process, one that focuses on change and improvement as well as reinforcing areas of strength. Figure 7.1 provides a visual display of the role of a performance appraisal in the human resources management process. This process, of course, includes staff development.

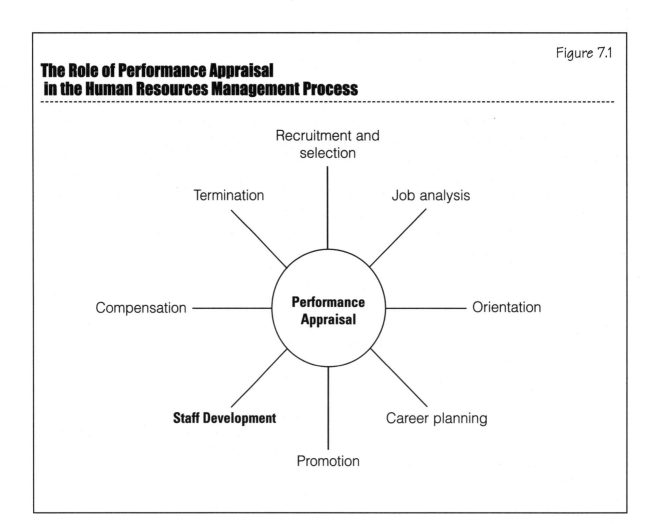

Figure 7.1

**The Role of Performance Appraisal
in the Human Resources Management Process**

Recruitment and
selection

Termination

Job analysis

Compensation

**Performance
Appraisal**

Orientation

Staff Development

Career planning

Promotion

If a performance appraisal plays such a vital role in organizational effectiveness, why is it that many directors dread the responsibility and see it as time consuming and burdensome? Employees as well seem to share this ambivalence and often complain that the process is arbitrary and sometimes humiliating. This section provides a rationale for viewing the performance appraisal processes of a center as a central vehicle for achieving centerwide change. It looks at the principles underlying an effective performance appraisal and presents guidelines for implementing a performance appraisal system in your center.

Principles Underlying
Effective Performance Appraisal

An effective performance appraisal depends on the following variables: the teacher, the evaluator, and

the context of the situation. For example, the background of the teacher with respect to educational level and experience will dictate the kinds of information used in the performance appraisal process. As evaluator, your values, attitudes, and your personal philosophy about evaluation certainly affect how you interpret that information. And the context of the situation in which you work will impact how that information is put to use. By understanding how these variables are defined differently in each situation, you can see why it is so important to individualize the performance appraisal process.

A number of excellent resources exist that identify effective performance appraisal processes: Danielson and McGreal (2000), Peterson (1995), Johnston (1988), Schwind (1987), Smither (1998), to name a few. All underscore key principles that will help you make the evaluation process a productive one—one that is both individualized and individually guided.

Performance appraisal must be thorough. Time is such a scarce commodity for administrators of early care and education programs. That is why many directors think that taking the time to conduct staff evaluations is a luxury they can't afford. But when viewed through the lens of program effectiveness, the time you allocate to evaluating your staff pays tremendous dividends later on. Better teaching performance, higher morale, and lower turnover are but a few of the payoffs that come with reallocating your time in order to provide feedback to staff through a performance appraisal. Interestingly, this is also an area that teachers feel strongly about. The following scenario captures the sentiments of a typical teacher.

Mary, a Head Start teacher, was observed with her class at lunchtime on three different occasions during the year. Her annual performance review stated that she showed poise, good manners, and self-control. On the basis of this assessment, her teaching was regarded as excellent. To the director's surprise, Mary was unhappy with this evaluation of her performance. She felt the evaluation was very cursory, and that the director's limited observation during lunchtime could not possibly give her a representative sample of her true performance. Even though the ratings were quite positive, Mary felt shortchanged. She had worked hard preparing her lessons and providing an enriching classroom experience for the children. She really wanted all her hard work to be validated.

Performance appraisal must be fair. One of the quirks of human nature is our tendency to let our personal biases cloud our judgment. In most situations the consequences are innocuous. In evaluating staff performance, however, this tendency can be both damaging and counterproductive. The personal biases we bring to the evaluation task often serve to make the process unfair and viewed as arbitrary from the teacher's perspective. The following example serves to illustrate this point.

Before Ramona became a director, she had taught kindergarten for 15 years. Ramona included poetry as an integral part of her teaching and felt that other teachers of young children should do the same. As a director, Ramona provided her teachers with poetry collections and often used poetry as part of staff meetings. Every week she would also post a new poem on the staff bulletin board. Ramona clearly valued poetry.

Carlo, an experienced teacher in the 4-year-old room, did not share this same enthusiasm for poetry. Ramona would often suggest appropriate poems for use in his classroom. The suggestions were ignored. Carlo believed that the children's own writing should be the foundation for early literacy. He felt strongly that he should display books and songs the children had created. On Carlo's performance appraisal form, he was rated "seldom" in promoting literacy. Carlo felt the rating was unfair, that Ramona was using her high value of poetry as the basis for this judgment. He felt strongly that he provided a literacy-rich environment—just not the kind of literacy that Ramona preferred.

Staff should be actively involved in developing evaluation standards. Because the context of each early childhood program is different, the performance appraisal criteria used need to reflect the unique values, culture, and goals of the program. If the evaluation methods are to accurately measure the knowledge, skills, and attitudes of the staff, then teachers need to have an integral role in determining how their performance should be evaluated.

The teachers of the public school prekindergarten program were surprised to find "dresses appropriately" on the performance appraisal form to be used to assess their teaching performance. After a team meeting, they met with the principal to get more clarity about how "dresses appropriately" would be defined. The principal listened to the teachers' rationale for why an informal mode of dress was appropriate for teachers at the preschool level. As a result, a description was added to the criteria that acknowledged the special needs of prekindergarten teachers to wear comfortable, informal attire on the job.

Performance appraisal should build on the competencies of the individual. The perceptions of the performance appraisal process held by both you and the teacher being evaluated are crucial. A sense of mutual trust and respect is essential. Evaluation must be viewed as a helping process—a time for building awareness and aspiring to new goals—rather than as a punitive process. From a motivation standpoint, focusing exclusively on a teacher's deficits is simply counterproductive. Feedback is most helpful when it focuses on strengths rather than weaknesses. Strengths change the nature of the interaction to one of looking at potential. In the end, this is what moves individuals to higher levels of performance and a stronger sense of self-efficacy and confidence.

After observing Shawna struggle with the organization and management of her classroom block area, Stewart, the education coordinator of the center, shared the problems he had faced in his own classroom years before. "NAEYC has a great publication, the Block Book, that you may want to take a look at, Shawna," he said. "I found a lot of good ideas that helped me. Would you like me to track down a copy for you?" When Shawna expressed an interest in the publication, Stewart was prompt in getting the book to her within a few days. The following week he observed again and, noticing new strategies in the block area, complimented Shawna specifically on the techniques he had observed. By using classroom observations as a vehicle to initiate change, Stewart was able to accent the positive and help Shawna become a better teacher. Shawna was empowered by seeing that her decisions and actions the classroom made a difference.

Performance appraisal should focus on behavior and results rather than on personal traits. When we try to evaluate traits such as cooperativeness, loyalty, sociability, trustworthiness, initiative, creativity, or thoroughness, we find that it is next to impossible to pinpoint exactly what those qualities mean. What we are left with is a subjective judgment based on the evaluator's interpretation of these traits. Consequently, what typically happens is that the evaluator ends up making an overall judgment of the person and rates the specific trait items consistent with the judgment.

Jessica had worked as the toddler teacher for four years. She had a pleasant disposition and smiled easily. The parents loved her. Bonnie, the program administrator, noticed that Jessica was less than careful about washing her hands when caring for the children. In fact, over the past six months, she had detected a rash of colds passed from one child to another in Jessica's classroom. Bonnie reminded Jessica of the importance of careful hand washing. She checked supplies to make sure soap and towels were always available and modeled good health habits when she visited the room. But there seemed to be no change in Jessica's behavior and illness continued to spread. The annual performance appraisal form used at the center only focused only on personality traits such as "is pleasant" and "displays positive attitude." Bonnie had to rate Jessica as excellent based on these criteria. This appraisal was unfortunate because Jessica's behavior in the area of providing a healthful environment clearly needed to be improved.

Traits are qualities that individuals bring to the job. They should not be the sole basis for performance appraisal because they are too subjective. Instead, attention should focus on behaviors, those critical incidents that can be noted and assessed in terms of how frequently they occur. In defining behaviors, be mindful that the specific criteria are sufficiently precise so as to provide a useful benchmark for performance. For example, *communicates with parents* as a criterion for judging performance is too vague to measure. Does this mean a "hello" and "goodbye" as parents drop off their children each day, or does it mean weekly progress notes home, a monthly newsletter, and two parent conferences a year? Without more specific behavioral descriptors added to the criteria, a director and teacher may have conflicting expectations of just what *communicates with parents* really means.

Results relating to teaching effectiveness such as the degree to which children are actively involved, the gains children achieve on competence measures, or the degree to which parents are satisfied with the program are important and useful ways to assess performance. But one must be cautious when interpreting certain outcome measures. Many programmatic outcomes in early childhood education are difficult to measure; others may be misleading. Take the case of Christine at The Children's Corner.

Case Study: The Children's Corner

Christine was a new teacher whom Martha had just hired. Martha had seen Christine in action at her previous preschool. She was a wonderful teacher, very much in touch with the needs of the young children. Her classroom was a child-centered learning environment, rich in opportunities for free exploration and discovery. In a nutshell, Christine represented Martha's ray of hope for converting the other teachers to implementing more developmentally appropriate practices. Much to Martha's surprise, the parents were not happy with Christine's performance. They complained to Martha that Christine was not getting their children "ready for school." They wanted to know why Christine was not sending home schoolwork like some of the other teachers.

Martha's experience shows us that results (in this case the parent's level of satisfaction with Christine's performance) can be misleading. The problem here is clearly not the teacher's performance, but rather the center's lack of communication to parents about how the philosophy and educational objectives of a developmentally appropriate program are translated into practice.

Multiple sources of evidence improve the reliability of a performance appraisal. As professionals, we know the value of using multiple sources of information for assessing the progress of young children. When it comes to adults, however, we tend to rely on single instruments as the totality of our evaluation process. Particularly in early childhood centers where directors wear both hats—supervisor and evaluator—it is imperative that they use multiple sources of evidence to evaluate the performance of staff.

The kinds of evidence used in a comprehensive performance appraisal will be both formal and informal and include different stakeholders. Some refer to this kind of comprehensive process as *multipoint feedback* or *360-degree feedback* (Edwards & Ewen, 1996; Jude-York & Wise, 1997). Certainly your assessment and teachers' assessments of how well the goals in their Goals Blueprint have been met will serve as one source of evaluation information. But there are many other sources of evidence that can be gathered to provide a holistic view of a teacher's performance. The following provides a menu of suggestions:

▶ *Standardized performance appraisal forms rating overall performance:* Once a year it is wise to use at least one standardized evaluation instrument rating teachers on their overall performance. This instrument should include some form of classroom observation as well as the evaluator's ratings on different pre-established criteria. Later in this chapter you'll learn how job descriptions can be used as the basis for constructing such an instrument.

▶ *Feedback from parents:* Feedback from the parents of students provides a rich source of evidence of the teacher's performance. You might want to send out a short questionnaire once a year (see Assessment Tool #11, for an example) or have the teacher gather together samples of parent notes and other correspondence that document parents' level of satisfaction.

▶ *Feedback from fellow teachers:* Feedback from colleagues is another important source of data about a teacher's performance. This feedback can be in the form of informal anecdotal notes that have been kept during the year or more formal peer observations that have been conducted. You may find Worksheet #10, "Peer Observation," in Appendix B useful for this purpose. Lead teachers who supervise other teachers or teachers serving in a mentoring role to other teachers should be provided with an opportunity to give formal feedback on the individual's performance annually.

▶ *Self-assessment:* If you are serious about wanting to make the performance appraisal process meaningful, it is essential that you help teachers assess their own growth and performance. Journal reflections written during the course of the year may be one way to gather this kind of data. At least annually teachers should do a more formal self-appraisal.

▶ *Videotaped segments of classroom instruction:* The wonders of technology can support your efforts to evaluate teaching performance. Some directors make a camcorder available so their teachers can assemble a montage of different activities conducted during the year. When the teacher has control over the production of the videotape, the process is non-threatening. This videotape not only will serve as an excellent source of evidence regarding the teacher's performance, but will no doubt also become a treasured memento as the teacher looks back on his or her teaching career.

▶ *Examples of professional activities:* Teachers can keep copies of the programs from conferences they attend as well as their notes from in-service workshops. They may also have certificates for specialized training they received outside the center. These and other artifacts provide evidence of teachers' professional growth during the year.

Effective performance appraisal depends on clear job descriptions. A clear and concise job description provides the foundation for fair and accurate evaluation. When job descriptions are clearly written and discussed at the initial hiring interview, the staff member has a better understanding of exactly what is expected in everyday performance. When job expectations are clearly understood right from the start, later evaluation is also easier and less biased; the whole process becomes a more effective tool for helping the employee be successful. A clear job description can provide baseline data for the level of expected performance because job descriptions, when done right, provide a concise picture of the competencies the employee needs.

The Child Development Associate (CDA) competency standards (CPR, 2001) detailing six competency goals in early childhood settings can serve as a useful guide for constructing job descriptions for the teaching staff at your center. Table 7.1 illustrates how these categories have been used to create a job description. This job description details the tasks for a teacher of preschool-age children. The precise responsibilities indicated under each category would need to be modified depending on the age level of children with whom the teacher was working. Thus job descriptions for teachers of infants, toddlers, or school-age children would be slightly different.

A good job description includes the following components: job title; a brief description of the job; accountability—to whom the individual holding the position reports; minimum qualifications for the position; and essential job functions and responsibilities required of the position. Writing job descriptions is tricky because you want enough detail so it is clear how the job is to be carried out, but you also want it concise enough to be useful. Job descriptions that are too brief and vague or too detailed and wordy tend to get filed away and ignored. If a job description is to be useful, it must be able to fit the individual holding the position. That means your center will have some generic job descriptions for each category of jobs, in addition to specific detailed ones that reflect the scope of an individual position held by a specific person.

Table 7.1

Job Description—Preschool Teacher

Description:

The Teacher is a member of the teaching team who shares responsibility with the Lead Teacher for the care and education of an assigned group of children. The Teacher is responsible for implementing curriculum, supervising children, communicating with parents, and providing a healthy and safe environment for children.

Accountability:

The Teacher reports to the Education Coordinator.

Minimum qualifications:

Successful completion of 30 semester hours of college coursework, including or supplemented by 12 semester hours of credit in child development or early childhood education or the completion of a training program to acquire the CDA (CPR, 2001) or CCP Credential (NCCA, 1991).

Responsibilities:

To establish and maintain a safe and healthy learning environment

1. Designs appropriate room arrangement to support the goals of the classroom
2. Plans and implements a nutritious snack program
3. Promotes healthy eating practices
4. Maintains a safe environment
5. Posts necessary information to ensure the safety and well being of the children
6. Maintains an orderly learning environment

To advance physical and intellectual competence

1. Provides a balance between child-initiated and teacher-initiated activities
2. Provides a balance between quiet and active learning activities
3. Uses equipment and materials for indoor and outdoor play that promote children's physical development
4. Involves children in planning and implementing learning activities
5. Provides an integrated curriculum that meets the needs of individual children
6. Plans and implements experiences that promote language and literacy development
7. Plans and implements activities that promote the acquisition of number concepts

To support social and emotional development and provide positive guidance

1. Plans and implements hands-on activities that develop positive self-esteem
2. Plans and implements hands-on activities that develop social skills
3. Plans and implements culturally diverse experiences
4. Uses and promotes positive guidance techniques
5. Provides a wide variety of creative and expressive activities
6. Establishes routines with smooth transition periods
7. Communicates with children at their developmental level
8. Encourages children to be independent

To establish positive and productive relationships with families

1. Relates assessment information to parents and offers support for dealing with children at different developmental stages
2. Plans and conducts home visits
3. Promotes communication with parents through weekly progress notes, a monthly newsletter, and semi-annual parent conferences
4. Provides a variety of ways that families can participate in the program
5. Encourages parents to participate in the program

To ensure a well-run, purposeful program responsive to participant needs

1. Assesses program supplies and materials needed before implementing activities
2. Coordinates and helps supervise aides and volunteers working in the classroom
3. Maintains written plans on a weekly basis
4. Assesses children's needs and developmental progress on an ongoing basis
5. Uses the results of assessment to plan activities

To maintain a commitment to professionalism

1. Promotes the center's philosophy and educational objectives
2. Supports the center's code of ethical conduct
3. Engages in ongoing staff development to improve personal and professional skills
4. Supports the professional growth and development of colleagues by sharing materials and information and providing helpful feedback and encouragement
5. Attends staff meetings, workshops, and in-service training provided by the center

Personal Qualities and Special Job Characteristics:

Must be physically able to perform the job of a preschool teacher (e.g., able to lift children and/or equipment up to 40 lbs; able to stoop, bend, sit, and stand for extended periods of time). Must have a warm, supportive attitude toward children. Must be reliable. Must be flexible in receiving assignments or adapting to changes in the program. Must be willing to accept supervision in order to improve work performance. Must be willing to perform other duties as required.

In writing a job description, Albrecht (2002) recommends that you think about what competence means in relation to the specific job. What general and specific knowledge does the person need to have? What skills are necessary to perform the job satisfactorily? What dispositions are essential or desirable to be successful in the position? What specific physical and mental requirements need to be included as special job characteristics? Summarize these items in the last section of the job description. Be sure to add a general statement about "other duties as required" to underscore the point that the responsibilities listed are not all-inclusive.

There are several excellent resources you may want to refer to when writing the job descriptions for your program (Albrecht, 2002; Sciarra & Dorsey, 2002; Storm, 1985; Travis & Perreault, 1981). Remember, however, that government agencies and courts regard job descriptions as prime evidence of job requirements. Consult an employment attorney or human resources consultant to review your center's job descriptions and update them annually.

Concise, well-written job descriptions are essential because they can serve as a template for designing a performance appraisal form for each role. Appendix B provides a blank performance appraisal form (Worksheet #11) for the position of Preschool Teacher. You can use this form as an example when constructing your own. This section includes sample peer observation and performance appraisal forms completed for Shelly at The Children's Corner.

Note how the performance appraisal form focuses on the frequency of behavior (from *seldom* to *always*) and on specific results the individual has achieved rather than providing a subjective evaluation (*poor* to *excellent*) of traits or behaviors. This is purposeful. If you really believe that the primary goal of evaluation is to help your teachers improve, then your subjective judgments of their performance become less important. Your role should not be one of conferring judgment, but rather one of providing clear and honest feedback about behavior. The most useful part of this performance

appraisal form will be the anecdotal notes you write in the comments section. It is here that you provide a summary of the informal and formal observational data you have accumulated during the year as well other data that has been collected which pertains to the specific criterion being evaluated.

Conducting the Performance Appraisal Conference

At least once a year you will want to schedule a formal performance appraisal conference. This session includes a discussion about the progress made on staff development action plans throughout the year. The scope of this conference is larger, however, than merely evaluating the progress of the teacher's action plan; it includes an appraisal of the teacher's overall performance during the year.

Teachers should be asked to complete a performance appraisal themselves and bring it to the conference with whatever documentation they wish. Particularly teachers at the consolidation, renewal, and maturity stages of their careers should be encouraged to develop portfolios as a means of compiling and tracking their activities and improvements during the previous year. This shift of responsibility is purposeful. It changes the nature of the teacher's role in the performance appraisal process from a passive one to an active one. The point is that the director should not be the only one held responsible for reviewing performance. Performance appraisal is the joint responsibility of the teacher and director and should be promoted as such.

If performance appraisal is perceived as an ongoing process throughout the year that culminates at the annual performance appraisal conference, then there should be no surprises for the employee. In other words, because the individual has had regular informal feedback through the year and has played an active role in documenting level of performance and areas in need of improvement, the director's role is dramatically altered from one of conferring judgment and assigning blame to one of nurturing reflection and problem solving. Certainly the director and teacher will want to discuss those areas where there may be

Peer Observation

Name of colleague observed ___Shelly___   Date: ___April 23___

As you observe, please note comments about the following aspects of the classroom environment: interactions between the teacher and children; interactions between the teacher and other co-workers or volunteers; interactions between the teacher and parents; the physical arrangement of space; the curriculum; and health, nutrition, and safety aspects of the classroom.

Aspects of this classroom I was impressed with include . . .

1. Wonderful gross motor activities! The obstacle course was a real hit with the children.

2. Great looking bulletin boards. Nicely organized science area too. The butterfly display is impressive.

3. The post office theme kit stimulated some wonderful interactions between the children in the dramatic play corner this morning.

Aspects of this classroom that might be improved include . . .

1. You could include a few more books and pictures that promote cultural diversity.

2. Try not to schedule two art projects on the same day that require so much adult supervision.

3. You could use a few more challenging puzzles for your older 4s. Check with me. I have some you can borrow.

Signed ___Christine___

Performance Appraisal—Preschool Teacher

Name: _Shelly_ Date _May 20_

To establish and maintain a safe and healthy learning environment

	Seldom	Sometimes	Frequently	Always	Comments
1. Designs appropriate room arrangement			✓		Excellent progress in meeting target goal
2. Plans and implements a nutritious snack program				✓	Nice parent comments about snacks 11/10, 4/23
3. Promotes healthy eating practices		✓			Don't forget the hand washing!
4. Maintains a safe environment			✓		Peer comment 1/12 about cleaning supplies
5. Posts necessary health and safety information				✓	Contributed an article from Young Children to resource bulletin board
6. Maintains an orderly learning environment			✓		Has begun to label learning centers; nice science area—peer comment 4/23

To advance physical and intellectual competence

	Seldom	Sometimes	Frequently	Always	Comments
1. Provides a balance between child- and teacher-initiated activities		✓			Moving in this direction. Still somewhat inflexible in adapting plans, 1/15 observation
2. Provides a balance between quiet and active learning activities				✓	Excellent music activities, peer comment 4/10
3. Uses equipment and materials for indoor and outdoor play that promote children's physical development				✓	Great aerobics activities, obstacle course, peer comment 4/23
4. Involves children in planning and implementing activities		✓			Moving toward this. Have observed increase in involvement of children during circle time
5. Provides an integrated curriculum that meets the needs of individual children		✓			Still too much emphasis on whole-group instruction in literacy and science content areas
6. Plans and implements experiences that promote language and literacy development				✓	Excellent drama/story reenactment, observations 1/15, 3/14
7. Plans and implements activities that promote the acquisition of number concepts			✓		Shared math article with staff; improved use of math manipulatives since February

To support social and emotional development and provide positive guidance

	Seldom	Sometimes	Frequently	Always	Comments
1. Plans and implements hands-on activities that develop positive self-esteem		✓			Activities still too craft oriented
2. Plans and implements hands-on activities that develop social skills			✓		From observations 1/15, 3/14 and from your journal reflections, good growth in this area
3. Plans and implements culturally diverse experiences	✓				Peer observation 4/23. We'll be having a workshop on this topic in the fall
4. Uses and promotes positive guidance techniques			✓		Greatly improved ★★★ Good job!!
5. Provides a wide variety of creative and expressive activities				✓	Wonderful dramatic play theme kits
6. Establishes routines with smooth transition periods			✓		Journal reflections show improvement
7. Communicates with children at their developmental level			✓		Interactive skills show improvement since December
8. Encourages children to be independent		✓			Encourage children to serve snack

To establish positive and productive relationships with families

	Seldom	Sometimes	Frequently	Always	Comments
1. Relates assessment information to parents and offers support for dealing with children at different stages			✓		Parent interactions sometimes abrupt and rushed at the end of the day
2. Plans and conducts home visits				✓	On schedule too! Great
3. Promotes communication with parents through progress notes, monthly newsletter, and parent conferences		✓			Be sure to let Pat proofread your newsletters. Many typos ☺
4. Provides a variety of ways that families can participate in the program		✓			It is natural to feel uncomfortable in this area during your first year of teaching
5. Encourages parents to participate in the program		✓			This will be easier next year

To ensure a well-run, purposeful program responsive to participant needs

	Seldom	Sometimes	Frequently	Always	Comments
1. Assesses program supplies and materials needed before implementing activities				✓	Well-organized system
2. Coordinates and helps supervise aides and volunteers working in the classroom			✓		This will become easier as routines are established
3. Maintains written plans on a weekly basis				✓	Always available and on time!
4. Assesses children's needs and developmental progress on an ongoing basis			✓		Increased observation time has aided this process; anecdotal notes show progress
5. Uses the results of assessment to plan activities			✓		Improving

To maintain a commitment to professionalism

	Seldom	Sometimes	Frequently	Always	Comments
1. Promotes the center's philosophy and objectives			✓		This will be easier in subsequent years
2. Supports the center's code of ethical conduct			✓		Watch the sharing of confidential information; one parent very upset
3. Engages in ongoing staff development to improve personal and professional skills				✓	Your enthusiasm and stamina in sticking to your action plan is commendable!
4. Supports the professional growth and development of colleagues by sharing materials and information				✓	Excellent! Very open and supportive; shares ideas and resources freely
5. Attends staff meetings, workshops, and in-service training provided by the center				✓	Didn't miss a single staff meeting!

Additional comments: Shelly has experienced tremendous growth professionally this year. She established a good working relationship with her mentor, Pat. As a result, the organization and flow of her classroom saw a marked improvement. Her observation skills have aided in providing more individualized planning and a better managed learning environment.

Supervisor Martha

discrepant perceptions about the teacher's level of performance, but usually these are minor if a trusting, open relationship has existed throughout the year.

Albrecht (1989) underscores the importance of separating competency and compensation issues in a center's performance appraisal system. Performance appraisal that focuses on competency must be perceived by teachers as ongoing, involving informal feedback about the achievement of goals on the staff development action plan and more formal discussions such as the performance appraisal conference where overall performance is reviewed. Compensation, on the other hand, is discussed upon hiring and then again on a semi-annual or annual basis, with the outcome of the review being the determination of salary or wage adjustment.

Albrecht believes this allows the director to tie compensation to the larger context of the center. She states, "Whereas competency discussions focus on an individual's teaching skills, compensation discussions focus on the individual's connection with and contribution to the center as a whole" (p. 38).

Tact is making a point without making an enemy

Albrecht goes on to say that compensation variables include regularity of attendance, initiative, progress toward completion of additional education and training, possession of special skills, special contributions to the management of the program, special training or certificates, and assignment of hours, in addition to overall teaching performance.

The performance appraisal conference should focus on the future. If a teacher needs improvement, it makes little sense to dwell on the past. Concentrating on the past seldom motivates people to improve their performance. Concentrating on the future, however, gives the teacher a blueprint for achieving change.

Perhaps most important to keep in mind is that your performance appraisal of each employee is a legal document. As such, it should chronicle performance and provide a time frame for needed improvements. This information may become critical should it become necessary to initiate an disciplinary action or terminate an employee at some future date.

Common Errors in Conducting Performance Appraisal

Research conducted in business and industry about potential pitfalls of the performance appraisal (Shaw et al., 1995; Schwind, 1987) is also relevant to the field of early childhood education. The following are several potential shortcomings of the performance appraisal that you must keep in mind if the process is to be a productive one.

Irrelevant or meaningless criterion. It seems so obvious that the criteria that form the basis for performance appraisal must be relevant and meaningful, yet many performance appraisal instruments fall short in this area. *Promotes an understanding of number concepts* may be a valid criterion for a preschool teacher, but would need to be modified as a criterion for an infant teacher. The best way to ensure that the performance appraisal criteria are relevant is to make sure they are derived from the job description—a job description in which the employee has had input.

Inappropriate scale anchors. The scale anchors used to assess performance (e.g., *poor* to *outstanding* or *sometimes* to *always*) must be appropriate for the specific criterion. Most behaviors are best assessed using a frequency scale (*seldom, sometimes, frequently, always*). Using a scale such as poor to outstanding is not wise because it implies a qualitative judgment that is more difficult to define. In other words, what constitutes outstanding when you are measuring a behavior like *promotes an understanding of number concepts*? Using such scale anchors can lead to misinterpretation about expectations for behavior.

Leniency. No one likes to play the role of the bad guy. Particularly in early childhood education, we pride ourselves on being empathetic and nurturing. But directors' desire to be liked by their employees can get in the way of an effective performance appraisal. While candid, honest feedback is difficult to give, successful directors understand it is necessary if teachers are to improve.

Undersampling. Perhaps the most frequent complaint voiced by teachers is that their administrators base their evaluations on too little evidence. "She observed me the morning that Michael decided to have a temper tantrum right in the middle of circle time!" "Wouldn't you know, it was raining, the gym was being painted and was off limits, so there I was trapped in the classroom with these hyper kids all day when my supervisor came to evaluate me." No doubt these frustrations surface when teachers feel their directors base their decisions about performance on an insufficient sampling of behavior. An annual performance appraisal that is based on just one or a few days of observation cannot possibly provide a full and accurate picture of a teacher's performance. As mentioned earlier, multiple sources of evidence gathered over an extended period of time are the best protection for ensuring that undersampling doesn't occur.

The halo effect. Another pitfall of the performance appraisal is the tendency of evaluators to let one dominant or salient characteristic of a teacher cloud their judgment about behavior in other areas. Bonnie's appraisal of Jessica's performance in the vignette shared earlier was in part due to the halo effect. Jessica's enthusiastic and friendly disposition with the children and parents led Bonnie to overlook her shortcomings in the area of maintaining a healthful environment. Just being conscious of this tendency can help you decrease the possibility of letting the halo effect impact your judgment. Precise criteria also help.

The recent-event effect. Given the complexity of the director's job and the countless number of interactions that demand attention every day, it is easy to forget events that transpired a week, a month, or a year ago. Consequently, there is a tendency to remember the more recent, critical events in a teacher's performance. This could be a problem if the recent events are not representative

of overall performance for the year. If a parent has just complained to you about a teacher, for example, you are likely to weight that piece of evidence more heavily than earlier assessments of the teacher's performance. Anecdotal notes and frequent recorded observations can serve to provide a more accurate profile of a teacher's overall performance throughout the year. Such records also help you see patterns in behavior rather than focusing on single recent incidents.

Refining Your Present Performance Appraisal System

Danielson and McGreal (2000) remind us that teachers change their behavior in the classroom only when they want to do so. They must perceive themselves as partners in the system. The best way to establish and/or change your methods of performance appraisal is to ask for help from your teachers. If your staff is large, recruit a representative group. Try to include a variety of teachers at different career stages. A good place to begin is to ask which components of the present performance appraisal system they like, which parts they don't, and why not.

A necessary part of this review should be the critical examination of current job descriptions and performance appraisal forms. The examples provided in Appendix B can provide a template for you and your staff to refine those that you already have in place. By starting with an analysis of each job, teachers will be intimately involved in structuring the support systems needed to guarantee higher levels of performance in the future. In addition, this kind of cooperative endeavor will set a precedent for future collaborative improvement projects that you might want to consider.

Linking Staff Development to Your Center's Career Ladder

Staff development and performance appraisal practices cannot exist in a vacuum. They need an organizational framework to support them. A career ladder is such a framework. Establishing a career ladder for personnel in your early childhood organization is a logical step for a program wishing to implement a comprehensive model of professional development. A career ladder provides the organizational framework to support good staff development and performance appraisal practices. The differentiated staffing patterns that comprise a career ladder occur when job roles are clearly defined and delineated. Each level in the ladder has certain expectations and specific responsibilities, indicating a minimum level of education. The experience necessary for the position is also indicated. Salary and benefits are commensurate with the level of the job within the career ladder.

Salary scales and career ladders, by definition, place the employee with the lowest amount of education and experience at the base of the vertical scale. Job responsibilities, salary, and benefits would also be at the lowest level. As the education, experience, and responsibilities of the employee increase, the worker progresses up the career ladder. Salary, benefits, and duties increase accordingly (Bloom, 1993a, 1993b; Neugebauer, 1994).

A career ladder clearly establishes the guidelines for advancement within the organization. In this way it supports the personal and professional development of the individual. The value of a career ladder model for an early childhood program is that individuals, in consultation with their supervisors, are allowed to move at their own pace, setting personal priorities and goals that are consistent with the overall goals and mission of the center. The model supports equity and fairness in pay and opportunities for promotion. Further, by tracking the upward career movement of staff, a director can better anticipate staffing needs and implement leadership succession plans.

Assumptions About Career Ladders

Although career ladders are relatively new in the field of early childhood, a substantial amount of research has been conducted regarding career ladders in public school programs at the elementary and secondary level (ATE, 1985; Brandt, 1990; Burden, 1987). From this research, several reasons emerge as a rationale for implementing a career ladder in early childhood organizations.

▶ A career ladder strengthens and unifies the structure and organization of a center and improves the teaching/learning process by providing clear job responsibilities. When workers know what is expected of them, they are able to do a better job. This, in turn, empowers teachers and helps them be more effective.

▶ A career ladder results in a more effective use of teachers' talents and abilities. A hierarchy of roles and responsibilities rewards teachers who are good and provides incentive for those who need improvement. Identifying the most capable teachers on a staff allows administrators to use these teachers as mentors for others. For example, a teacher who is gifted at nurturing children's artistic expression should be encouraged (and rewarded) for sharing this ability with others.

▶ A career ladder provides incentives for staff at different career stages. Currently the teaching profession is front-loaded—that is, most rewards are given to teachers within the first five years of service. This practice discourages longevity in the field. Promotion within the ranks of teaching results in a stronger commitment to the profession and a greater retention of competent teachers.

▶ A career ladder encourages a better pattern of initial teacher induction and gives focus to on-the-job development. By firmly establishing a system of teachers who serve as mentors to younger, less experienced staff, the beginning teacher is automatically provided with a support system to aid and encourage development.

Mertens and Yarger (1988) view the differentiation of staffing as a way to make teaching more professional and a more attractive career. They concur with other educational leaders that "career ladders provide ways staff members can rise to positions of importance with more responsibility, leadership, and status within a setting" (p. 33). In sum, a considerable amount of evidence points to the conclusion that career ladders provide a way to empower teachers and encourage them to stay in the field of early childhood education.

Developing a Career Ladder for Your Center

Because each early childhood program is unique in its philosophy, goals, and needs, each center must develop its own distinctive version of a career ladder. By reviewing the roles and responsibilities of staff, budget limitations, and the professional goals of your center, you can design a career ladder that is responsive to your center's unique character.

A good career ladder provides a hierarchy based on differing roles for personnel within the center. The education and experience needed for each role must be clearly defined, as are corresponding salaries and benefits. The five-step progression of professional categories presented in Table 7.2 provides a useful model from which to develop a career ladder for your center. The structure of this model is consistent with the professional categories proposed by the National Association for the Education of Young Children (1993).

Table 7.2 begins with Level I, Step I, an apprentice teacher/aide position with the minimum qualifications required to work in a teaching position at a center. While a few individuals will be hired with the minimal qualifications required of this position, most employees will enter the organization with higher qualifications. At the time of initial hiring, an assessment of overall qualifications can be made and a decision regarding the appropriate level of entry. For example, a teacher having just completed a baccalaureate degree in early childhood education with no formal experience might need to begin work at Level II, Step 3. Then as the teacher achieves one year of experience, advancement to Level III, Step 1 would be appropriate.

While this model is broad and intended to encompass a wide range of positions in a center, it can be tailored to meet the specific demands of your early childhood program. Each step requires the professional to achieve the needed education and experience before applying for the next level within the organization. A variety of roles are avail-

able at each of the five professional levels, leaving options for those career professionals at the higher levels who choose to stay in the classroom yet want to diversify their service within the center.

Step 1. Identify roles. Earlier in this chapter in discussing the performance appraisal process, the responsibilities for a typical preschool teacher in a center-based program were defined. Table 7.3 provides a brief description of the other professional roles that may exist in a program along with requisite qualifications. The role titles and qualifications for teaching and administrative staff are consistent with those promoted in the *Program Administration Scale* (Talan & Bloom, 2004) and NAEYC's teacher education guidelines (Hyson, 2003). The different roles at any particular center will vary, of course, depending on the size of the program and the needs of the center. A small program may not necessitate a family resource coordinator. Likewise, in a small program, the director may serve as both education coordinator and program administrator.

One of the strongest benefits resulting from an established set of professional categories is greater consistency in the nomenclature used in early childhood programs around the country. The lack of consistency in job titles in the field of early childhood education is one of the principal roadblocks to achieving professional status. There still exists much confusion from program to program about job titles and requisite qualifications. When fully implemented, a comprehensive career lattice for the field that uses agreed-upon professional categories with corresponding roles and job titles should help eliminate this confusion.

Step 2. Set salaries. Using an index scale, salaries can be included as part of your center's career ladder. With 1.00 as the baseline for the professional employee at Level I, Step I, the index allows the center administrator to set a prorated system that increases salaries as the staff member moves up the ladder during his or her career. For example, in Table 7.2, if the salary index of 1.00 equaled $13,000 per year, the index of 1.25 would equal $16,250 and the highest paid position at an

Table 7.2

Professional Categories

Level	Step	Index	Education	Experience	Roles
V	1	4.00	PhD or EdD in early childhood education or related discipline	5 or more years	Administrator Education Coordinator Family Resource Coordinator
IV	3	3.75	Master's degree, 21 s.h. in cd/ece, and 21 s.h. in area of specialization	3 or more years	Administrator Education Coordinator Family Resource Coordinator
	2	3.50	Master's degree, 21 s.h. in cd/ece, and 15 s.h. in area of specialization	2 or more years	Administrator Education Coordinator Family Resource Coordinator
	1	3.25	Enrollment in master's degree program, 21 s.h. in cd/ece, and 9 s.h. in area of specialization	1 or more years	Administrator Education Coordinator Family Resource Coordinator Lead Teacher
III	3	3.00	Baccalaureate degree, 21 s.h. in cd/ece, and 21 s.h. in area of specialization	3 or more years	Administrator Educational Coordinator Family Resource Coordinator Lead Teacher
	2	2.75	Baccalaureate degree, 21 s.h. in cd/ece, and 15 s.h. in area of specialization	2 or more years	Administrator Educational Coordinator Family Resource Coordinator Lead Teacher
	1	2.50	Baccalaureate degree or 90 s.h. college credit, 21 s.h. in cd/ece, and 9 s.h. in area of specialization	1 or more years	Lead Teacher Teacher
II	3	2.25	Associate degree or 60 s.h. college credit with 30 s.h. in cd/ece	2 or more years	Teacher
	2	2.00	Associate degree or 60 s.h. of college credit with 21 s.h. in cd/ece	1 or more years	Teacher
	1	1.75	30 s.h. of college credit with 12 s.h. in cd/ece or CDA/CCP		Teacher Apprentice Teacher/Aide
I	3	1.50	15 s.h. of college credit with 9 s.h. in cd/ece	2 or more years	Apprentice Teacher/Aide
	2	1.25	9 s.h. of college credit with 6 s.h. in cd/ece	1 or more years	Apprentice Teacher/Aide
	1	1.00	High school diploma or GED plus enrollment in cd/ece course		Apprentice Teacher/Aide

Table 7.3

Differentiated Staffing Roles for a Center-Based Program

Apprentice Teacher/Aide

Description: The Apprentice Teacher/Aide is a member of the teaching team who assists in the implementation of classroom activities under the direct supervision of a Teacher or Lead Teacher. The Apprentice Teacher/Aide performs the daily, routine tasks that establish the basic foundation for a healthy and safe environment.

Minimum qualifications: The Apprentice Teacher/Aide position is an entry-level position requiring no formal experience in child development or early childhood education. The Apprentice Teacher/Aide must be 18 years of age and possess a high school diploma or GED, and be enrolled in a credit-bearing child development or early childhood course.

Teacher

Description: The Teacher is a member of the teaching team who shares responsibility with the Lead Teacher for the care and education of an assigned group of children. The Teacher is responsible for implementing curriculum, supervising children, communicating with parents, and providing a healthy and safe environment for children.

Minimum qualifications: Successful completion of 30 semester hours of college coursework including or supplemented by 12 semester hours in child development or early childhood education or the completion of a training program to acquire the CDA or CCP Credential.

Lead Teacher

Description: The Lead Teacher is the member of the teaching team with the highest educational qualifications assigned to teach a group of children. She/he is responsible for daily lesson planning, parent conferences, child assessment, and curriculum planning. The Lead Teacher functions as the team leader and supervises other members of the teaching team.

Minimum qualifications: A baccalaureate degree or 90 semester hours of college credit including or supplemented by 21 semester hours of coursework in child development or early childhood education and 9 semester hours in an area of specialization.

Administrator

Description: The Administrator is the person located on-site who has the primary responsibility for planning, implementing, and evaluating the early care and education program. The Administrator monitors the administrative systems of the center, including the fiscal management of the program, recruitment and development of personnel, facility management, board relations, marketing, and public relations. The Administrator also serves as liaison to professional organizations and regulatory agencies.

Minimum qualifications: A baccalaureate degree including or supplemented by 21 semester hours of coursework in child development or early childhood education and 15 semester hours of specialized coursework in administration (e.g., human resources management, legal issues, licensing and regulations, leadership, program evaluation, financial management, marketing, grant writing, advocacy, technology). This position requires two years of experience working in early childhood education.

Education Coordinator

Description: The Education Coordinator is responsible for implementing the educational goals and objectives of the center. The Education Coordinator oversees the planning and implementation of the curriculum; assists with supervision, training, and evaluation of staff; and supports program evaluation and accreditation.

Minimum qualifications: A baccalaureate degree including or supplemented by 21 semester hours of coursework in child development or early childhood education and 15 semester hours of coursework in an area of specialization (e.g., staff supervision, curriculum design, child assessment, mentoring and coaching, program evaluation). This position requires two years of experience working in early childhood education.

Family Resource Coordinator

Description: The Family Resource Coordinator is responsible for planning and implementing the parent involvement and parent education component of an early childhood program. The Family Resource Coordinator also oversees the implementation of child and family services including health nutrition guidance, counseling, and special needs.

Minimum qualifications: A baccalaureate degree including or supplemented by 21 semester hours of coursework in child development or early childhood education and 15 semester hours of specialized coursework in an area of specialization (e.g., family systems theory, family support, parent involvement, counseling, social work). This position requires two years of experience working in early childhood education.

---

index of 4.00 would equal $52,000. By using an index as a basis for salary increases, fair and equitable advancements can be incorporated into the center's organizational structure. Budget planning becomes easier as the present and projected salary needs become clear.

Because advancement to the next professional category largely depends on the attainment of additional education and training, a center may also want to include a parallel system of small increments within each step that are based on years of working experience at the center. It is important that such a system not undermine the intent of the career ladder—to encourage individuals to increase their level of education and training.

Unfortunately, implementing a career ladder doesn't automatically solve the perennial issue facing directors of how to increase the total pool of money allocated for salaries; it only allows one, as Jensen (1979) noted, to "distribute dissatisfaction more equitably." This book does not touch upon how to increase funding, but organizations such as the Center for the Child Care Workforce (CCW/AFTEF) have a number of excellent resources that can help you find creative ways to raise salaries. The popular management magazine for early childhood administrators, *Child Care Information Exchange*, is also a good source of articles on this topic.

Step 3. Establish a menu of benefits. Providing ample employee benefits is problematic for most small businesses in this country. Centers that are part of a large agency network or those sponsored by a parent corporation are fortunate in that they may already have in place a comprehensive benefits plan for their employees. But even small centers can work to increase the amount and variety of benefits offered to staff. Some benefits, like paid preparation time or free lunches, can be provided to all employees. Other benefits, however, can be tied to longevity at the center and an individual's position on the center's career ladder. One way to accomplish this is to establish an indexed menu of benefits.

An index of benefits operates in much the same way as a salary index. Two categories of benefits, professional and personal, can be offered to employees. *Professional benefits* include such things as membership in professional organizations, subscriptions to professional journals, paid days to observe other programs, reimbursement for college classes, and paid conference registrations. *Personal benefits* include such things as health insurance, dental insurance, retirement/pension, child care tuition, paid vacation days, and sick days. Table 7.4 provides a list of the possible personal and professional benefits and an example of how the distribution of benefits could be awarded according to the employee's index level.

How such a benefit system is actually implemented varies from center to center. For example, you could decide that an employee at the 1.00 index level could choose one benefit from each of the personal and professional categories. At the 1.25 index level, another benefit choice could be added; and still another at 1.50. Under such a system, each employee would have the opportunity to choose from the menu of professional and personal benefits. From year to year, choices may change as the needs of the employee change. For example, an employee with a young child may be more interested in health insurance and partial payment of child care tuition. An older employee may choose dental insurance and reimbursement for conference fees. The attractiveness of such a plan is that it is not only equitable, but it also accommodates the changing needs of the individuals working at the center.

While the record keeping involved may be viewed as cumbersome, offering a menu of benefits is clearly advantageous to the employer. Increasing the type and variety of benefits offered to employees can have a direct impact on their level of commitment to the center. By assessing the kinds of benefits employees select from year to year, you can plan a budget for benefits that meets the changing needs of staff. A center with a staff of young teachers who are using child care tuition as a major benefit each year would be able to plan for the lost revenue on child care slots within the center. A center with a staff of older employees who are interested in extended vacations or released time to observe other centers would be able to budget for the hiring of substitutes. Accommodating staff's changing needs in this fashion can't help but increase employee satisfaction and reduce turnover.

Step 4. Determine how individuals advance within the center. The final step in developing a career ladder for your center is to decide on the configuration and progression of steps for advancement. Table 7.5 provides an example of a career ladder configuration for a center. By plotting where each teacher is on the career ladder, you can plan staffing configurations and budget salaries and benefits. For example, Table 7.6 shows the staffing pattern of a full-day program with 140 preschool children divided into 7 classrooms of 20 children each. In this center, the education coordinator also assumes the role of family resource coordinator. In a smaller center, individuals may have additional overlapping roles. The education coordinator and the program administrator could be the same person.

The professional categories listed earlier in Table 7.2 designate a natural progression to be followed as an employee advances within the center. By obtaining education and/or job experience, the employee becomes eligible to assume new roles and responsibilities. Because salaries and benefits are indexed according to each of the steps within the career levels, the incentive to advance is clearly seen by the employee and can be used in charting new staff development goals.

At the time when progress toward achieving staff development goals is assessed, short-term

Table 7.4

Personal and Professional Benefits

Each of these items constitutes one UNIT of benefit.

Personal

- ▶ 25% health insurance
- ▶ 25% disability insurance
- ▶ 25% dental insurance
- ▶ 25% life insurance
- ▶ 25% vision insurance
- ▶ 25% retirement/pension plan
- ▶ 25% child care tuition
- ▶ 25% maternity leave
- ▶ 5 vacation/personal days
- ▶ 5 sick days

Professional

- ▶ membership in a professional association
- ▶ 1/4 tuition reimbursement for a college class
- ▶ 1 day released time to observe other centers
- ▶ conference or workshop registration
- ▶ credential or certification fees
- ▶ subscription to professional journals

Benefit Index

Employees may choose according to their individual needs using the following guidelines:

Index Level

1.00 = 1 personal unit and 1 professional unit
1.25 = 1 personal unit and 2 professional units
1.50 = 2 personal units and 2 professional units
1.75 = 2 personal units and 3 professional units
2.00 = 3 personal units and 3 professional units
2.25 = 3 personal units and 4 professional units
2.50 = 4 personal units and 4 professional units
2.75 = 4 personal units and 5 professional units
3.00 = 5 personal units and 5 professional units
3.25 = 5 personal units and 6 professional units
3.50 = 6 personal units and 6 professional units
3.75 = 6 personal units and 7 professional units
4.00 = 7 personal units and 7 professional units

For example, an employee at the 2.50 index level may choose to use 4 personal units for health insurance (50% paid) plus 10 sick days and 4 professional units for 2 paid days to observe another school plus 1/2 tuition reimbursement for a college class.

Career Ladder Configuration for Professional Staff

Table 7.5

Level	Role — Apprentice Teacher/Aide	Teacher	Lead Teacher	Education Coordinator*	Administrator
V				Step 1	Step 1
IV			Step 1	Step 3 / Step 2 / Step 1	Step 3 / Step 2 / Step 1
III		Step 1	Step 3 / Step 2 / Step 1	Step 3 / Step 2	Step 3 / Step 2
II	Step 1	Step 3 / Step 2 / Step 1			
I	Step 3 / Step 2 / Step 1				

* Family Resource Coordinator career ladder configuration is the same as the Education Coordinator

Table 7.6

Sample Staffing Pattern for Center with 140 Students

TEACHING STAFF

Classroom	Position	Career Level		Index
1.	Lead Teacher	Level III,	Step 3	3.00
	Teacher	Level II,	Step 2	2.00
	Aide	Level I,	Step 1	1.00
2.	Lead Teacher	Level IV,	Step 1	3.25
	Teacher	Level II,	Step 1	1.75
	Aide	Level I,	Step 1	1.00
3.	Lead Teacher	Level III,	Step 1	2.50
	Teacher	Level II,	Step 3	2.25
	Aide	Level I,	Step 3	1.50
4.	Lead Teacher	Level III,	Step 2	2.75
	Teacher	Level II,	Step 2	2.00
	Aide	Level I	Step 2	1.25
5.	Lead Teacher	Level III,	Step 2	2.75
	Teacher	Level II,	Step 2	2.00
	Aide	Level I,	Step 2	1.25
6.	Lead Teacher	Level IV,	Step 1	3.25
	Teacher	Level II,	Step 1	1.75
	Aide	Level I,	Step 1	1.00
7.	Lead Teacher	Level III,	Step 3	3.00
	Teacher	Level II,	Step 2	2.00
	Aide	Level I,	Step 1	1.00

SPECIALTY ROLES

Education Coordinator/Parent Resource Coordinator	Level III,	Step 3	3.00
Program Administrator	Level IV,	Step 2	3.50

SUPPORT STAFF

Administrative assistant
Cook

and long-term professional opportunities for the staff member should be discussed. Helping an employee reach new professional goals is the responsibility of both the employer and the employee. Together a plan can be implemented to aid the professional advancement of each staff member. In this way a center shows a commitment to staff and a willingness to retain and improve the quality of work life for its employees.

A Final Word

In this chapter we have seen how the performance appraisal process and a career ladder for professional growth can serve as the organizational framework to support staff development. Together these two aspects of center operations can help ensure that goals for individual change become a reality.

The performance appraisal process detailed in this chapter rest on the premise that all employees, regardless of how outstanding their current teaching performance, can stretch and grow. The constructive feedback gleaned from the performance appraisal conference provides the rationale for different areas that need to be addressed in a teacher's staff development action plan. The entire nature of the experience is changed from an adversarial one to a supportive one. When done properly, the performance appraisal process thus serves a dual purpose—it acknowledges and rewards teachers' strengths while helping expand their field of vision of what they can become.

If staff development and performance appraisal processes are tied in with a career ladder for professional advancement, then true changes in teachers' level of professional competence are more likely to occur. By setting clear standards and rewards for advancement, a center's career ladder helps individuals make decisions based on personal needs and goals. In essence, teachers are helped to take control of their own career development. When implemented, these organizational structures and processes serve as the supporting framework to energize employees to higher levels of professional competence and job satisfaction.

One thing worse than training people and losing them is not training them and keeping them.

Zig Ziglar

Chapter 8

Connecting Individual and Organizational Needs

The point has been stressed in this book that the development of individuals within a center and the development of the center itself are inextricably related. Understanding your center as an integrated whole composed of many interconnected parts will help you see the big picture—how the issues confronting your center relate to the issues experienced by staff. As an agent of change, you are the one who sets the tone, shapes the expectations, and creates the climate of collaboration that connects individual efforts with the larger vision of the center. Figure 8.1 visually captures this dynamic relationship.

How does this meshing of organizational and individual needs happen? This chapter explores the issue from two perspectives. First it looks at some of the steps you can take to reduce people's resistance to change; then it provides suggestions for ways you can nurture norms of collaboration in the work environment. The result is a professional learning community—a place where people come together with a shared purpose of constructing new understandings together. To set the stage for this discussion, let's return to our case study, The Children's Corner, as an example of the change process in action.

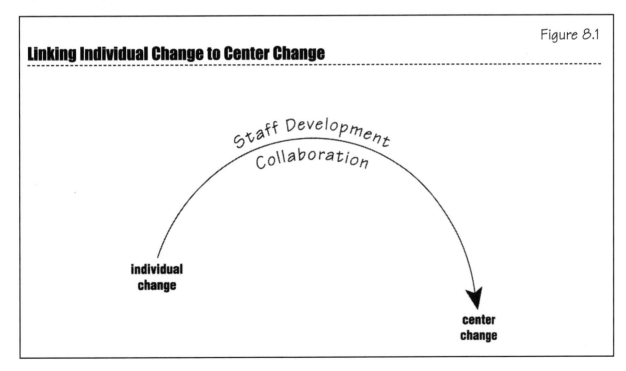

Figure 8.1

Linking Individual Change to Center Change

Staff Development
Collaboration

individual change

center change

Martha was pleased. Her decision to keep anecdotal notes and develop an individual profile for each teacher helped her get to know each of her teachers better. It also helped her understand why some individuals on her staff embraced change while others resisted so strongly. Creating opportunities for teachers to learn more about each other's personal lives, their previous work experiences, career aspirations, and special interests was beginning to break down the norms of isolation and competition that had characterized staff relations. Her efforts were also beginning to dissipate some of the negativity that had fueled tension between certain cliques of teachers. Martha was particularly pleased with her decision to have Shelly observe in Georgia's classroom. This decision bolstered Georgia's confidence and reduced some of her resistance to new ideas.

At her goal-setting conference with each teacher in the fall, Martha asked the teachers to assess their own strengths and the areas they felt could be improved. Together they set professional development goals that built on the teacher's strengths. Martha still felt that there were many issues that needed to be addressed at the center, but she also understood that change would not come swiftly. She simply could not rush the process. She was hopeful that if she could win her teachers' trust on a one-to-one basis, she could then get them to begin to work more cooperatively and collaboratively as a group.

Overcoming Resistance to Change

Change may be implemented at an organizational level, but it is experienced on an individual level. While there is certainly a difference between voluntary and imposed change, all real change involves loss, anxiety, and struggle. Failure to recognize this phenomenon as natural means that you may end up ignoring important aspects of the change process or missing opportunities to support individuals in dealing with the issues that accompany the change process.

Resistance to change occurs for a variety of reasons, but most often resistant behaviors are rooted in fears of loss of autonomy and self-esteem or fear that one might fail in the midst of the change process. Dealing with resistance involves not only an understanding of the change process, but also an awareness of what the change represents to individuals on a personal level. Early childhood administrators who work objectively to depersonalize resistance try to build rapport with teachers and support them with an empathic point of view (Saxl, 1989).

Tuning in to the Psychological Element

It is tempting to think of change in early childhood programs as an impersonal event rather than a highly personal process. But when you acknowledge the fact that organizational change can only come about through changes in the way people think and act, it becomes clear that you can't ignore the psychological element. Each person on your staff is different and will respond to change in his or her own idiosyncratic way. The degree to which you are attuned to the psychological states of teachers involved in the change process will help determine one of the conditions for successful change. As a change agent you set the stage for change when you cue into teachers' levels of concern, the problems they perceive as inherent in the change process, and the resistance they exhibit.

Hopkins (1990) studied school climate and the psychological state of individual teachers. He assessed how teachers with different psychological states who worked in different school climates used or ignored new educational ideas. He describes teachers' psychological states in terms of their level of confidence, their overall interest in growth, their interest in seeking out new experiences, and their sense of collegiality within the group. He found that those teachers who performed at a higher level of self-fulfillment and who were situated in schools that valued collaboration and collegiality were more likely to make use of new educational ideas. Hopkins concluded that when a school is committed to a more democratic work climate in which collegiality, collaboration, and communication are prevalent forms of school management, individual teachers adapt more readily to school changes.

What is perhaps most relevant from Hopkins's research to our present discussion of change in early care and education programs is his analysis of how teachers change in their psychological states.

Hopkins analyzed four categories of teachers with respect to their psychological states. Teachers at the lowest self-actualizing level expressed a lack of self-confidence. Their main concern was focused on protecting themselves from losing control of their class. Hopkins found that these teachers were far less able to implement new ideas in practice than more confident teachers who had a strong self-concept and whose energy was focused on growth. He stresses that for teachers demonstrating a low-level of self-actualization, it is important to introduce change slowly and in small doses.

The connection between center climate and a teacher's psychological state cannot be overemphasized. Your role as leader is crucial in establishing a positive, open atmosphere that actively supports teachers' growth. Dogmatic directors, as well as those who give only passive support, inhibit teachers from embracing change and achieving their personal and professional goals. Unquestionably, teachers' degree of receptiveness to change is significantly affected by their perception of their administrator's support. It follows, then, that expanding opportunities for teachers to formally discuss, help plan, and implement new educational ideas provides the climate of administrative support for change to take hold.

Understanding the Risk-of-Failure Factor

Tynette Hills once quipped, "Each time we ask a person to change, we ask her or him to take a journey into incompetence." So true. One of the most common reasons why people avoid change is that it represents a personal risk of failure. For many on your staff, the bold changes you may be proposing represent a leap into the unknown. Wallenberg (1980) echoes these sentiments. He says that new beginnings, no matter how simple, are experienced by teachers as both fearful and hopeful. Fear of the unknown can overwhelm a teacher. "I just can't do this." "I'm too old to learn something new." "I've always done it this way. Why should I change now?" These phrases capture the reluctance teachers feel to put themselves on the line, to be vulnerable, to feel incompetent. Change raises the specter of failure in a highly personal way. Many times

these feelings are at a subconscious level. Teachers may not even be aware of why they feel intimidated, angry, or so opposed to a specific change.

Carol, a talented veteran teacher, was given a new age-group of children to teach. She had difficulty adjusting since her tried-and-true curriculum activities just weren't appropriate for younger children. Patricia, her supervisor, visited Carol's class to see how things were going. She expected to see the competent, experienced teacher she knew. Instead, she saw a chaotic room and a teacher whose healthy self-esteem seemed shattered. Patricia resolved to visit more often. Carol saw these visits as intrusive and not supportive. She began to dread her supervisor's observations and just couldn't seem to do anything right when Patricia was there. She became angry, uncooperative, and resistant. Patricia felt rejected by Carol and annoyed at what appeared to be Carol's negative reaction to her new teaching assignment. She began to think that Carol might not be such a good teacher after all.

What can be done to remedy this situation? Patricia, the supervisor, is caught up in her own subjective point of view and thus is unable to help Carol assess her situation objectively. Working with the new age-group of children represents personal failure for Carol. Even experienced teachers like Carol begin to doubt themselves when faced with new situations in which they are not immediately successful. New situations can psychologically remove teachers from areas in which they feel highly successful to areas of unfamiliarity in which they feel unsuccessful, even out of control. Consequently, oppositional behavior such as passive and active withdrawal of support for proposed changes, limiting resources of time and energy, blocking, stalling, and procrastinating may be exhibited. Saxl (1989) says these behaviors serve the function of preventing teachers from viewing themselves as failures.

> *Habits can't be thrown out the upstairs window. They have to be coaxed down the stairs one step at a time.*
>
> Mark Twain

Let's return now to our vignette about Carol and her supervisor to see how their situation might be handled in a proactive, positive way.

Patricia was worried about the difficult relationship she had with Carol, but she was determined to turn this potentially explosive situation around and make it a positive growth experience. She knew Carol was a teacher with extensive background and a great deal of experience. Ordinarily she demonstrated independence and autonomy. Because of Carol's need to adjust to a new age-group of children, Patricia decided, for the time being, that Carol needed additional supervisory support.

Patricia initiated another conversation with Carol in which she acknowledged how difficult it must be for Carol to make the transition to a new age-group. She asked Carol what strategies might be implemented to assist her in building her confidence level. Carol stated that she had felt so physically exhausted lately that she had not had time to track down the books and curriculum aids she wanted to use with the children. Patricia felt she could offer direct help in this area. She then asked Carol if she would like to observe another teacher at the center who taught the same age level. When Carol enthusiastically agreed, Patricia said she thought she could adjust schedules so the two teachers could share information and plan together.

Acknowledging Change as Loss

Change often represents a personal loss for individuals. It may be as simple as a change in secretarial support or a change in the way a classroom is staffed. These seemingly uneventful changes may be experienced as a temporary loss of security until familiarity in the new situation is established. Change requires adjustment—adjustment in new relationships or adjustment in unlearning or modifying old behaviors. When change is introduced, individuals often feel that their former work was not worthwhile in the eyes of administrators or that it was not appreciated. The loss of what was formerly done becomes personally intimidating. "I have never done group time like

that!" "Your idea for a math curriculum will never work here." "We've tried a substitute system like that before, and it didn't work at all."

Change can be perceived as a loyalty conflict where individuals feel that by embracing new approaches, they must reject the old. Unlearning old behaviors is a difficult process, one that involves the feelings and personal concerns of individuals. It is a wise director who understands the link between center change and personal change and views resistance as a means for the individual to preserve autonomy and a feeling that one's work is worthwhile and successful. Resistance is another way for teachers to say, "Your changes threaten my sense of security." Resistance, then, is a form of protection for teachers who worry that not only their work, but their ideas, philosophy, and personal beliefs are threatened by the proposed changes.

Accepting the Fact That Not Everyone Sees Things the Same Way

We've shared several vignettes in this book that provide colorful examples of how individuals view the same situation in vastly different ways. Differing perceptions of reality occur because individuals come to any situation with varied experiences, diverse values and beliefs, and different expectations. Individuals holding different positions in a center have access to different types of information. This in itself can contribute to different perceptions of events. Because not everyone sees things the same way, the likelihood for resistance to change is increased.

Danielson and McGreal (2000) assert that a major hindrance to change in teacher performance is related to the incongruence between organizational expectations and what teachers are in fact required to do. For example, supervisors may expect teachers to improve classroom performance by conducting complicated screening procedures for children and keeping detailed records. Teachers may also be expected to perform these record-keeping procedures during class time when children are present, thus effectively hindering change in classroom performance. Resistance to change may simply be the teachers' only means of protesting unrealistic workload expectations.

Establishing a Collaborative Environment

Collaboration is the vehicle for linking individual change to organizational change and achieving a professional learning community. Saxl (1989) defines collaboration as creating relationships in which influence is mutually shared. Establishing a collaborative work environment involves structuring specific workplace conditions that support cooperative relationships. The process is achieved by developing goal consensus and supporting opportunities for shared decision making. These elements enable teachers to reduce resistance and see the change process as their own.

Working Toward a Common Vision— Achieving Goal Consensus

Achieving lasting organizational change can only occur when individuals in a center feel a sense of commitment and connection to the center. In other words, they share a common vision of what the center could and should be. But before a staff can achieve a common vision, they need to achieve some degree of consensus as to just how a center's philosophy is put into practice through its goals and educational objectives. Having a clear, agreed-upon set of purposes directly affects the center's ability to carry out its mission. If a center's goals are ambiguous, then teachers will feel uncertain about their own teaching practices.

Educational goals and objectives really center on priorities—those things we want children to do, to be, or to have as a result of their early childhood experience. Because teachers have different values, their educational priorities may be different. Goal consensus in many ways reflects both a consensus of value orientations and the ability of individuals to compromise and tolerate differences of opinion. When teachers share goals in work settings, it is an indication that a harmony of purpose exists among the individuals in the center.

A good place to begin in establishing goal consensus among staff is with the center's stated philosophy. This statement can serve as a starting point to help discern differences in interpretation.

This is more difficult than it may appear on the surface. Most philosophical statements are written in vague, abstract language. They are filled with jargon like *child-centered, developmentally appropriate, family friendly,* and *individualized instruction.* These are important concepts, but if true goal consensus is to be achieved, staff need to be able to articulate in behavioral terms just what they mean by each of these phrases.

Involving Staff in Decision Making

Directors who are intent on building a collaborative work environment need to see shared decision making as a priority by setting aside time for teachers to meet concerning different aspects of the program. It is the interaction itself, more than the invitation, that leads to collaboration (Bloom, 2000). Involvement in decision making can take a variety of forms. Joint planning, problem solving, and evaluating are but a few of the ways that staff can work together.

Rosenholtz (1989) notes some of the ways teachers benefit from shared decision making. She states that when teachers have the opportunity to debate issues, they clarify and broaden their own point of view when confronted with their colleagues' varied perspectives. When staff can reason through problems together, it reinforces the notion that a mutual exchange of ideas is the best way to improve everyone's teaching practice. The most valuable benefit derived from shared decision making, however, is that teachers find out that their colleagues have competencies and special skills that complement their own. The process can help teachers identify with and take pleasure in the work of their colleagues. This cannot help but strengthen their connection to others in the center.

> *The most efficient route to bold change is the participation of everyone, every day in incremental change.*
>
> Tom Peters

Setting Conditions for Collaboration

Collaborative work environments don't just happen. Learning to work cooperatively takes skill—skill that may not be in a teacher's repertoire of behaviors. Some teachers may be products of previous work

Martha planned several in-depth staff meetings for the sole purpose of "dissecting our philosophy to arrive at a shared understanding of why we do what we do with children in our classrooms." The first meeting was an unmitigated disaster. Every teacher seemed to be on the defensive. This was particularly true of some of the old timers, who used the forum for espousing their point of view. Martha felt no one was really listening to anyone else. At the second meeting, however, things improved. Martha asked Bea to facilitate the discussion. All of a sudden, what had been a defensive, resistant posture on her behalf now became one of support and encouragement. Martha was heartened. She really felt some progress was being made in the group dynamics among the teachers.

At the third meeting, the teachers really began to open up. The discussion now focused on how individual teachers translated the center's philosophy into specific curricular practices. As the discussion unfolded, some concerns began to surface. Margaret, one of the younger teachers, admitted that she felt intimidated by the parents—most of whom she felt had unrealistic expectations for their children. "They equate learning with worksheets! I just don't know how to respond when they expect that I should be giving their 4-year-olds direct instruction in reading," she confessed. Margaret's comment opened a floodgate of similar concerns. Several other teachers stated that they felt *developmentally appropriate* was a fuzzy term and weren't really sure what it meant precisely.

Martha suggested that since the staff had identified a problem, maybe they should collect some data to find some possible solutions. Teachers agreed to fill out questionnaires about their values and beliefs as well as their perceptions about the center's degree of goal consensus. They also suggested that Martha do a formal observation of teaching practices in each classroom to see how the staff differed in their approaches. Without exception, the teachers expressed an interest in learning more about developmentally appropriate teaching practices.

In a subsequent meeting, when some of the data were shared, Martha couldn't believe the growth in self-analysis that took place. Teachers began to connect general philosophical terms such as *child-initiated* and *individualized instruction* to specific teaching practices. They analyzed their behavior in how they scheduled children's time, how they arranged their classroom space and materials, and how they interacted with children.

Previously the teachers had stated that their problem was parents who had unrealistic expectations for their kids. Now the problem was being recast. Instead of assigning blame to the parents, the teachers were beginning to see that the problem was their own inability to articulate and defend developmentally appropriate practices. Collectively they decided that the best place to start figuring out appropriate teaching practices might be to get involved in NAEYC's program accreditation process. Martha agreed that the self-study phase of accreditation was an excellent place to start. She was confident that as the teachers increased their own awareness of developmentally appropriate practices, their level of confidence would also increase. This in turn would change the adversarial relationship they were experiencing with parents into one in which they could perceive themselves as helping to educate parents as partners in the education of their children.

environments that fostered competition rather than cooperation, where alienation and isolation—the "everyone for himself" attitude—prevailed. Without experience in collaborative decision making, teachers may not know how to adjust their own point of view to support group planning.

Learning to work cooperatively also takes time. It is not uncommon for teachers first introduced to cooperative group experiences to become frustrated with the slowness of the process. It takes time to nurture reciprocity, trust, and supportive relationships. This means that directors must structure multiple opportunities for staff to make decisions together, to solve staff problems together, and to work together in the mutual exchange of instructional ideas and materials that help improve program practices.

Rosenholt (1989) explains why some teachers do not readily collaborate with their colleagues. Most individuals avoid situations that threaten to expose or highlight their instructional uncertainty. She says, "Indeed, under conditions of high uncertainty, colleagues are most apt to interpret requests for help as clear evidence of performance inadequacy" (p. 43). Teachers may or may not be willing to seek help from one another or from their director if they perceive the result will be embarrassing or threatening to their self-esteem. This is probably why in the previous vignette, Carol resisted the initial attempts of her supervisor to help her.

One way to help teachers work collaboratively is to acquaint them with current research on professional learning communities and cooperative learning (DuFour, 2004; Johnson, 1987; Roberts & Pruitt, 2003; Slavin, 1990). Staff development programs that focus on how to develop learning communities and the benefits of cooperative learning encourage teachers to learn and model collaborative behaviors as they develop strategies to use with the children in their classrooms. As they learn about different instructional learning strategies for children, a conscious parallel is drawn between their actions and children's behavior. Collaboration emphasizes highlighting teachers' common goals and arranging tasks so that goals can be achieved only by pooling the collective talent of individuals.

In a professional learning community there is a shift in emphasis from teaching to learning. This means creating opportunities for discussion of practice at every level of the organization. This kind of job-embedded professional development can only happen if there is sufficient opportunity for conversation, reflection, and inquiry. The early childhood programs of Reggio Emila, Italy provide a wonderful case study of professional learning communities in action—where children, teachers, and parents are involved in sharing ideas, engaging in active dialogue, and construction new meanings.

Another way that norms of collaboration can be nurtured is to acquaint teachers with the research on learning styles, behavioral styles, and temperament (Gregorc, 1982; McCarthy, 1996; Myers, 1998; Bolton & Bolton, 1996). Sharing this information with staff and allowing them opportunities to assess their own learning styles and temperaments can increase their appreciation for differences among people. Appreciating individual differences is the first step in building the sense of cohesion that binds people together in a cooperative spirit. It was for this reason that Martha included a staff

in-service session on the topic of learning styles as one of her objectives on the action plan that you read at the end of Chapter 4.

Team teaching and mentoring are also powerful tools for increasing helping behaviors among teachers. Individuals who team teach together, sharing classroom responsibilities, have built-in, ongoing opportunities to talk about their educational objectives and instructional strategies. In contrast to teachers in isolated settings, Rosenholtz (1989) says team teachers communicate more, are more experienced in decision making, and work more closely with their supervisors regarding decisions. She also believes that team teaching results in a substantial increase in the teachers' ability to give and take advice.

Mentoring has also been shown to be particularly effective in reducing teacher isolation and increasing staff cohesiveness. The supportive role that the mentor plays in guiding the professional development of a less-experienced teacher has the ancillary effect of reducing some of the supervisory responsibility of directors. Driscoll, Peterson, and Kauchak (1985) state, "What separates new teachers from experienced professionals is not only years of experience, but also the knowledge and skills that have developed over those years. Mentoring systems provide a process for passing on this knowledge to beginning teachers in a systematic rather than haphazard way" (p. 108).

In their research, Driscoll and her colleagues found that mentoring programs increase not only teachers' productivity, but also their commitment to the profession, thus preventing teacher attrition. This is important because the foundation for collegial, cooperative relationships rests in large part on the sense of staff stability at a center. Centers that experience high turnover will have more difficulty in both initiating and sustaining collaboration.

What Have We Learned From The Children's Corner?

Let's review the case study we've shared in this book and see what lessons we can learn from Martha's experience. We've followed her progress over her first year as director of The Children's Corner. Clearly the most important lesson Martha learned was that change takes time. In September Martha was confronted with the challenge of reducing the discrepancy between the stated philosophy of the center (structure) and the everyday teaching practices (processes) that were in place. She was also confronted with some teachers who were uncooperative and occasionally hostile. But Martha was patient and determined.

Martha began with a top-down model of change in order to modify the center norms of isolation and resistance. She hoped her efforts would create a more collaborative climate for teachers. Her goal was to build a unified team out of her staff. She began by making some changes in her own administrative behavior that would model the collaborative, open, and trusting behavior she hoped to nurture in her staff.

As the year progressed, Martha and her staff implemented individual action plans that furthered the goal of achieving a collaborative environment for the center. Teachers began sharing resources, observing each other's classrooms, and working together to try out new ideas. Staff meetings evolved from a top-down directed approach to one where teachers took a more active role in determining the agenda and facilitating the discussions.

It was not until the spring that teachers internalized a collective sense of responsibility for center change and improvement. When it happened, though, the effect was powerful. Martha was amazed at how the teachers zeroed in on a fundamental problem in the center—the lack of a shared vision of what developmentally appropriate practice really meant in action. Martha facilitated the problem clarification discussion, helped the teachers articulate a goal, and assisted them in deciding where they wanted to direct their energies the following year. Martha felt their action plan was a bit too ambitious, but she also knew good action plans are not carved in stone. This one could be modified as activities were initiated the following September.

Case Study: The Children's Corner

Martha did not want to lose the momentum generated at the last few staff meetings. She feared that if summer vacation came without a well-thought-out plan of action committed to paper, the enthusiasm and cooperation she had seen during the previous month might be lost. She sent a memo to the staff suggesting a half-day retreat on a Saturday in mid-May. Initially Bea and Mary indicated that they had conflicting plans, but when Georgia and the rest of the staff enthusiastically supported the idea, even Bea and Mary rearranged their schedules to be available.

At the retreat, Martha and the teachers spent some time deciding how they might adjust schedules to conduct the self-study phase of accreditation. They looked at the possibility of purchasing new equipment and how to allocate dollars in the following year's budget for this purpose. They also decided to begin a peer-mentoring program based on Shelly's and Pat's successful mentoring experience. Finally, several younger teachers made a case for getting substitute teachers so that staff could observe other centers. They felt these visits would give them a basis for comparison with their own program. They were particularly eager to observe some accredited centers and speak to the teachers in those programs. They anticipated that the whole accreditation process would take about eighteen months. The teachers met on two more occasions to develop a center action plan so that work could be divided equitably. Individual goal-setting conferences were planned. The individual and organizational change process was underway.

In the meantime, Martha was busy meeting with individual teachers to develop their goals blueprints and staff development action plans for the following year. At their orientation meeting in late August, she would be prepared to show them how their individual goals meshed with the center's goals. Included are copies of Martha's working papers, Worksheets #4 and #12, to show you how she did this.

All in all, Martha's experience was a positive one. She grew professionally in learning how to practice the collaborative skills she embraced philosophically. She looked forward to her second year at The Children's Corner with a sense of pride and anticipation. She knew there was still a lot to do, but she felt ready and eager to handle the

Action Plan

Goal: Staff will have a shared vision of developmentally appropriate practice and be able to communicate that vision to parents.

Objectives	Action Steps	Person Responsible	Time	Resources Needed (people, materials, $$$)	Evaluation Checkpoints
To clarify the center's philosophy and educational objectives	1. complete Assessment Tools #2 and #5 2. committee write drafts of philosophy; bring to whole staff 3. read *Developmentally Appropriate Practices*; discuss at 6 staff meetings	1. all staff; Martha tabulates results 2. Pat, Christine, Georgia, Scott 3. Two teachers lead each meeting	1. ½ hr for teachers; 1 hr. Martha 2. 20 hrs during fall 3. 3 hrs to read book; 2 hrs to prepare group discussion	1. photocopying $10 2. each committee member to get 4 hrs released time Read on own time; discussion leaders to get 2 hrs prep time; books = $10 each	1. August 2. draft philosophy in November; final in December 3. do Assessment Tool #10 after each meeting; do Assessment Tool #5 in December
To initiate the self-study phase of NAEYC center accreditation	1. get materials from NAEYC 2. get approval from board 3. conduct classroom observations (Assessment Tool #12)	1. Martha 2. Martha 3. Bea and Shelly to coordinate observations	1. 1 hr 2. 2 hr to write proposal 3. 3 hrs to observe each classroom x 2 times x 7 classes	1. initial fee + misc. expenses $600 2. photocopying for board and copies of NAEYC accreditation guidelines $125 3. released time for observations; substitutes = $200	1. by Sept. 15 2. presentation in October 3. ½ observations done by 12/31, rest done by 5/31
To increase parents' understanding of developmentally appropriate practices	1. photocopy handouts for monthly newsletter 2. conduct 6 parent education meetings 3. distribute Assessment Tool #11 to parents	1. Scott 2. Pat to coordinate parent meetings 3. Martha	1. during planning time 2. Pat: 1 hr/mo; 5 hrs each team 3. 2 hrs to tally	1. approx. $60/mo. 2. paid planning time 30 hrs; food = $150; misc. supplies $50 3. photocopying $10, postage $20	1. one article per month 2. workshops Nov. to April 3. distribute Tool #11 again in May

Working Toward a Common Vision

Center goal

Staff will have a shared vision of developmentally appropriate practice and be able to communicate that vision to parents.

Objectives

▶ To clarify the center's philosophy and educational objectives
▶ To initiate the self-study phase of NAEYC center accreditation
▶ To increase parents' understanding of developmentally appropriate practices

Date: June 15

Name: Pat
▶ chair committee for parent workshops
▶ conduct one workshop on block play
▶ serve on committee to rewrite the center's philosophy

Name: Shelly
▶ with Bea coordinate classroom observations
▶ conduct 4 observations
▶ conduct staff meeting with Margaret on DAP

Name: Georgia
▶ chair committee to rewrite philosophy
▶ conduct parent workshop on guidance
▶ coordinate refreshments for staff meetings

Name: Bea
▶ with Shelly coordinate classroom observations
▶ conduct 4 observations
▶ make posters announcing parent workshops

Name: Scott
▶ select articles for parent newsletter
▶ conduct staff meeting with Christine on DAP
▶ conduct 4 observations

Name: Christine
▶ serve on committee to rewrite the center's philosophy
▶ conduct staff meeting with Scott on DAP
▶ coordinate refreshments for parent workshops

challenges ahead. In one year she had made enormous strides in cultivating the norms of a professional learning community that would help her program improve from the inside out.

A Final Word

In collaborative early childhood work environments, organizational change is a shared goal between the director and teachers. Teachers view one another as mutual facilitators in achieving individual professional goals and the collective goals of the center. Collaboration offers many benefits to a center-based program. Positive interpersonal relationships increase teachers' self-esteem and encourage them to support the work of colleagues. Acceptance and instructional sharing, in turn, lead to a shared vision, greater productivity, and cohesion as a staff. Center-based change is achieved when individuals begin to embrace the goals of the center as their own.

In this book you've seen that an important part of creating a climate for change depends on how events are planned and how effectively time is used during the change process. Teachers and directors need enough time to identify pressing problems, gather data, develop an action plan, implement it, and evaluate progress. Not allocating sufficient time for any one of these steps in the change process can jeopardize the entire process.

Individuals also need time to get to know one another, share ideas and information, and learn how to work together. If teachers are eager to work on implementing a new curriculum but meetings are sporadic and only twenty minutes long, then it will be difficult for them to feel they can successfully complete their work. Time is such a precious resource. Ensuring a realistic time line for the change process is a necessary condition for successful change.

Before embarking on a course of change, it is important to consider whether the center can provide the resources needed to accomplish its intended goals. Financial resources are necessary for materials and equipment, for hiring substitutes, for evaluation materials, and for a host of other related expenses. Other necessary resources include energy and expertise. And you can't neglect the human element. It is a tremendously important energy resource to give teachers undivided attention to listen to their concerns. Allowing time to develop relationships with staff and support their needs is a precondition for successful change. Information and expertise may also be seen as resources. Building a network of consultants and links to the community through parents, professionals, and professional associations that can provide expertise is a necessary element in the change process.

Successful change, as we have seen, is dependent on concrete action plans. The action plans must begin with a clear statement of the proposed goal so that staff will have a common vision of what the changes will be. Explicitly delineating objectives, the activities, and who will carry out the activities is essential to the smooth implementation of the change process. In addition, carefully planning evaluation procedures helps participants see that progress is being made. Disorganized and haphazard action plans make it difficult to avoid ambiguity, role confusion, and conflict.

Finally, in order to improve programs, changes are needed in the structures and processes of the center that will support and sustain change in individuals. This book has shown that the professional development of staff is the vehicle for achieving center-based change. A holistic view of change that meshes individual needs and goals with center needs and goals is tied to an understanding that a program is an integrated whole made up of different, though interrelated, parts. Such a systems view can help you understand why people resist change and the conditions necessary for successfully accomplishing the change process. Lasting change will occur only when the participants build a shared vision linking organizational needs to the needs of individual people. Collaboration, shared decision making, and building a cohesive sense of purpose as a professional learning community are all elements that will help ensure this happens.

Effective leadership means more than simply knowing what to do—it's knowing when, how, and why to do it. Effective leaders understand how to balance pushing for change while at the same time, protecting aspects of culture, values, and norms worth preserving.

Tim Waters

References

Abbott-Shim, M. (1990, January). In-service training: A means to quality care. *Young Children, 45*(2), 14–18.

Albrecht, K. (2002). *The right fit: Recruiting, selecting, and orienting staff.* Lake Forest, IL: New Horizons.

Albrecht, K. (1989, December). Helping teachers grow: Separating competency from compensation. *Child Care Information Exchange,* 37–38.

Alessandra, T., & O'Connor, M. (1994). *People smarts.* San Diego: Pfeiffer & Company.

American Academy of Pediatrics. (1993). *Model child care health policies.* Elk Grove Village, IL: Author.

APQC (American Productivity & Quality Center). (1993). *Managing complex change.* Houston: Author.

Arbuckle, M., & Murray, L. (1989). *Building systems for professional growth: An action guide.* Andover, MA: The Regional Laboratory for Educational Improvement of the Northeast and Islands.

ATE (Association of Teacher Educators). (1985). *Developing career ladders in teaching.* Reston, VA: Author.

Ayers, W. (1989). *The good preschool teacher.* New York: Teachers College Press.

Bandura, A. (1997). *Self-efficacy: The exercise of self-control.* New York: Freeman.

Baratta-Lorton, M. (1994). *Mathematics their way.* Lebanon, IN: Pearson Learning.

Barbe, W., & Swassing, R. (1988). *Teaching through modality strengths concepts and practices.* Columbus, OH: Zaner Bloser.

Barker, L., Wahlers, K., & Watson, K. (2001). *Groups in process* (6th ed.). Boston: Allyn & Bacon.

Bean, R., & Clemes, H. (1978). *Elementary principal's handbook: New approaches to administrative action.* Upper Saddle River, NJ: Prentice Hall.

Beer, M. (1980). *Organization change and development: A systems view.* Glenview, IL: Scott, Foresman.

Berman, P., & McLaughlin, M. W. (1976). Implementation of educational innovations. *Educational Forum, 40,* 345–70.

Blake, R. R., & Mouton, J. (1994). *The managerial grid.* Houston: Gulf Professional Publishing.

Bloom, P. J. (2003). *Leadership in action: How effective directors get things done.* Lake Forest, IL: New Horizons.

Bloom, P. J. (2002). *Making the most of meetings: A practical guide.* Lake Forest, IL: New Horizons.

Bloom, P. J. (2000). *Circle of influence: Implementing shared decision making and participative management.* Lake Forest, IL: New Horizons.

Bloom, P. J. (1997). *A great place to work: Improving conditions for staff in young children's programs.* Washington, DC: National Association for the Education of Young Children.

Bloom, P. J. (1996). *Improving the quality of work life in the early childhood setting: Resource guide and technical manual for the Early Childhood Work Environment Survey.* Wheeling, IL: The McCormick Tribune Center for Early Childhood Leadership, National-Louis University.

Bloom, P. J. (1993a). Full cost of quality report. "But I'm worth more than that!" Addressing employee concerns about compensation. *Young Children, 48*(3), 65J68.

Bloom, P. J. (1993b). Full cost of quality report. "But I'm worth more than that!" Implementing a comprehensive compensation system. *Young Children, 48*(4), 67–72.

Bloom, P. J. (1989, Winter). Professional orientation: Individual and organizational perspectives. *Child and Youth Care Quarterly, 18*(4), 227–40.

Bloom, P. J. (1988a). Closing the gap: An analysis of teacher and administrator perceptions of organizational climate in the early childhood setting. *Teaching and Teacher Education: An International Journal of Research and Studies, 15*(4), 9–11.

Bloom, P. J. (1988b). Factors influencing overall job satisfaction and organizational commitment in early childhood work environments. *Journal of Research in Early Childhood Education, 3(2)*, 107–22.

Bloom, P. J. (1986, July). Organizational norms—Our blueprint for behavior. *Child Care Information Exchange*, 5–9.

Bloom, P. J. (1982). *Avoiding burnout: Strategies for managing time, space, and people in early childhood education.* Lake Forest, IL: New Horizons.

Bloom, P. J., & Ford, M. (1988). Factors influencing administrators' decisions regarding the adoption of computer technology. *Journal of Educational Computing Research, 4*(1), 31–47.

Bolton, R., & Bolton, D. G. (1996). *People styles at work.* New York: American Management Association.

Bowditch, J., & Buono, A. (1982). *Quality of work life assessment.* Boston: Auburn House.

Brandt, R. (1990). *Incentive pay and career ladders for today's teachers: A study of current programs and practices.* Albany: State University of New York Press.

Bredekamp, S., & Copple, C. (Eds.). (1997). *Developmentally appropriate practice in early childhood programs* (Rev. ed.). Washington, DC: National Association for the Education of Young Children.

Bridges, W. (1991). *Managing transitions: Making the most of change.* Reading, MA: Perseus Books.

Bronfenbrenner, U. (1979). *The ecology of human development.* Cambridge, MA: Harvard University Press.

Buckingham, M., & Clifton, D. (2001). *Now, discover your strengths.* New York: The Free Press.

Burden, P. R. (1987). *Establishing career ladders in teaching.* Charles Thomas.

Carter, M. (1998, March). Principles and strategies for coaching and mentoring. *Child Care Information Exchange,* 82–85.

Carter, M., & Curtis, D. (2000). *The art of awareness.* St. Paul, MN: Redleaf.

Carter, M., & Curtis, D. (1998). *Visionary director: A handbook for dreaming, organizing, and improvising in your center.* St. Paul, MN: Redleaf.

Carter, M., & Curtis, D. (1994). *Training teachers: A harvest of theory and practice.* St. Paul, MN: Redleaf Press.

Caruso, J. J., & Fawcett, M. T. (1999). *Supervision in early childhood education: A developmental perspective* (2nd ed.). New York: Teachers College Press.

Conner, D. R. (1993). *Managing at the speed of change.* New York: Villard Books.

Corwin, R. G. (1965). Professional persons in public organizations. *Educational Administration Quarterly, 1,* 19–28.

CPR (Council for Professional Recognition). (2001). *Child Development Associate assessment system and competence standards for preschool caregivers.* Washington, DC: Author.

Curtis, D., & Carter, M. (2003). *Designs for living and learning.* St. Paul, MN: Redleaf.

Danielson, C., & McGreal, T. (2000). *Teacher evaluation: To enhance professional practice.* Alexandria, VA: Association for Supervision and Curriculum Development.

Deal, T., & Peterson, K. (1999). *Shaping school culture: The heart of leadership.* San Francisco: Jossey-Bass.

Dillon-Peterson, B. (1981). *Staff development/ organizational development.* Alexandria, VA: Association for Supervision and Curriculum Development.

Dodge, D. T., Colker, L., & Heroman, C. (2002). *The Creative Curriculum* (4th ed.). Washington, DC: Teaching Strategies.

Driscoll, A., Peterson, K., & Kauchak, D. (1985). Designing a mentor system for beginning teachers. *Journal of Staff Development, 6*(2), 108–17.

DuFour, R. (2004, May). What is a professional learning community? *Educational Leadership, 61*(8), 6–11.

Dunn, R., & Dunn, K. (1978). *Teaching students through their individual learning styles.* Reston, VA: Reston Publishing.

Dyer, W. G. (1984). *Strategies for managing change.* Reading, MA: Addison Wesley.

Edwards, M., & Ewen, A. (1996). *360° feedback.* New York: AMACOM.

Erikson, E. H. (1968). *Identity: Youth and crisis.* New York: W. W. Norton.

Fessler, R., & Christensen, J. (1992). *The teacher career cycle: Understanding and guiding the professional development of teachers.* Boston: Allyn & Bacon.

Firestone, W. A., & Corbett, W. (1988). Planned organizational change. In N. Boyan (Ed.). *Handbook of research on educational administration* (pp. 321–40). White Plaines, NY: Longman.

Fliegel, F., & Kivlin, J. (1966). Attributes of an innovation as factors in diffusion. *American Journal of Sociology, 72*, 235–48.

Fullan, M. (2001). *Learning in a culture of change.* San Francisco: Jossey-Bass.

Fuller, F. (1969). Concerns of teachers: A developmental conceptualization. *American Educational Research Journal, 6*, 207–26.

Gehreke, N. J. (1988, January-February). On preserving the essence of mentoring as one form of teacher leadership. *Journal of Teacher Education, 3*(1), 43–45.

Getzels, J., & Guba, E. G. (1957, Winter). Social behavior as an administrative process. *The School Review, 65*, 423–41.

Giammatteo, M. C. (1975). *Training package for a model city staff.* Field paper no. 15. Portland, OR: Northwest Regional Educational Laboratory.

Gladwell, M. (2000). *The tipping point: How little things can make a big difference.* Boston: Little, Brown.

Glickman, C. D. (2004). *Supervision and Instructional leadership: A developmental approach.* Boston: Allyn & Bacon.

Gregorc, A. (1982). *An adult's guide to style.* Maynard, MA: Gabriel Systems.

Gronland, G., & Engel, B. (2001). *Focused portfolios.* St. Paul, MN: Redleaf.

Hall, G., & Hord, S. (2001). *Implementing change: Patterns, principles, and potholes.* Boston: Allyn & Bacon.

Hall, J. (1988). *The competence connection.* The Woodlands, TX: Woodstead Press.

Harms, T., Clifford, R., & Cryer, D. (1998). *Early Childhood Environment Rating Scale—Revised.* New York: Teachers College Press.

Harms, T., Cryer, D., & Clifford, R., (2003). *Infant/Toddler Environment Rating Scale—Revised.* New York: Teachers College Press.

Havelock, R. G., & Havelock, M. C. (1973). *Training change agents.* Ann Arbor, MI: Institute for Social Research.

Helburn, S., & Bergmann, B. (2002). *America's child care problem: The way out.* New York: St. Martin Press.

Helm, J. H., Beneke, S., & Steinheimer, K. (1997). *Windows on learning: Documenting young children's work.* New York: Teachers College Press.

Hemmeter, M. L., Joseph, G. E., Smith, B. J., & Sandall, S. (Eds.). (2001). *DEC recommended practices program assessment: Improving practices for young children with special needs and their families.* Longmont, CO: Sopris West.

Heifetz, R. A. (1998). *Leadership without easy answers.* Cambridge, MA: Belknap.

Hendry, J., & Johnson, G. (1994). *Strategic thinking: Leadership and the management of change.* Somerset, NJ: John Wiley.

Herman, B. (1999). *Teach me—reach me!* Deerfield, IL: Pathways to Learning.

Hersey, P., Blanchard, K., & Johnson, D. E. (2001). *Management of organizational behavior* (8th ed.). Upper Saddle River, NJ: Prentice-Hall.

Herzberg, F. (1966). *Work and the nature of man.* New York: World Publishing.

High/Scope Educational Research Foundation. (2003). *Preschool Program Quality Assessment (PQA)*. Ypsilanti, MI: Author.

Hirsh, E. S. (1984). *The block book* (Rev. ed.). Washington, DC: National Association for the Education of Young Children.

Hollas, B. (2001, November). Keeping your staff motivated. *Principal, 81*(2), 6–15

Hohmann, M., & Weikart, D., (2002). *Educating young children: Active learning practices for preschool and child care programs* (2nd edition). Ypsilanti, MI: High/Scope.

Hopkins, D (1990). Integrating staff development and school improvement: A study of teacher personality and school climate. In B. Joyce (Ed.), *Changing school culture through staff development* (pp. 41–67). Reston, VA: Association for Supervision and Curriculum Development.

House, L. J. (2004, July). *Teacher dispositions: Can we reach agreement?* Paper presented at the Annual Congress of the International Council on Education for Teaching, Hong Kong.

Hoy, W., & Miskel, C. (2005). *Educational administration: Theory research and practice* (7th ed.). New York: McGraw-Hill.

Hunsaker P., & Alessandra, A. (1980). *The art of managing people*. New York: Simon & Schuster.

Hunt, D. E., Butler, L., Noy, J., & Rosser, M. (1978). *Assessing conceptual level by the paragraph completion method*. Toronto: Ontario Institute for Studies in Education.

Huszczo, G. (1996). *Tools for team excellence: Getting your team into high gear and keeping it there*. Palo Alto, CA: Davies-Black.

Hyson, M. (Ed.). (2003). *Preparing early childhood professionals: NAEYC's standards for programs*. Washington, DC: National Association for the Education of Young Children.

Jablon, J., Dombro, A., & Dichtelmiller, M. (1999). *The power of observation*. Washington, DC: Teaching Strategies.

Jensen, J. (1979). *Basic guide to salary management*. Los Angeles: The Grantsmanship Center.

Johnson, D. (1987). *Learning together and alone: Cooperative, competitive, and individualistic learning*. Upper Saddle River, NJ: Prentice-Hall.

Johnston, J. (1984, March). Assessing staff problems: Key to effective staff development. *Child Care Information Exchange*, 1–4.

Johnston, J. (1988, September). A performance based approach to staff evaluation. *Child Care Information Exchange*, 10–13.

Jones, E. (1993). *Growing teachers: Partnerships in staff development*. Washington, DC: National Association for the Education of Young Children.

Jones, A. P., & James, L. R. (1979). Psychological climate: Dimensions and relationships of individual and aggregated work environment perceptions. *Organizational Behavior and Human Performance, 23*, 201–50.

Jude-York, D., & Wise, S. (1997). *Multipoint feedback: A 360 catalyst for change*. Menlo Park, CA: Crisp.

Jung, C. (1923). *Psychological types*. New York: Harcourt Brace.

Kagan, S. L. (1990). *Policy perspectives: Excellence in early childhood education—Defining next-decade strategies.* Washington, DC: U.S. Department of Education, Office of Research and Improvement, Information services.

Kagan, S. L., & Neuman, M. J. (2003, April). Integrating early care and education. *Educational Leadership, 60*(7), 58–63.

Kast, F. E., & Rosenzweig, J. E. (1985). *Organization and management: A systems and contingency approach.* New York: McGraw-Hill.

Katz, L. (1993). *Helping others with their teaching.* Urbana, IL: ERIC Clearinghouse on Elementary and Early Childhood Education.

Katz, L. (1993, April). *Dispositions: Definitions and implications for early childhood practices.* Urbana, IL: ERIC Clearinghouse on Elementary and Early Childhood Education.

Katz, L. (1972). Developmental stages of preschool teachers. *Elementary School Journal, 73,* 50–55.

Kegan, R. (2000). What "form" transforms? A constructive-developmental approach to transformative learning. In J. Mezirow (Ed.), *Learning as transformation* (pp.35–69). San Francisco: Jossey-Bass.

Keirsey, D. (1998). *Please understand me II: Temperament, character, intelligence.* Del Mar, CA: Prometheus Nemesis.

Kilman, R. H. (1984). *Beyond the quick fix.* San Francisco: Jossey-Bass.

Kirton, M. J. (1976). Adaptors and innovators: A description and measure. *Journal of Applied Psychology, 61,* 622–29.

Kotter, J. (1996). *Leading change.* Boston: Harvard Business School Press.

Kroeger, O., Thuesen, J., & Rutledge, H. (2002). *Typetalk.* New York: Dell.

Lally, R., Griffin, A., Fenichel, E., Segal, M., Szanton, E., & Weissbourd, B. (2003). *Caring for infants and toddlers in groups: Developmentally appropriate practice.* Washington, DC: Zero to Three.

Lawrence, G. (1993). *People types and tiger stripes* (3rd ed.). Gainesville, FL: Center for Applications of Psychological Type.

Levine S. (1989). *Promoting adult growth in schools.* Boston: Allyn & Bacon.

Lewin, K. (1951). *Field theory in social sciences.* New York: Harper & Row.

Lightfoot, S. (1983). *Good high schools: Portraits of character and culture.* New York: Basic Books.

Little, J. W. (1982). Norms of collegiality and experimentation: Workplace conditions of school success. *American Educational Research Journal, 19,* 325–340.

Loevinger, J. (1976*). Ego development.* San Francisco: Jossey-Bass.

Lombardi, J. (2002). *Redesigning child care to promote education, support families, and build communities.* Philadelphia: Temple University Press.

Loucks-Horsley, S. (1987). *Continuing to learn: A guidebook for teacher development.* Andover, MA: Regional Laboratory for Educational Improvement of the Northeast and Islands.

Luft, J., & Ingham, H. (1973). The Johari Window. *Annual handbook for group facilitators*. San Diego, CA: University Associates.

Maslow, A. A. (1954). *Motivation and personality*. New York: Harper & Row.

McCarthy, B. (1996). *About learning*. Oak Brook, IL: Excel.

McGregor, D. (1960). *The human side of enterprise*. New York: McGraw-Hill.

Meisels, S. J., Jablon, J., Marsden, D., Dichtelmiller, M., &. Dorfman, A. (1994). *The Work Sampling System*. Ann Arbor, Mi: Rebus Planning Associates.

Merrill, D., & Reid, R. (1981). *Personal styles and effective performance*. Radnor, PA: Chilton.

Mertens, S., & Yarger, S. (1988, January-February). Teaching as a profession: Leadership, empowerment and involvement. *Journal of Teacher Education*, 32–37.

Meyer, J. P., & Allen, N. J. (1997). *Commitment in the workplace: Theory, research, and application*. Thousand Oaks, CA: Sage.

Miles, M. B. (1965). Planned change and organizational health: Figure and ground. In M. Miles (Ed.), *Change processes in the public schools* (pp. 11–34). Eugene, OR: University of Oregon, Center for Advanced Study of Educational Administration.

Mowday, R., Steers, R., & Porter, L. (1979). The measurement of organizational commitment. *Journal of Vocational Behavior, 14*, 224–47.

Myers, I. B. (1998). *Introduction to type* (6th ed.). Palo Alto, CA: Consulting Psychologists Press.

Myers, I. B. (1980). *Gifts differing*. Palo Alto, CA: Consulting Psychologists Press.

Nadler, D., & Tushman, M. (1983). A general diagnostic model for organizational behavior: Applying a congruence perspective. In J. R. Hackman, E. Lawler, & L. Porter (Eds.), *Perspectives on behavior in organizations* (pp. 112–24). New York: McGraw Hill.

National Association for the Education of Young Children. (1998). *Code of ethical conduct and statement of commitment* (rev. ed.). Washington, DC: Author.

National Association for the Education of Young Children. (2004, June). *NAEYC draft early childhood program standards*. Online: www.naeyc.org/accreditation/next_era. asp#standards.

National Association for the Education of Young Children. (1993). *A conceptual framework for early childhood professional development*. Washington, DC: Author.

NCCA (National Child Care Association). (1991) *Certified Childcare Profession (CCP) credential*. Atlanta: Author.

Neugebauer, R. (1994, May). Guidelines for fine tuning your salary schedule. *Child Care Information Exchange, 55–64*.

Neugebauer, B. (1990, September/October). Are you listening? *Child Care Information Exchange*, 62.

Neugebauer, B. (1990, August). Evaluation of director by staff. *Child Care Information Exchange*, 20–21.

Norton, R. (1983). *Communicator style: Theory, applications, and measures*. Beverly Hills, CA: Sage.

Oakley, E., & Krug, D. (1991). *Enlightened leadership: Getting to the heart of change.* New York: Simon & Schuster.

Oshry, B. (1996). *Seeing systems: Unlocking the mysteries of organizational life.* San Francisco: Berrett-Koehler.

Owens, R. G. (2000). *Organizational behavior in education.* (7th edition). Boston: Allyn & Bacon.

Parkay, F., & Damico, S. (1989, Spring). Empowering teachers for change through faculty-driven school improvement. *Journal of Staff Development, 10*(2), 8–14.

Peters, D. L., & Kostelnik, M. (1981). Current research in day care personnel preparation. In S. Kilmer (Ed.), *Advances in Early Education and Day Care* (vol. 2, pp. 29–60). Greenwich, CT: JAI.

Peters, T. J., & Waterman, R. H. (1982). *In search of excellence: Lessons learned from America's best-run companies.* New York: Random House.

Peterson, K. D. (1995). *Teacher evaluation: A comprehensive guide to new directions and practices.* Thousand Oaks, CA: Corwin.

Public Management Institute. (1980*). Non-profit management skills for women managers.* San Francisco: Author.

Reddin, W. J. (1970). *Managerial effectiveness.* New York: McGraw-Hill.

Ritvo, R., Litwin, A., & Butler, L. (Eds.). (1995). *Managing in the age of change.* New York: Irwin Professional Publishers.

Rizzo, J., House, R., & Lirtzman, S. (1970). Role conflict and role ambiguity in complex organizations. *Administrative Science Quarterly, 15,* 150–63.

Roberts S., & Pruitt E. (2003). *Schools as professional learning communities: Collaborative activities and strategies for professional development.* Thousand Oaks, CA: Corwin.

Rogers, E. (2003). *Diffusion of innovations* (5th ed.). New York: The Free Press.

Rosenholtz, S. (1989). *Teachers' workplace.* New York: Longman.

Russo, E. M. (1995). *What's my communication style?* King of Prussia, PA: Organization Design and Development.

Rust, F., & Freidus, H. (2001). *Guiding school change: The role and work of change agents.* New York: Teachers College Press.

Saxl, E. (1989). *Assisting change in education: Trainer's manual.* Alexandria, VA: Association for Supervision and Curriculum Development.

Schein, E. (2004). *Organizational culture and leadership* (3rd edition*).* San Francisco: Jossey-Bass.

Schmuck, R. A., & Runkel, P. J. (1994). *The handbook of organization development in schools and colleges* (4th ed.). Long Grove, IL: Waveland.

Schweinhart, L. J., Montie, J., Xiang, Z., Barnett, W. S., Belfield, C. R., & Nores, M. (2005). *Lifetime effects: The High/Scope Perry Preschool study through age 40.* (Monographs of the High/Scope Educational Research Foundation, 14). Ypsilanti, MI: High/Scope Press.

Schwind, H. (1987). Performance appraisal: The state of the art. In S. Dolan and R. Schuler (Eds.), *Personnel and human resources management in Canada* (pp. 197–210). Toronto: West Publishing.

Sciarra, D. J., & Dorsey, A. G. (2002). *Leaders and supervisors in child care programs.* Albany, NY: Delmar.

Scott, C., & Jaffe, D. (1989). *Managing organizational change.* Menlo Park, CA: Crisp.

Seashore, S. E., Lawler, E., Mirvis, P., & Cammann, C. (1983). *Assessing organizational change.* New York: John Wiley.

Seligson, M., & Stahl, P. (2003). *Bringing yourself to work: A guide to successful staff development in after-school programs.* New York: Teachers College Press.

Senge, P. (1994). *The fifth discipline: The art and practice of the learning organization.* New York: Currency.

Shaw, D. G., Schneier, C., Beatty, R., & Baird, L. (Eds.). (1995). *Performance, measurement, management, and appraisal sourcebook.* Amherst, MA: HRD Press.

Slavin, R. E. (1990). *Cooperative learning: Theory, research, and practice.* Upper Saddle River, NJ: Prentice-Hall.

Smither, J. W. (1998). *Performance appraisal: State of the art in practice.* San Francisco: Jossey-Bass.

Spector, P. E. (1997). *Job satisfaction: Application, assessment, causes, and consequences.* Thousand Oaks, CA: Sage.

Storm, S. (1985). *The human side of child care administration.* Washington, DC: National Association for the Education of Young Children.

Stonehouse, A. (1986). *For us, for children: An analysis of the provision of in-service education for child care centre personnel in Australia.* Camberra: Australian Early Childhood Association.

Stremmel, A. J. (2002, September). Nurturing professional and personal growth through inquiry. *Young Children, 57*(5), 62–70.

Talan, T., & Bloom, P. J. (2004). *The Program Administration Scale: Measuring early childhood leadership and management.* New York: Teachers College Press.

Teaching Strategies. (2003). *Implementation checklist: The Creative Curriculum for Preschool.* Washington, DC: Author

Tobias, C. (1994). *The way they learn.* Colorado Springs, CO: Focus on the Family Publishing.

Travis, N., & Perreault, J. (1981). *Day care personnel management.* Atlanta, GA: Save the Children.

VanderVen, K. D. (1988). Pathways to professional effectiveness for early childhood educators. In B. Spodek, O. Saracho, & D. Peters (Eds.), *Professionalism and the early childhood practitioner* (pp. 137–60). New York: Teachers College Press.

Vartuli, S., & Fyfe, B. (1993, May). Teachers need developmentally appropriate practices too. *Young Children, 48*(4), 36–43.

Vygotsky, L. S. (1978). *Mind in society: The development of higher psychological processes.* Cambridge, MA: Harvard University Press.

Wallenberg, I. (1980). *The emotional experience of learning and teaching.* London: Routledge & Kegan Paul.

Waters, T., Marzano, R., & McNulty, B. (2003). *Balanced leadership.* Aurora, CO: McREL.

Weiner, B. (1980). *Human motivation.* New York: Holt, Rinehart & Winston.

Wonder, J., & Donovan, P. (1984). *Whole-brain thinking.* New York: William Morrow.

Wu, P. C. (1988, Spring). Why is change difficult? Lessons for staff development. *Journal of Staff Development, 9*(2), 10–14.

Yukl, G. A. (2002). *Leadership in organizations* (5th ed.). Upper Saddle River, NJ: Prentice Hall.

Zachary, L. J. (2000). *The mentor's guide.* San Francisco: Jossey-Bass.

Zmuda, A., Kuklis, R., & Kline, E. (2004). *Transforming schools: Creating a culture of continuous improvements.* Alexandria, VA: Association for Supervision and Curriculum Development

----

Internet Resources for Staff Development

Association for Supervision and Curriculum Development (ASCD)
www.ascd.org

Center for the Child Care Workforce (CCW/AFTEF)
www.ccw.org

Child Care Information Exchange (CCIE)
www.ccie.com

Council for Professional Recognition
www.cdacouncil.org

Council for Exceptional Children (CEC)
www.cec.sped.org

Early Head Start National Resource Center
www.ehsnrc.org

Harvest Resources
www.ecetrainers.com

High Scope Foundation
www.highscope.org

McCormick Tribune Center for Early Childhood Leadership
www.nl.edu/cecl

National Association for the Education of Young Children (NAEYC)
www.naeyc.org

National Association of Child Care Professionals (NACCP)
www.naccp.org

National Association of Child Care Resource and Referral Agencies (NACCRRA)
www.naccrra.net

National Child Care Association (NCCA)
www.nccanet.org

National Child Care Information Center (NCCIC)
www.nccic.org

National Head Start Association
www.nhsa.org

National School Age Care Alliance
www.nsaca.org

National Staff Development Council (NSDC)
www.nsdc.org

Teaching Strategies
www.teachingstrategies.com

Transforming Learning Communities
www.ode.state.oh.us/tlc

Zero to Three
www.zerotothree.org

Assessment Tools

The assessment tools included in this appendix are also included on the CD-ROM accompanying this book. These masters may be freely reproduced for professional development activities at your center. Permission for systematic large-scale reproduction for other training and research purposes or for the inclusion in other publications must be obtained from the publisher, New Horizons. This appendix includes the following assessment tools:

1. Reacting to Change

2. Concerns About an Innovation

3. Organizational Climate

4. Leadership Style

5. Goal Consensus and Communication Processes

6. Collegiality and Collaboration

7. Decision-Making Processes

8. Supervision and Evaluation Processes

9. Organizational Norms

10. Group Meeting Processes

11. Parent Satisfaction

12. Preschool Teaching Practices

13. Infant-Toddler Teaching Practices

14. Learning Style

15. Psychological Type

16. Beliefs and Values

17. Communication Style

18. Job Satisfaction

19. Professional Orientation

20. Role Clarity

21. Role Clarity (new staff)

22. Organizational Commitment

23. Perceived Problems

24. Flexibility and Openness to Change

25. Supervisory Beliefs

26. Goal-Setting Motivation

Reacting to Change

Rationale:

Assessing employee reactions to a proposed organizational change is the first step in identifying initial concerns staff might have about change. This is important because organizational change implies altering established ways of thinking about one's job. The information gleaned from such an assessment can help directors tap into staff's feelings, assumptions, fears, and concerns about a proposed change. Assessment Tool #1 is an informal measure of how individuals anticipate the impact a proposed change will have on their work, their self-perception, and their relationships with others. This instrument was adapted from the work of W. J. Reddin (1970).

Directions:

Distribute the "Change-Reaction Checklist" and a blank envelope to all staff who will be affected by a proposed change. Place a box labeled Questionnaire Return Box in your center's office or staff room and ask respondents to place their completed surveys in this box. Ensure staff of the confidentiality of their responses.

Scoring:

This instrument can be scored in two ways.

1. To generate an average positive impact (+), negative impact (–) and no impact (n/i) score for the center, add together all the individual staff scores (at the bottom of the checklist) for each of these three categories, then divide each of the three sums by the total number of respondents who completed surveys.

2. To do an item analysis, tally the number of times staff indicated a positive (+), negative (–), and no impact (n/i) for each item. Items with the highest negative impact scores are areas where staff express the deepest concern about a proposed change.

The results of this informal assessment can be used as a springboard for discussion at a staff meeting about the proposed organizational change.

Change-Reaction Checklist

Proposed change: _____

In the space provided after each statement, indicate if you anticipate the proposed change will have a positive (+) impact, a negative (–) impact, or no impact (n/i) with respect to your work, yourself, and your relationships with others.

Work

1.	The amount of work I do	_____
2.	My interest in my work	_____
3.	The importance of my work	_____
4.	The challenge of my work	_____
5.	My physical surroundings	_____
6.	My hours of work	_____

Self

7.	My advancement possibilities	_____
8.	My salary	_____
9.	My future with this center	_____
10.	My formal authority	_____
11.	My ability to predict the future	_____

Others

12.	My relationship with my co-workers	_____
13.	My relationship with my supervisor	_____
14.	My relationship with the children	_____
15.	My relationship with the parents	_____

total + _____

total – _____

total n/i _____

Concerns About an Innovation

Rationale:

Because change is experienced differently by every person, the concerns associated with implementing any proposed organizational change vary from one individual to another. Hall and Hord (2001) have identified seven stages of concern about implementing educational innovations. These concerns move from self, to task, to the innovation's impact. Assessment Tool #2 is an abbreviated version of their concerns questionnaire. The goal of this instrument is to provide a quick assessment of an individual's most intense concerns about a proposed innovation. This shortened version uses the Work Sampling System as an example of an early childhood innovation.

Directions:

The "Concerns Questionnaire" will need to be adapted for the specific innovation you are planning to implement. In each instance where Work Sampling System is noted, the name or type of innovation being considered can be substituted. Distribute the "Concerns Questionnaire" and a blank envelope to all staff who will be involved in implementing the proposed change or innovation. Place a box labeled Questionnaire Return Box in your center's office or staff room and request that respondents place their completed, signed questionnaires in this box.

Scoring:

On the scoring sheet provided, put the number of points the individual assigned next to the corresponding number of the questionnaire item. (The item numbers are ordered in columns indicating stage or type of concerns rather than chronologically.) Then tally the points for each column. This score will represent the individual's total score for that type (stage) of concern. Scores for each type of concern will vary from 0 to 15. Note the two or three areas where the individual scored highest. At the end of the instrument are suggestions for facilitating change in each of these seven areas for individuals who have strong concerns.

Since facilitating change should be handled on an individual basis, it is not recommended that scores be combined to generate an aggregate staff profile. A centerwide average on this instrument can mask the enormous variation that can exist in the type of concerns that individuals experience.

Concerns Questionnaire

Name _____

The purpose of this questionnaire is to determine how you feel about using the Work Sampling System. Please respond to the items in terms of your present concerns, or how you feel about your involvement or potential involvement with the Work Sampling System. Some of the items on this questionnaire may have little relevance to you at this time. For the completely irrelevant items, please circle 0 on the scale. Other items will represent those concerns you do have, in varying degrees of intensity, and should be marked higher on the scale.

Irrelevant	Not true of me now		Somewhat true of me now		Very true of of me now
0	1	2	3	4	5

1. I am concerned about how the students will react to the Work Sampling System.   0 1 2 3 4 5

2. I know of some other assessment approaches that might work better than the Work Sampling System.   0 1 2 3 4 5

3. I don't even know what the Work Sampling System is.   0 1 2 3 4 5

4. I am concerned about not having enough time to organize myself to implement this assessment system.   0 1 2 3 4 5

5. I would like to help the other teachers in their use of the Work Sampling System.   0 1 2 3 4 5

6. I am concerned about how I can carry out all my responsibilities with respect to the Work Sampling System.   0 1 2 3 4 5

7. I would like to know who will make decisions regarding implementing the Work Sampling System.   0 1 2 3 4 5

8. I would like to explore the possibility of using the Work Sampling System.   0 1 2 3 4 5

9. I would like to know what resources are available to support me in using the Work Sampling System.   0 1 2 3 4 5

10. I am concerned about my inability to manage all that the Work Sampling System requires.   0 1 2 3 4 5

11. I am concerned about evaluating my impact on students' learning with respect to the Work Sampling System.   0 1 2 3 4 5

12. I am too occupied with other things right now to consider implementing the Work Sampling System.　　　0　1　2　3　4　5

13. I would like to modify and revise the Work Sampling System assessment approach.　　　0　1　2　3　4　5

14. I would like to coordinate my efforts with other staff to maximize the effects of the Work Sampling System.　　　0　1　2　3　4　5

15. I would like to have more information on the time and energy commitment required to implement the Work Sampling System.　　　0　1　2　3　4　5

16. I would like to know what other teachers are doing with respect to implementing the Work Sampling System.　　　0　1　2　3　4　5

17. At this time, I am not really interested in learning about the Work Sampling System.　　　0　1　2　3　4　5

18. I would like to determine how to supplement and enhance the use of the Work Sampling System in this center.　　　0　1　2　3　4　5

19. I am interested in getting feedback from students and parents to improve the way I implement the Work Sampling System.　　　0　1　2　3　4　5

20. I would like to know how my role will change if I implement the Work Sampling System.　　　0　1　2　3　4　5

21. I would like to know how the Work Sampling System is better than the assessment strategies we use now.　　　0　1　2　3　4　5

When I think of the Work Sampling System, my primary concern is …

Adapted from Hall, G., & Hord, S. (2001). *Implementing change: Patterns, principles, and potholes.* Boston: Allyn & Bacon.

186

Concerns Questionnaire Scoring Sheet

Stage 0 Awareness Concerns	Stage 1 Informational Concerns	Stage 2 Personal Concerns	Stage 3 Management Concerns	Stage 4 Consequence Concerns	Stage 5 Collaboration Concerns	Stage 6 Refocusing Concerns
3 _____	8 _____	7 _____	4 _____	1 _____	5 _____	2 _____
12 _____	9 _____	15 _____	6 _____	11 _____	14 _____	13 _____
17 _____	21 _____	20 _____	10 _____	19 _____	16 _____	18 _____
_____ total	_____ total	_____ total	_____ total	_____ total	_____ total	_____ total

Facilitating Change for Individuals at Different Stages of Concern

Stage 0 – Awareness Concerns

▶ Involve teachers in discussions and decisions about the innovation and its implementation.

▶ Share enough information to arouse interest, but not so much that it overwhelms.

▶ Acknowledge that a lack of awareness is expected and reasonable, and that no questions about the innovation are foolish.

▶ Encourage individuals in this category to talk with colleagues who know more about the innovation.

▶ Take steps to minimize gossip and inaccurate sharing of information about the innovation.

Stage 1 – Informational Concerns

▶ Provide clear and accurate information about the innovation.

▶ Use a variety of ways to share information—verbally, in writing, and through any available media.

▶ Communicate with individuals and with small and large groups.

▶ Have individuals who have used the innovation in other settings visit with your teachers. Visits to other centers could also be arranged.

▶ Help teachers see how the innovation relates to their current practices, both in regard to similarities and differences.

▶ Be enthusiastic and enhance the visibility of others who are excited.

Stage 2 – Personal Concerns

▶ Legitimize the existence and expression of personal concerns; knowing that their concerns are common and that others have them can be comforting to individuals.

▶ Use personal notes and conversations to provide encouragement and reinforce personal adequacy.

▶ Connect these teachers with others whose personal concerns have diminished and who will be supportive.

▶ Show how the innovation can be implemented sequentially rather than in one big leap. It is important to establish expectations that are attainable.

▶ Do not push innovation use, but encourage and support it while maintaining expectations.

Stage 3 – Management Concerns

▶ Clarify the steps and components of the innovation.

▶ Provide answers that address the small specific how-to issues that are so often the cause of management concerns.

▶ Demonstrate exact and practical solutions to the logistical problems that contribute to these concerns.

▶ Help teachers sequence specific activities and set timelines for their accomplishment.

▶ Attend to immediate demands of the innovation, not what will be or could be in the future.

Stage 4 – Consequence Concerns

▶ Provide these teachers with opportunities to visit other settings where the innovation is in use and to attend conferences on the topic.

▶ Give these individuals positive feedback and needed support.

▶ Find opportunities for these individuals to share their skills with others.

▶ Share relevant research relating to the outcomes of the innovation.

Stage 5 – Collaboration Concerns

▶ Provide these individuals with opportunities to develop the skills necessary for working collaboratively.

▶ Bring together people, both within and outside the center, who are interested in collaboration.

▶ Help the collaborators establish reasonable expectations and guidelines for the collaborative effort.

▶ Use these people to provide technical assistance to others who need assistance.

▶ Encourage the collaborators, but don't attempt to force collaboration on those who are not interested.

Stage 6 – Refocusing Concerns

▶ Respect and encourage the interest these individuals have for finding a better way.

▶ Help these individuals channel their ideas and energies in ways that will be productive rather than counterproductive.

▶ Encourage these individuals to act on their concerns for program improvement.

▶ Help these people access the resources they may need to refine their ideas and put them into practice.

▶ Accept the fact that these individuals may replace or significantly modify the innovation.

Organizational Climate

Rationale:

Organizational climate describes the collective perceptions of staff regarding the overall quality of work life at the center. Assessment Tool #3 is the short form of the *Early Childhood Work Environment Survey* (Bloom, 1996). It is designed to measure staff's perceptions about 10 different dimensions of organizational climate: co-worker relations, opportunities for professional growth, supervisor support, clarity, reward system, decision-making structure, goal consensus, task orientation, physical environment, and innovativeness. (The table on the following page provides a fuller description of these 10 dimensions.) The instrument is short and can be administered to staff annually to take a quick pulse of organizational functioning.

Centers wishing to have a fuller profile of staff's perceptions regarding the dimensions of organizational life may want to administer the longer version of this instrument. It can be obtained from the McCormick Tribune Center for Early Childhood Leadership at National-Louis University (www.nl.edu/cecl).

Directions:

Distribute the short form of the *Early Childhood Work Environment Survey* to all staff who work a minimum of 10 hours per week at the center. In addition to the teaching staff, this will probably include some support staff (e.g., secretary, nutritionist, social worker). Each individual should also be given a blank envelope. Designate one person on your staff to be responsible for collecting completed surveys. Before distributing the survey to your staff, decide who will be tabulating the results and summarizing the data. Let the staff know who this person will be.

Scoring:

The organizational climate scores on this survey will range from 0 to 100. Tabulate individual scores by simply adding up the numbers next to each statement. To determine the average organizational climate score, add together the organizational climate individual scores and divide the sum by the number of individuals completing the survey.

This instrument is most useful when used as a pre and post assessment of staff's perceptions of the quality of work life. If the center is engaged in any kind of center improvement effort, the information gleaned from comparing pre and post scores on this assessment will provide helpful information as to the success of the center improvement efforts.

Ten Dimensions of Organizational Climate

Dimension	Definition
Collegiality	Extent to which staff are friendly, supportive, and trust one another; peer cohesion and esprit de corps of the group.
Professional growth	The degree of emphasis placed on personal and professional growth.
Supervisor support	The degree of facilitative leadership that provides encouragement, support, and clear expectations.
Clarity	The extent to which policies, procedures, and responsibilities are clearly defined and communicated.
Reward system	The degree of fairness and equity in the distribution of pay, benefits, and opportunities for advancement.
Decision making	The degree of autonomy given to the staff and the extent to which they are involved in centerwide decisions.
Goal consensus	The degree to which staff agree on the philosophy, goals, and objectives of the center.
Task orientation	The emphasis placed on good planning, efficiency, and getting the job done.
Physical setting	The extent to which the spatial arrangement of the center helps or hinders staff in carrying out their responsibilities.
Innovativeness	The extent to which the center adapts to change and encourages staff to find creative ways to solve problems.

From: Bloom, P. J. (1996). *Improving the quality of work life in the early childhood setting: Resource guide and technical manual for the Early Childhood Work Environment Survey.* Wheeling, IL: The McCormick Tribune Center for Early Childhood Leadership, National-Louis University.

Early Childhood Work Environment Survey

(Short Form)

This survey is designed to find out how you feel about this early childhood center as a place to work. The success of this survey depends on your candid and honest responses. Please know that your answers are completely confidential; you do not need to sign the form. When you have completed the questionnaire, put it in the attached plain envelope, seal it, and give it to your staff representative. Indicate in the space provided the numeral (0–5) that most accurately describes how you feel about each statement.

Never	Seldom	Sometimes	Somewhat regularly	Frequently	Always
0	1	2	3	4	5

_____ Staff are friendly and trust one another.

_____ Morale is high. There is a good team spirit.

_____ Staff are encouraged to learn new skills and competencies.

_____ The center provides guidance for professional advancement.

_____ Supervisor(s) are knowledgeable and competent.

_____ Supervisor(s) provide helpful feedback.

_____ Communication regarding policies and procedures is clear.

_____ Job responsibilities are well defined.

_____ Salaries and fringe benefits are distributed equitably.

_____ Promotions are handled fairly.

_____ Teachers help make decisions about things that directly affect them.

_____ People feel free to express their opinions.

_____ Staff agree on school philosophy and educational objectives.

_____ Staff share a common vision of what the center should be like.

_____ The program is well planned and efficiently run.

_____ Meetings are productive. Time is not wasted.

_____ The work environment is attractive and well organized.

_____ There are sufficient supplies and equipment for staff to do their jobs.

_____ Staff are encouraged to be creative and innovative in their work.

_____ The center implements changes as needed.

What three words describe the climate of this center as a place to work?

What do you perceive to be the greatest strengths of this center?

What areas do you feel could use some improvement?

Thank you!

Leadership Style

Rationale:

The leadership style of the director of an early childhood program is perhaps the most critical factor influencing organizational effectiveness. The director must create an environment based on mutual respect in which individuals work together to accomplish collective goals. The success of this endeavor depends in large part on the director's ability to balance organizational needs with individual needs. Research in this area suggests that leaders who head the most effective organizations tend to be those who apply an integrated leadership style—the ability to adjust their style to the demands of each situation so that both organizational needs and individual needs are met.

Part I of this assessment was adapted from the work of Blake and Mouton (1994); Giammatteo (1975); Hersey, Blanchard, & Johnson (2001); and Yukl (2002). It assesses three different leadership styles: the task-oriented style emphasizing organizational needs; the people-oriented style focusing on people and their individual needs; and the integrated style stressing an appropriate emphasis on both the center's needs and the individual worker's needs, depending on the situation. Part II of Assessment Tool #4 provides staff with an opportunity to assess the degree to which you the director exhibit 25 different leadership traits. It was adapted from the work of Neugebauer (1990).

Directions:

Distribute the *"My Director..."* feedback form and a blank envelope to all employees who work at your center more than 10 hours per week. (If you are a male, the gender of pronouns in some of the questions will first need to be changed.) You may also choose to give the form to other individuals (e.g., board members, supervisors, center owner) whom you feel have an important perspective on your performance. Be sure to complete the assessment yourself so you can compare your responses with the collective perceptions of others.

Place a box labeled Questionnaire Return Box in your center's office or staff room, and ask respondents to put the envelopes holding their completed, unsigned surveys in this box. Reassure individuals about the confidentiality of their responses.

Scoring:

The composite results of Part I summarize your staff's perceptions of your dominant leadership style. The following scoring sheet includes a brief description of the three leadership styles assessed by this questionnaire. To score Part I, tally the responses by noting with a mark each time a staff member checked a particular response:

1. _____	9. _____	17. _____
2. _____	10. _____	18. _____
3. _____	11. _____	19. _____
4. _____	12. _____	20. _____
5. _____	13. _____	21. _____
6. _____	14. _____	22. _____
7. _____	15. _____	23. _____
8. _____	16. _____	24. _____

Now total the marks for the following groups of responses. These totals will indicate how your leadership style is perceived.

Task-oriented: 1, 6, 8, 10, 14, 17, 19, 22   Total _____

Achieving center goals is most important in a task-oriented leadership style. The director exhibits a strong concern for high performance and accomplishing tasks. Emphasis is on planning, directing, following procedures, and applying uniform standards and expectations for all. This director may be viewed as too structured, bureaucratic, and inflexible.

People-oriented: 2, 4, 7, 11, 15, 18, 20, 24   Total _____

Achieving harmonious group relations is foremost in a people-oriented leadership style. The director places a strong emphasis on maintaining comfortable, friendly, and satisfying working conditions and allowing staff to exercise control and be self-directed with minimal intrusion of centerwide policies. Staff working in centers with this style of leadership may complain about the lack of order and coordination.

Integrated: 3, 5, 9, 12, 13, 16, 21, 23   Total _____

Achieving both center goals and maintaining high morale is important in an integrated leadership style. This director is flexible and fair, recognizing that different situations may require a different emphasis on centerwide needs or individual needs.

To score Part II, use the Summary Form to record your own scores and those of each rater.

- ▶ Enter your own score for each of the 25 items in the column headed "Self-rating."
- ▶ In the columns A to J under the heading "Other raters," enter the scores for each individual who completed Part II of the *"My Director..."* feedback form.
- ▶ For each trait, generate an average score by totaling the respondents' ratings and then dividing the total by the number of respondents. Record the result under the "Average" heading in the far right column. Do this for each of the 25 traits.
- ▶ Generate an average rating by each respondent by adding the scores going down each column. (The totals will range from 25–125.) Then divide each total (near the bottom of the form) by 25 (the number of traits).
- ▶ Generate an average overall rating for the "Other raters" by adding the individual average ratings (at the bottom) and dividing by the total by the number of respondents.

Interpreting the ratings: As you compare your own ratings with the average ratings of your colleagues, look for four themes:

- ▶ Agreed-upon strengths—traits that both you and your staff rated high.
- ▶ Unrealized strengths—traits that you rated low, but your staff rated high.
- ▶ Areas for growth—traits that both you and your staff rated low.
- ▶ Blind spots—traits that you rated high, but your staff rated low.

For a fuller discussion about how to interpret your leadership style, see *Leadership in Action: How Effective Directors Get Things Done* (Bloom, 2003).

"My Director ..."

Dear Staff:

One of the hallmarks of an effective early childhood professional is the ability to reflect on his or her or her performance. Your feedback about my leadership style is important in helping me grow professionally. Please take a few minutes to complete this leadership style evaluation form. When you have finished, insert it in the attached envelope and put it in the Questionnaire Return Box in the office. There is no need for you to put your name on the form.

Thank you.
(Your signature)

PART I: Place a check (✔) in front of the statement that most nearly reflects your director's leadership style in different situations. *(Check only one response in each group).*

With respect to planning, my director...

1. _____ does most of the planning herself by setting goals, objectives, and work schedules for staff to follow. She then works out procedures and responsibilities for staff to follow.

2. _____ does very little planning, either by herself or with the staff. She tells the staff she has confidence in them to carry out their jobs in a responsible way.

3. _____ gets staff members together to assess centerwide problems and discuss ideas and strategies for improvement. Together they set up goals and objectives and establish individual responsibilities.

With respect to work assignments and the day-to-day operation of the center, my director...

4. _____ checks with staff regularly to see if they are content and if they have the things they need. She does not see the necessity of precise job descriptions, preferring instead to let the staff determine the scope and nature of their jobs.

5. _____ is flexible in adapting job descriptions and changing work assignments as needed. Updates center polices and procedures depending on the needs of the staff, parents, children, and board.

6. _____ tends to go by the book. Expects staff to adhere to written job descriptions. Follows policies and procedures precisely.

With respect to leadership philosophy, my director...

7. _____ tends to emphasize people's well-being, believing that happy workers will be productive workers.

8. _____ tends to emphasize hard work and a job well done. We are a results-oriented program.

9. _____ tends to emphasize both what we do and what we need as people.

During meetings, my director...

10. _____ keeps focused on the agenda and the topics that need to be covered.

11. _____ focuses on each individual's feelings and helps people express their emotional reactions to an issue.

12. _____ focuses on differing positions people take and how they deal with each other.

The primary goal of my director is...

13. _____ to meet the needs of parents and children while providing a healthy work climate for staff.

14. _____ to keep the center running efficiently.

15. _____ to help staff find fulfillment.

In evaluating the staff's performance, my director...

16. _____ attempts to assess how each individual's performance has contributed to center-wide achievement of goals.

17. _____ makes an assessment of each person's performance and effectiveness according to predetermined established criteria applied equally to all staff.

18. _____ allows people to set their own goals and determine performance standards.

My director believes the best way to motivate someone who is not performing up to his/her ability is to...

19. _____ point out to the individual the importance of the job to be done.

20. _____ try to get to know the individual better in an attempt to understand why the person is not realizing his/her potential.

21. _____ work with the individual to redefine job responsibilities to more effectively contribute to centerwide goals.

My director believes it is her role to...

22. _____ make sure that staff members have a solid foundation of knowledge and skill that will help them accomplish center goals.

23. _____ help people learn to work effectively in groups to accomplish group goals.

24. _____ help individuals become responsible for their own education and effectiveness, and take the first step toward realizing their potential.

What three words or phrases most accurately describe the leadership style of your director:

_____   _____   _____

PART II. Circle the numeral from 1 to 5 (1 = *strongly disagree*, 5 = *strongly agree*) that most nearly represents your assessment of my performance in each of the areas described.

My director is ...	Strongly disagree				Strongly agree
accessible—is available when staff, parents, or community representatives need to reach him/her.	1	2	3	4	5
collaborative—encourages staff to participate in centerwide decisions impacting their welfare.	1	2	3	4	5
confident—has a can-do spirit and sense of optimism about the future.	1	2	3	4	5
creative—looks for new and novel ways to solve problems and keep things interesting.	1	2	3	4	5
dependable—can be counted on to follow through on commitments and responsibilities.	1	2	3	4	5
direct—is clear and forthright in both oral and written communication.	1	2	3	4	5
empathetic—is genuinely concerned about the well-being of the staff and children.	1	2	3	4	5
enthusiastic—has the energy and stamina to handle the daily demands of the director's job.	1	2	3	4	5
ethical—demonstrates integrity in both words and actions.	1	2	3	4	5
fair—looks at all sides of an issue and takes into consideration equity factors when making tough decisions.	1	2	3	4	5
flexible—is willing to make accommodations when necessary to support staff and families.	1	2	3	4	5
friendly—displays a warm and gracious manner to staff, parents, and visitors to the center.	1	2	3	4	5

	Strongly disagree				**Strongly agree**

good listener—knows how to listen respectfully
and attentively to others.

1 2 3 4 5

inspiring—has high expectations and helps people
achieve their personal best.

1 2 3 4 5

knowledgeable—keeps current about new developments
and best practices in the field of early childhood education.

1 2 3 4 5

objective—makes decisions after seeking different perspectives
and weighing the advantages and disadvantages of each.

1 2 3 4 5

open—shares important information about the center
with staff and parents.

1 2 3 4 5

optimistic—has a positive attitude and keeps things
in a healthy perspective.

1 2 3 4 5

organized—knows how to create organizational systems
to ensure the smooth functioning of the program.

1 2 3 4 5

predictable—ensures that expectations are clearly
defined and policies are consistently enforced.

1 2 3 4 5

problem solver—gathers needed data to solve
problems in a systematic and timely manner.

1 2 3 4 5

resourceful—knows how to tap community resources
to get things done.

1 2 3 4 5

respectful—treats each employee as a unique and special
person and appreciates diversity as an organizational asset.

1 2 3 4 5

supportive—promotes the professional growth of staff by
providing opportunities for ongoing training and development.

1 2 3 4 5

visionary—has a sense of mission and communicates
a clear vision for the future.

1 2 3 4 5

Summary Form

Trait	Self-rating	Other raters										Average
		A	B	C	D	E	F	G	H	I	J	
Accessible												
Collaborative												
Confident												
Creative												
Dependable												
Direct												
Empathetic												
Enthusiastic												
Ethical												
Fair												
Flexible												
Friendly												
Good listener												
Inspiring												
Knowledgeable												
Objective												
Open												
Optimistic												
Organized												
Predictable												
Problem solver												
Resourceful												
Respectful												
Supportive												
Visionary												

Total												
Average rating												

Agreed-upon strengths: _____

Unrealized strengths: _____

Areas for growth: _____

Blind spots: _____

Goal Consensus and Communication Processes

Rationale:

The hallmark of any successful organization is a shared sense among its members about what they are trying to accomplish. Agreed-upon goals and ways to attain them provide the foundation for rational planning and action. One cannot assume, however, that just because a center's goals and objectives are committed to paper there will be uniform agreement among staff about their importance. Assessment Tool #5 assesses staff's rankings of various educational goals and objectives. From this information you will be able to determine the degree of goal consensus that exists among your staff. The six educational objectives included on this questionnaire are common objectives for most early childhood programs. Feel free to reword them to make them more appropriate for your program.

Goal consensus depends largely on the effectiveness of communication in the center. Communication of information takes many forms in early care and education programs. It can be oral or written, formal or informal, personal or impersonal. Communication networks also vary in centers. They may be vertical (from supervisor to teacher) or horizontal (between teachers). Assessment Tool #5 also assesses staff's perceptions of the effectiveness of communication at the center. The questions on this assessment tool were adapted from the work of Bean and Clemes (1978), Bloom (1996), and Rosenholtz (1989).

Directions:

Distribute the "Goal Consensus and Communication Processes Questionnaire" and a blank envelope to all teaching staff who work at the center more than 10 hours per week. Place a box labeled Questionnaire Return Box in your center's office or staff room and ask staff to put their completed, unsigned questionnaires in this box.

Scoring:

Tally the results of Part I by noting the number of individuals who ranked each educational objective as 1, 2, 3, 4, 5, 6. When you have completed the tally, you will have a profile of the distribution of staff's perceptions of the importance of different educational objectives. If there is strong goal consensus among your staff, the responses should cluster. In other words, you should see a strong agreement among staff about which one or two educational objectives are most important and which objective is least important. Even in centers where there is strong goal consensus, it is rare to see strong agreement in the third, fourth, and fifth rankings. Remember, the larger your staff, the more difficult it is to achieve goal consensus. Thus large programs (with more than 20 staff completing the questionnaire) should expect to see a wider distribution of responses.

For Part II of the questionnaire, for each statement tally the number of individuals who checked the statement as being an accurate reflection of center practices. Divide this number by the total number of respondents to find the percentage of staff who agree with the statement.

For Part III total the scores of individual respondents. They will range from 10 to 50. Then add together all respondents' scores and divide by the number of staff completing the questionnaire. This will yield an average score. Average scores between 40 and 50 indicate that staff perceive the communication processes of the center to be quite positive. Average scores between 10 and 20 indicate that staff feel this is an area that may need some improvement.

Goal Consensus and Communication Processes Questionnaire

This questionnaire has three parts. Part I assesses your perceptions of the priority of different goals and educational objectives in the center. Part II asks you to indicate which statements accurately reflect how you feel about goal consensus at the center. Finally, Part III assesses your attitudes about the effectiveness of different communication processes in the center. Your honest and candid responses to these questions are appreciated. When you have completed your questionnaire, please put it in the envelope you have received and place it in the Questionnaire Return Box in the office. There is no need to include your name.

PART I. Rank order the following program objectives according to how important you feel they are at this center. Put a 1 by the most important, a 2 by the next most important and so on until you get to 6 for the least important. *Each objective must only have one numeral next to it.*

_____   to help children develop language and problem-solving skills

_____   to help children build strong friendships and learn to share

_____   to help children master concepts needed for reading and arithmetic

_____   to help children develop skill and independence in caring for themselves

_____   to help children develop physical coordination

_____   to help children develop a healthy self-esteem and positive self-concept

PART II. Please check (✔) all statements that accurately describe how you feel.

_____   At this center we agree on the objectives we're trying to achieve with students.

_____   The director's values and philosophy of education are similar to my own.

_____   Most teachers at this center have an educational philosophy and personal values similar to my own.

_____   There are clear guidelines at this center about the things teachers should emphasize in their teaching.

_____   Discussion about center goals and the means of achieving them are a regular part of our staff meetings.

_____   Before teachers are hired at this center, they are asked about their philosophy of teaching.

PART III. Circle a number from 1 (*strongly disagree*) to 5 (*strongly agree*) to indicate for each of the following statements how you feel about the statement:

	Strongly disagree				*Strongly agree*
Written communication at this center is clear	1	2	3	4	5
Staff seem well informed most of the time	1	2	3	4	5
The information I receive is usually accurate	1	2	3	4	5
Families seem well informed about issues and events	1	2	3	4	5
Communication between teachers is open and direct	1	2	3	4	5
Communication between the director and staff is open	1	2	3	4	5
Expressing my ideas and feelings is easy to do here	1	2	3	4	5
People feel comfortable disagreeing with one another	1	2	3	4	5
The director makes an effort to solicit feedback	1	2	3	4	5
Policy manuals and written procedures are clear	1	2	3	4	5

What suggestions do you have for improving communication processes at the center?

Collegiality and Collaboration

Rationale:

Collegiality is esprit de corps, that feeling of sharing and caring for one another that is so essential to a team effort in improving center functioning. Assessment Tool #6 assesses staff's perceptions about their overall co-worker relations, specifically, the extent to which they feel teaching at the center is a team effort directed toward the collaborative goal of improving center effectiveness. Rosenholtz (1989) states that "collaborative norms undergird achievement-oriented groups, they bring new ideas, fresh ways of looking at things, and a stock of collective knowledge that is more fruitful than any one person's work alone" (p. 41).

Whether or not teachers work mutually depends in large part on the harmony of their interests within the center—the degree to which they hold similar values and share similar educational goals for children and families. It should not be surprising, then, if the results of this assessment are similar to those of the goal consensus (Assessment Tool #5). The questions on this assessment tool were adapted from the work of Rosenholtz (1989).

Directions:

Distribute the "Collaboration Index" and a blank envelope to all teaching and support staff who work at the center more than 10 hours per week. Place a box labeled Questionnaire Return Box in your center's office or staff room and ask staff to put their completed, unsigned questionnaires in this box.

Scoring:

Since many of the questions on this instrument deal with sensitive social relationship issues, it is wise to have an outside person tabulate the results and summarize the responses to the open-ended question. The scores for this instrument will range from 0 to 10. To determine the center's collaboration index,

a. For each respondent tally the number of checks next to items 1, 3, 5, 6, 9   Total _____ (a)

b. For each respondent tally the number of checks next to items 2, 4, 7, 8, 10   Total _____ (b)

c. A respondent's individual total score is (a) – (b) + 5 = _____ (c)

d. Add together all the individual total scores (c) and divide by the total number of staff completing the questionnaire to determine your center's collaboration index. A score of 7 to 10 indicates that your staff has quite positive feelings about teamwork at your center. A score lower than 4 indicates that there is room for improving the climate of collaboration.

Collaboration Index

This questionnaire assesses your perceptions of the degree to which the staff functions as a team. Your honest and candid responses to these questions are appreciated. When you have completed your questionnaire, please put it in the envelope provided and place it in the Questionnaire Return Box in the office. It is not necessary for you to include your name.

Put a check (✓) next to those items which accurately reflect how you feel.

_____ 1. Other teachers at this center regularly seek my advice about professional issues and problems.

_____ 2. I don't offer advice to other teachers about their teaching unless they ask me for it.

_____ 3. I regularly share teaching ideas, materials, and resources with other teachers at this center.

_____ 4. I believe that good teaching is a gift; it isn't something you can really learn from anyone else.

_____ 5. If teachers at this center feel that another teacher is not doing a good job, they will exert some pressure on her/him to improve.

_____ 6. The director encourages teachers to plan together and collaborate on instructional units, field trips, and classroom activities.

_____ 7. Substitutes at this center often do not know what is expected of them.

_____ 8. Most of the time the other teachers at this center don't know what I do in my classroom with my group of children.

_____ 9. I see myself as part of a team and share responsibility for our center's successes and shortcomings.

_____ 10. I can go for days at this center without talking to anyone about my teaching.

Select the three words that most accurately describe other staff at this center:

cooperative	friendly	isolated	cautious
competitive	trusting	guarded	helpful
caring	cliquish	open	mistrustful

What suggestions do you have that might increase opportunities for collaboration and teamwork at our center (e.g., modifying work schedules, changing the layout of space)?

Decision-Making Processes

Rationale:

The opportunity to participate in centerwide decision making is an important factor impacting the morale of teachers. It is also an essential ingredient in achieving a collaborative model of center improvement. Since every center is unique, the nature of decision-making processes will also be unique. Thus the roles that teachers and director play in the decision-making process will vary according to the nature of the issue being considered and the background and interests of the parties involved. Not all teaching staff want the same degree of decision-making influence in all areas of program functioning.

Assessment Tool #7 is designed to assess staff's perceptions of their current and desired levels of decision-making influence in 10 areas. The purpose of this assessment is to measure the discrepancy between perceived levels of current and desired decision-making influence. Assessment Tool #7 also includes questions about how staff perceive the decision-making processes of the center. The information gleaned from this instrument will give you a clearer picture of the areas in which staff desire a greater role in decision making. The questions on this assessment tool were adapted from the decision-making assessment tool in *Circle of Influence: Implementing Shared Decision Making and Participative Management* (Bloom, 2000).

Directions:

Distribute the "Decision-Making Influence Questionnaire" and a blank envelope to all teaching staff who work at the center more than 10 hours per week. Place a box labeled Questionnaire Return Box in your center's office or staff room and ask staff to place their completed, unsigned questionnaires in this box.

Scoring:

Tally the results of Part I by assigning the following point values: 0 = *very little influence*, 1 = *some influence*, 2 = *considerable influence*. To determine a discrepancy score between current and desired levels of decision-making influence, make the following calculations:

a. Calculate the current decision-making influence score for each respondent (scores will range from 0 to 20).

b. Calculate the desired decision-making influence score for each respondent (scores will range from 0 to 20).

c.   Add together all the current decision-making influence scores for respondents and divide by the total number of respondents to get an average current decision-making influence score. The average current decision-making influence score will range from 0 to 20.

d.   Add together all the desired decision-making influence scores for respondents and divide by the total number of respondents to get an average desired decision-making influence score. The average desired decision-making influence score will range from 0 to 20.

e.   For most programs the average desired decision-making influence score is greater than the average current decision-making influence score. Subtract the average current decision-making influence score from the average desired decision-making influence score to determine the discrepancy between current and desired levels of decision-making influence. The strength of this discrepancy will help you understand how strongly staff feel about wanting greater input into the decision-making processes at the center. A discrepancy score of greater than 10 would indicate that staff have strong feelings about their perceived current and desired levels of influence.

Occasionally teachers will voice concern that they desire less decision-making influence than they currently have. In this case the desired decision-making influence score will be lower than the current decision-making influence score.

For Part II, tally the total number of checks for each item and divide by the total number of questionnaires completed. This will yield a percentage of staff who feel that the statement characterizes decision-making processes at the center.

Decision-Making Influence Questionnaire

This questionnaire has two parts. Part I assesses your perceptions about your current and desired levels of decision-making influence. Part II assesses your perceptions about the way decisions are made at this center. Your honest and candid responses to these questions are appreciated. When you have completed your questionnaire, please put it in the envelope provided and place it in the Questionnaire Return Box in the office. There is no need to include your name.

PART I. Read the attached handout "Types of Decisions in the Early Childhood Setting." Then in the space below indicate (✔) how much influence you *currently have* and how much influence you would *like to have* in each of the 10 areas listed.

TYPE OF ORGANIZATIONAL DECISIONS	CURRENT INFLUENCE			DESIRED INFLUENCE		
	Very little influence	Some influence	Considerable influence	Very little influence	Some influence	Considerable influence
Staff supervision and professional development						
Instructional practices and scheduling						
Enrollment and grouping						
Fiscal policies and practices						
Human resource allocation						
Centerwide goals and educational objectives						
Family relations						
Community relations						
Facilities management						
Evaluation practices (child, staff, center)						

PART II. Check (✔) all statements that describe how decisions are made at this center most of the time.

_____ Teachers are asked their opinions on important issues.

_____ The director likes to make most of the decisions.

_____ People don't feel free to express their opinions.

_____ Everyone provides input on the content of staff meetings.

_____ People provide input, but decisions have already been made.

_____ Teachers make decisions about things that directly affect them.

_____ Decisions are made by those who know most about the problem or issue.

What suggestions do you have for promoting shared decision making at this center?

From: Bloom, P. J. (2000). *Circle of influence: Implementing shared decision making and participative management.* Lake Forest, IL: New Horizons. Reprinted with permission.

Types of Decisions in the Early Childhood Setting

Staff supervision and professional development
- establish guidelines and procedures for staff orientation
- establish guidelines for supervision of teaching staff
- establish guidelines for supervision of support staff
- determine the type and frequency of in-service training
- establish career ladder guidelines

Instructional practices and scheduling
- determine the daily schedule of classroom activities
- select instructional materials and equipment
- determine the content of the curriculum
- determine the type and frequency of special events
- establish an annual calendar

Enrollment and grouping
- determine enrollment criteria and policies
- determine group size and patterns (e.g., mixed-age grouping)
- determine grouping assignments
- determine adult-child ratios
- determine the placement of children with special needs

Fiscal policies and practices
- determine tuition and fees
- determine salaries and benefits
- set priorities for center and classroom expenditures
- determine fund-raising priorities and goals
- determine the procedure for accounts payable and accounts receivable

Human resource allocation
- determine the qualifications for different positions
- determine staff hiring criteria and procedures
- determine the staffing pattern and teaching assignments
- set staff work schedules
- determine the criteria for promotion and advancement

Centerwide goals and educational objectives

► determine the center's philosophy
► determine the educational objectives for different age groups
► determine the frequency and scheduling of staff meetings
► determine staff meeting agendas
► establish a code of conduct (e.g., dress, confidentiality)

Family relations

► determine who serves as primary contact with the family
► set expectations for family involvement
► determine the format and frequency of parent conferences
► determine the type and frequency of parent education
► determine the content of the family newsletter

Community relations

► determine the type of contacts with community agencies
► establish marketing and public relations priorities
► determine the content of press releases
► establish a risk management plan
► determine the type of contact with local schools

Facilities management

► determine how space is allocated
► determine how space is arranged
► establish food service procedures and contracts
► determine capital improvement priorities
► determine maintenance procedures and contracts

Evaluation practices (child, staff, center)

► determine the type and frequency of child assessments
► determine guidelines for staff performance appraisals
► determine the type and frequency of programwide evaluations
► determine the center's accreditation timeline and procedures
► determine the use and distribution of evaluation data

Supervision and Evaluation Processes

Rationale:

It is customary in early childhood work settings for staff to be evaluated by their supervisors. Seldom, however, are teachers and support staff given the opportunity to offer feedback to their supervisors about the quality of the supervision and evaluation they receive. This is unfortunate, because a teacher's ability, interest, and desire to improve often depends on the quality of the relationship the teacher has established with his/her supervisor. Without solid supervisory and evaluation processes in place, individual and collective change simply cannot take place.

Assessment Tool #8 measures staff's perceptions of the extent to which the supervisory and performance appraisal processes of the center pose constraints or opportunities for professional growth. This assessment focuses on the individual employee's relationship with his or her immediate supervisor. This could be a lead teacher, education coordinator, or the director if he/she has immediate supervisory responsibility for the employees. It is important to remember that this assessment measures perceptions and these perceptions may or may not mirror yours or someone else's notion of objective reality. Perceptions are important, though, because how people perceive any given situation or working relationship shapes their behavior. The questions on this instrument were adapted from the work of Bean and Clemes (1978), Bloom (1996), and Neugebauer (1990).

Directions:

Distribute the "Supervisory Behavior Questionnaire" and a blank envelope to each employee who works at the center more than 10 hours per week. (For nonteaching staff, it may be necessary to revise sections of this questionnaire to accurately reflect the nature of their jobs.) Before distributing the survey, indicate the name of the supervisor you want the employee to evaluate. This may be the lead teacher of a single classroom or the education coordinator who supervises several classrooms. In centers where the director is the primary supervisor of staff, the director's name will appear on the surveys.

To get accurate feedback from staff, you should stress the importance of providing honest, candid responses to all questions. Assure them of the confidential nature of their responses.

Scoring:

Since the nature of this assessment is sensitive, you may want to designate an outside person to tabulate the results and summarize the findings. This summary can then be given to the individual supervisors. The results of this assessment will need to be coded separately for each supervisor assessed.

To score Part I, add up the number of items checked on each completed survey for each supervisor being rated. The scores will range from 0 to 25. Total all scores for each supervisor and divide by the number of respondents rating that supervisor. This will yield an average supervisory behavior score for each supervisor.

Scores greater than 20 indicate that the respondents have very positive attitudes about the opportunities for professional growth that are available, the fairness of performance appraisal procedures used at the center, and the support and helpful encouragement they receive from their supervisor. Scores lower than 10 indicate that respondents have generally unfavorable perceptions about the supervisory and evaluation processes at the center.

It may also be helpful to do an item analysis for this section of the instrument. This can be done by tallying the total number of respondents who checked each statement. Divide this number by the total number of respondents to get a percentage of participants who responded affirmatively to the statement.

Part II of this assessment tool focuses on the supervisor's listening behavior. To derive a supervisory listening quotient, score each questionnaire in the following manner.

a.   For each respondent add up the number of checks next to items #1, 4, 7, 8, 11, 12, 13, 15, 19, 20

     total _____ (a)

b.   For each respondent add up the number of checks for items #2, 3, 5, 6, 9, 10, 14, 16, 17, 18

     total _____ (b)

c.   The supervisor's listening quotient on each survey (c) equals (a) – (b) + 10

     total _____ (c) (scores will range from 0–20)

d.   Add together all the individual respondents' scores (c) for a particular supervisor and divide by the number of respondents to yield an average listening quotient for that supervisor.

Scores between 15 and 20 indicate that respondents feel their supervisor is attentive, genuinely interested, and supportive when engaged in conversation. Scores lower than 5 signal the need for supervisors to build stronger listening and communication skills. This same instrument could be used as a posttest measure at a later date to determine if the staff's perceptions of the supervisor's listening skills had improved.

Supervisory Behavior Questionnaire

The purpose of this questionnaire is to give you an opportunity to provide feedback about the supervisory and evaluation processes at this center. In answering the questions that refer to a specific person, please provide feedback regarding the individual whose name appears below. When you have completed all three parts of this questionnaire, please put it in the envelope provided and give it to your staff representative. You do not need to sign it. The results of this survey will be tabulated, and a written summary will be given to your supervisor and center director.

Name of supervisor _____

PART I. Check (✓) all those statements with which you agree.

_____ At this center, I have many opportunities to learn new things.
_____ Evaluation of my teaching is used to help me improve.
_____ The standards by which my teaching is evaluated are clear and well specified.
_____ The methods used in evaluating my teaching are objective and fair.
_____ I know what I'm being evaluated on at this center.

My supervisor...

_____ provides suggestions to help me become the best possible teacher.
_____ encourages me to try out new ideas.
_____ encourages me to be independent and self-reliant.
_____ spends enough time in my classroom observing my teaching.
_____ sets high but realistic expectations.
_____ takes a strong interest in my professional development.
_____ displays a strong interest in improving the quality of our program.
_____ helps me understand the sources of important problems I face.
_____ provides the resources I need to help me improve my performance.
_____ provides constructive suggestions that help me deal with problems I encounter.
_____ uses praise appropriately.
_____ communicates effectively.
_____ is dependable and reliable.
_____ is friendly and sociable.
_____ is ethical, honest, and trustworthy.
_____ is patient and supportive.
_____ is knowledgeable about early childhood education.
_____ uses time wisely.
_____ is available when I need her/him.
_____ stays calm in difficult situations.

PART II. Check (✓) the statements that reflect your appraisal of your supervisor's listening behavior.

When you and I are talking together...

1. _____ you make me feel as if this is the most important thing you could be doing right now.

2. _____ your attention is often divided; you interrupt our conversation by answering the phone or addressing the needs of others.

3. _____ you sometimes begin shaking your head or saying "no" before I finish my thought.

4. _____ you refer to our previous conversations; there is a history to our communication.

5. _____ you fidget and squirm and look at the clock as though you can't wait to get on to other more important projects and conversations.

6. _____ you begin asking questions before I finish my message.

7. _____ you look me in the eye and really focus attention on me.

8. _____ you ask thoughtful questions that let me know you were really listening.

9. _____ you finish my sentences for me as though nothing I have to say is new to you.

10. _____ you change the agenda by taking over and changing the content of the conversation.

11. _____ you follow up on what we discussed and keep me posted on what is happening.

12. _____ you are sensitive to the tone of what I have to say and respond respectfully.

13. _____ you give me credit for ideas and projects that grow out of our communications.

14. _____ you try to speed things up and leap ahead with conclusions as though we're in a rush.

15. _____ you smile at me and make me feel comfortable and valued.

16. _____ you make jokes about things that are serious to me and thereby belittle my concerns.

17. _____ you get defensive and argue before I can fully explain my point.

18. _____ you often make me feel I have nothing worthwhile to say.

19. _____ you ask questions that demonstrate your efforts to understand what I have to say.

20. _____ whether or not you agree with me, you make me feel my opinions and feelings are respected.

Part II is adapted from Neugebauer, B. (1990, September/October). Are you listening? *Child Care Information Exchange*, p. 62. Reprinted with permission.

Organizational Norms

Rationale:

Norms are standards or codes of expected behavior—shared assumptions about the way things are done at the center. Most norms are seldom verbalized or made explicit in writing, yet they still serve as powerful regulators of behavior. When an individual violates a norm, others in the group will probably respond with some kind of sanction or subtle reminder that the behavior is out of bounds. Such enforcement can be in the form of joking or kidding, ignoring the individual, or taking the person aside to give a cautionary warning. Some norms are useful; they provide staff with implicit guidelines about what to do in different situations. Other norms, though, may be counterproductive, obsolete, irrelevant, or actually prevent the center from achieving its stated goals.

Periodically assessing staff's perceptions of the dominant norms that exist in the center can provide useful data about the degree to which certain norms are shared by members of the staff. Such an inventory also helps staff identify the norms that may need to be altered if center improvement efforts are to take hold. Assessment Tool #9 was adapted from the work of Bloom (1986) and Schmuck and Runkel (1994).

Directions:

Distribute a blank envelope and the assessment "The Way Things Are Done Around Here..." to all teaching and support staff who work at the center more than 10 hours per week. Place a box labeled Questionnaire Return Box in the center's office or staff room and ask staff to place their completed surveys in the box. Let staff know that although they will be writing their responses by hand, their anonymity will be maintained because an outside party will be summarizing the data.

Scoring:

Because of the potentially sensitive nature of some of the responses to this assessment, it is recommended that an outside party summarize the data. Summarizing the responses is a fairly straightforward process. Create a separate summary page for each of the seven categories included on the assessment. On each page, list all the norms that were mentioned by respondents along with the corresponding +, –, or 0. If a norm is mentioned by more than one individual, do not list it twice, merely indicate an additional +, –, or 0 next to it. Norms that are mentioned by several people indicate they are fairly established, shared norms. Those mentioned by only one person may indicate a misperception by that individual of center expectations.

You'll need to decide how to use the data generated from the results of this assessment. If a climate of trust has been established at the center, the summarized results can serve as a wonderful springboard for a staff meeting discussion. Sharing the results of this assessment can serve to free individuals to examine the norms that are beneficial and those that may need to be changed.

While acknowledging that the director has a significant role in both creating and sustaining norms, changing norms requires the collaboration of the entire staff. The group must have a shared perception of the value of the change, otherwise efforts to change will be fruitless. Changing a norm usually means changing the way people behave. This requires consensus not only about what the new behavior will be but also how that new behavior will be reinforced. The value of doing this goes beyond the specific norm being changed. In the process staff will become conscious of the group dynamic and grow together in structuring collaborative change.

"The Way Things are Done Around Here..."

When individuals work together in a work setting, implicit agreement develops about the way things are supposed to be done. Over time these shared patterns of behavior become standards and define the appropriate range of acceptable behavior in a variety of situations. The term norm is used to describe these shared assumptions and expectations. Norms include things we are expected to do and things we should not do. Every center varies in the kinds of norms it has and in the intensity with which they are felt.

This assessment asks you to think about some of the do's and don'ts of your center. It is divided into seven different areas. Under each category, think of some of the norms (the do's and don'ts) that you feel are shared expectations.

Everyday demeanor (Includes expectations about appropriate dress, whether or not smoking is allowed, the amount of noise tolerated, and the degree of formality in everyday manners)

_____   _____

_____   _____

_____   _____

Use of space and materials (Includes such things as expectations for sharing of supplies, who cleans up when and how often, and the amount of clutter tolerated)

_____   _____

_____   _____

_____   _____

Time and task orientation (Includes such things as assumptions about workload, expectations for promptness in beginning meetings, and the degree of participation expected)

_____   _____

_____   _____

_____   _____

Professional conduct with children and families (Includes expectations about the type of guidance used with children, the teacher's classroom behavior, and the degree of parental involvement)

_____   _____

_____   _____

_____   _____

Collegiality (Includes assumptions that govern social interaction among staff, such as the degree to which staff are open or reserved in displaying emotions, the extent to which people talk about their personal lives, and how new teachers and substitutes are treated)

_____   _____

_____   _____

_____   _____

Communication and decision making (Includes expectations about the topics staff feel free to discuss, taboo subjects, how much griping is allowed, how decisions are made, and the degree to which people are frank, open, and free to disagree with one another)

_____   _____

_____   _____

_____   _____

Change and experimentation (Includes expectations for individual and group improvement, the degree of risk taking tolerated, and openness to new ideas and ways of doing things)

_____   _____

_____   _____

_____   _____

Now go back through each category and in front of each norm you have written, indicate whether or not you think this is a useful norm. In other words, does the norm support the goals of the center and enhance the staff's ability to carry out their work? If you feel it is a positive norm, indicate so by putting a + in front of it. If you feel the norm deters the center in any way from achieving its goals, indicate so by putting a – in front of it. If the norm is neutral, neither positive nor negative, put an 0 in front of the norm.

When you have completed this assessment, put your unsigned survey in the blank envelope provided and place it in the Questionnaire Return Box in the office.

Thank you!

Group Meeting Processes

Rationale:

Because staff meetings are the primary vehicle for decision making and problem solving in early childhood programs, it is important to regularly assess staff perceptions about the meetings' effectiveness. Assessment Tool #10 assesses staff's perceptions about the organization, content, and flow of a recent staff meeting. It also asks for feedback about the roles that individuals played during the meeting.

While the ostensible purpose of this assessment is to elicit information that will help you plan and conduct future meetings more effectively, it also serves as a useful professional development tool in helping staff appreciate the important role they play as participants in ensuring successful meeting outcomes. For a more comprehensive treatment of this topic, see *Making the Most of Meetings* (Bloom, 2002).

Directions:

It is probably useful to conduct this assessment only twice a year. The day following a typical staff meeting, distribute a blank envelope and the two-page "Checklist for Effective Staff Meetings" to those who attended the meeting. Place a box labeled Questionnaire Return Box in the office or staff room and ask staff to place the envelopes containing their completed, unsigned surveys in the box.

Scoring:

Tabulate the results of Part I by simply adding up the number of checks in the *yes* column. Scores will range from 0 to 20. Add together all respondents' scores and divide by the number of respondents. This will yield an average score.

A score higher than 15 indicates that staff were generally pleased with the organization, content, and flow of the meeting. Scores lower than 10 indicate there are some areas in the planning and meeting facilitation process that could be improved.

It is important with this type of assessment to also note the range of scores (the highest and lowest score). It is possible that the group average will mask a strong variation in responses. In other words, some people may be quite happy with the meeting, while others were dissatisfied. It is also helpful to do an item analysis noting the two or three items that consistently achieved a *yes* rating by staff and those that were consistently rated *no*. This will help you determine what areas need improvement.

Part II provides insights into the staff's perceptions of the different roles people played during the meeting. This section is perhaps most useful as a check against your own perceptions of how supportive individuals were in guiding the flow of the meeting in a positive way.

Checklist for Effective Staff Meetings

PART I. Check (✔) *yes* or *no* to indicate your reaction to the following questions:

	Yes	No
1. Were all participants informed ahead of time with a written agenda?	____	____
2. Did the meeting start on time?	____	____
3. Did the meeting begin on a positive note?	____	____
4. Was the room arranged to facilitate interaction between members?	____	____
5. Was the content of the meeting relevant to all participants?	____	____
6. Did the group have enough background, information, and expertise to make necessary decisions?	____	____
7. Did all participants have a chance to express their opinions and offer suggestions if they wanted to?	____	____
8. Was the facilitator successful in keeping the discussion focused and on track?	____	____
9. Did the facilitator restate and summarize issues when necessary?	____	____
10. Was an understanding or consensus achieved on one issue before moving on to the next issue?	____	____
11. Was there sufficient time allotted for each item?	____	____
12. Did the facilitator allow enough room and flexibility to adapt the agenda to the needs of the group?	____	____
13. Was the facilitator able to guide discussion so that it did not get bogged down in trivia or turn to petty gossip?	____	____
14. Did participants listen respectfully to each other?	____	____
15. Did most participants express themselves openly, honestly, and directly?	____	____
16. Were differences of opinion on issues openly explored and constructively managed?	____	____
17. When a decision was made, was it clear who would carry it out and when?	____	____
18. Did the meeting end on a positive note?	____	____
19. Did the meeting end on time?	____	____
20. Overall, do you feel your time was well spent at this meeting?	____	____

From Bloom, P. J. (2002). *Making the most of meetings: A practical guide.* Lake Forest, IL: New Horizons, p. 99. Reprinted with permission.

PART II. In your judgment, which members of our staff contributed the most to meeting effectiveness by: [*list names of participants*]

Helping to get the meeting started on time?

_____ _____ _____

Sticking to the agenda?

_____ _____ _____

Performing acts of encouragement, warmth, friendly interest, and support?

_____ _____ _____

Bringing in ideas, information, and suggestions?

_____ _____ _____

Helping us stay on track, summarizing, and checking to make sure we understood one another?

_____ _____ _____

What suggestions do you have for improving our staff meetings in the future?

Parent Satisfaction

Rationale:

Parents are an integral piece of the overall program quality equation in early childhood organizations. How the parental role is understood and acknowledged by the director and staff has a strong bearing on how the center functions. Open, trusting relationships with parents and other child guardians are built on mutual respect. Such environments actively seek to elicit feedback from parents and guardians about different program practices. Assessment Tool #11 is designed as an easy-to-use survey to elicit parental feedback about center policies, procedures, and the overall quality of program services.

Directions:

To ensure that this questionnaire does not get lost among the artwork, story dictations, and other miscellaneous treasures that make their way home in children's tote bags, it is probably best to mail this survey directly to each family. A stamped return envelope addressed to the center should be included. You may even want to include a separate cover letter letting parents know the importance of providing accurate, candid feedback to the center and the date by which you would like the question-naire returned. Let them know that their signature is optional. Two weeks should be sufficient time.

It is recommended that this questionnaire be administered annually. More often than that will burden families and yourself with unnecessary paperwork. Most directors find that late spring is the best time to conduct this assessment.

Scoring:

You will probably find it useful to do an item analysis and note the percentage of respondents who either strongly agree or strongly disagree with each item on the survey. After you have tabulated the data, it is important to share a summary of the results (both positive and negative) with the families in your program. In the summary you provide, try not to overwhelm people with too many details, but be sure to highlight the five or six most noteworthy findings.

Without revealing the identity of respondents, it is also good to include a few quotes in your summary about how children have benefited from the program and about areas that were suggested to be in need of improvement. Such a published summary will convey a strong message to families about your earnest interest in their feedback, both positive and negative. Such information can only help enhance your center's overall reputation.

To determine how parent perceptions of your program improve over time, you may want to derive a total mean score for the assessment. The numerical scores will range from 8 to 40 with a high score indicating more positive perceptions. Add together the parents' total scores and divide by the number of respondents to yield a mean score.

Parent Feedback Survey

Dear Parents and Guardians,

This questionnaire is designed to find out how we are meeting the needs of families enrolled in our program. Your candid and honest responses will enable us to improve communication and services for you and your child. Please circle the number from 1 (*strongly disagree*) to 5 (*strongly agree*) that best represents your feelings about each of the statements below.

	Strongly disagree				*Strongly agree*
1. I have received adequate information about program policies and procedures.	1	2	3	4	5
2. My child received a warm welcome into the program.	1	2	3	4	5
3. Teachers encourage me to be actively involved in my child's learning.	1	2	3	4	5
4. I am regularly informed about my child's growth and development.	1	2	3	4	5
5. Classroom newsletters and teachers' written notes keep me well informed.	1	2	3	4	5
6. I have had sufficient opportunity for conversations with the teaching and administrative staff.	1	2	3	4	5
7. My parent-teacher conferences have provided me with useful insights about my child.	1	2	3	4	5
8. I have been invited to participate in classroom activities and field trips.	1	2	3	4	5

How has your child benefited from his/her experience at this center?

In what ways could we improve the program to better meet your child's needs?

Thank you!

Preschool Teaching Practices

Rationale:

Assessing teaching practices at the classroom level provides a fresh opportunity to ask the central questions that go to the core of our work in early care and education: Is this a good place for children? Is this a place where children thrive—an environment that is safe; an environment that fosters friendship, learning, self-esteem, and joy? Periodically assessing preschool teaching practices will highlight strengths in the way your program is run as well as those areas that may need improvement.

Assessment #12 focuses on four areas of preschool programming: interactions among teachers and children; the curriculum; the physical environment; and health, safety, and nutrition. Although indicators in this assessment are clustered into these four subscales, there is certainly some conceptual as well as practical overlap between subscales.

- **Interactions Among Teachers and Children:** Optimal development in all domains—social, emotional, cognitive, and physical—depends on positive, supportive, individualized relationships with adults. Young children also develop socially and intellectually through peer interaction. Taking time to periodically observe classroom interactions among staff and children is one way to monitor the quality of program services.

- **Curriculum:** The curriculum consists of the program goals, the daily schedule, planned activities, the availability and use of materials, transitions between activities, and the way in which routine tasks of classroom life are implemented. The curriculum of an early childhood program should be consistent with the center's philosophy and mission.

- **Physical Environment:** Research in the area of environmental psychology confirms what we already know from our daily interactions at home and in the workplace—that the arrangement and use of space can have a profound effect on adults and children. The quality of the physical environment in early care and education programs includes the spatial arrangement of classrooms and support space, the adequacy and accessibility of equipment and materials, and the overall aesthetic appeal of the environment. Because the early childhood physical environment can have such a strong impact on children's behavior and teachers' morale, the arrangement and use of space should be evaluated on a regular basis.

- **Health, Safety, and Nutrition:** A safe and healthy environment is essential in the provision of quality early childhood programming. High-quality programs meet the nutritional needs of children with appetizing and healthful foods; they help prevent illness and accidents and are able to deal with emergencies when they occur; and they educate children concerning health and safety practices.

Assessment Tool #12 is based on professional standards of developmentally appropriate practices in early childhood programs (Bredekamp & Copple, 1997). Specific items were adapted from several valid and reliable evaluation instruments (see resources on the following page). Some of the items included in this assessment are beyond the individual teacher's control; they fall under the responsibilities of a center's management. This underscores the important point that achieving and maintaining high-quality learning environments is the shared responsibility of administrative and teaching staff.

Directions:

Separate forms should be used for each preschool classroom observed. You will probably want to collect this observational data over three or four days and at different times during the day. This is important because a particular part of a day's activities may not accurately reflect all the teaching practices included on the assessment tool. After observing each item, indicate your rating by circling the appropriate numeral from 1 (*little evidence*) to 5 (*a great deal of evidence*).

Scoring:

After completing your observation, total all the ratings of individual items to generate scores for each of the four subscales: interactions among teachers and children; curriculum; physical environment; and health, safety, and nutrition. The scores for each subscale will range from a low of 20 to a high of 100. Add together the four subscale scores to generate a total preschool teaching practices score. This total score will range from a low of 80 to a high of 400.

The results from this assessment can be used to identify those teaching practices related to each of the four subscales in which a particular teacher or group of teachers may need improvement. This information will help you modify administrative and supervisory procedures to support more positive preschool teaching practices.

Assessment Tool #12 is particularly useful as a pre and post measure documenting changes in teaching practices as they relate to preschool classrooms. The observed score on the first observation can serve as baseline data from which to measure change in the way an individual teacher or group of teachers interact with children. If theinstrument is used in this way, it is important that the same observer conduct both the pre and post assessments.

Resources:

American Academy of Pediatrics. (1993). *Model child care health policies.* Elk Grove Village, IL: Author.

Bredekamp, S., & Copple, C. (Eds.). (1997). *Developmentally appropriate practice in early childhood programs* (Rev. ed.). Washington, DC: National Association for the Education of Young Children.

Harms, T., Clifford, R., & Cryer, D. (1998). *Early Childhood Environment Rating Scale—Revised.* New York: Teachers College Press.

Hemmeter, M. L., Joseph, G. E., Smith, B. J., & Sandall, S. (Eds.). (2001). *DEC recommended practices program assessment: Improving practices for young children with special needs and their families.* Longmont, CO: Sopris West.

High/Scope Educational Research Foundation. (2003). *Preschool Program Quality Assessment (PQA).* Ypsilanti, MI: Author.

National Association for the Education of Young Children. (2004, June). *NAEYC draft early childhood program standards.* Online: www.naeyc.org/accreditation/next_era.asp#standards.

Talan, T., & Bloom, P. J. (2004). *The Program Administration Scale: Measuring early childhood leadership and management.* New York: Teachers College Press.

Teaching Strategies. (2003). *Implementation checklist: The Creative Curriculum for Preschool.* Washington, DC: Author.

Classroom Observation—Preschool

Interactions Among Teachers and Children	Little evidence		Some evidence		A great deal of evidence
1. Teachers show warmth and affection in their interactions with children through hugs, smiles, tone of voice, and eye contact.	1	2	3	4	5
2. Teachers listen to children with attention and respect, responding to their questions and requests in a friendly, courteous manner.	1	2	3	4	5
3. Teachers capitalize on opportunities to help children build vocabulary.	1	2	3	4	5
4. Teachers engage in meaningful conversations with individual children, encouraging them to share ideas and personal experiences.	1	2	3	4	5
5. Teachers ask open-ended questions, encouraging children to solve problems, consider consequences, and extend their thinking.	1	2	3	4	5
6. Teachers provide comfort to children who are hurt, disappointed, or upset.	1	2	3	4	5
7. Teachers initiate activities and discussions that promote positive self-identity and the valuing of differences.	1	2	3	4	5
8. Teachers treat children of all races, religions, and cultures with equal respect and consideration.	1	2	3	4	5
9. Teachers provide boys and girls with equal opportunities to take part in all activities.	1	2	3	4	5
10. Teachers encourage independence and self-help as children are ready.	1	2	3	4	5
11. Teachers use positive approaches to help children deal with anger and frustration.	1	2	3	4	5
12. The overall sound of the group is pleasant most of the time.	1	2	3	4	5
13. Teachers vary their instructional strategies based on children's differing abilities, learning styles, interests, and temperaments.	1	2	3	4	5
14. Children are generally comfortable, relaxed, and happy.	1	2	3	4	5
15. Children learn to resolve conflicts by identifying feelings, describing problems, negotiating differences, and generating solutions.	1	2	3	4	5
16. Teachers support children's friendships by helping them learn to share, take turns, listen to one another, and provide comfort when needed.	1	2	3	4	5
17. Teachers encourage and recognize children's work and accomplishments.	1	2	3	4	5
18. Teachers guide children's behavior by modeling desired behavior, establishing rules, encouraging cooperation, offering reminders, and redirecting unacceptable behavior.	1	2	3	4	5
19. Teachers never use corporal punishment, threats, derogatory remarks, or withholding of food as a means of guidance.	1	2	3	4	5
20. Teachers develop a sense of community by allowing children to participate in decisions about classroom rules, planning activities, and group celebrations.	1	2	3	4	5

Comments:

Subscale score _____ **/100**

Curriculum	Little evidence		Some evidence		A great deal of evidence
1. The written curriculum framework is consistent with the program's philosophy statement, goals, and educational objectives. (check written documents)	1	2	3	4	5
2. The written curriculum framework delineates age-appropriate child outcomes that address central aspects of child development. (check written documents)	1	2	3	4	5
3. The daily schedule provides a balance between quiet and active activities, fine-motor and large-motor activities, and indoor and outdoor activities.	1	2	3	4	5
4. The daily schedule provides a balance between child-initiated and teacher-initiated activities.	1	2	3	4	5
5. The daily schedule provides consistency in routines, yet is flexible, allowing variations to accommodate the individual needs of children.	1	2	3	4	5
6. The curriculum reflects the culture, values, traditions, and language of the children served.	1	2	3	4	5
7. The curriculum goals for children are based on assessment of individual needs and interests.	1	2	3	4	5
8. The curriculum promotes active exploration, experimentation, and discovery.	1	2	3	4	5
9. Interest centers and learning materials are organized to support independent use and are rotated regularly to accommodate new interests and skill levels.	1	2	3	4	5
10. Classroom displays, books, dolls, and learning materials depict cultural and racial diversity, special needs, and nonstereotyped role models.	1	2	3	4	5
11. Teachers provide a variety of age-appropriate experiences (discussions, field trips, hands-on activities) that foster positive self-concepts in children.	1	2	3	4	5
12. Teachers provide a variety of age-appropriate materials and learning experiences that encourage children to think, reason, question, and experiment.	1	2	3	4	5
13. Teachers provide a variety of activities (group storytime, independent reading, story dictations, field trips) that encourage literacy and language development.	1	2	3	4	5
14. Teachers provide a variety of age-appropriate learning experiences to help children understand basic number concepts, geometric shapes, and measurement.	1	2	3	4	5
15. Teachers provide a variety of equipment and activities (games, dance, outdoor play, obstacle courses) that enhance children's physical development.	1	2	3	4	5
16. Teachers provide a variety of age-appropriate activities (cooking, gardening, field trips, stories) that promote sound health, safety, and nutritional practices.	1	2	3	4	5
17. Teachers provide a variety of age-appropriate activities (dramatic play, art, music, field trips, dance) that encourage creative expression and appreciation of the arts.	1	2	3	4	5
18. Teachers conduct smooth and unregimented transitions between activities. The environment is prepared so children do not have to wait.	1	2	3	4	5
19. Routine tasks such as toileting, eating, dressing, and napping are handled in a relaxed and individualized manner.	1	2	3	4	5
20. Teachers use a variety of media and technology to enrich the curriculum and extend learning (computer, digital camera, tape recorder, CD player, video).	1	2	3	4	5

Comments:

Subscale score _____ **/100**

Physical Environment	Little evidence		Some evidence		A great deal of evidence
1. There is ample space indoors and outdoors so children are not crowded.	1	2	3	4	5
2. The indoor space is arranged to accommodate individual children, small groups, and large groups.	1	2	3	4	5
3. A wide variety of age-appropriate equipment and materials are available for children indoors and outdoors.	1	2	3	4	5
4. Individually labeled space is provided for each child's personal belongings.	1	2	3	4	5
5. Private areas where children can work alone or with a friend are available indoors and outdoors.	1	2	3	4	5
6. The environment includes soft, washable items (pillows, rugs, cushions).	1	2	3	4	5
7. Sound-absorbing materials such as ceiling tile, rugs, and drapes are used to cut down noise.	1	2	3	4	5
8. The classroom space is divided into well-defined interest areas.	1	2	3	4	5
9. Materials are arranged and labeled on low, open shelves to encourage children to use them independently.	1	2	3	4	5
10. The outdoor play area is protected from access to streets and other dangers.	1	2	3	4	5
11. Indoors and outdoors there are clear pathways available for children to move from one activity to another.	1	2	3	4	5
12. Tables and chairs are the appropriate size for the age level of children.	1	2	3	4	5
13. Overall, the classroom is aesthetically pleasing (freshly painted, washed floors, minimal clutter, no offensive odors).	1	2	3	4	5
14. Children's artwork, posters, bulletin boards, and documentation panels are attractively displayed and updated regularly.	1	2	3	4	5
15. The indoor and outdoor environments comply with ADA standards and accommodate children with disabilities.	1	2	3	4	5
16. The classroom provides a clearly defined space where families can sign in and get information about their child's day or upcoming events.	1	2	3	4	5
17. Space is provided for teachers and support staff to store their personal belongings.	1	2	3	4	5
18. Teachers have access to a computer, printer, and photocopier.	1	2	3	4	5
19. There is an adult-size bathroom conveniently located for teachers.	1	2	3	4	5
20. There is a separate space with adult-size furniture where teachers can relax, plan, and prepare materials or conduct a parent conference.	1	2	3	4	5

Comments:

Subscale score _____ **/100**

Health, Safety, and Nutrition

		Little evidence		Some evidence		A great deal of evidence

1. Teachers are able to supervise children at all times by sight and sound.   1   2   3   4   5

2. Children are dressed appropriately for indoor and outdoor play and sunscreen is applied in hot weather and on sunny days.   1   2   3   4   5

3. Teachers and children keep areas reasonably clean and uncluttered.   1   2   3   4   5

4. Toileting areas are clean and sanitary.   1   2   3   4   5

5. A sink with running hot and cold water is in close proximity to the toileting areas.   1   2   3   4   5

6. Teachers wash their hands with soap and water on arrival, before serving food, and after assisting children with toileting or wiping noses.   1   2   3   4   5

7. Children wash their hands with soap and water after toileting, before meals, after playing in the water table, and after wiping their noses.   1   2   3   4   5

8. The indoor equipment and furniture are secure, safe, and well maintained.   1   2   3   4   5

9. Equipment and learning materials are safe for the age of children (e.g., three-year-olds use scissors with blunt tips).   1   2   3   4   5

10. Toilets, drinking water, and hand-washing facilities are easily accessible.   1   2   3   4   5

11. A clear evacuation plan is posted in the classroom.   1   2   3   4   5

12. The indoor space is well lighted, ventilated, and maintained at a comfortable temperature.   1   2   3   4   5

13. Teachers sanitize tables before and after meals.   1   2   3   4   5

14. A fully equipped first-aid kit is readily available in the classroom.   1   2   3   4   5

15. Electrical outlets are covered with protective caps.   1   2   3   4   5

16. Outdoor climbing structures, swings, and other equipment are safe and secure; cushioning materials such as mats, wood chips, and sand are used under structures, slides, and swings.   1   2   3   4   5

17. Children under 4 are not offered whole or sliced hot dogs, whole grapes, nuts, popcorn, hard pretzels, spoonfuls of peanut butter, raw carrot chunks, or meat not cut into small pieces.   1   2   3   4   5

18. Potentially dangerous products such as medicines or cleaning supplies are stored in locked cabinets out of the reach of children.   1   2   3   4   5

19. Snack and mealtimes are pleasant social and learning experiences for children. Adults sit and interact with children during meals.   1   2   3   4   5

20. Mealtimes encourage independence and self-help in children.   1   2   3   4   5

Comments:

Subscale score _____ **/100**

Subscale scores

▶ **Interactions among teachers and children** _____

▶ **Curriculum** _____

▶ **Physical environment** _____

▶ **Health, safety, nutrition** _____

Total score _____ **/400**

Infant-Toddler Teaching Practices

Rationale:

Over the past decade there has been a dramatic increase in the demand for infant and toddler care. Although licensing standards vary from state to state in their technical definitions of *infancy* and *toddlerhood*, most early childhood educators define infancy as that period from birth until the child learns to walk, at about 12–15 months. Toddlerhood then continues until the child turns 3 years of age.

The care and education of infants and toddlers differs from that of preschool-age children in several important ways. These differences relate to the special needs of the youngest children in early care and education programs. Their care is more intense and personal, requiring more one-to-one physical contact and focused responsiveness from adults. How time is spent in caregiving routines is also qualitatively different in infant and toddler settings. Interactions with teachers during the basic routines of eating, playing, dressing, and napping are the essence of the infant-toddler curriculum—a time to build language, nurture self-awareness, and expand understanding of the world. Because infants are so vulnerable and toddlers are so mobile, the use and arrangement of space in infant-toddler classrooms is also distinctively different from that in preschool classrooms. In sum, engaging and enriching learning environments for infants and toddlers are not simply scaled-down versions of a good preschool program for 3- to 5-year-olds.

Assessment #13 assesses the quality of teaching practices in infant and toddler classrooms. It includes indicators assessing adult-child relationships, daily experiences, the environment, health, safety, and nutrition. Items are organized into three sections: those that applying to both age groups, infants and toddlers; those applying to toddlers only; and those applying to infants only.

Assessment Tool #13 is based on developmentally appropriate practice in early childhood programs (Bredekamp & Copple, 1997). Specific items are adapted from several sources of professional standards (see resources on the following page). Some of the items on Assessment #13 are beyond the individual teacher's control and fall under the responsibilities of a center's management. This underscores the important point that achieving and maintaining high-quality learning environments for infants and toddlers is the shared responsibility of administrative and teaching staff.

Directions:

Separate forms should be used for each infant or toddler classroom observed. You will probably want to observe these items over three or four days and at different times during the day. This is important because a particular part of a day's activities may not accurately reflect all the teaching practices included on the scale. After observing each item, indicate your rating by circling the appropriate number from 1 (*little evidence*) to 5 (*a great deal of evidence*).

Scoring:

After completing your observation, add up all the ratings of the first 60 infant-toddler items to generate an infant-toddler subtotal. Scores will range from a low of 60 to a high of 300. Then total the additional ratings for the toddler-only items (10 items) or the infant-only items (10 items), depending on the age group observed. Add this second subtotal to the initial infant-toddler subtotal to generate a total infant teaching practices score or a total toddler teaching practices score (ranging from a low of 70 to a high of 350).

The information gleaned from this assessment should prove useful in modifying administrative and supervisory procedures to support more positive teaching practices in infant and toddler classrooms. Assessment Tool #13 can also be used as a pre and post measure documenting changes in teaching practices as they relate to infant and toddler classrooms. The observed score on the first observation can serve as baseline data from which to measure change in the way an individual teacher or group of teachers interacts with infants and toddlers. If the instrument is used in this way, it is important that the same observer conduct both the pre and post assessments.

Resources

American Academy of Pediatrics. (1993). *Model child care health policies.* Elk Grove Village, IL: Author.

Bredekamp, S., & Copple, C. (Eds.). (1997). *Developmentally appropriate practice in early childhood programs* (Rev. ed.). Washington, DC: National Association for the Education of Young Children.

National Association for the Education of Young Children. (2004, June). *NAEYC draft early childhood program standards.* Online: www.naeyc.org/accreditation/next_era.asp#standards.

Harms, T., Cryer, D., & Clifford, R. (2003). *Infant/Toddler Environment Rating Scale—Revised.* New York: Teachers College Press.

Hemmeter, M. L., Joseph, G. E., Smith, B. J., & Sandall, S. (Eds.). (2001). *DEC recommended practices program assessment: Improving practices for young children with special needs and their families.* Longmont, CO: Sopris West.

Lally, R., Griffin, A., Fenichel, E., Segal, M., Szanton, E., & Weissbourd, B. (2003). *Caring for infants and toddlers in groups: Developmentally appropriate practice.* Washington, DC: Zero to Three.

Talan, T., & Bloom, P. J. (2004). *The Program Administration Scale: Measuring early childhood leadership and management.* New York: Teachers College Press.

Classroom Observation—Infant-Toddler

		Little evidence		Some evidence		A great deal of evidence
1.	Teachers show warmth and affection in their interactions with children through hugs, smiles, tone of voice, and eye contact.	1	2	3	4	5
2.	Teachers quickly respond to infants' and toddlers' cries or other signs of distress by providing physical comfort and needed care.	1	2	3	4	5
3.	Teachers act to avoid problems before they occur (provide duplicate toys, direct children to a new activity, intervene to avoid falls or other accidents).	1	2	3	4	5
4.	Infants, toddlers, and their parents are greeted warmly each morning.	1	2	3	4	5
5.	Teachers are sensitive and patient in supporting children's separation from parents.	1	2	3	4	5
6.	Teachers are able to supervise children at all times by sight.	1	2	3	4	5
7.	Teachers treat children of all races, religions, and cultures with equal respect and consideration.	1	2	3	4	5
8.	Teachers support infants' and toddlers' communication in their family language.	1	2	3	4	5
9.	Teachers encourage independence and self-help as children are ready.	1	2	3	4	5
10.	Teachers engage infants and toddlers in individualized play that includes simple rhymes, songs, and interactive games (peek-a-boo).	1	2	3	4	5
11.	Teachers never use corporal punishment, threats, derogatory remarks, or withholding of food as a means of managing an infant's or toddler's behavior.	1	2	3	4	5
12.	Information is provided to parents on a daily basis regarding their child's activities, developmental milestones, and caregiving issues.	1	2	3	4	5
13.	Grouping and scheduling supports stability in caregiver relationships. Infants and toddlers and their teachers are encouraged to stay together for at least a year.	1	2	3	4	5
14.	Routines are flexible and individualized to meet infants' and toddlers' needs. Children are not rushed during transitions or made to wait as a group.	1	2	3	4	5
15.	Teachers provide a variety of age-appropriate experiences that help infants and toddlers develop an emerging sense of self-awareness.	1	2	3	4	5
16.	Daily experiences for infants and toddlers are based on an assessment of each child's individual needs and take into consideration the desires and concerns of parents.	1	2	3	4	5
17.	Photographs and pictures of children and their families are displayed at children's eye level.	1	2	3	4	5
18.	Classroom displays, books, dolls, and learning materials depict cultural and racial diversity, special needs, and nonstereotyped role models.	1	2	3	4	5
19.	Extra diapers and clothing are available for each child.	1	2	3	4	5
20.	Routine tasks such as diapering, eating, dressing, and napping are handled in a relaxed and individual manner.	1	2	3	4	5

	Little evidence		Some evidence		A great deal of evidence
21. Teachers encourage infants' and toddlers' active exploration and sensory-motor learning.	1	2	3	4	5
22. Teachers use language and read books that build awareness of mathematical concepts (more and less, big and small, counting); they encourage children to see and touch different shapes, sizes, and patterns.	1	2	3	4	5
23. Infants and toddlers have opportunities to express themselves creatively by moving to music and engaging in pretend play.	1	2	3	4	5
24. Teachers support the foundations for early literacy by reading picture books and making durable books available for children's independent exploration.	1	2	3	4	5
25. Teachers support infants' and toddlers' attempts to communicate ("I know you are hungry; let's get a snack").	1	2	3	4	5
26. Teachers engage in pretend play with infants and toddlers (talk on toy telephone, feed a baby doll).	1	2	3	4	5
27. A wide variety of age-appropriate equipment and materials are available for infants and toddlers indoors and outdoors.	1	2	3	4	5
28. There is ample space indoors and outdoors, so infants and toddlers are not crowded.	1	2	3	4	5
29. Furniture and supplies are accessible and convenient (cots are easy for adults to access; diapering supplies are near diapering table; cubbies are near classroom entrance).	1	2	3	4	5
30. Adults have a comfortable place to sit while holding and feeding infants or rocking and comforting toddlers.	1	2	3	4	5
31. The environment includes many soft, washable elements (pillows, rugs, cushions).	1	2	3	4	5
32. Sound-absorbing materials such as ceiling tile, rugs, and drapes are used to cut down noise.	1	2	3	4	5
33. Overall, the classroom is aesthetically pleasing (freshly painted, washed floors, minimal clutter, no offensive odors).	1	2	3	4	5
34. The outdoor play area is protected from access to streets and other dangers.	1	2	3	4	5
35. An easily accessibly outdoor area where infants and toddlers are separated from older children is used at least an hour daily year-round, weather permitting.	1	2	3	4	5
36. Rocking chairs and glider chairs are placed in locations that will prevent injury to children who may be on the floor.	1	2	3	4	5
37. Infants are placed in individual, labeled cribs for sleeping. Toddlers' naptime is personalized (crib or cot is labeled and placed in the same place; a special blanket or cuddly toy is provided).	1	2	3	4	5
38. The indoor and outdoor environments comply with ADA standards and accommodate children with disabilities.	1	2	3	4	5
39. Space is provided for teachers and support staff to store their personal belongings.	1	2	3	4	5

	Little evidence		Some evidence		A great deal of evidence
40. There is an adult-size bathroom conveniently located for teachers.	1	2	3	4	5
41. There is a separate space with adult-size furniture where teachers can relax, plan and prepare materials, or conduct a parent conference.	1	2	3	4	5
42. The classroom provides a clearly defined space where families can sign in and get information about their child's day or upcoming events.	1	2	3	4	5
43. Bathrooms have barriers to prevent entry by unattended infants and toddlers.	1	2	3	4	5
44. Children are dressed appropriately for indoor and outdoor play and sunscreen is applied in hot weather and on sunny days.	1	2	3	4	5
45. Teachers keep areas reasonably clean and uncluttered.	1	2	3	4	5
46. Diapering and toileting areas are clean and sanitary.	1	2	3	4	5
47. A sink with running hot and cold water is in close proximity to the diapering and toileting areas.	1	2	3	4	5
48. Teachers wash their hands with soap and water on arrival, before serving food, after diapering or assisting children with toileting, and after wiping noses.	1	2	3	4	5
49. The indoor equipment and furniture are secure, safe, and well maintained.	1	2	3	4	5
50. A clear evacuation plan is posted in the classroom.	1	2	3	4	5
51. The indoor space is well lighted, ventilated, and maintained at a comfortable temperature.	1	2	3	4	5
52. A fully equipped first-aid kit is readily available in the classroom.	1	2	3	4	5
53. Electrical outlets are covered with protective caps.	1	2	3	4	5
54. Outdoor climbing structures, swings, and other equipment are safe and secure; cushioning materials such as mats, wood chips, or sand are used under structures, slides, and swings.	1	2	3	4	5
55. Children are not offered whole grapes, nuts, popcorn, hard pretzels, spoonfuls of peanut butter, raw carrot chunks, or meat that is not cut into small pieces.	1	2	3	4	5
56. Potentially dangerous products such as medicines or cleaning supplies are stored in locked cabinets out of the reach of children.	1	2	3	4	5
57. The classroom is free of objects or small toys that could be choking hazards.	1	2	3	4	5
58. Mouthed toys are sanitized after a child puts them in his or her mouth and before another child has the opportunity to play with them.	1	2	3	4	5
59. Teachers sanitize high chairs or tables before and after a child has eaten.	1	2	3	4	5
60. Safety straps are used in high chairs, strollers, swings, and car seats.	1	2	3	4	5

Comments:

Subtotal _____ **/300**

	Little evidence		Some evidence	A great deal of evidence	

Additional items for toddlers only

61. Teachers use positive approaches to help toddlers control impulses and frustration. 1 2 3 4 5

62. Teachers support toddlers' emerging language by introducing new vocabulary, reading books, engaging in conversations, and listening attentively. 1 2 3 4 5

63. Teachers facilitate positive interactions and friendships among toddlers. 1 2 3 4 5

64. Toddlers are given appropriate art materials such as large crayons, water-based markers, and large paper. Emphasis is placed on exploration of materials, not on finished product. 1 2 3 4 5

65. Toddlers wash their hands with soap and water after toileting, before meals, after playing in the water table, and after wiping their noses. 1 2 3 4 5

66. Snack and mealtimes are pleasant social and learning experiences for toddlers. Adults sit and interact with children during meals. 1 2 3 4 5

67. Mealtimes encourage independence and self-help in toddlers. 1 2 3 4 5

68. Toddlers do not carry bottles or sippy cups while walking around the classroom. 1 2 3 4 5

69. Toilets, drinking water, and hand washing facilities are easily accessible for toddlers. 1 2 3 4 5

70. Tables and chairs for toddlers are child size. 1 2 3 4 5

Subtotal _____ /50

Additional items for infants only

61. Teachers give one-to-one attention to infants when engaging in caregiving routines. 1 2 3 4 5

62. Infants are fed when they are hungry, not according to a group or preset schedule. 1 2 3 4 5

63. The program supports breastfeeding by storing and serving mothers' expressed milk and/or providing a comfortable, secluded place for mothers who are breastfeeding. 1 2 3 4 5

64. After one hour any formula or human milk is discarded if it has been served but not completely consumed or refrigerated. 1 2 3 4 5

65. No milk, including human milk, and no other infant foods are warmed in a microwave oven. 1 2 3 4 5

66. Teachers wipe infants' hands and face with sterile cloth after feeding. 1 2 3 4 5

67. Unless otherwise ordered by a physician, infants are placed on their backs to sleep on a firm surface manufactured for sale as infant sleeping equipment. 1 2 3 4 5

68. Infants and toddlers do not have bottles while in their cribs. 1 2 3 4 5

69. Sides of cribs are kept in a raised position; latches and locks on the drop side are fastened. Pillows, quilts, comforters, and stuffed toys are not allowed in infants' cribs. 1 2 3 4 5

70. Before walking on surfaces that infants use, adults and children remove or cover with clean foot coverings any shoes they have worn outside. 1 2 3 4 5

Subtotal _____ /50

Total score _____ /350

Learning Style

Rationale:

Styles of thinking and approaches to learning vary among any group of individuals. These differences determine why learning experiences may be stimulating and interesting to some people while down right boring to others. Understanding differences in learning styles is important for any director who is interested in tailoring staff development activities to the needs of individual teachers.

Assessment Tool #14 draws on the work of several researchers whose approaches to assessing learning style have been particularly useful in educational settings (Barbe & Swassing, 1988; Dunn & Dunn, 1978; Gregorc, 1982; McCarthy, 1996). Part I looks at an individual's preference for processing and organizing information. Part II looks at the environmental, emotional, sociological, and physical elements of a person's preferred learning style. Part III assesses an individual's preferred perceptual modality—visual, auditory, or kinesthetic.

Directions:

This learning style assessment tool is particularly useful to administer to new employees as you prepare their staff development profile for the first time. The individual should be allowed to take the assessment home and spend as much time to complete it as necessary. The directions included in each part of the tool are self-explanatory. Since learning style is a fairly stable construct (it doesn't change from day to day), it will not be necessary to administer the assessment again for two or three years.

Scoring:

It is suggested you do the scoring of this assessment together with the teacher who has completed it. This will provide a good opportunity for the two of you to talk about the meaning of different learning styles as they relate to your specific work setting.

For Part I, add up the number of circled words in each column—A, B, C, and D. The column with the most circled words is the individual's preferred style, as described below:

- ► Column A corresponds to a practical (concrete-sequential) learning style
- ► Column B corresponds to an analytic (abstract-sequential) learning style
- ► Column C corresponds to an imaginative (abstract-random) learning style
- ► Column D corresponds to an inventive (concrete-random) learning style

A description of each style and suggested learning strategies can be found in Chapter 5. In scoring this section of the assessment, look for the strength of the person's scores as they relate to each style. Some people will have a clear dominant style, while others may be more evenly balanced between two or three styles.

There are no specific scoring directions for Part II. This section provides a wealth of data, however, that will give you a more comprehensive picture of the teacher's preferred learning style. This will be particularly useful as you design and implement staff development opportunities for that person.

To score Part III, transcribe the person's rating for each item (0, 1, or 2) onto the scoring template provided below. (Note that the item numbers are not in sequential order). Total the numbers in each column—visual, auditory, and kinesthetic. Scores in each modality—visual, auditory, kinesthetic—will range from 0 to 20. The column with the highest score is the person's primary perceptual modality. The second highest score indicates the individual's secondary preferred modality. Some people will have a distinct dominance in one of the modalities, while others may be more evenly balanced among two or all three of the modalities. For a fuller description of this aspect of learning style, refer to Chapter 5.

Scoring Template

Visual	Auditory	Kinesthetic
3. _____	1. _____	2. _____
4. _____	6. _____	5. _____
8. _____	9. _____	7. _____
11. _____	12. _____	10. _____
14. _____	15. _____	13. _____
18. _____	17. _____	16. _____
20. _____	19. _____	21. _____
24. _____	22. _____	23. _____
27. _____	25. _____	26. _____
29. _____	30. _____	28. _____
Total _____	**Total** _____	**Total** _____

Appreciating Individual Differences

The purpose of this assessment is to help you gain greater insight into your preferred learning style. Set aside some quiet time when you won't be interrupted or distracted. Remember, there are no right or wrong answers.

Part I. The following table includes 60 words and phrases organized into 15 rows. Each row includes four descriptors. From each row, select the one word or phrase that best captures how you would describe yourself as a learner. When you have completed this part, you will have 15 circled descriptors, one in each row.

	A	B	C	D
1.	realistic	systematic	adaptable	investigative
2.	organized	critical	imaginative	inquisitive
3.	gets to the point	debates	relates	creates
4.	practical	academic	personal	adventurous
5.	precise	analytical	flexible	inventive
6.	orderly	sensible	sharing	independent
7.	perfectionist	logical	cooperative	intuitive
8.	hard-working	intellectual	emotional	risk-taking
9.	product-oriented	quality-oriented	people-oriented	problem-oriented
10.	memorizes	thinks through	collaborates	originates
11.	wants direction	evaluates	spontaneous	changes
12.	cautious	reasons	communicates	discovers
13.	practices	examines	cares	challenges
14.	completes work	gains ideas	sees possibilities	interprets
15.	persistent	rational	aesthetic	experimental

PART II. In this section of the assessment you have an opportunity to reflect on your learning preferences. Write down your answers to each of the questions in as much detail as possible.

Environmental Elements

Sound: Do you learn best with music playing in the background, or do you need absolute quiet to concentrate? Are you able to screen out people's conversations and other extraneous environmental noise when you read or concentrate on a task?

_____

_____

_____

Light. Do you find either bright or dim lights distracting? Do you work best in natural filtered daylight? Describe your preference.

_____

_____

_____

Temperature. Are you affected by extremes in ambient temperature? Do you prefer cool, warm, or moderate temperatures in which to learn?

_____

_____

_____

Design. When you read something that requires your full attention, do you prefer to sit in an easy chair or a hard-back chair, or do you like to stretch out on the floor? Do you prefer a formal or informal room arrangement when you attend a workshop or lecture? Describe your preference.

_____

_____

_____

Emotional Elements

Motivation. Under what learning conditions do your sources of motivation differ? When do you need extrinsic reinforcement (praise, grades, pay bonus) to encourage you to tackle new knowledge and skill areas? Under what conditions are you intrinsically motivated to learn something new?

_____

_____

_____

Persistence. How would you describe yourself with respect to your level of persistence in learning new things? Do you prefer to set short, achievable goals or do you have a level of persistence that allows you to tackle long-range goals?

_____

_____

_____

Responsibility. Under what conditions are you most likely to take responsibility for your own learning?

_____

_____

_____

Structure. Do you like to have new areas of learning highly structured and tightly supervised, or do you prefer to set your own goals and monitor your own progress?

_____

_____

_____

Sociological Elements

Grouping. Which types of things do you learn best on your own, in small groups, or in large groups? What kinds of collegial staff development experiences do you find most rewarding?

_____

_____

_____

Physical Elements

Intake. How important is it to you to have something to eat or nibble on when you focus on a new task? Do you like to chew gum or drink something when you master something new?

_____

_____

_____

Time. Some people are more alert in the morning; others prefer to tackle new learning tasks in the afternoon or evening. Describe your preference.

_____

_____

_____

Mobility. When you attend a staff development workshop, do you need to get up and move around at regular intervals? When you work at a computer or when you read, do you like to take frequent breaks to stretch your muscles, or can you sit and concentrate for long periods?

_____

_____

_____

Part III. This final section focuses on your preferred perceptual modality. For each item, indicate the degree to which the statement describes you (0 = *not at all like me*, 1 = *somewhat like me*, 2 = *exactly like me*).

	Not at all like me	Somewhat like me	Exactly like me
1. I can remember the details of what was said at lectures, sermons, and speeches I've attended.	0	1	2
2. I enjoy making things and working with my hands.	0	1	2
3. Even a week after a meeting, I can remember the details of what people wore and where they sat in the meeting room.	0	1	2
4. When attending a workshop, I like to sit up front so I can see the speaker, flip charts, and overhead transparencies.	0	1	2
5. When attending a workshop, I like to sit near the back of the room so I can get up and move around if necessary.	0	1	2
6. When attending a workshop, I focus on the speaker's tone of voiceand how words and phrases are crafted.	0	1	2
7. During workshops, I like to take lots of notes or doodle while I am listening.	0	1	2
8. During workshops and meetings, I rely on handouts, flip charts, and overhead transparencies to help me process information.	0	1	2
9. I prefer listening to the news on the radio to reading about it in the newspaper.	0	1	2
10. People would describe me as a touchy-feely kind of person.	0	1	2
11. I am skillful at making eye-catching charts and graphs.	0	1	2
12. When someone gives me directions, I don't need to write them down to remember them.	0	1	2
13. When people give me directions, I write down the details so I remember them.	0	1	2
14. I'm good at reading maps.	0	1	2
15. I'm good at learning foreign languages.	0	1	2

	Not at all like me	Somewhat like me	Exactly like me
16. While studying, I tap a pencil, chew on an eraser, fiddle with objects, bite my nails, or run my fingers through my hair.	0	1	2
17. When solving a problem, I weigh options by talking to myself.	0	1	2
18. When I want to recall someone's name, I try to see it pictured in my head.	0	1	2
19. I enjoy listening to books on tape.	0	1	2
20. I would rather read about a new subject than have someone tell me about it.	0	1	2
21. In workshops, I really enjoy interactive exercises and hands-on activities.	0	1	2
22. I'm good at remembering poems, rhymes, and jingles from radio commercials.	0	1	2
23. Some of my best thinking happens when I am running, swimming, walking, or actively moving.	0	1	2
24. I am distracted by visual clutter in a room.	0	1	2
25. I am distracted when participants engage in side conversations while a lecture or presentation is being made.	0	1	2
26. I learn best by doing—actively trying out a new skill.	0	1	2
27. I tend to be neat and detail oriented.	0	1	2
28. I gesture or move around a lot when I speak.	0	1	2
29. I am a good speller. I recognize words by sight.	0	1	2
30. I've always been a whiz at phonics.	0	1	2

Psychological Type

Rationale:

People differ in fundamental ways; they have distinct preferences for how they take in information and reach conclusions about the world. These different preferences for how we function are important because they govern both behavior (how we act in different situations) and beliefs (how we feel about different situations). A theory to explain these personality differences was first proposed by Carl Jung (1923). Jung believed that individuals could be typed by their preference for a certain way of functioning. Jung's theory was popularized by the work of Isabel Briggs Myers, who developed the Myers-Briggs Type Indicator (MBTI). The work of Jung and Myers is important because an understanding of the different psychological types can elicit a deeper appreciation for those who function differently from us.

Assessment Tool #15 is a self-assessment of psychological type along four dimensions: extraversion/introversion, sensing/intuition, thinking/feeling, and judging/perceiving. While the theoretical framework for this assessment tool is drawn from the work of Jung (1923) and Myers (1980, 1998), several other sources were useful in clarifying the concepts associated with psychological type (Keirsey, 1998; Kroeger, Thuesen, & Ruthledge, 2002; Lawrence, 1993). Assessment Tool #15 is not a substitute for the kind of thorough analysis of psychological type that can come from the administration of the Myers-Briggs Type Indicator. Rather, it is designed as a brief introduction to the concept and terminology. Directors interested in a more precise assessment of psychological type are encouraged to contact a psychologist or counselor who is professionally qualified to administer the MBTI.

Directions:

Like Assessment Tool #14 this assessment is useful to administer to new employees as you prepare their staff development profile for the first time. Since one's psychological type is a fairly stable construct (it does not change from month to month), it is not be necessary to administer this assessment tool more than once every four or five years. When you distribute the assessment to your staff, ask them to take it home and complete it when they have no distractions. Emphasize that there are no right or wrong answers.

The information gleaned from this assessment will assist you in identifying the different psychological types represented by your staff. It can also help you appreciate the importance of hiring diverse staff who represent different psychological typologies.

Scoring:

Directions for scoring this assessment are included on the instrument itself. Also included is a handout that describes the 16 typologies resulting from different combinations of preferences. In addition to the interpretation of psychological type provided here, it is highly recommended that you obtain copies of two or three of the following resources for a more complete description of the different psychological typologies.

References:

Myers, I. B. (1998). *Introduction to type* (5th ed.). Palo Alto, CA: Consulting Psychologists Press.

Myers, I. B. (1980). *Gifts differing.* Palo Alto, CA: Consulting Psychologists Press.

Lawrence, G. (1993). *People types and tiger stripes* (3rd ed.). Gainesville, FL: Center for Applications of Psychological Type, Inc.

Keirsey, D. (1998). *Please understand me II: Temperament, character, intelligence.* Del Mar, CA: Prometheus Nemesis.

Kroeger, O., Thuesen, J., & Rutledge, H. (2002). *Typetalk.* New York: Dell.

Tuning In to Your Psychological Type

Just as each of us has distinctive fingerprints, so too do we have different preferences for how we perceive the world and make decisions that guide our everyday behavior. These preferences, in large part, shape our personality. The purpose of this survey is to provide a brief profile of your personality preferences with respect to four different dimensions: extraversion/introversion, sensing/intuition, thinking/feeling, and judging/perceiving. The labels associated with each of these dimensions are value free. In other words, a preference for a pattern of behavior associated with one end of a continuum is not necessarily better than the other. Likewise in some dimensions, you may exhibit a strong preference, while in other dimensions you may be more evenly balanced in your preferences. The most important thing to keep in mind is that there are no right or wrong answers.

As you read each statement, use the following coding system to indicate your responses. A description and interpretation of each dimension follows each section.

0 = Not like me at all   1 = Somewhat like me   2 = Exactly like me

Extraversion   _____   Most of my social activities occur in the context of a group.
_____   I readily offer my opinion on issues.
_____   I feel comfortable initiating conversations with people.
_____   I enjoy working with others on projects and tasks.
_____   I find listening more difficult than talking.
_____   I feel energized when I am with a lot of people.
_____   I thrive on action and variety.
_____   I rely on a telephone answering machine so I won't miss a call.
_____   I get impatient when things aren't happening.
_____   I don't mind interruptions when I am working.
_____   **Total Extraversion (E) score**

Introversion   _____   I am perceived as a good listener.
_____   I prefer a few close friends to a large number of casual acquaintances.
_____   I usually wait until I am approached before engaging in conversation.
_____   I often rehearse things before I say them.
_____   I relish having quiet time during the day to reflect and think.
_____   I rely on a telephone answering machine so I can screen my calls.
_____   In school I preferred written assignments to oral presentations.
_____   I dislike interruptions.
_____   I prefer to work alone on projects and tasks.
_____   I can concentrate for a long time on a single task.
_____   **Total Introversion (I) score**

The Extraversion/Introversion dimension has to do with the source, direction, and focus of one's energy. Extraverts are energized by the outer world. They are actively involved with people and things around them. For introverts, reflection, introspection, and solitude produce energy, focus, and attention. Introverts are more involved with concepts and ideas. They turn to the inner world of ideas and private thoughts.

Write the letter of the pattern that best describes you, Extraversion (E) or Introversion (I)? _____
(If your scores on the Extraversion and Introversion scales are the same, put an X in the space provided.)

Sensing _____ I am good at recalling facts and details.

_____ I carry out directions by completing each task in the order given.

_____ I avoid conversations having to do with global ideas or abstractions.

_____ I am a keen observer.

_____ I am a realist—a practical sort of person.

_____ I prefer the known to the unknown.

_____ I like jobs that produce tangible results.

_____ I get frustrated when people don't give clear instructions.

_____ I do my job without worrying about how it fits into the larger scheme of things.

_____ I like utilizing and refining the skills I have rather than learning new ones.

_____ **Total Sensing (S) score**

Intuition _____ I enjoy discussing conceptual schemes, ideas, and theories.

_____ When I read a report, I look for the implications of the ideas presented.

_____ I get impatient with routine tasks.

_____ I have a vivid imagination.

_____ While reading a magazine, I jump randomly from article to article.

_____ I dislike reading directions; precise details bother me.

_____ I enjoy trying to solve problems.

_____ I've never enjoyed balancing my checkbook.

_____ I'd rather learn a new skill than refine an old one.

_____ I like to see the interconnections between things and come up with new possibilities.

_____ **Total Intuition (N) score**

The Sensing/Intuition dimension has to do with how we gather information and perceive reality. Sensing types look at facts and details. They tend to be down-to-earth, very literal, and realistic. Sensing types are sequential in their thinking and rely on their five senses as a means of gathering information. They prefer the practical and enjoy hands-on, tangible experiences. Intuition types, on the other hand, are concerned with the big picture, the grand scheme of things. They are more abstract in the way they process information. Intuition types tend to look at the relationships between things. They strive to understand the meaning of situations to order to achieve insight and solve problems.

Write the letter of the pattern that best describes you, Sensing (S) or Intuition (N)?_____
(If your scores on the Sensing and Intuition scales are the same, put an X in the space provided.)

Thinking _____ I am very rational in my decision making.

_____ I rank and weigh factors before making a decision.

_____ I am comfortable with orderly rules.

_____ I believe it is more important to be fair minded than warm hearted.

_____ I can remain cool and calm in almost any situation.

_____ I am very logical in the way I approach issues.

_____ I keep my feelings to myself.

_____ My style is brief and businesslike.

_____ You can count on me to give constructive criticism.

_____ I base decisions on what is fair and equitable and not what makes people happy.

_____ **Total Thinking (T) score**

Feeling   _____   I believe the best decisions consider other people's feelings.

_____   I get impatient with people who plod through logical processes.

_____   Harmonious interpersonal relations are a high priority for me.

_____   In conversations, I tend to focus on the who rather than the what.

_____   I am a very empathetic person.

_____   I go out of my way to accommodate other people.

_____   My heart guides my decision making.

_____   People sometimes take advantage of me.

_____   I show my feelings freely.

_____   I can usually predict how others will feel.

_____   **Total Feeling (F) score**

The Thinking/Feeling dimension relates to how we make decisions about the information we've gathered. Thinking types tend to be very objective and analytical. They are logical in their decision-making processes and purposefully impersonal. Thinking types weigh facts objectively, considering all sides of an issue, including the consequences of a decision. Feeling types are more subjective, using their personal value system for making decisions. Understanding people, achieving harmony, and feeling compassion are important to feeling types. They tend to need approval and personal support more than they need to achieve in intellectual tasks. Don't let the labels for this dimension mislead you. Thinking types certainly have feelings and feeling types surely have a capacity to think. When making decisions, however, their preferences for how to arrive at a decision are very different.

Write the letter of the pattern that best describes you, Thinking (T) or Feeling (F)?_____
(If your scores on the Thinking and Feeling scales are the same, put an X in the space provided.)

Judging   _____   I make decisions easily and quickly.

_____   Most of my daily activities are planned.

_____   Sometimes I make decisions too hastily.

_____   I work well with deadlines.

_____   I like to finish one project before starting another.

_____   I like things settled and decided.

_____   I am methodical and organized.

_____   It bothers me when people are not on time.

_____   I am more planned than spontaneous.

_____   I love the feeling that comes with completing a project.

_____   **Total Judging (J) score**

Perceiving   _____   I like to examine an issue from all sides before making a decision.

_____   Sometimes I put off making decisions.

_____   I need little structure in my daily activities.

_____   I take life at a leisurely pace.

_____   I am able to adapt to almost any situation.

_____   I do just fine without a to-do list.

_____   I am easily distracted.

_____   Some people think of me as being disorganized.

_____   I pride myself on being flexible.

_____   I sometimes have a problem finishing tasks.

_____   **Total Perceiving (P) score**

The final dimension, Judging/Perceiving, has to do with how we structure our lives—it is our lifestyle orientation. Judging types tend to have rather structured, scheduled, and organized personal and professional lives. They see a right way to do things and proceed accordingly. Judging types are also decisive and deliberate when making decisions. Perceiving types, on the other hand, need variety, novelty, and change. They prefer to stand back and use a wait-and-see style when confronted with the need to make a decision. They often have a poor concept of time and feel comfortable with a go-with-the-flow attitude toward life. They are more flexible, spontaneous, and adaptive than judging types.

Write the letter of the pattern that best describes you, Judging (J) or Perceiving (P)?_____
(If your scores on the Judging and Perceiving scales are the same, put an X in the space provided.)

Determining Your Typology

Write the four letters that make up your typology:

_____	_____	_____	_____
E or I	S or N	T or F	J or P

With the four pairs of preferences, there are 16 different possible combinations. Each typology is different from the others. There is no one best typology.

Circle your typology:

ISTJ	ISFJ	INFJ	INTJ
ISTP	ISFP	INFP	INTP
ESTP	ESFP	ENFP	ENTP
ESTJ	ESFJ	ENFJ	ENTJ

If your scores where the same on any one of the dimensions and you indicated an X for your preference, then circle the two typologies for that dimension (for example, if your type was EXTP, then you would circle ENTP and ESTP).

The following table provides a brief description of the combinations of different preferences. Remember, however, that these brief descriptions do not capture the richness and complexity of each typology. For a more complete description of each typology, several references are noted in the introduction to this assessment. These references will provide a fuller treatment of psychological types.

Description of Different Typologies

ISTJ	ISFJ	INFJ	INTJ
Serious, quiet, earn success by concentration and thoroughness. Practical, orderly, matter-of-fact, logical, realistic, and dependable. See to it that everything is well organized. Take responsibility. Make up their own minds as to what should be accomplished and work toward it steadily, regardless of distractions.	Quiet, friendly, responsible, and conscientious. Work devotedly to meet their obligations. Lend stability to any project or group. Thorough, painstaking, accurate. May need time to master technical subjects. Can be patient with necessary details. Loyal, considerate, perceptive, and concerned with how people feel.	Succeed by perseverance, originality, and desire to do whatever is needed or wanted. Put their best efforts into their work. Quietly forceful, conscientious, and concerned for others. Respected for their firm principles. Likely to be honored and followed for their clear visions as to how best to serve the common good.	Have original minds and great drive for their own ideas. Have long-range vision and quickly find meaningful patterns in external events. In fields that appeal to them, they have a fine power to organize a job and carry it through. Skeptical, critical, independent, determined, and have high standards for competence and performance.

ISTP	ISFP	INFP	INTP
Cool onlookers—quiet, reserved, observing and analyzing life with detached curiosity and unexpected flashes of original humor. Usually interested in cause and effect, how and why mechanical things work, and in organizing facts using logical principles. Excel at getting to the core of a practical problem and finding a solution.	Retiring, quietly friendly, sensitive, and modest about abilities. Shun disagreements, do not force opinions or values on others. Usually do not care to lead but are loyal followers. Often relaxed getting things done because they enjoy the present moment and do not want to spoil it by undue haste or exertion.	Quiet observers, idealistic, and loyal. Important that outer life be congruent with inner values. Curious, quick to see possibilities. Often serve as catalysts to implement ideas. Adaptable, flexible, accepting unless a value is threatened. Want to understand people and ways of fulfilling human potential. Little concern with possessions or surroundings.	Quiet and reserved. Especially enjoy theoretical or scientific pursuits. Like solving problems with logic and analysis. Interested mainly in ideas, with little liking for parties or small talk. Tend to have very sharply defined interests. Need career where some strong interests can be used and useful.

ESTP	ESFP	ENFP	ENTP
Good at on-the-spot problem solving. Like action, enjoy whatever comes along. Tend to like mechanical things and sports, with friends on the side. Adaptable, tolerant, pragmatic; focused on getting results. Dislike long explanations. Are best with real things that can be worked, handled, taken apart, or put back together.	Outgoing, accepting, friendly, enjoy everything and make things more fun for others by their enjoyment. Like action and making things happen. Know what's going on and join in eagerly. Find remembering facts easier than mastering theories. Are best in situations that need sound common sense and practical ability with people.	Warmly enthusiastic, high-spirited, ingenious, imaginative. Able to do almost anything that interests them. Quick with a solution for any difficulty and ready to help anyone with a problem. Often rely on their ability to improvise instead of preparing in advance. Can always find compelling reasons for whatever they want.	Quick, ingenious, good at many things. Stimulating company, alert and outspoken. May argue for fun on either side of a question. Resourceful in solving new challenging problems, but may neglect routine assignments. Apt to turn to one new interest after another. Skillful in finding logical reasons for whatever they want.

ESTJ	ESFJ	ENFJ	ENTJ
Practical, realistic, matter-of-fact, with a natural head for business and mechanics. Not interested in abstract theories; want learning to have direct and immediate application. Like to organize and run activities. Often make good administrators; are decisive, quickly move to implement decisions; take care of routine details.	Warm-hearted, talkative, popular, conscientious, born cooperators, active committee members. Need harmony and may be good at creating it. Always doing something nice for someone. Work best with plenty of encouragement and praise. Main interest is in things that directly and visibly affect people's lives.	Responsive and responsible. Feel real concern for what others think and want, and try to handle things with due regard for the others. Can present a proposal or lead a group discussion with ease and tact. Sociable, popular, sympathetic. Responsive to praise and criticism. Like to facilitate others and enable people to achieve their potential.	Frank, decisive, leaders in activities. Develop and implement comprehensive systems to solve organizational problems. Good in anything that requires reasoning and intelligent talk, such as public speaking. Are usually well informed and enjoy adding to their fund of knowledge.

From Myers, 1. B. (1998). *Introduction to type* (5th ed.). Reproduced by special permission of the publisher, Consulting Psychologists Press, Inc., Palo Alto, CA 94303. All rights reserved.

Beliefs and Values

Rationale:

Teachers' beliefs about children provide the foundation for their philosophy of teaching. Because beliefs are grounded in one's values, they have a strong impact on shaping behavior. Teachers' values also govern how they react when confronted with the ethical dilemmas that occur from time to time. Your role as director is to ensure that the values and beliefs of the teachers on your staff are consistent with the core values and mission of your organization.

Assessment Tool #16 asks teachers to reflect on their attitudes and beliefs about children, parents, and their role in the classroom. The information gleaned from this self-assessment will help you to better understand the underlying values and beliefs that drive the teaching practices you observe in the classroom. Without clarification of these values, it is difficult to set goals for changing behaviors.

Directions:

Since teachers' attitudes and feelings about their teaching role change over time, it is important to administer this assessment every year or two. It will provide you with valuable insight as you create a staff development profile for each teacher. Assure your teachers of the confidentiality of their responses. You may even want to let them take the assessment home to complete it when they have more time and fewer distractions. Emphasize that there are no right or wrong answers.

Scoring:

No quantitative score is generated by this assessment. Rather, the answers themselves should be used to generate discussion between you and your teachers about how values and beliefs provide the foundation for their philosophy of teaching.

Values Clarification

Values are enduring beliefs—ideas that we cherish and regard highly. Values influence the decisions we make and the courses of action we follow. Some values we prize more deeply than others; they become standards by which we live. The purpose of this assessment is to provide an opportunity for you to share the values and beliefs that guide your teaching practices.

PART I. Complete the following sentences.

1. I think children are generally _____

2. When children are unhappy, it's usually because _____

3. I get angry when children _____

4. The most important thing a teacher can do is _____

5. Children should not _____

6. All children are _____

7. I wish parents would _____

8. When parents _____ I feel _____

PART II. Circle the five traits you would like children to be or have as a result of their preschool experience with you.

adventurous	appreciation of beauty	determined
affectionate	inquisitive	energetic
polite	respectful	friendly
altruistic	self-starter	obedient
caring	sense of humor	spontaneous
honest	industrious	persistent
assertive	creative	proud
confident	independent thinker	risk taker
cheerful	desire to excel	open-minded

Communication Style

Rationale:

Working in early childhood is intense work. Every day, teachers have hundreds of interactions with children, parents, and co-workers. Opportunities for being misunderstood are many. Effective interpersonal relationships are the glue that holds early childhood programs together. An understanding of different communication styles can assist teachers in working together with greater appreciation of the nuances that shape the way a message is sent, received, and interpreted.

Assessment Tool #17 is a quick and easy-to-use instrument to promote greater self-awareness and sensitivity to others' communication styles. This assessment draws on the seminal work of David Merrill (Merrill & Reid, 1981) and Russo's (1995) application of Merrill's work to the area of communication. Russo conceptualizes communication style along two dimensions—assertiveness and expressiveness. The dimension of assertiveness is the effort that a person makes to control the thought or actions of others. Assertive communicators tend to be direct, task-oriented, and confident. Nonassertive communicators defer; they are more reserved, deliberate, and easygoing. The dimension of expressiveness describes the degree to which people exhibit or control their emotions and feelings while communicating. People who are expressive tend to show more vocal variation in their speech patterns and are more outgoing and demonstrative when talking. The intersection of these two dimensions results in four communication styles: direct, spirited, considerate, and systematic.

Directions:

Distribute the "Communication Style Audit" to each staff member. The directions included in the tool are self-explanatory. You may want to do this assessment prior to a staff meeting. The results should serve as a springboard for a lively discussion about how people interact.

Scoring:

Scoring is straightforward. In Part I, simply add up the number of circled words in each column—A, B, C, and D.

- ▶ Column A corresponds to a **direct** communication style
- ▶ Column B corresponds to a **spirited** communication style
- ▶ Column C corresponds to a **considerate** communication style
- ▶ Column D corresponds to a **systematic** communication style

The column with the most circled words is the individual's preferred communication style. In interpreting the results, look for the strength of the person's scores as they relate to each style. Some people will have a clear dominant style, while others may be more evenly balanced between two styles or three styles. A more complete description of each style can be found in Chapter 5.

There are no specific scoring directions for Part II. This section provides useful information, however, that will give you a more complete picture of a teacher's communication style. This should prove useful as you design and implement professional development opportunities for that person.

Communication Style Audit

The purpose of this assessment is to help you gain greater insight into your communication style. Set aside some quiet time when you won't be interrupted or distracted. Remember, there are no right or wrong answers.

Part I. The following table includes 60 words. From the entire list, circle the 15 words that best describe your communicate style.

A	B	C	D
Advocate	Influencing	Steady	Cautious
Decisive	Optimistic	Patient	Restrained
Frank	Enthusiastic	Caring	Exact
Determined	Talkative	Accommodating	Serious
Assertive	Animated	Easygoing	Precise
Achiever	Friendly	Warm	Objective
Take charge	Spontaneous	Counselor	Accurate
Pragmatic	Outgoing	Supportive	Logical
Fast paced	Enjoys the spotlight	Good listener	Orderly
No nonsense	Lively	Sympathetic	Persistent
Honest	Cheerleader	Sensitive	Analytical
Independent	Motivator	Team player	Problem solver
Outspoken	Presenter	Mentor	Organized
Candid	Popular	Sentimental	Detailed
Risk taker	Charismatic	Cooperative	Focused

Part II. In this section you have an opportunity to reflect on your communication style. Write down your answers to each of the questions in as much detail as possible.

✏️➤ Describe the ways you prefer to receive and give information. For example when someone gives you directions, do you prefer to have it in writing or just hear it? What is your preference with respect to using different technologies—voice mail, e-mail, text messaging?

_____

_____

_____

_____

_____

✏️➤ What do you consider to be the most positive aspects of your communication style? Share some examples of how these positive aspects have benefited you in your relationships.

_____

_____

_____

_____

_____

✏️➤ What are some aspects of your communication style that have hindered your effectiveness in interpersonal relationships? What can you do to reduce or eliminate these hindrances?

_____

_____

_____

_____

_____

Job Satisfaction

Rationale:

Job satisfaction can be defined as an individual's evaluation of his or her job. It is a kind of psychological contract between the worker and the demands of the workplace that is influenced by personal needs, values, and expectations (Jones & James, 1979; Bloom, 1988b; Spector, 1997). Put simply, job satisfaction is the discrepancy between real conditions and ideal conditions. When job satisfaction is high, the discrepancy between existing and ideal conditions is small. But job satisfaction is more than just a global feeling that things are going well or not so well. Indeed, many aspects of teachers' work contribute to their feelings of professional fulfillment; and it is possible that they may feel quite content in one facet of their work yet feel discouraged or frustrated in another.

Assessment Tool #18 is a modified version of the *Early Childhood Job Satisfaction Survey* (Bloom, 1988b). Individual staff members use the "Work Attitudes Questionnaire" to assess five facets of job satisfaction: co-worker relations, supervisor relations, the nature of the work itself, working conditions, and pay and promotion opportunities. The following page provides a description of each facet. The staff member then summaries the results of his or her questionnaire in an individual job satisfaction profile.

Directions:

It is important to convey to staff that the "Work Attitudes Questionnaire" is a self-assessment tool designed to help each employee explore those areas of his or her job that are most satisfying. The employee is responsible for scoring the assessment and developing his or her own personal profile. This profile may then be brought to the goal-setting conference and used as a springboard for discussing the individual's feelings about the job.

Examining the interaction between the nature of the work setting and individual attitudes may facilitate effective job restructuring. The goal, of course, is to implement organizational practices that facilitate a good fit. Sometimes, however, the analysis may lead to the realization that the fit is not right—that the individual and the center have differing goals and expectations. Many new teachers, for example, have unrealistic expectations about their jobs. During the goals-setting conferences, directors can ask questions that relate specifically to workers' conceptions of their ideal job with respect to each job facet. Such information may help reduce the incidence of mismatch in perceptions of what the role and work setting can offer and thus promote greater professional fulfillment.

Scoring:

Directions for scoring the "Work Attitudes Questionnaire" are explained in "Developing Your Job Satisfaction Profile."

Five Facets of Job Satisfaction

Satisfaction with...	Definition
Co-worker relations	The extent to which a worker has formed close relationships with colleagues; the degree of mutual trust and respect.
Supervisor relations	Perceived quality and quantity of feedback, encouragement, and helpful support from supervisor; the worker's assessment of the supervisor's overall competence.
The nature of the work itself	Includes various job components as they relate to the nature of the work experience (degree of challenge, variety, autonomy, and control) as well as the sheer quantity of tasks to be done and the time frame in which to do them; the extent to which the job provides intrinsic enjoyment and fulfills one's needs for recognition, creativity, and skill building. Also includes task identity (the perceived importance of the work).
Working conditions	Includes both the structure of the work experience (flexibility of hours, teacher:child ratio, adequacy of breaks, substitutes, and teaching materials) as well as the context in which the work is performed (the aesthetic quality of the physical environment, overall noise level, heat, ventilation, light, and spatial arrangement).
Pay and promotion opportunities	Concerns the adequacy of pay as well as the perceived equity and fairness of policies regarding the distribution of pay, fringe benefits, and opportunities for advancement. Also includes the worker's perceived job security.

From Bloom, P. J. (1988). Factors influencing overall job satisfaction and organizational commitment in early childhood work environments. *Journal of Research in Childhood Education, 3*(2), 107–122. Reprinted with permission.

Work Attitudes Questionnaire

This survey is designed to find out how you feel about different facets of your job. The purpose of this assessment is to help you become more aware of those aspects of your work that contribute most to your job satisfaction and those you would like to improve. The value of this assessment depends on your candid and honest responses.

After you have scored your survey, you will develop a personal job satisfaction profile. This summary profile will be useful when you meet with your supervisor or director to plan your professional goals.

PART I. Check (✓) the corresponding space (*strongly disagree* to *strongly agree*) to indicate how you feel about each of the statements in the categories below:

		Strongly disagree				*Strongly agree*
My co-workers...						
1.	care about me.	___	___	___	___	___
2.	encourage and support me.	___	___	___	___	___
3.	share their personal concerns with me.	___	___	___	___	___
4.	are hard to get to know.	___	___	___	___	___
5.	are critical of my performance.	___	___	___	___	___
6.	are competitive.	___	___	___	___	___
7.	are not very helpful.	___	___	___	___	___
8.	share ideas and resources with me.	___	___	___	___	___
9.	can't be trusted.	___	___	___	___	___
10.	are enjoyable to work with.	___	___	___	___	___
My supervisor...						
11.	respects my work.	___	___	___	___	___
12.	is too busy to know how I'm doing.	___	___	___	___	___
13.	supervises me too closely.	___	___	___	___	___
14.	gives me helpful feedback.	___	___	___	___	___
15.	asks for my opinion.	___	___	___	___	___
16.	is tactful.	___	___	___	___	___
17.	is not very dependable.	___	___	___	___	___
18.	encourages me to try new ideas.	___	___	___	___	___
19.	makes me feel inadequate.	___	___	___	___	___
20.	is unpredictable.	___	___	___	___	___

	Strongly disagree				Strongly agree

My work...

21. is stimulating and challenging.
22. is respected by the parents of my students.
23. involves too much paperwork and record keeping.
24. does not have enough variety.
25. is not very creative.
26. makes an important difference in my students' lives.
27. does not match my training and skills.
28. gives me a sense of accomplishment.
29. There is too little time to do all there is to do.
30. I have control over most things that affect my satisfaction.

Working conditions

31. My work schedule is flexible.
32. The teacher:child ratio is adequate.
33. I always know where to find the things I need.
34. I feel too cramped.
35. I need some new equipment/materials to do my job well.
36. The decor of my center is drab.
37. This center meets my standards of cleanliness.
38. I can't find a place to carry on a private conversation.
39. This place is too noisy.
40. The center's policies and procedures are clear.

Pay and promotion opportunities

41. My pay is adequate.
42. My pay is fair considering my background and skills.
43. My pay is fair considering what my co-workers make.
44. I'm in a dead-end job.
45. My fringe benefits are inadequate.
46. I feel I could be replaced tomorrow.
47. I have enough time off for holidays and vacations.
48. I'm being paid less than I deserve.
49. Opportunities for me to advance are limited.
50. I expect to receive a raise during the next year.

PART II. If you could design your ideal job, how closely would your present position resemble your ideal job with respect to the following:

	Not like my ideal at all		Somewhat resembles my ideal		Is my ideal
	1	2	3	4	5
Relationship with co-workers	____	____	____	____	____
Relationship with supervisor	____	____	____	____	____
The work itself	____	____	____	____	____
Working conditions	____	____	____	____	____
Pay and promotion opportunities	____	____	____	____	____

PART III. Different people value different aspects of their work. Below is a list of some of the ways that jobs can be rewarding and contribute to personal and professional fulfillment. Put a check (✓) next to the three job characteristics that you value the most.

_____ Colleagues—working with people I like
_____ Altruism—helping others
_____ Achievement—that feeling of accomplishment from doing a job well
_____ Pay—earning a good living to pay for the things I need
_____ Intellectual stimulation—learning new things
_____ Variety—the opportunity to do different kinds of things
_____ Challenge—the opportunity to master new skills
_____ Security—the assurance that my position is secure
_____ Creativity—developing new ideas, creating new things
_____ Autonomy—being independent in making decisions
_____ Recognition—getting respect and acknowledgement from others
_____ Environment—working in pleasant surroundings
_____ Leadership—having the opportunity to guide and influence the work of others
_____ Promotion—having the opportunity for advancement
_____ Other: _____

PART IV. What are the two most satisfying things about your present job? What are to two most frustrating things about your present job?

Satisfactions	*Frustrations*
1. _____	1. _____
2. _____	2. _____

Developing Your Job Satisfaction Profile: Instructions for Scoring

Step #1   Assign points (1, 2, 3, 4, or 5) to each statement in Part I of the "Work Attitudes Questionnaire" according to the following formula:

Co-worker relations (questions 1–10)
Score questions #1, 2, 3, 8, 10:   1 (*strongly disagree*) to 5 (*strongly agree*)
Score questions #4, 5, 6, 7, 9:   5 (*strongly disagree*) to 1 (*strongly agree*)

Supervisor relations (questions 11–20)
Score questions #11, 14, 15, 16, 18:   1 (*strongly disagree*) to 5 (*strongly agree*)
Score questions #12, 13, 17, 19, 20:   5 (*strongly disagree*) to 1 (*strongly agree*)

The nature of the work itself (questions 21–30)
Score questions #21, 22, 26, 28, 30:   1 (*strongly disagree*) to 5 (*strongly agree*)
Score questions #23, 24, 25, 27, 29:   5 (*strongly disagree*) to 1 (*strongly agree*)

Working conditions (questions 31–40)
Score questions #31, 32, 33, 37, 40:   1 (*strongly disagree*) to 5 (*strongly agree*)
Score questions #34, 35, 36, 38, 39:   5 (*strongly disagree*) to 1 (*strongly agree*)

Pay and promotion opportunities (questions 41–50)
Score questions #41, 42, 43, 47, 50:   1 (*strongly disagree*) to 5 (*strongly agree*)
Score questions #44, 45, 46, 48, 49:   5 (*strongly disagree*) to 1 (*strongly agree*)

Step #2   Now add up the scores above in each category in Part I. These job satisfaction facet scores will range from 10 to 50.

Co-worker relations   total score = _____
Supervisor relations   total score = _____
The nature of the work itself   total score = _____
Working conditions   total score = _____
Pay and promotion opportunities   total score = _____

Step #3   Plot your job satisfaction facet scores from Step #2 on the Part I profile chart on the next page.

Step #4   Add up the total number of points for Part II:

Total congruence with ideal = _____ (score will range from 5 to 25)

Step #5   Plot your congruence with ideal score from Step #4 on the Part II profile chart on the following page.

Step #6   Transfer the information from Part III and Part IV to the corresponding spaces on the profile on the next page.

See the job satisfaction profile sample for clarification.

Job Satisfaction Profile for _____

PART I. Facets of Job Satisfaction

```
High   50 ┤
        -
       40 ┤
        -
       30 ┤
        -
       20 ┤
        -
Low    10 └─────────────────────────────────────────────
         Co-worker   Supervisor   Work    Working     Pay/promotion
         relations   relations    itself  conditions  opportunities
```

PART II. Congruence with Ideal

```
Is my ideal        25 ┤

                   20 ┤

Somewhat like
my ideal           15 ┤

                   10 ┤

Not like my
ideal at all        5 └──────────────────
```

PART III. Occupational Values

1. _____

2. _____

3. _____

PART IV. Primary Satisfactions and Frustrations

Satisfactions	*Frustrations*
1. _____	1. _____
2. _____	2. _____

Job Satisfaction Profile for _Margaret_

SAMPLE

PART I. Facets of Job Satisfaction

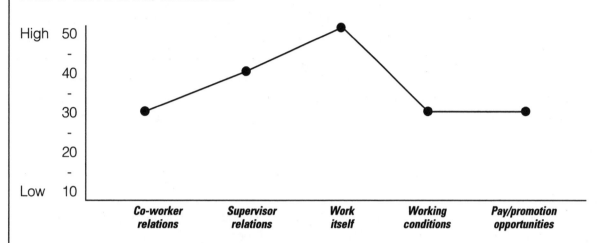

High 50				
-				
40				
-				
30				
-				
20				
-				
Low 10				

Co-worker relations   Supervisor relations   Work itself   Working conditions   Pay/promotion opportunities

PART II. Congruence with Ideal

Is my ideal   25

20

Somewhat like my ideal   15

10

Not like my ideal at all   5

PART III. Occupational Values

1. _challenge_

2. _altruism_

3. _security_

PART IV. Primary Satisfactions and Frustrations

Satisfactions

1. _opportunity to learn new skills_

2. _watching children grow and learn_

Frustrations

1. _parents who have unrealistic expectations for their children_

2. _low pay_

Professional Orientation

Rationale:

The involvement of teachers and administrators in professional development activities promotes growth and change, knowledge-based skill, reference-group orientation, and achievement of goals. Individuals who have a strong professional orientation also tend to have a stronger commitment to the center and demonstrate more enthusiasm about their work. Assessment Tool #19 assesses the type and variety of activities an individual engages in that promote professionalism. Reliability and validity data and a comparison to national norms can be found in "Professional Orientation: Individual and Organizational Perspectives" (Bloom, 1989).

Directions:

The kind of information elicited on the "Professional Activities Questionnaire" provides important background data on prospective candidates for employment at your center. Once the teachers are employed, you will probably want to administer this assessment biannually to see how they are progressing in their level of professional orientation. Staff and candidates for employment should be instructed to answer the 13 questions as honestly as possible.

Scoring:

The total score for this instrument ranges from a low of 0 to a high of 20. The following may be used as a guide for scoring the 13 questions.

1. just a job = 0, a career = 1
2. no = 0, yes = 1
3. no = 0, yes = 1
4. 0 to 5 hrs. = 0, 6 to 10 hrs. = 1, more than 10 hrs. = 2
5. Give 1 point for each different organization noted, up to 2 points (note that NAEYC and its Affiliates, such as ILAEYC, CAEYC, HAEYC, are considered as only one organization).
6. Give 1 point for each educational magazine or journal noted, up to 2 points.
7. none = 0, 1–3 = 1, 4 or more = 2
8. none = 0, 1 = 1, 2 or more = 2
9. none = 0, 1–3 = 1, 4 or more = 2
10. none = 0, 1 = 1, 2 or more = 2
11. 1 point if title and publisher are noted
12. no = 0, yes = 1
13. no = 0, yes = 1

Professional Activities Questionnaire

Please answer the following questions candidly and honestly.

1. Do you consider your work _____ just a job, or _____ a career?

2. Did you enroll in any college courses for credit last year?   no _____ yes _____

3. Are you currently working toward a college degree or CDA credential?   no _____ yes _____

4. On the average, how many hours per week do you spend **over and above what you are paid for** in activities related to early childhood? _____ hours

5. What professional organizations do you currently pay dues to?

   _____   _____

6. What professional journals and/or magazines do you currently subscribe to?

   _____   _____

7. How many professional books did you read last year?

   _____ none   _____ 1 to 3   _____ 4 or more

8. How many advocacy letters to elected representatives or to the editor of your local newspaper have you written during the past year?

   _____ none   _____ 1   _____ 2 or more

9. How many professional conferences or workshops did you attend last year?

   _____ none   _____ 1 to 3   _____ 4 or more

10. How many workshops or lectures did you present to professional groups during the past year (not counting your own staff)?

    _____ none   _____ 1   _____ 2 or more

11. Have you published any articles or books on early childhood education?

    Title/publisher _____

12. Do you expect to be working in the field of early childhood three years from now?

    _____ no _____ yes   If no, why? _____

13. If you could do it all over again, would you choose a career in early childhood education?

    _____ no _____ yes   Why? _____

                                            Name _____

Role Clarity

Rationale:

Central to program effectiveness is a clear understanding about who does what, when, and where. While job descriptions provide the broad framework for organizational functioning, everyday issues about the scope and nature of responsibilities often get blurred. Conflict between individuals at a center often arises when their definition of their own role responsibilities differs from the way in which others look upon their role. In addition, the way in which others perform their roles affects one's ability to perform at optimal levels. Role conflict occurs when a person's formal position has conflicting organizational expectations. Role ambiguity results when there are vague or ambiguous job descriptions, operating policies, or procedures. Assessment Tool #20 assesses staff's perceptions about their jobs. It is adapted from the work of Dyer (1984); Rizzo, House, and Lirtzman (1970); and Seashore, Lawler, Mirvis, and Cammann (1983).

Directions:

Distribute the "Role Perception Questionnaire" to all staff who have worked at the center for more than three months. Be sure to give each person a blank envelope. Ensure staff of the confidentiality of their responses. Place a box labeled Questionnaire Return Box in your center's office or staff room, and ask respondents to deposit their completed, unidentified questionnaires in that box. If you feel that staff will not be as candid in their responses to the open-ended questions if they know you are tabulating the results, you may want an outside person to summarize the responses. It is recommended that this assessment be administered annually.

Scoring:

Total the individual scores for respondents. To do this, add up the numerals circled for all items except #5, 7, and 11. Because these three items are worded negatively, reverse the scoring (seldom = 5, always = 1) and add them to the total. A respondent's total score on this assessment tool will range from 12 to 60.

Next add together all the staff's scores and divide by the total number of respondents to get an average role clarity score. A high average score (48–60) indicates that staff perceive that their jobs are clearly defined and they seldom experience conflicting demands and role expectations. A low average score (12–24) indicates that confusion exists about lines of authority and role assignments.

Role Perception Questionnaire

Please circle the response that most nearly describes your feelings about your present job.

		Seldom		*Sometimes*		*Always*
1.	I am clear about what my responsibilities are.	1	2	3	4	5
2.	I am certain about how much authority I have.	1	2	3	4	5
3.	I am given a chance to do the things I do best.	1	2	3	4	5
4.	I have an opportunity to develop my own special abilities.	1	2	3	4	5
5.	I spend time on unnecessary, irrelevant tasks.	1	2	3	4	5
6.	Clear planned goals and objectives exist for my job.	1	2	3	4	5
7.	I receive conflicting expectations from people about my job.	1	2	3	4	5
8.	I have the knowledge and skills to do my job well.	1	2	3	4	5
9.	I have enough resources to do my job well.	1	2	3	4	5
10.	There is enough time to do my job well.	1	2	3	4	5
11.	I ignore certain policies in order to carry out my job.	1	2	3	4	5
12.	I get the support I need to do my job well.	1	2	3	4	5

What keeps you from being as effective as you would like to be in your position?

If you had the power to change anything about your job, what would you change? Why would this be an improvement over existing conditions?

What suggestions do you have for improving schedules, routines, and procedures so staff can function as a more effective team?

Role Clarity
New Staff

Rationale:

Confusion about roles and expectations often begins in the first days (even the first hours) that an employee starts a new job. Tapping into staff's perceptions about their new positions can create the beginning of a relationship based on mutual trust and respect. It can also circumvent potential problems before they have a chance to grow into full-blown job grievances. Assessment Tool #21 is designed for new staff employed at your center. Ideally, it should be given to them approximately four weeks after they have begun in their new position.

Directions:

Distribute the "Staff Orientation Assessment" to all new staff approximately four weeks after they have begun working at your program. It is advised that the individual have the opportunity to take the assessment home and complete it without the distractions of the classroom.

Scoring:

Since the responses on this assessment tool are open-ended, they will vary from individual to individual. The results should serve as a springboard for discussion during an orientation feedback conference with each new employee. Issues that surface from this assessment will alert you to potential misunderstandings about the scope and nature of the position. The results can also prove helpful in modifying orientation policies for new employees in the future.

Staff Orientation Assessment

Please take a few minutes to answer the questions below. Your honest, candid responses will help us continue to meet the needs of new staff in our center.

1. Were you made to feel comfortable and welcome at the center on your first day on the job? Did other staff know you were coming?   ❑ no   ❑ yes

    Comments:

2. Were you given enough information about the particulars of our school environment (parking, supplies, storage, lunch routines, schedules, etc.) to help you through those first difficult days?   ❑ no   ❑ yes

    Comments:

3. Were you given sufficient background on the center's policies, goals, and philosophy?   ❑ no   ❑ yes

    Comments:

4. Were you made to feel that others had a personal interest in your progress? Have other staff made you feel like you are part of the team?   ❑ no   ❑ yes

    Comments:

5. Are there any policies or procedures you would like to know more about?   ❑ no   ❑ yes

    Comments:

Organizational Commitment

Rationale:

High-quality early childhood programs can't happen without highly committed staff. Teachers' levels of organizational commitment directly affect their willingness to exert an effort on behalf of the program and their desire to remain working at the center. Level of commitment is a direct reflection of their acceptance of the center's goals, values, and working conditions. Assessment Tool #22 was designed to help you tap into your staff's level of commitment. It was adapted from the work of Bloom (1988b); Meyer and Allen (1997); and Mowday, Steers, and Porter (1979).

Directions:

Because many of the questions included on the "How Committed Am I?" questionnaire are sensitive, it is recommended that individuals use it as a self-assessment tool to reflect on their personal level of commitment to the center. Emphasize to staff that you are not interested in their answers to specific questions, but rather in their total score. For this reason, they should be responsible for scoring the instrument themselves. Reassure them of the confidential nature of their score and that your interest in knowing their total score is to help you get a sense of the collective commitment of the staff and whether that commitment has fluctuated over time.

Scoring:

The total scores for this instrument range from a low of 15 to a high of 75. A score between 60 and 75 indicates that the individual has quite positive feelings about the center as a place to work. From the employee's perspective, the match between what they bring to the center and what the center can offer is good. A score lower than 30 indicates there are strong feelings on the part of the individual that the center may not be the best place to work. From the other data you have collected, you will be able to discern if the person is a candidate for burnout and needs to be re-energized or if there is truly a mismatch between the needs and expectations of the person and what the program can offer. This type of situation may necessitate the person's leaving the center to find a more satisfying and fulfilling place to work.

"How Committed Am I?"

Below are a series of statements that represent possible feelings that individuals may have about this early childhood center as a place to work. With respect to your own feelings about the center, please indicate your degree of agreement or disagreement with each statement using the scale below:

Strongly disagree				Strongly agree
1	2	3	4	5

_____ 1.   I am willing to put in a great deal of effort beyond that normally expected in order to help the center be successful.

_____ 2.   I talk about this center to my friends as a great place to work.

_____ 3.   I feel a great deal of loyalty to this center.

_____ 4.   I would accept almost any type of job assignment in order to keep working for this center.

_____ 5.   I find that my values and the center's values are very similar.

_____ 6.   I am proud to tell others that I work for this center.

_____ 7.   It would not be the same working for another center even if the type of work I did was similar.

_____ 8.   This center really inspires the very best in me in the way of job performance.

_____ 9.   It would take a big change in my present circumstances to cause me to leave this center.

_____ 10.   I am extremely glad that I chose to work at this center over other options I was considering at the time I started.

_____ 11.   Most of the time I agree with this center's policies on important matters relating to its employees.

_____ 12.   I really care about the future of this center.

_____ 13.   For me this is the best of all possible organizations to work for.

_____ 14.   Even if I were offered a slightly higher paying job, I wouldn't leave this job.

_____ 15.   I intend to work here at least two more years.

Perceived Problems

Rationale:

One approach to providing meaningful, individualized staff development is to identify the day-to-day problems teachers experience as they go about their work. With this information in hand you will be better able to design individual staff development experiences that specifically address those problems. Engaging teachers in the process of identifying and articulating problem areas also communicates your desire to personalize the process and help teachers take ownership of their professional development. Assessment Tool #23 was developed by John M. Johnston (1984). It includes 60 areas that have been identified by preschool teachers as problematic.

Directions:

Distribute the "Preschool Teacher Problem Checklist" to those teachers for whom you feel the issues addressed are appropriate. Ask the teachers to read through the 60 problems carefully. This will take some time, so you may want them to take the assessment home so they can have enough time to read and reflect. Be sure to let the teachers know that the problem statements included on this survey were generated by preschool teachers. This may help reduce their level of anxiety about identifying their most problematic areas. When teachers have completed this assessment, they will have identified the 10 problems that they perceive as most troublesome in their own practice. These can then be discussed at your annual planning conference as you develop new goals for the following year.

Scoring:

The 60 problems can be grouped into seven major problems areas: subordinate staff relations, control and nurturance of children, remediation, supervisor relations, parent cooperation, management of time, and management of routines. The 10 problems selected by the teacher can be reviewed in light of these seven areas to determine if they focus more on one particular area. Such analysis can lead to a discussion of individual staff development strategies for the teacher to foster improvement in that area.

Alternative purpose and scoring:

Assessment Tool #23 may also be used as a basis for staff development plans for the center as a whole. Using a scale of 1 (this is not a problem) to 5 (this is a serious problem), have the staff assign a rating to each item. Tally all the staff's ratings for each item and divide by the number of staff. This will yield an average score for each item. The items with the highest average score represent problems of importance to the staff as a whole. Several teachers may share the same problem. These identified issues can form the basis for small-group staff development activities. Other problems shared by all teachers can form the basis for centerwide staff development activities.

Preschool Teacher Problems Checklist

Read through the following list of 60 problems that preschool teachers have identified as troublesome. As you read through the list, preface each problem statement with the phrase, "I have a problem..." Put a check next to those that seem to be most troublesome for you. When you are finished, go back through your list and put a star next to the 10 most troublesome problems you experience.

I have a problem...

____ 1. getting children to do what I ask them to do.

____ 2. controlling the noise or energy level in the room.

____ 3. understanding the reason for children's problem behavior.

____ 4. getting parents to supply accurate, up-to-date information for our files.

____ 5. getting children to share or take turns.

____ 6. providing for communication among staff.

____ 7. getting parent cooperation in solving their children's preschool-related problems.

____ 8. orienting new staff to all aspects of the program and their job.

____ 9. knowing how to handle children's aggressive behavior.

____ 10. getting parents to drop off or pick up their children on time.

____ 11. dealing with a child who cries or whines frequently.

____ 12. promoting effective mutual communication between home and center.

____ 13. getting staff to follow through on assigned responsibilities.

____ 14. getting parents to keep their children home when they are sick.

____ 15. getting children to clean up.

____ 16. motivating myself to be involved in outside professional activities.

____ 17. dealing with parents who say their children are toilet-trained when they are not.

____ 18. providing adequate staff to meet all program needs.

____ 19. knowing how to help the special or atypical child.

____ 20. spending personal time doing necessary classroom tasks or administrative tasks.

____ 21. contending with interruptions while I am working.

____ 22. meeting the required staff:child ratios at all times during the day.

____ 23. getting children to learn and follow classroom rules and routines.

____ 24. finding time away from children for planning and preparation.

____ 25. getting children to use words and not hit others when they are angry.

____ 26. getting parents to follow policies on enrollment or fee payments.

____ 27. keeping children's attention during group time.

____ 28. getting parent cooperation with toilet training.

____ 29. getting children to sleep or rest quietly at nap time without disturbing others.

____ 30. working with my supervisor.

____ 31. getting parents to provide appropriate clothing from home.

____ 32. finding qualified substitute staff.

____ 33. feeling positive toward a child who frequently misbehaves.

____ 34. getting my supervisor to respect my professional judgment.

____ 35. being able to stay home when I am sick.

____ 36. keeping one child's problem behavior from affecting other children.

____ 37. finding workshops that are appropriate to my level of skill and knowledge.

____ 38. meeting an individual child's needs without neglecting the group.

____ 39. getting children who are toilet trained not to wet their pants.

____ 40. helping parents understand and deal appropriately with their child's behavior.

____ 41. getting staff to model appropriate behavior for children.

____ 42. getting staff to work in a cooperative fashion.

____ 43. helping parents of atypical children recognize and adjust to their child's needs.

____ 44. getting parents to come to scheduled events or conferences.

____ 45. getting my supervisor to give me feedback about my job performance.

____ 46. getting my supervisor to include me in decision making on issues relating to my classroom.

____ 47. knowing how to counter a child's negative home environment.

____ 48. meeting the needs of the children when the room is short staffed.

____ 49. working with equipment or facilities that are in poor condition.

____ 50. getting all children to participate in group activities.

____ 51. knowing if parents are abusing or neglecting their children.

____ 52. finding time for cleaning and other nonteaching tasks.

____ 53. involving the passive child in activities.

____ 54. getting staff to recognize and act on children's needs.

____ 55. dealing with unfair criticism from my supervisor.

____ 56. meeting the needs of all children in a multi-age group.

____ 57. giving adequate attention to the special-needs child without neglecting the other children.

____ 58. getting staff to understand and deal appropriately with young children's behavior.

____ 59. dressing and undressing children for cold weather outdoor play.

____ 60. understanding the public's attitude that child care is just babysitting.

From Johnston, J. (1984, March). Assessing staff problems: Key to effective staff development. *Child Care Information Exchange*, pp. 1–4. Reprinted with permission from Exchange Press.

Flexibility and Openness to Change

Rationale:

Gaining insight into one's attitudes and behaviors relative to change is an important first step in identifying potential resistance to new ideas. When we think about attitudes toward change, it is useful to visualize of a continuum from a flexible (typically more open-minded) approach to a more conservative (typically more cautious) approach. Knowing a teacher's orientation on this continuum can help you structure the pace and timing of staff development experiences to accommodate individual needs. Assessment Tool #24 is a modified version of an instrument developed by the Public Management Institute (1980).

Directions:

You will probably want to administer the "Flexibility Index" to your staff about once every two or three years. This instrument is designed to be self-administered and self-scored by the individual staff member. Using the scoring directions below, a flexibility profile can be generated. This profile can then be brought to the planning conference and used to stimulate discussion about the individual's openness to change.

Scoring:

Instruct teachers how to use the "Chart Your Flexibility Profile" to record their *yes* and *no* answers and create an individual profile showing regarding their orientation to change. To analyze the results, consider that a flexibility profile with fewer than 6 yes answers indicates a dynamic, change-oriented approach to work. The greater the number of yes answers, the more conservative (and possibly resistant) the person may be regarding change.

Flexibility Index

Answer *yes* or *no* to the 20 questions below, using the introductory words "I generally..." before each phrase. There are no right or wrong answers to this questionnaire. The responses should reflect your preferred orientation with respect to change.

		Yes	No
I generally...			
1.	try to cope with things as they are.	_____	_____
2.	feel there is a right way and a wrong way to teach young children.	_____	_____
3.	think change usually interrupts the efficiency of my classroom routine.	_____	_____
4.	must believe I will succeed before I will try something new.	_____	_____
5.	believe that changes in routine only makes teaching more difficult.	_____	_____
6.	believe a rational approach to problem solving is best.	_____	_____
7.	choose alternatives according to their risk factors.	_____	_____
8.	believe I'm not particularly creative in my teaching.	_____	_____
9.	believe if I fail to manage my classroom well, I'll probably lose my job.	_____	_____
10.	tend to set short-term rather than long-term goals.	_____	_____
11.	have trouble evaluating alternatives quickly.	_____	_____
12.	am skeptical of plans that will change the basic routine of my classroom.	_____	_____
13.	believe that change happens so slowly that in the end it is ineffective.	_____	_____
14.	like my job for security reasons.	_____	_____
15.	believe that routine is an important element of teaching.	_____	_____
16.	feel the old way of doing things works just as well or better.	_____	_____
17.	feel that many changes don't make any real difference.	_____	_____
18.	believe that most people are quite satisfied with the way things are.	_____	_____
19.	see most risks as win/lose situations.	_____	_____
20.	must understand every facet of the problem before I make a decision.	_____	_____

Chart Your Flexibility Profile

Referring to your responses to the 20 statements on the previous page ("Flexibility Index"), circle the statement number in either the *Yes* or *No* row on the profile below.

Conservative

Yes 1   2   3   4   5   6   7   8   9   10   11   12   13   14   15   16   17   18   19   20

No 1   2   3   4   5   6   7   8   9   10   11   12   13   14   15   16   17   18   19   20

Flexible

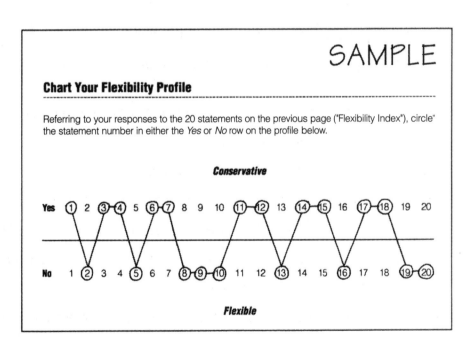

Adapted from Public Management Institute. (1980). *Non-profit management skills for women managers.* San Francisco, CA: Author, pp. 173–75. Reprinted with permission.

Supervisory Beliefs

Rationale:

Before choosing a supervisory approach to use with a teacher, it is important to assess your own beliefs about supervision and staff development. Although most supervisors use directive, collaborative, and nondirective styles at one time or another, one style is usually dominant. This assessment will help you become aware of you strongest orientation. Other professional staff who serve in supervisory roles, such as lead teacher or education coordinator, may also benefit from doing this assessment. Assessment Tool #25 was developed by Carl Glickman (2004).

Directions:

This inventory is designed to be self-administered and self-scored. As you read the questions, circle one of two options: A or B for each item. You may not completely agree with either choice, but choose the one that is closest to how you feel.

Scoring:

Step 1. Circle your answers from the inventory in the three columns below:

Column I	Column II	Column III
1B	1A	
	2B	2A
3A	3B	
4B		4A
	5B	5A
6A		6B
	7A	7B
8A		8B
9A	9B	
10B		10A
11A		11B
12A	12B	
	13B	13A
14B	14A	
	15A	15B

Step 2. Total the number of circled items in each column and multiply by 6.7.

(2.1) Total responses in Column I _____ x 6.7 = _____

(2.2) Total responses in Column II _____ x 6.7 = _____

(2.3) Total responses in Column III _____ x 6.7 = _____

Interpretation

The product you obtained in Step 2.1 is an approximate percentage of how often you take a directive approach to supervision. The product you obtained in Step 2.2 is an approximate percentage of how often you take a collaborative approach, and that in Step 2.3 is an approximate percentage of how often you take a nondirective approach.

The Supervisory Beliefs Inventory

Circle either A or B for each item. You may not completely agree with either choice, but choose the one that is closer to how you feel.

1. A. Supervisors should give teachers a large degree of autonomy and initiative within broadly defined limits.
   B. Supervisors should give teachers directions about methods that will help them improve their teaching.

2. A. It is important for teachers to set their own goals and objectives for professional growth.
   B. It is important for supervisors to help teachers reconcile their personalities and teaching styles with the philosophy and direction of the school.

3. A. Teachers are likely to feel uncomfortable and anxious if the objectives on which they will be evaluated are not clearly defined by the supervisor.
   B. Evaluations of teachers are meaningless if teachers are not able to define with their supervisors the objectives for evaluation.

4. A. An open, trusting, warm, and personal relationship with teachers is the most important ingredient in supervising teachers.
   B. A supervisor who is too intimate with teachers risks being less effective and less respected than a supervisor who keeps a certain degree of professional distance from teachers.

5. A. My role during supervisory conferences is to make the interaction positive, to share realistic information, and to help teachers plan their own solutions to problems.
   B. The methods and strategies I use with teachers in a conference are aimed at our reaching agreement over the needs for future improvement.

6. In the initial phase of working with a teacher
   A. I develop objectives with each teacher that will help accomplish school goals.
   B. I try to identify the talents and goals of individual teachers so they can work on their own improvement.

7. When several teachers have a similar classroom problem, I prefer to
   A. have the teachers form an ad hoc group and help them work together to solve the problem.
   B. help teachers on an individual basis find their strengths, abilities, and resources so that each one finds his or her own solution to the problem.

8. The most important clue that an in-service workshop is needed occurs when
   A. the supervisor perceives that several teachers lack knowledge or skill in a specific area, which is resulting in low morale, undue stress, and less effective teaching.
   B. several teachers perceive the need to strengthen their abilities in the same area.

9. A. The supervisory staff should decide the objectives of an in-service workshop since they have a broad perspective on the teachers' abilities and the school's needs.
   B. Teachers and supervisory staff should reach consensus about the objectives of an in-service workshop before the workshop is held.

10. A. Teachers who feel they are growing personally will be more effective than teachers who are not experiencing personal growth.
    B. The knowledge and ability of teaching strategies and methods that have been proved over the years should be taught and practiced by all teachers to be effective in their classrooms.

11. When I perceive that a teacher might be scolding a student unnecessarily,
    A. I explain, during a conference with the teacher, why the scolding was excessive.
    B. I ask the teacher about the incident, but do not interject my judgments.

12. A. One effective way to improve teacher performance is to formulate clear behavioral objectives and create meaningful incentives for achieving them.
    B. Behavioral objectives are rewarding and helpful to some teachers but stifling to others; some teachers benefit from behavioral objectives in some situations but not in others.

13. During a preobservation conference,
    A. I suggest to the teacher what I could observe, but I let the teacher make the final decision about the objectives and methods of observation.
    B. the teacher and I mutually decide the objectives and methods of observation.

14. A. Improvement occurs very slowly if teachers are left on their own, but when a group of teachers work together on a specific problem, they learn rapidly and their morale remains high.
    B. Group activities may be enjoyable, but I find that individual, open discussion with a teacher about a problem and its possible solutions leads to more sustained results.

15. When an in-service or staff development workshop is scheduled,
    A. all teachers who participated in the decision to hold the workshop should be expected to attend it.
    B. teachers, regardless of their role in forming a workshop, should be able to decide if the workshop is relevant to their personal or professional growth and, if not, should not be expected to attend.

From Glickman, C. (2004). *Supervision and instructional leadership.* Boston: Allyn & Bacon, pp. 120–22. Reprinted with permission.

Goal-Setting Motivation

Rationale:

Whether it's a New Year's resolution to lose 10 pounds or a promise to a favorite aunt that you'll call more often, we have all set goals and made promises to change our behavior. But often our goals go unfulfilled, our promises go unkept. Somewhere along the way we lost our will to see them through. Sometimes this happens because we do not take the time to accurately assess our true motivation in reaching our goals. Setting goals for oneself is only the first step to changing behavior. We also need to determine what reasons might affect our motivation to achieve the goal. Otherwise, goal setting and action plans are merely a paper exercise.

Assessment Tool #26 was designed to help you assist staff in assessing their level of motivation for achieving the goals they have set as part of their staff development action plan. This assessment is a modified version of a goal-setting motivation questionnaire developed by Dyer (1984).

Directions:

After you have met with your staff at their annual planning conference to target goals for the coming year, distribute the questionnaire "How Motivated Am I?" and ask them to complete it. This questionnaire is designed to encourage reflection on their part about the level of commitment they have for achieving the goals that have been drawn up on their action plan. There is no need to collect this self-administered assessment after the individual has completed it.

Scoring:

This questionnaire is designed to be self-scored by the teacher completing it. The most important part of the assessment is the goal-motivation continuum at the bottom of the page. The individual should determine his or her overall level of motivation for achieving the goals on the staff development action plan that has been drawn up. Let teachers know that if they rate their overall motivation as 3 or lower on this scale, it will be important for them to meet with you again to revise the action plan to more accurately reflect those areas in which they are sincerely motivated to accomplish.

"How Motivated Am I?"

The two lists below show some of the reasons people make a change (payoffs) or don't make a change (blocks). As you set your goals and write your action plan, identify those reasons that might affect your motivation to achieve your goals.

Blocks	**Payoffs**
Fear of the unknown	Greater recognition
Complacency	More freedom and autonomy
Lack of skill	Increased productivity
Takes too much time	Greater efficiency
Don't want more responsibility	More responsibility
Don't see a need for change	Increased feelings of self-worth
Too much effort required	Opportunity to be of help to others
Fear of rejection	Better interpersonal relationships
Forced to make the change	More control over what I am doing

other _____   other _____

Which of the blocks affects you the most?

_____

In what ways can you reduce the impact of these blocks?

_____

_____

What is the payoff for you for taking on this goal?

_____

_____

On a scale of 1 to 7, assess the strength of your motivation to achieve the goals you have set.

(low) 1   2   3   4   5   6   7 (high)

Adapted from Dyer, W. (1984). *Strategies for managing change*. Reading, MA: Addison-Wesley, pp. 101–02. Reprinted with permission.

► Appendix B ◄

Worksheets

The worksheets included on the following pages are also included on the CD-ROM accompanying this book. These forms may be freely reproduced for professional development purposes at your center. Permission for systematic large-scale reproduction for other training and research purposes or for inclusion in other publications must be obtained from the publisher, New Horizons. .

1. Identifying the Problem

2. Analyzing the Situation

3. Generating Possible Solutions

4. Action Plan

5. Individual Profile

6. Observations

7. Preparing for the Planning Conference

8. Goals Blueprint

9. Staff Development Action Plan

10. Peer Observation

11. Performance Appraisal—Preschool Teacher

12. Working Toward a Common Vision

Identifying the Problem

Problem:_____
_____
_____

Symptoms: _____
_____
_____
_____

Results of data collection: _____
_____
_____
_____
_____
_____
_____
_____
_____
_____
_____
_____
_____

Goal (ideal situation): _____
_____
_____
_____
_____

Analyzing the Situation

Goal (ideal situation): _____

_____

_____

_____

_____

Helping Forces   **Hindering Forces**

Present Situation

Generating Possible Solutions

Goal (ideal situation): _____

_____

_____

_____

_____

Proposed Solution   **Possible Consequences**

_____ ▶   _____

_____ ▶   _____

_____ ▶   _____

_____ ▶   _____

_____ ▶   _____

_____ ▶   _____

Action Plan

Goal: _____

Objectives	Action Steps	Person Responsible	Time	Resources Needed (people, materials, $$$)	Evaluation Checkpoints

Individual Profile

Name: _____ Age: _____

Personal history _____
_____
_____

Education/training_____
_____
_____

Work experience _____
_____
_____

Interests and special talents _____
_____
_____

Beliefs and values _____
_____
_____

Dispositions _____
_____
_____

Flexibility and openness to change _____
_____
_____

Energy level _____
_____
_____

Cognitive capacity _____
_____
_____

Learning style _____

_____

_____

Psychological type _____

_____

_____

Communication style _____

_____

_____

Self-efficacy _____

_____

_____

Needs and expectations _____

_____

_____

Adult development stage _____

_____

_____

Career stage _____

_____

_____

Level of commitment and motivation _____

_____

_____

Professional orientation _____

_____

_____

Concomitant roles_____

_____

_____

Observations

Name _____

Date: _____

_____

_____

_____

_____

_____

_____

Date: _____

_____

_____

_____

_____

_____

_____

Date: _____

_____

_____

_____

_____

_____

_____

Preparing for the Planning Conference

Dear Staff member:

As you prepare for our planning conference, think about the following:

▶ What aspect of your job gives you the greatest personal satisfaction?

▶ What aspect of your job is most frustrating?

▶ What keeps you from being as effective as you would like to be in your position?

▶ If you had the power to change anything about your job, what would you change? Why would this be an improvement over existing conditions?

▶ What do you see yourself doing five years from now?

▶ What new skills or knowledge would you like to learn this next year?

▶ How can I or other staff help you achieve your personal and professional goals?

Goals Blueprint

Teacher's name: _____   Date: _____

Strengths as a teacher

1. _____

   _____

2. _____

   _____

3. _____

   _____

Identified growth areas

1. _____

   _____

2. _____

   _____

3. _____

   _____

Goal: _____

   _____

Objectives

1. _____

   _____

2. _____

   _____

3. _____

   _____

Staff Development Action Plan

Name _____ Date _____

Objective #1 _____

Activities	Time Needed	Resources Needed

Evaluation (how/when) _____

Objective #2 _____

Activities	Time Needed	Resources Needed

Evaluation (how/when) _____

Objective #3 _____

Activities	Time Needed	Resources Needed

Evaluation (how/when) _____

Peer Observation

Name of colleague observed _____   Date: _____

As you observe, please note comments about the following aspects of the classroom environment: interactions between the teacher and children; interactions between the teacher and other co-workers or volunteers; interactions between the teacher and parents; the physical arrangement of space; the curriculum; and health, nutrition, and safety aspects of the classroom.

Aspects of this classroom I was impressed with include . . .

1. _____
   _____

2. _____
   _____

3. _____
   _____

Aspects of this classroom that might be improved include . .

1. _____
   _____

2. _____
   _____

3. _____
   _____

Signed _____

Performance Appraisal—Preschool Teacher

Name: _____

Date _____

	Seldom	Sometimes	Frequently	Always	Comments

To establish and maintain a safe and healthy learning environment

1. Designs appropriate room arrangement
2. Plans and implements a nutritious snack program
3. Promotes healthy eating practices
4. Maintains a safe environment
5. Posts necessary health and safety information
6. Maintains an orderly learning environment

To advance physical and intellectual competence

1. Provides a balance between child- and teacher-initiated activities
2. Provides a balance between quiet and active learning activities
3. Uses equipment and materials for indoor and outdoor play that promote children's physical development
4. Involves children in planning and implementing activities
5. Provides an integrated curriculum that meets the needs of individual children
6. Plans and implements experiences that promote language and literacy development
7. Plans and implements activities that promote the acquisition of number concepts

299

To support social and emotional development and provide positive guidance

	Seldom	Sometimes	Frequently	Always	Comments
1. Plans and implements hands-on activities that develop positive self-esteem					
2. Plans and implements hands-on activities that develop social skills					
3. Plans and implements culturally diverse experiences					
4. Uses and promotes positive guidance techniques					
5. Provides a wide variety of creative and expressive activities					
6. Establishes routines with smooth transition periods					
7. Communicates with children at their developmental level					
8. Encourages children to be independent					

To establish positive and productive relationships with families

	Seldom	Sometimes	Frequently	Always	Comments
1. Relates assessment information to parents and offers support for dealing with children at different stages					
2. Plans and conducts home visits					
3. Promotes communication with parents through progress notes, monthly newsletter, and parent conferences					
4. Provides a variety of ways that families can participate in the program					
5. Encourages parents to participate in the program					

Comments

To ensure a well-run, purposeful program responsive to participant needs

	Seldom	Sometimes	Frequently	Always
1. Assesses program supplies and materials needed before implementing activities				
2. Coordinates and helps supervise aides and volunteers working in the classroom				
3. Maintains written plans on a weekly basis				
4. Assesses children's needs and developmental progress on an ongoing basis				
5. Uses the results of assessment to plan activities				

To maintain a commitment to professionalism

	Seldom	Sometimes	Frequently	Always
1. Promotes the center's philosophy and objectives				
2. Supports the center's code of ethical conduct				
3. Engages in ongoing staff development to improve personal and professional skills				
4. Supports the professional growth and development of colleagues by sharing materials and information				
5. Attends staff meetings, workshops, and in-service training provided by the center				

Additional comments:

Supervisor _____

Working Toward a Common Vision

Center goal

_____
_____
_____
_____
_____
_____

Objectives

_____
_____
_____
_____
_____
_____
_____
_____
_____

Date: _____

Name: _____
_____
_____
_____

Name: _____
_____
_____
_____

Name: _____
_____
_____
_____

Name: _____
_____
_____
_____

Name: _____
_____
_____
_____

Name: _____
_____
_____
_____

Index

▶ Notes ◀

► Notes ◄

► Notes ◄

▶ Notes ◀

Available from New Horizons

▶ *Avoiding Burnout: Strategies for Managing Time, Space, and People*

▶ *A Great Place to Work: Improving Conditions for Staff in Young Children's Programs*

▶ *Blueprint for Action: Achieving Center-Based Change Through Staff Development*

▶ *Workshop Essentials: Planning and Presenting Dynamic Workshops*

The Director's Toolbox:
A Management Series for Early Childhood Administrators

▶ *Circle of Influence: Implementing Shared Decision Making and Participative Management*

▶ *Making the Most of Meetings: A Practical Guide*

▶ *The Right Fit: Recruiting, Selecting, and Orienting Staff*

▶ *Leadership in Action: How Effective Directors Get Things Done*

A Trainer's Guide is also available for each topic in the Director's Toolbox Series. Each guide provides step-by-step instructions for planning and presenting a dynamic and informative six-hour workshop. Included are trainers' notes and presentation tips, instructions for conducting learning activities, reproducible handouts, transparencies, and a PowerPoint CD.

To place your order or receive additional information
on prices and quantity discounts, contact:

NEW HORIZONS
P.O. Box 863
Lake Forest, Illinois 60045-0863
(847) 295-8131 ●(847) 295-2968 FAX
newhorizons4@comcast.net ● www.newhorizonsbooks.net